GILBERT IMLAY:
CITIZEN OF THE WORLD

GILBERT IMLAY:
CITIZEN OF THE WORLD

BY

Wil Verhoeven

LONDON
PICKERING & CHATTO
2008

Published by Pickering & Chatto (Publishers) Limited
21 Bloomsbury Way, London WC1A 2TH

2252 Ridge Road, Brookfield, Vermont 05036-9704, USA

www.pickeringchatto.com

BRITISH LIBRARY CATALOGUING IN PUBLICATION DATA

Verhoeven, Wil
Gilbert Imlay: citizen of the world
1. Imlay, Gilbert, 1754?–1828? 2. Adventure and adventurers – United States
– Biography
I. Title
973.4'092

ISBN-13: 9781851968596

Typeset by Pickering & Chatto (Publishers) Limited
Printed in the United Kingdom at the University Press, Cambridge

CONTENTS

FOR

Emory Elliott

ACKNOWLEDGEMENTS

Like the subjects they write about, biographers have their own genealogies. I am proud to acknowledge my indebtedness to my predecessors in the search for the elusive Gilbert Imlay, notably Richard Garnett (1903), John Wilson Townsend (1907), Ralph Leslie Rusk (1923), Oliver Farrar Emerson (1924), W. Clark Durant (1927) and Joseph Lewis Fant III (1984).

The research for this book spans the best part of ten years and was carried out in libraries and manuscript collections all over the United States and Europe. During that time I have worked with innumerable (reference) librarians, archivists, curators, archive researchers, cataloguers and bibliographers, not to mention scores of historians, biographers, genealogists and other fellow archives' rats – whom I have found to be extremely knowledgeable, committed, resourceful and always willing to help, offer advice and honour my endless requests for copies, scans or photographs. Inevitably, over the years I have incurred massive debts of gratitude: quite literally, without the people that make the archives work, this book would not exist today.

Following Imlay's trail has led me on several research trips to Kentucky and over the past few years I have come to appreciate the state and its people as equally congenial and welcoming. I spent a few extraordinarily fruitful and enjoyable weeks at the Filson Historical Society in Louisville, an institution that oozes the history of the Ohio River Valley. I want to thank the Society's Executive Director Mark Wetherington and his expert staff, particularly Jim Holmberg, Curator of Special Collections, Judith Partington, Head Librarian, Mike Veach and Robin Wallace, Special Collections Assistants, and Pen Bogert, Reference Specialist. No-one can claim to have an inkling of local Kentucky history who has not consulted Neil O. Hammon. I harassed him with many an email and phone call, but Neil always had the answers. I also thank him for generously sharing his own extensive research data with me, and for saving me from making some glaring mistakes. Mary Ellen Moore and Dolores Salsman, archive researchers at the Nelson County Court Archives, Bardstown, have provided stacks of photocopies of old court cases. It was a great pleasure to finally meet them in the vaults of the Court House and to join them in the hunt for further traces of Gilbert Imlay in the largely unsorted, uncatalogued and partially burnt records of Nelson County Court. I want to thank Walter Bowman, archivist at the Kentucky Department for Libraries and Archives in Frankfort, for guiding me through the complex world of the District of Kentucky Supreme Court and Court of Appeals Deed Books. Doug Davies helped me locate important documents in the Archives and Records Department of Jefferson County Circuit Court, Louisville. At the Kentucky Historical Society, Frankfort, Library Branch Manager Jim Kastner, Manuscripts Archivist and Curator Lynne Hollingsworth and Staff Researcher Elizabeth Wills generously provided advice, copies and research leads. Kandie Adkinson at the Land Office Division at the Office of the Secretary of State, Frankfort, has been crucial in sorting out the complexities surrounding Imlay's land patents. I am deeply grateful to her for nominating me to be commissioned a Kentucky Colonel by the Governor and the Secretary of State, an honour bestowed on 'individuals in recognition of noteworthy accomplishments and outstanding service to a community, state or the nation'. On a rare break from the archives, my friend John G. Cawelti offered me a splendid dinner and company after taking me to see the forks of Beargrass Creek, winding their way through what is now Louisville's East End before flowing in the Ohio River just north of the Falls – the area where Imlay had planned his utopian community of 'Bellefont' (and where in the end he did *not* take Mary Wollstonecraft).

The state of New Jersey may have, shall we say, a 'mixed' reputation in the United States, but I confess I am thrilled that my search for Gilbert Imlay's roots has taken me on several occasions along the by-ways and high-ways of the Garden State (including the infamous New Jersey Turnpike). Thomas J. Imlay shared some of his own explorations into his family roots, and I cannot thank him enough for putting me in touch with Leslie V. Meirs. I had long suspected that the family papers that in 1881 were in the possession of Mrs Elizabeth Imlay would still be in some relative's drawer or shoebox – and they were. Leslie Meirs graciously entrusted the Bruere-Imlay papers to me for my perusal. I am grateful to Joan Ruddiman for introducing me to John Fabiano, president of the Allentown-Upper Freehold Historical Society, who spent hours with me at the Allentown Public Library going through the local history collection and the microfilm copies of the Charles Hutchinson collection. At Special Collections and University Archives, Rutgers University Libraries, Albert C. King, Manuscripts Curator, and David Kuzma took the trouble to advise me on Imlay holdings. Margaret Sherry Rich, Reference Librarian and Archivist at Rare Books and Special Collections, Princeton University Library, helped me find my way through the Lee Family manuscripts (thanks, also, to AnnaLee Pauls and Lisa Dunkley). I have benefited much from the help and advice of Gary Saretzky, County Archivist, and Mary Ann Kiernan, Reference Specialist, both at the Monmouth County Archives in Manalapan, New Jersey. I would also like to thank Tim Decker, Collections Manager at the New Jersey Historical Society; Carla Z. Tobias, Monmouth County Historical Association, Freehold, New Jersey; and New Jersey historian David Fowler.

Elsewhere in the United States I have received support, advice and encouragement from scores of people I have worked with over the years; many of whom have responded efficiently and graciously to my endless requests for copies, scans and microfilms. Charles W. Royster at Louisiana State University was kind enough to answer my queries about Light-Horse Harry Lee. Dr Nicholas Butler, Special Collections Manager at Charleston County Public Library, helped me find material on Imlay and Freneau in those Charleston records not destroyed in the city's various fires, hurricanes, earthquakes and military sieges. Kathie Ludwig, Librarian at the David Library of the American Revolution, Washington Crossing, Pennsylvania, always promptly answered my reference questions and provided countless photocopies. Thanks, too, to Meg McSweeney, Chief Operating officer at the David Library, for inviting me to work there. For helping me locate sources and pointing out further avenues of research I am also grateful to William S. Poole, Professor of Southern History at the College of Charleston; Lisa Reams, Librarian, South Carolina Historical Association, Charleston; Elizabeth Gallow, Assistant Special Collections Librarian, Maryland Historical Society, Baltimore, Maryland; Leah Prescott, Manuscripts and Archives Librarian, Wendy Schnur, Reference Manager, and Peggy Tate Smith, Rights and Reproductions and Sales Coordinator, all at the G. W. Blunt White Library of the Mystic Seaport Museum (Mystic, Connecticut); Janet Bloom, at the William L. Clements Library, University of Michigan; Ward J. Childs, City Archivist, at the Philadelphia City Archives; Matthew Edney, Director of the History of Cartography Project, Department of Geography, University of Wisconsin; Sister Benedicta Mahoney, of the Sisters of Charity of Cincinatti Archives Department; Professor Daniel Schaefer of the University of North Florida; Kristina Perez of the Missouri Historical Society, St Louis, Missouri; Nancy Mulhern of the Wisconsin Historical Society; Cindy VanHorn, Library Assistant, at The Lincoln Museum, Fort Wayne, Indiana; John McClure, Reference Department Manager, and Toni M. Carter, Assistant Librarian at the Virginia Historical Society, Richmond, Virginia. I would like to thank Fredrika Teute, Editor of Publications, Omohundro Institute of Early American History and Culture, for her interest in my work and for suggesting that Imlay would take over my life if I did not write this book; Jack P. Greene, Emeritus Professor of Early American History at Johns Hopkins University, for his friendship, his superb scholarship and his irreverent wit; and Frank Shuffleton, Professor of English at the University of Rochester, for donating a reprint copy of the 1797 London edition of Imlay's *Topographical Description* in the earlier days of this project.

In the European theatre I am deeply indebted to Jud Campbell, who on more than one occasion sacrificed his valuable research time at the Archives Nationales, Paris, and the Institute of Historical Research, London, to gather key information and documents for me. Historian Gunnar Molden is a leading expert on eighteenth- and nineteenth-century trade and shipping links between Scandinavia and Western Europe, and over the years has generously shared with me his vast knowledge of the subject and his many fascinating discoveries in this area. I want to thank him for this and for keeping up a long email correspondence with me. I would like to thank David Dobson for his expert advice on the Scottish emigration to America and John Urie of the Aberdeen and North-East Scotland Family History Society for providing information on the Imlays of Aberdeenshire. Professor Rosa María García-Barroso, at the Research Institute for North American Studies of the University of Alcalá, has directed me to archives in Spain, while Professor Franklin Kopitzsch of the University of Hamburg answered queries about archives in Hamburg and Altona. Lyndall Gordon, Senior Research Fellow, St Hilda's College, Oxford, was very kind to send me some of the Imlay material she had collected for her recent biography of Mary Wollstonecraft. At the Ministry of Foreign Affairs, Paris, I am grateful to Françoise Watel, Curator of Diplomatic Archives, and Isabelle Richefort, Chef du département des archives historiques, for helping me locate key documents relating to American blockade runners. Sylvie Barot, Chief Curator at the Archives municipales du Havre, patiently answered my questions about the registers of the 'état-civil', and Laurent Durel was so kind as to photograph Fanny Imlay's birth certificate for me. Linda Romeril, Head of Archives and Collections of the Jersey Heritage Trust, St Helier, Jersey, kindly granted me permission to reproduce material from the Jersey Archive. Toby Chiang, Archives Assistant at the Jersey Archive, did valuable research for me in the court archives and the St Brelade burial records. A special thanks to Janet Todd, Professor of English at the University of Aberdeen and biographer *par excellence*, whose outstanding work on Mary Wollstonecraft has been an inspirational example to me and who has supported my work on Imlay these past few years.

Much of the material for the early chapters of this book was gathered during the many months I spent at the John Carter Brown Library, at Brown University, Providence, Rhode Island, first as a Library Associates' Research Fellow (2002) and subsequently during my stint as the inaugural Charles H. Watts II Professor in the History of the Book and Historical Bibliography (2003). Then Director Norman Fiering and his dedicated staff provided a uniquely welcoming research environment for archival scholars, and I will never forget his kindness, encouragement and loyal support. I was fortunate to be able to continue my work at the John Carter Brown Library as an Invited Research Scholar in 2004 and 2005. Further funding for my research was provided by a C. Ballard Breaux Visiting Fel-

lowship from the Filson Historical Society, Louisville, Kentucky (2004). A grant
from the Netherlands Organisation for Scientific Research (2004) enabled me to
write sections of this book.

I would like to thank the following institutions for granting me permission to
reproduce the images to which they hold the copyright: the G. W. Blunt White
Library Collection, Mystic Seaport Museum, Mystic Seaport, Connecticut,
for the Bill of Sale of Human Cargo; the Collections of The New Jersey Historical Society, Newark, New Jersey, for the plat of Robert Imley's Plantation;
the Department of Rare Books and Special Collections, Princeton University
Library, Princeton, New Jersey, for the Shingled Plots near Huston's Fork of
South Fork on Licking River, Kentucky; the Wisconsin Historical Society, Madison, Wisconsin, for the letter of Gilbert Imlay to Daniel Boone, 21 September
1786; the Houghton Library, Harvard College Library, Harvard University,
Cambridge, Massachusetts, for the letter of Joel Barlow to Ruth Barlow, 19 April
1793; Archives municipales du Havre, France, for the birth certificate of Fanny
Imlay; the Jersey Heritage Trust, St Helier, Jersey, and the Reverend Mark Bond,
Rector of St Brelade's Parish, Jersey, for the burial record of Gilbert Imlay.

I am grateful to the following institutions for granting me permission to
quote from manuscripts in their collections: Allentown-Upper Freehold Historical Society (Allentown, New Jersey); Archives des Affaires Étrangères (Paris);
Archives Municipals du Havre (Le Havre); Archives Nationales (Paris); Archivo
Histórico-Nacional (Madrid); Beinecke Rare Book and Manuscript Library,
Yale University (New Haven, Connecticut); Bodleian Library (Oxford); Dan-
ish National Archives; David Library of the American Revolution (Washington
Crossing, Pennsylvania); Filson Historical Society (Louisville, Kentucky); Guild-
hall Library (London); G. W. Blunt White Library, Mystic Seaport Museum
(Mystic, Connecticut); Houghton Library, Harvard University (Cambridge,
Massachusetts); Jefferson County Circuit Clerk's Office (Louisville, Kentucky);
Jersey Archive (St Helier, Jersey); Kentucky Historical Society, Special Col-
lections and Archives Library (Frankfort, Kentucky); Kentucky Land Office
(Frankfort, Kentucky); Kentucky State Archives (Kentucky Department for
Library and Archives, Frankfort, Kentucky); Library of Congress (Washington,
DC); Library of Virginia (Richmond, Virginia); Lincoln Museum (Fort Wayne,
Indiana); Maryland Historical Society (Baltimore, Maryland); Massachusetts
Historical Society (Boston, Massachusetts); Monmouth County Archives
(County Clerk's Office, Manalapan, New Jersey); Monmouth County His-
torical Association (Freehold, New Jersey); National Archives (formerly Public
Record Office, Kew, United Kingdom); National Archives and Records Admin-
istration (Washington, DC); Nelson County Circuit Clerk's Office (Bardstown,
Kentucky); New Jersey Historical Society (Newark, New Jersey); New Jersey
State Archives (Trenton, New Jersey); New Jersey State Library (Trenton, New

Jersey); New York Public Library; Princeton University Library, Rare Books and Special Collections (Princeton, New Jersey); Rhode Island Historical Society (Providence, Rhode Island); Rutgers University Library (New Brunswick, New Jersey); South Carolina Department of Archives and History (Columbia, South Carolina); South Carolina Historical Society (Charleston, South Carolina); Statsarkivet i Kristiansand (Kristiansand, Norway); Stockholm Riksarkivet (Stockholm, Sweden); University of Virginia (Charlottesville, Virginia); Virginia Historical Society (Richmond, Virginia); William L. Clements Library, University of Michigan (Ann Arbor, Michigan); Wisconsin Historical Society (Madison, Wisconsin). Chris Grasso, editor of the *William and Mary Quarterly*, kindly granted me permission to reprint pages that originally appeared, in different form, in the journal. Portions of the manuscript were delivered at conferences and institutions in Europe and the United States; I want to thank various hosts and audiences for their invitations, their attentiveness and their questions.

At Pickering & Chatto, I would like to thank Publishing Director Mark Pollard for believing in this book and for graciously extending the deadline when I was squeezed. As always, it has been a pleasure to work with Editorial Manager Julie Wilson, whose professionalism compensates for any author's slackness.

I would like to acknowledge an irredeemable debt to Simone and Nathan, for missing out on years of their childhood, and to Amanda Gilroy, for everything. Finally, my Dutch warmblood, Peco, has kept me balanced when writing was pushing me to the edge.

I dedicate this book to Emory Elliott, Distinguished Professor of English and Director of the Center for Ideas and Society, University of California, Riverside, in appreciation of two decades of inspiration and encouragement in the study of early American culture.

WMV
Westport Point, MA, January 2008

LIST OF FIGURES

PROLOGUE: THE MANY LIVES OF GILBERT IMLAY

How can you love to fly about continually – dropping down, as it were, in a new world – cold and strange! – every other day? Why do you not attach those tender emotions round the idea of home, which even now dim my eyes?
Mary Wollstonecraft to Gilbert Imlay, 10 June 1795[1]

Consciousness does not determine life, but life determines consciousness
Karl Marx, from *The German Ideology*, 1845–6[2]

The American Gilbert Imlay (*c.* 1754–*c.* 1828) was a man of many talents and trades. Described by one commentator as 'unscrupulous, independent, courageous, a dodger of debts to the poor, a deserter, a protector of the helpless, a revolutionist, a man of enlightenment beyond his age, a greedy and treacherous land booster',[3] Gilbert Imlay was all of these and more. In many ways a prototype of the American conman, Imlay constantly had to reinvent himself as he tried to survive on the murky margins of a late eighteenth-century transatlantic world deeply divided by international political rivalry, ideological conflict and military tension. Although by no means a major historical figure in his own right, Imlay unwittingly acted as an interface between figures of much greater historical significance. Their diverse and often mutually exclusive ideas and ambitions, dreams and schemes he frequently borrowed and then disseminated across continents and across the Atlantic, whilst invariably serving his own, usually less honourable interests.

An officer in the American Revolutionary Army, Imlay set out to try his luck across the Allegheny Mountains in the Ohio Valley not long after hostilities between Britain and her American colonies had ended, most probably in the early spring of 1783. As a deputy surveyor for Jefferson County, Imlay was soon deeply invested in the Kentucky land bubble, rubbing shoulders with prominent historical figures – as well as wholesale land-jobbers – such as Daniel Boone, Richard Henderson, John Filson, General George Rogers Clark, Benjamin Sebastian, General James Wilkinson and Henry ('Light-Horse Harry') Lee. Of these, Imlay could count Wilkinson, Sebastian and Lee among his closest friends and trusted legal representatives; they were also his partners in business, as well as in crime. Having piled up more debts than he could handle while successfully eluding sheriffs' summonses and court writs, Imlay quietly left the West in late 1785. Back East, Imlay invested – and lost – his remaining assets in a venture in the triangular trade, after which he disappeared from America some time during the summer of 1787. It is not known what he did or where he was during the next few years, but evidently he put his experiences in Kentucky to good use. When we next hear from him, in 1792, he is in London and the author of *A Topographical Description of the Western Territory of North America*, which quickly became one of the decade's most widely disseminated and influential books on America's trans-Alleghenian West. In 1793 Imlay followed up on the success of his *Topographical Description* with an epistolary novel, *The Emigrants*, America's first frontier novel, and the nation's only Jacobin novel.

Widely regarded in Europe as an expert on the topographical conditions and commercial potential of the American West and as a friend of the French Revolution, Imlay on the eve of the Terror gained access to the group of intellectuals and revolutionaries that had gathered around the notorious radical Thomas Paine at his Paris home in the Faubourg Saint-Denis – a group that included such Francophile expatriates and Revolution tourists as the radical scientist and philosopher Thomas Cooper, the novelist Helen Maria Williams and her lover, the radical publisher and merchant John Hurford Stone, the poet, land-jobber and merchant Joel Barlow, the businessman and co-editor of the liberal *Analytical Review* Thomas Christie, and Mary Wollstonecraft, the founder of modern feminism. During his stay in France, Imlay is also known to have had dealings with a number of prominent French politicians, including the minister of foreign affairs, Lebrun, and the Girondist leader Brissot de Warville, as well as the Venezuelan freedom fighter General Francisco de Miranda and Hector St John de Crèvecoeur, French diplomatic, merchant and renowned author of *Letters from an American Farmer*.[4] Most scholars of the Romantic era would associate Imlay with his tempestuous and ill-fated liaison with Wollstonecraft; less well known is Imlay's involvement in the spring of 1793 in the Girondist cabal – masterminded by Brissot – to launch a rebellion in Kentucky against the Spanish interests in Louisiana. Imlay prepared two reports on the West for the French government, in the first of which he proposes to take a small army of saboteurs into Louisiana to destabilize Spanish rule there.[5] The documents were duly presented to the notorious Committee of Public Safety, but nothing was done with them for soon afterwards the Girondists were ousted from the National Convention, Brissot went to the guillotine, and Genet, the Minister Plenipotentiary of the French Republic to the United States, was recalled to France. After a last chance meeting with Wollstonecraft on the New Road in London in the spring of 1796, Imlay disappeared from her life and by and large from public life altogether. As Imlay embarked on a succession of progressively shadier trades and business ventures, the initial impact of his topographical writings continued to be felt in the decade's political debates and polemics in both Britain and the United States, leaving a long trail in the print history of the period.

Space and mobility were central to Imlay's life and activities. He was a man who moved often and who moved fast. In the early 1780s, when the Appalachian Mountains still formed a formidable barrier between the East and the West, Imlay was slipping into and out of the Kentucky back country as easily as the hero of his novel *The Emigrants* moves across the vast regions of the 'Old North West'. Contemporary correspondence from, to and about Imlay reveals a picture of a man who is said to have been sighted in Richmond, or believed to be in New Jersey; presumed to have been in New York, but expected soon in Baltimore; just left Charleston but thought to be en route to Louisville or Lexington. In Europe, Imlay moved with equal ease in and between England and France, despite restrictions imposed on domestic and international travel during the Anglo-French War. He was a man who was seldom where he said he would be, and when he was, would not be there for long. His itinerant lifestyle was the mark of a man who was invariably involved in clandestine and often plainly illegal mercantile activities – varying from land-jobbing to racketeering and from slave-trading to blockade running. Inevitably, Imlay was not someone to leave many lasting impressions, let alone documented traces of his presence and activities.

This relative paucity of source material has rendered it hard to reconstruct the complete story of Imlay's life. Except for the three years of his life that he lived in the shadow of Mary Wollstonecraft, the known facts about Gilbert Imlay's life have until now been sketchy, as well as scattered over an extraordinarily wide range of archives and other depositories. Given the illegitimate nature of his business activities, much of the source material for this book has been located in court archives, notably in Kentucky. A substantial part of that material has so far been untapped by researchers (indeed, it is not infrequently unsorted and uncatalogued). Another major source of information has been the private and business correspondence of individuals who had dealings with Imlay. Even so, since Imlay's side of the correspondence is often missing, writing this biography has been somewhat similar to trying to prove the existence of a black hole: more often than not, Imlay's presence and movements can only be established vicariously by observing the movement of satellites orbiting him.

Over the past few decades, Wollstonecraft's biographers have thoroughly researched the three years Imlay spent with her – roughly, from March 1793 to March 1796. It was unavoidable that they should have been primarily guided in their explorations by Wollstonecraft's surviving letters to her lover. However, Wollstonecraft's letters to Imlay have put him at a double disadvantage. Not only have Imlay's letters to her not survived – so his side of the story is missing – but her letters to Imlay were also carefully edited prior to publication by her then husband, William Godwin.[6] Mourning the recent death of his wife, Godwin was eager to present her to the world as a woman capable of extraordinary empathy and sensibility, who was driven to distraction in a world dominated by material-ism, greed and soul-destroying trade – a world epitomized, in Godwin's mind, by Gilbert Imlay. Unsurprisingly, scholars in the field of British Romantic stud-ies have come to know Imlay above all as the philanderer who abandoned Mary Wollstonecraft – and their infant daughter – and drove her to attempt suicide twice. No one's reputation and character would have emerged unscathed from the kind of heart-rending account that Wollstonecraft gives of her affair with Imlay in her letters to him. Taking their cue from Godwin, most Wollstonecraft scholars have therefore generally concurred with Godwin that in rejecting Woll-stonecraft's love, Imlay behaved like 'the base Indian [who threw] a pearl away, richer than all his tribe'.[7]

Without aspiring to materially challenge or replace it, this book aims to correct and nuance the abiding image of Imlay as Wollstonecraft's infamous lover. But, more importantly, *Citizen of the World* wants to complement existing accounts of Imlay by recounting the full story of his life. Relatively little research has been done into Imlay's life after his relationship with Wollstonecraft ended, and hardly any into the thirty-five years, or so, which he spent in America before he came to Europe. In the final analysis, Imlay may be one of the main chapters in Wollstonecraft's biography, but even during the rosy days of their affair, Mary Wollstonecraft played second fiddle to Imlay's true mistress – speculative trade. This is the first study to treat the figure of Gilbert Imlay as an individual in his own right. Hence the research for this biography has been focused specifically on the underexposed and largely unexplored periods in Imlay's life, particularly his American years.

Gilbert Imlay was in many ways a paradigmatic figure of his time. He belonged to that generation of Americans, born in the 1750s, whose lives were crucially shaped by the revolutions in America and France – the two historical events that sent cataclysmic shock-waves through the late eighteenth-century circumatlantic world order and that, it is generally accepted, ushered in politi-cal modernity and marked the birth of the modern subject. Swept along by the strong current of historical events, this generation was indelibly marked by its historical moment. The dawn of liberty may have boosted human agency, but, ironically, the revolutionary process that paved the way for liberty largely dic-tated the experiences of those caught up in it. Hence the lives of many men of Imlay's generation – Joel Barlow, James Swan, Samuel Blackden, Nathaniel Cut-ting, Mark Leavenworth, Benjamin Hichborn and scores of others – evolved along remarkably similar lines. It was their active involvement in America's bid for liberty and republicanism that gave these men direct access to the revolutionary process that would later unfold in France; it was their neutral American passports that would enable them to amass fortunes in the wartime trade with the French Republic. In the case of Joel Barlow and Gilbert Imlay, the dictates of history and geography prescribed almost identical scenarios for their lives. Both Imlay and Barlow served in the Revolutionary Army, after which they became speculators in western land; in Europe they became avowed republicans, combining a career in trade with a life of letters; during the Anglo-French war they became purveyors to the French government and proposed plans to help France reconquer Louisiana, after which they drifted into relative anonymity.

Gilbert Imlay's life in all probability began on 9 February 1754 in the township of Upper Freehold, Monmouth County, New Jersey, where the Imlay family had been established since the late seventeenth century – lending their name to present-day Imlaystown, Monmouth County. As far as we know, it ended on 20 November 1828 in the parish of St Brelade's, on the Channel Island of Jersey. Yet the neat geographical symmetry suggested by his place of birth (New Jersey) and death (Jersey) is an ironic counterpoint to the lack of reliable information Imlay's biographers have had to contend with.[8] How did this New Jersey-born adventurer become a citizen of the world before finding his last resting place on the Isle of Jersey? The answer is contained in a curious tale of reverse transatlantic emigration.

1 WAR CHILD AND SOLDIER

New Jersey – 'Crossroads of the American Revolution'
Proverbial saying

We all live the histories that produced us. Gilbert Imlay's life took shape in the unfolding of two dominant historical narratives. One is a story of war and conflict, played out on a regional, national and transnational stage; the other, a story of dissent and diaspora, written into a family of emigrants and settlers. From both he inherited an awareness that harmony is only discord contained, settlement but displacement delayed. Too much history can be a bad thing; the eighteenth century had so much history, it either overwhelmed people, or it released them – from the local, the personal, the here-and-now. For Imlay, speculation, risk-taking and rootlessness were the stuff of life – the same stuff history is made of. Citizens of the world are not born – they are ineluctably made in historical experience. Gilbert Imlay was such a citizen.

Gilbert Imlay was in more than one sense a war child. Born in 1754, Imlay's entry into the world coincided with the start of the French and Indian War, as the North American theatre of the Seven Years War between France and England was called; he came of age amidst the turmoil of the Revolutionary War, during which New Jersey saw more armed engagements than any other state in the union. Directly or indirectly, both historical events would have a deeply formative impact on Imlay's future life. His experiences in the New Jersey militia and, perhaps even more so, his exposure to the near meltdown of social and legal order during the lawless years following the retreat of British forces from the province, honed his survival skills and seems to have somewhat insensitized him to the ethical and legal niceties of conventional life. Without the Herculean struggle between England and France for control over North America, the shock-waves of which were keenly felt in New Jersey and other seaboard colonies at the time, Imlay could not have become the *agent provocateur* who would mastermind for the post-Bastille French government the military plot that would – ostensibly – hand back to them the western territory of North America they had lost to the British.

'It is the nature of great events to obscure the great events that came before', Francis Parkman observed in his monumental study of 'the Old French War'; 'The Seven Years War in Europe is seen but dimly through revolutionary convulsions and Napoleonic tempests; and the same contest in America is half lost to sight behind the storm-cloud of the War of Independence'.[1] Yet the outcome of the titanic struggle between the two rival imperial powers would decide not just who would win supremacy over the North American continent, but also who would gain ascendancy in the wider world beyond. The outcome of the Seven Years War, Parkman mused in 1884,

> made England what she is. It crippled the commerce of her rival, ruined France in two continents, and blighted her as a colonial power. It gave England the control of the seas and the mastery of North America and India, made her the first of commercial nations, and prepared that vast colonial system that has planted new Englands in every quarter of the globe. And while it made England what she is, it supplied to the United States the indispensable condition of their greatness, if not of their national existence.[2]

In hindsight, the result of the conflict seems to have been a foregone conclusion; but to those who fought the war and to those who got caught up in the turmoil it generated, it was far from being so.

At the heart of the geopolitical conflict between France and Britain was the question which side would gain control over the vast trans-Alleghenian western territory. The French were firmly established in the north – Canada – and the south – Louisiana. A chain of military posts, circling through the western wilderness nearly three thousand miles, precariously connected the Gulf of St Lawrence with the Gulf of Mexico. Midway between New France and Louisiana lay the valley of the Ohio. If the British were to claim the West, they would have to seize the Ohio Valley and thereby sever the chain of French posts; if the French were to consolidate their presence in the Ohio Valley, they would effectively shut the British between the Alleghenies and thus curb further British expansion on the North American continent. The key to the great West was the fork of the Ohio River, where the Monongahela River joins the Allegheny – today the site of Pittsburgh. A band of English backwoodsmen had already started to build a fort there in the early spring of 1754, when a French contingent of around five hundred men arrived at the spot, claimed it for France, and started building what would become Fort Duquesne. Part of a regiment of the Virginia militia on orders from Governor Dinwiddie of Virginia to warn the French to stop erecting fortresses close to the British territory arrived too late on the scene. In late May a small contingent of the Virginia regiment, under the command of George Washington, then a twenty-two-year-old newly commissioned lieutenant-colonel, advanced upon the fort and clashed with a French reconnaissance force. Though only ten French soldiers and one Virginian were killed, 'this obscure skirmish began the war that set the world on fire', as Parkman put it.[3] Eager to revenge their losses, the French on 3 July launched an attack on Fort Necessity (in present-day Fayette County, Pennsylvania), which had been hastily erected by Washington in the preceding weeks. Outnumbered by two-to-one, Washington agreed to surrender the Fort on 4 July, although the British were allowed to walk with all honours.

Despite the French occupation of the Ohio Valley, George Washington's defeat at Fort Necessity and Indian attacks on Virginia's frontier, frontier settlers were willing to risk their lives and property. But this was all to change after the defeat of Major General Edward Braddock's army at the Monongahela in the summer of 1755. In April 1755 Braddock set out on an extremely arduous wilderness expedition against the French-held Fort Duquesne. His force had to cut a road westward from Fort Cumberland, Maryland, the first road across the Allegheny Mountains: the same road that after the Revolution would become one of the main routes for emigrants from New Jersey and Pennsylvania across the mountains to the west – indeed, the very same route that Imlay would take on his way to Kentucky in 1783. Three hundred axemen led the way to cut and clear the road, which was twelve feet wide, and the line of march often extended four miles. George Washington, now a colonel and aide-de-camp, was among the 500 provincials and 1,400 British regulars under Braddock's command. It was Washington who proposed to split the army. The best troops, horses, wagons and a limited number of artillery pieces would push ahead while the rest of the force would bring up the supply train. As the British slowly and cautiously advanced through thick forests and swamps, a force was dispatched from Fort Duquesne to intercept them as they were fording the Monongahela at one of two crossings. The French force consisted of around 250 soldiers and Canadians and an assortment of around 600 allied Indians, mainly Hurons, Potawotomis, Ottawas, Shawnees, Missisaugas, Iroquois, Delaware and Mingos. The British managed to cross both fords, in force, unmolested. However, soon after they had crossed the Monongahela for the second time, the forward column of around 1,200 men was ambushed in a ravine about 7 miles south of the fort. With the Indians pursuing those who tried to flee and finishing off the wounded, casualties were horrific. Nearly all the officers and about two-thirds of the fighting men were either dead or wounded. The massacre left an indelible sorrow in the collective consciousness of colonial America – and beyond. Thus, in his novel *The Emigrants* (1793) Imlay would have his heroine, Caroline, on her journey across the Alleghenies to Pittsburgh, halt in respectful mourning at 'the spot which was made memorable by the defeat of the gallant Braddock' and pay tribute to 'the sepulchers of so many brave Englishmen'.[4]

In the wake of Braddock's defeat, the frontier was left unguarded. The first to suffer the consequences were the settlers in western Pennsylvania, who were soon exposed to a campaign of bloody raids by marauding Indians. As rumours of further impending Indian attacks spread, hundreds of settlers began fleeing eastward, many of them seeking refuge in the Jerseys. The wave of panic sweeping through the frontier settlements thus reverberated through the eastern provinces, where newspaper accounts of the military engagements and Indian incursions were eagerly read. Petitions poured into the New Jersey Assembly from the northern counties, which prompted legislators to provide funds to raise troops and build blockhouses along the Delaware River.

No engagement during the French and Indian War brought the conflict closer to the hearts and minds of the New Jerseymen than the attack and surrender of Fort William Henry in upstate New York. Situated on the south shore of Lake George, Fort William Henry was of key strategic importance to the defence of southern New England and the middle provinces against the combined threat of the French and Indian nations. In late July 1757 the French under the Marquis de Montcalm assembled a force of 3,081 regular troops, 2,946 Canadian militia, 188 artillery men and 1,806 Indians for an attack on Fort William Henry. By the time the siege began Lieutenant-Colonel George Monro had under his command around 2,200 men, including militias from Massachusetts and New Jersey. As in the case of Braddock's defeat on the Monongahela, what made the deepest impression on the colonials away from the battlefield was the brutal treatment of prisoners at the hands of the Indians. New Jersey militiamen served in the English army and fought at all major battles. In August 1756 a large part of the New Jersey regiment was captured during the siege and sacking of Fort Oswego, a strategic British stronghold on Lake Ontario, by a French force under Montcalm. In 1757 a detachment of the regiment was wiped out in a fight at Sabbath Day Point on Lake George. But nowhere did they suffer such heavy losses as during the siege of Fort William Henry. During the siege, around three hundred provincials, chiefly from New Jersey, set out from Fort William Henry under command of Colonel Parker to reconnoitre the French outposts. Having been discovered by Montcalm's scouts, a band of Indians ambushed the militiamen. About two hundred New Jersey provincials – about half of the province's troops – were massacred and of the ones they captured, the Indians ate three on the spot.[5] The atrocities at the fort earned an enduring place in the popular national imagination in James Fenimore Cooper's novel *The Last of the Mohicans*.

Accounts of Indian atrocities at Fort William Henry and of the 'calamitous Situation' of the provinces following the French victory quickly began to appear in local newspapers.[6] From just across the Raritan Bay, reports were coming in of great numbers of New Yorkers having gone upstate to defend Albany against an expected Indian attack: 'Long-Island is all in Motion; the neighbouring Counties embarking for Albany. West-Chester County, and all above the high Lands, are gone up.'[7] Increasingly newspapers were carrying accounts of murderous raids from across the Delaware River into New Jersey by marauding Indians, who were getting more and more brazen in their attacks on communities and blockhouses, particularly in the north-western counties. In its issue of 31 May 1758 the *New American Magazine* (published at Perth Amboy) reported a string of such Indian raids in Sussex County, while on 6 July 1758 the *Pennsylvania Gazette* printed 'A List of the Killed in Jersey, since May 1757'.[8] In the same issue the *Gazette* also reported that two hundred soldiers had been posted on 'our Frontiers' to keep 'the Inhabitants from leaving their Habitations'. This followed the decision of the New Jersey Assembly in June 1757 that a militia be immediately raised in the wake of the Sussex County murders perpetrated by Indians. In addition, the Assembly voted to bring the New Jersey regiment up to a strength of 1,000 men. The regiment was popularly known as the 'Jersey Blues', after the colour of their uniforms. By the autumn of 1758, the New Jersey Assembly had commissioned a line of defence to protect the population against such attacks, particularly in the north-western part of the province. The line of defence consisted of a chain of nine small forts or blockhouses and four smaller 'ranging posts', stretching along the east bank of the Delaware River from downstream of the Delaware Water Gap on the north-eastern border between New Jersey and Pennsylvania to the Neversink River Valley in southern New York. In practice, however, the forts did little to stop the attacks. Thus, the *Gazette* reported in July 1758 how 'Three of our Jersey Men went over the River to plow, near the Fort at Pequase, when a Party of Indians fell upon them, and murdered and scalped them'.[9] The *New American Magazine* reported in May that Governor Bernard had sent orders to the officers on the Sussex and Warren frontiers to restrain their soldiers from leaving their quarters and straying into the woods to hunt, as some of them had been shot and scalped by Indians.[10]

   The Assembly tried to reduce hostilities by passing acts aimed as relieving the grievances some of the New Jersey tribes had concerning land rights and illegal occupancy by white settlers (Gilbert's uncle, John Imlay, was a presiding judge during one of the land settlement cases).[11] However, a frontier guard of two hundred men was kept up for some time as late as the summer of 1764 in connection with a new wave of Indian raids on settler communities in Pennsylvania during Pontiac's War. Named after the Ottawa chief who was one of the many native leaders of the campaign, Pontiac's War (1763–4) was a coordinated uprising launched by warriors from various tribes who were unhappy with their treatment by the British following their victory over the French in the French and Indian War. The Indians sacked eight smaller British forts and staged lengthy, but unsuccessful, sieges of Fort Detroit and Fort Pitt. American Indian raids on frontier settlements escalated in the spring and summer of 1764, affecting communities in Pennsylvania as well as Virginia and Maryland. Retaliation by white vigilante groups such as the notorious Paxton Boys increased pressure on the borders with New Jersey, as Indian refugees from eastern Pennylvania – many of them Christians who had lived peaceably amongst the white settlers – were seeking a safe haven across the Delaware River.

In the relatively small province of New Jersey, with a population of only seventy to eighty thousand, well stocked with newspapers, a good infrastructure, bustling seaports and wedged in between the two largest colonial urban centres of Philadelphia and New York, news travelled far and fast. Aged ten by the time Pontiac's War drew to a close, Gilbert Imlay had been growing up with a constant stream of reports and rumours of bloody war, threats of French encroachments, of men, women and children having been killed, scalped or abducted, and of forts being erected and men – including some he may have known – being recruited to be stationed in them to protect the borders or to serve in the New Jersey militia. Nor can he have remained unaffected by the dire economic and social consequences of the war, which wreaked havoc upon people's everyday lives in New Jersey. In fact, the French and Indian War had left the province on the verge of bankruptcy.

In order to encourage the colonies to provide both raw materials (including precious metals) and markets for British mercantile expansion, Parliament had enacted laws that prohibited the export of British silver coinage. As a result, specie was extremely scarce in the colonies, which had detrimental effects on trade and manufacturing. In order to alleviate the squeeze on trade, Assemblies had been passing a series of acts allowing for the circulation of bills of credit and other forms of paper money – a process that was very closely monitored by the Crown, which would only permit issues of non-legal-tender paper money for the purpose of meeting provincial charges and wartime expenditures. By the spring of 1754 the Assembly had circulated so much paper money that the rate of exchange of the New Jersey currency had begun to indicate serious deflation. The Assembly wanted to issue more paper money but Governor Belcher shelved the plans. However, Belcher having died unexpectedly in August 1757 and senior Councilor Reading having become acting governor, the Assembly reverted to its favourite activity of increasing the paper money supply. The contingencies to be met following the outbreak of the French and Indian War – the need to provide border protection and calls from the British army to contribute men, material and supplies for distant military campaigns – persuaded the legislators that they should ignore royal instructions and hence they voted in a string of bills of credit. Pontiac's War alone necessitated an emission of £100,000 in 1764. As long as there was a threat from the French and their Indian allies, the Crown tended to authorize these emissions of paper money. Even Belcher's successor, Governor Bernard, conspired to have the regulations liberalized. But soon after peace was declared, the colony's exchequer was short of money again. The result of New Jersey's numerous paper-money issues has been described by one commentator as 'sufficiently perfect to satisfy a fairly orthodox quantity theorist' – that is:

> a large issue of paper money, unfavorable exchange rates for importers, real estate booms and other evidence of prosperity; then, as the notes were retired, debtors began to feel economically pinched, interest rates seemed high and lawyers' fees more excessive, debtors' prisons filled up; next legislation to relieve the situation was passed, chief of which was another paper-money bill; and the cycle was ready to begin again. It did not take the colony's creditor classes long to see the results of inflation, nor the debtors long to see the results of deflation and protest, but few persons, if anybody, saw that the method of suddenly expanding and gradually contracting the paper-money supply was largely responsible for both evils.[12]

Between 1754 and 1764 the small colony of New Jersey had authorized the issuing of £347,000 in paper money, a total exceeding that of any other colony on the continent. Not only that, but it also had one of the most inefficient tax collections. As a result, by 1765 New Jersey had mounted the largest deficit of all of the colonies – a total of £300,000.[13] The adoption by Parliament of the Currency Act of 1764 brought New Jersey to the brink of financial ruin, as the colony could no longer print itself into solvency.

With New Jersey's economy already in a deep depression, the British government's determination to make the colonies bear a large share of the debt it had incurred to fight the French and Indian War spelled more bad news. The Sugar Act of 1764 had a severely detrimental effect on the trade of the middle and New England colonies, while the Stamp Act of 1765 added an additional financial burden on business and trade. William Pitt's repeal of the Stamp Act in February 1766 brought little relief, as his Chancellor of the Exchequer, Charles Townsend, immediately replaced it with a system of import duties on a string of colonial products. However, despite grievances over monetary policy and trade regulation, rebellion against the mother country was as remote a notion in New Jersey as the Revolution itself was unexpected.

Lacking large commercial cities, New Jersey remained a predominantly rural colony, with its population of just under 130,000 at the start of the Revolution spread out over hundreds of small towns and villages. Neither the Boston Massacre in March 1770 nor the Boston Tea Party of December 1773 attracted much attention in New Jersey. The colony was more preoccupied with the Crown's decision on its latest paper money act than with any thought of rebellion against the Crown. And yet, because it held a key geographical position between Philadelphia and New York City, New Jersey was to see more engagements than any other state during the war.

New Jersey was known as the 'crossroads' of the American Revolution, with armies in it or crossing it throughout the war. In November 1776 Washington's troops started their retreat across New Jersey to the other side of the Delaware River, chased by the British after the fall of New York City. Between late December 1776 and mid January 1777 Washington's forces in turn chased the British out of most of New Jersey, gaining important victories at the first battle of Trenton and the battle of Princeton. In 1778, after they had abandoned Philadelphia, the British under Sir Henry Clinton crossed through New Jersey again, where Washington engaged them on 6 June at the battle of Monmouth. On the eve of the latter engagement, the largest one-day battle of the war and the last major engagement of the northern theatre, one column of Clinton's force encamped at Imlaystown, while another occupied Allentown. After French General Comte de Rochambeau and his troops joined Washington on the Hudson River in July 1781, the two armies marched through New Jersey on their way south to battle the British troops under Cornwallis in Virginia. In an attempt to oust Washington from his position in the Watchung Mountains, the British attacked the Americans around Springfield twice in July 1780.

In addition to the major actions that took place in New Jersey, there were hundreds of smaller battles, engagements, skirmishes, raids, ambushes and so on, involving regular troops as well as militia and loyalist units, vigilante groups and privateers. Bordering on the Hudson River as well as having a long sea coast with many small bays and ports, New Jersey in addition saw many engagements on its river shores and off the sea coast. The area along the Hudson River from above the New York border south to Sandy Hook was known as New Jersey's 'Neutral Ground'. Although its navy dominated the shore, the British could not occupy the area without risking being pushed back by the Americans; for their part, the Americans could not control the area because the close proximity of the British across the river meant that they could be under attack at any point in time. The Neutral Ground became the scene of a brutal conflict between Patriots (or 'rebels') and Loyalists (or the 'disaffected'), assisted by the armed forces of both sides.[14] New Jersey Patriots used whaleboats and small ships as privateers to raid British shipping and territories around New York City, Long Island and off Sandy Hook. Loyalists (or 'refugees') from British-held Manhattan, Staten and Long Islands would raid across the river into New Jersey, taking up arms against their former neighours and friends. Raids were both large and small in the Neutral Ground. Some involved only a few men, others were in fact invasions of a thousand or more men. The British frequently sent raids into New Jersey for military purposes and foraging. Loyalist and Hessian raids were usually carried out for plunder, retaliation, to capture prisoners for exchange, or simply out of hatred of the other side. Affording easy access from the sea in the north and east,

Monmouth County was more afflicted by refugee marauding parties than all the rest of the state combined.

The American Revolution in New Jersey was in many ways a nasty civil war, often with neighbour pitted against neighbour or family member against family member. In Monmouth County this intestine war was particularly brutal and vicious. Not infrequently, long-standing feuds between families or disputes between neighbours over land would be settled under the guise of wartime exigency. The Patriots looted the Tories, raided their strongholds, confiscated their lands and torched their homes, all under the auspices of the treason acts. The Loyalists retaliated in kind and would pass information about rebel activity to the British. At one time the refugees took possession of the village of Freehold, but were driven out after a week by the Whigs. Some of the refugees took to the swamps and woods, where Loyalist sympathizers would supply them with food and arms. Hiding by day in the recesses of the 'Pines' or amid the dunes of the seashore, marauding parties of these 'Pine Robbers' would ride at night to plunder and burn the homes of Whigs, kidnapping and summarily executing some. Many of the Pine Robbers belonged to a somewhat loosely structured military corps called the 'Associated Loyalists', which had been set up amongst refugees in New York City and which was led by William Franklin, an illegitimate son of Benjamin Franklin and the last royal governor of New Jersey. In June 1780 over four hundred inhabitants of Monmouth County formed a Patriot vigilante group known as the 'Association for Retaliation'. Apparently begun as a mutual protection league to defend its members against the depredations of Loyalists, the Association soon exceeded the spirit as well as the letter of the law by terrorizing, intimidating and plundering friends and foes alike. Members of many of Monmouth's prominent families joined the Association, which from 1780 to 1783 was chaired by Colonel David Forman, a former commanding officer of a regiment in the New Jersey militia.[15]

* * *

A fourth generation descendant of Scottish-Presbyterian immigrant stock, Gilbert Imlay was born in Imlaystown in or around 1754 into what was already an extended dynasty in Upper Freehold Township, Monmouth County, in the colony of East New Jersey. Tucked away among the gently undulating hills of central New Jersey, about sixteen miles south-east of Princeton, the present-day village of Imlaystown is an enduring memorial to the prominent status the Imlays once held in this part of the state. Imlaystown was founded in 1690 by the family's immigrant progenitor, Patrick Imlay, from whom the place derives its name. According to local folklore, the narrow, winding Main Street follows the pattern of an Indian village that once stood there, on the banks of Doctor's Creek. Around the time of Gilbert Imlay's presumed death on the Isle of Jersey, Imlaystown was described as a post-town containing '12 or 15 dwellings, a grist mill and saw mill, tannery, 1 tavern, 1 store, wheelwright and smith shop'.[16] The village nowadays consists of around thirty buildings that can trace their roots back to the mid-nineteenth century, although most of them were rebuilt after a fire in 1898 destroyed much of the property in the town. Most of the houses are two-storey wood-frame buildings, several of them still equipped with colonial-style cellar kitchens. One of the town's most striking buildings is an old grist mill known as 'Salter's Mill' – although the present construction, no longer in use as a mill, replaces several earlier mills that were burnt down at the same site. During much of the eighteenth century, the town was the hub of social, economic and political life in Upper Freehold, but its fortunes have since then been in a slow but steady decline. Along with the farms in the surroundings area that once supported the town, Imlaystown now threatens to fall prey to New Jersey's voracious urban sprawl. Ironically, ever since the village was added to the state and national registers of historic places in 1985, many of its buildings have fallen into further decay. Some properties are currently uninhabitable because of sanitation issues caused by the proximity of Doctor's Creek. Unsurprisingly, Imlaystown is currently on Preservation New Jersey's top-ten list of endangered historic sites in Monmouth County.[17]

The history of Monmouth County, and, indeed, that of the entire state of New Jersey, is inextricably bound up with the history of the persecution and dispossession of large numbers of English and Scottish Dissenters in the course of the seventeenth century, and their subsequent relocation in America. After the New Netherlands colony had been seized by Colonel Richard Nicolls in September 1664, Charles II granted the region between the St Lawrence River and the Delaware as a proprietary colony to his brother James, Duke of York, later James II. In June 1665 James in turn granted the territory between the Hudson River and the Delaware to two of his closest friends, John Berkeley, first Baron of Stratton, and Sir George Carteret. Both men had been loyal supporters of the Duke during the Civil War and were already the proprietors of the Carolinas.[18] The new province was named Nova Caesaria, or New Jersey, in compliment to Carteret, who, as governor of the Channel Island of Jersey, had been the last to surrender to the Commonwealth's forces in 1649. In February 1664 Carteret and Berkeley drew up a document which they later made public under the title of 'The Concessions and agreement of the Lords Proprietors of New Jersey, to and with all and every of the adventurers, and all such as shall settle and plant there'. To all intents and purposes a constitution for the colony of New Jersey, the 'Concessions and Agreement' described the structure of government for the new colony and the conditions on which colonists could settle there. However, the key aim of the proclamation was to entice more settlers to move to the colony, as this would allow the proprietors to maximize the profitability of their property by collecting so-called 'quitrents', or annual fees paid on granted lands. To encourage such settlement, the 'Concessions and Agreement' guaranteed

> that noe person ... within the said Province at any time shalbe any waies molested punished disquieted or called in Question for any difference in opinion or practice in matters of Religious concernements, who doe not actually disturbe the civill peace of the said Province, but that all and every such person and persons may from time to time and at all times truly and fully have and enjoy his and their Judgments and Conciences in matters of Religion throughout all the said Province.[19]

The promise of religious freedom acted as a strong incentive to many among Britain's dissenting sects to settle in the new colony, notably Quakers, Presbyterians and Baptists. Townships quickly began to spring up, including Bergen (1665), Elizabeth-Town (1664), Middletown and Shrewsbury (1665), Woodbridge (1666), Piscataway (1666) and Newark (1667). In March 1683 East Jersey was partitioned for administrative purposes into four counties, each with its own court: Bergen, Essex, Middlesex and Monmouth (Somerset was set off from Middlesex in 1688). The exact boundary line between the two sections of the proprietary colony was in dispute for many years, but the 1676 Quintipartite Deed more or less resolved the conflicting claims, thereby confirming the division of the original proprietory colony into East New Jersey and West New Jersey. After Carteret's death in 1680, his half of the province, East New Jersey, was sold to twelve people, eleven of whom were members of the Society of Friends, led by William Penn. Later in the same year (1682), the twelve purchasers each took on a partner in the venture, and the resulting twenty-four proprietors elected the Scottish Quaker apologist Robert Barclay to be the governor of East Jersey. While the quitrent of 2*d.* per acre (later reduced to 1*d.*) was required throughout East Jersey, it was never systematically or effectively collected. If the quitrent system proved to be highly unprofitable in East Jersey, it had never become prevalent in West Jersey in the first place. This had persuaded proprietor John Berkeley in 1674 to sell West Jersey for £1,000 to two English Quakers, John Fenwick and Edward Byllynge, after which substantial numbers of Quakers settled in Burlington, Gloucester and Salem. In April 1702 the East and West Jersey Proprietors surrendered governance rights to Queen Anne, and New Jersey became a single royal colony. However, the provincial capitals of Perth Amboy and Burlington continued as dual seats of government for the colony's eastern and western divisions, respectively. While the proprietors retained their land rights, deeds, surveys and other records would continue to refer to the provinces of East and West Jersey into the revolutionary period and beyond.

Patrick Imlay's arrival in East Jersey was coterminous with a large-scale exodus of Quakers, Presbyterians and other Dissenters from Scotland which reached its climax in the 1680s. The 'Covenanter Uprisings' during the Commonwealth had resulted in many militant Scottish Presbyterians ('Covenanters') being imprisoned and subsequently sold into service in the colonies. The bitter persecution of Scottish Presbyterians during the periods of Anglican Episcopal rule also contributed significantly to Scottish emigration to the American colonies in the latter half of the seventeenth century. Heavy fines were imposed for non-attendance of the state church, while the death penalty could be decreed for those attending 'conventicles', as clandestine religious gatherings were then called in Scotland. Troops were quartered in areas where Presbyterian dissent was strongest, prisons were filled to capacity, and many were banished to the colonies. Economic conditions, too, were very poor in Scotland at that time. By the early 1680s the situation had become so desperate that a number of prominent Dissenters among the nobility and gentry began to arrange for the settlement of large numbers of colonists in New Jersey (as well as the Carolinas).

The bulk of the Scottish Dissenter emigration to New Jersey took place between 1683 and 1688. Most Scottish emigrants came from the eastern districts, from places such as Edinburgh, Aberdeen, Montrose and Kelso, where it was the Quakers – highly localized in these areas – who organized the emigration to America. Among the most active of the Scottish proprietors in the settlement of East Jersey were James Drummond, fourth Earl of Perth, and his brother, John Drummond, first Earl of Melfort. While Perth and Melfort were more interested in land speculation than in providing an asylum for the persecuted, the person they had nominated as Governor of East Jersey, Robert Barclay, was a learned man and Friends' advocate who had himself suffered persecution and imprisonment. Although he never resided in New Jersey, Governor Barclay sponsored four major expeditions to the colony between 1683 and 1685. One of the communities set up to receive religious convicts from Scotland was founded in East New Jersey in 1682, where the proprietors' agents took up 6,000 acres of land on the Raritan opposite Ambo Point. In 1684 Perth – now Perth Amboy – was made the capital of the new Scottish settlement, so named in honour of the Earl of Perth.

One of the principle backers of the new settlement was George Scot, or Scott (d. 1685) of Pitlochie, a Presbyterian who had repeatedly been fined and imprisoned by the Privy Council of Scotland for attending conventicles. Fully persuaded to seek freedom of worship in the new world, Scot in 1685 published *The Model of the Government of the Province of East New Jersey, in America; and Encouragement for Such as Design to be concerned there*, in which he contrasted the advantages for settlers in East Jersey with the bleak future for Dissenters in Scotland. In recognition of this promotional tract, Scot received a grant of five hundred acres from the proprietors of East Jersey. In the course of 1685 Scot chartered a ship from Newcastle, the *Henry and Francis*, and instructed his agents to round up a hundred prospective settlers, described in an unkind contemporary source as a mixture of prisoners, debtors, poverty-stricken 'whoo-res and prodigal wasters', as well as some Dissenters of 'phanatical principles'.[20] In September of that year, the *Henry and Francis* sailed from Leith for Amer-ica, with captain Richard Hutton as master. Before they reached Land's End, a malignant fever broke out on board, and during the voyage all of the crew except the captain and the boatswain died, along with nearly half of the passengers. In total about seventy persons died, including Scot and his wife. After a voyage of fifteen weeks the survivors, many of whom were so feeble they were scarcely able to walk ashore, were landed at Perth Amboy, from where some of them found their way into Monmouth County.

It has been suggested by some that Patrick Imlay was among this group, although there is no conclusive evidence to support this claim.[21] Beside the *Henry and Francis*, two other vessels that were involved in transporting emigrants from eastern Scotland to East New Jersey between 1683 and 1685 have been positively identified: the *Exchange of Stockton* (which sailed in August 1683 via Aberdeen) and the *Thomas and Benjamin* (which sailed from Montrose in 1684). A third vessel – the *America* – may also have been involved.[22] Although the main body of emigrants on board were Quakers, to make up numbers aboard ship they took Covenanter prisoners and other Dissenters as indentured servants. Patrick Imlay may therefore have sailed on any of these vessels. He would certainly have been in the catchment area of the Quaker emigration schemes from east Scotland: Imlay is a relatively rare surname that is traditionally found in Aberdeenshire, where originally it was Imlach, probably a Gaelic surname.

If he did sail to America as an indentured servant, Patrick Imlay must have coped remarkably well with his replantation to the New World, for when we first come across him in the colonial records, he is neither a destitute dependent nor a socially uprooted exile. Thus, from the early 1690s onwards he was not only acquiring and selling significant tracts of land, first in northern and later in western Monmouth County, but he also appears to have established close rela-tions with several of the gentrified members of the Presbyterian community in the county. An ardent Presbyterian, Patrick Imlay is first found in Monmouth County in 1692, by which time, with some others, he had established a Presby-terian church at what is still known today as the 'Old Scotch Burying Ground' in Marlboro Township, in the north-western section of Monmouth County.[23] Continuing to exert his social status in the service of his faith, Imlay in Decem-ber 1705 joined with John Craig, Walter Ker and William Bennet 'on behalf of their brethren' in a petition to court to record the site of the Old Scots meeting house of the 'Protestant Desenters of Freehold called Presbyterians'.[24] In a deed dated 1 June 1727 Patrick Imlay is mentioned as one of the grantees for a piece of land near the site of the original structure to be used 'for a burying Yard and to keep a Presbyterian Meeting'.[25] Nor did Patrick Imlay ignore his civic duties to the local community. Thus, in November 1705 he was commissioned lieutenant of a company of militia in the eastern part of Freehold under the command of Captain Richard Saltar. It was from the same Richard Saltar that Patrick Imlay in September 1710 bought his first tract of land in the township of Freehold containing 480 acres for the considerable sum of £330. Reflecting Imlay's elevated social standing, the deed identifies him as a 'Gentleman' residing in the township of Freehold.[26] By 1730 he was referred to in deeds as 'Yeoman'.[27]

While in early provincial records he is commonly called 'Patrick Imlay', his name is sometimes rendered as 'Peter'. The family name is variously given as 'Imly', 'Imley', and in its present form of 'Imlay'.[28] Land speculation being America's oldest profession, it is not surprising to see Patrick Imlay's name appear with some regularity in the East and West Jersey deed books. The first conveyance of land to Patrick Imlay is recorded in a deed dated 17 June 1693, when Thomas Boel of Wickatunk conveyed a tract of land of 160 acres to 'Peter Imley' for the consideration of £32.[29] A locality of somewhat indefinite bounds, though apparently having comprised the country lying south of the Raritan River and east of South River, Wickatunk is mentioned in the minutes of the proprietors of East Jersey as a tract containing by estimation 36,000 acres, to be purchased from the Indians at the proposed price of about £250.[30] It had been plotted by the Surveyor General, George Keith, with lands at Topanhemus, and been divided into twenty-four lots, each proprietor to receive his plot by the drawing of lots. Wickatunk included the site of the town of Freehold, which was first formed on 31 October 1693. By deed dated 1710, Patrick Imlay and his wife, Margaret, later conveyed the Wickatunk property to Adrian Bennet for £210, after which they moved west to the Crosswicks area, where they bought the plantation on the south side of Doctor's Creek.[31] Imlay was to acquire several other sizeable tracts of land during his lifetime, including, in March 1700, an interest in a tract of land along the east side of the Matawan Creek,[32] and, in 1701, an interest in a patent for a lot on Winsunkneck, to be used for a landing and a road.[33] On 5 January 1714 Patrick Imlay was involved with William Montgomery and Peter Burnet, all of Freehold, in the purchase of Dr William Robieson's patent of 550 acres lying south of Allentown; on 15 August 1715 he sold his interest of 150 acres to Nathan Allen of Allentown for £30.[34] But it was the 480 acre tract of land on the southern bank of Doctor's Creek, which Imlay bought from Richard Saltar in September 1710, that remained the nucleus of the Imlay family's rapidly expanding landed presence in Imlaystown and the surrounding area.

The site of Imlaystown was part of a large tract of land of 2,100 acres patented by the proprietors to John Baker on 24 May 1690. When Baker died soon after, the tract, 'Intended to be called and known by the name of Manor of Buckhole', passed to George Willocks, one of the East Jersey proprietors, who sold it to Captain Richard Saltar in 1708.[35] Saltar built a grist mill on the site of the present building some time before 1700. Upon his death it passed to Richard Saltar, Jr, who, in April 1727, sold the 50-acre mill property, with 39 acres of mill-pond, to Patrick Imlay's eldest son, Peter, for £650.[36] With Peter, Jr, in possession of the valuable mill property, including 11 acres on the north side of the creek, on which the principal part of the village was located, and his father, Patrick, in possession of a 480-acre tract on the southern bank of Doctor's Creek, the Imlay dynasty was well and truly established in Monmouth County by the late 1720s.

Patrick Imlay died intestate some time prior to 1744, by which time the family's founding estate of 480 acres had been cut up into three different grants. Patrick had granted the easterly section of 111 acres to his second son, Robert, by deed dated 1 May 1715.[37] By deed dated 24 April 1730, Patrick Imlay, then 'of the City of Philadelphia, late of Freehold', and 'Margaret, his wife', conveyed the middle section of 172 acres to Joseph Cannaan. The same deed confirms that by that date the most westerly part of Patrick's original Imlaystown estate had been granted to his youngest son, John (see Figure 1).[38]

Of the four brothers, Robert appears to have inherited his father's patriarchal ambitions. Already the owner of the 111-acre plantation just south of Imlays-town and the 100 acres he acquired from John Runnels by deed dated 17 May 1720, Robert steadily continued to expand the home plantation. By deed dated 3 April 1749 he acquired 97 acres from Esther Lippencott, and 8⅔ acres from Thomas Saltar by deed of 6 May 1752.[39] He purchased a further 200 acres from John Clayton by deed dated 9 August 1746, and 125¾ acres adjoining his home plantation from Robert Gordon by deed dated 14 May 1743.[40] In addition to this, he owned tracts at Mount Pleasant and at Middletown Point (near Mata-wan), both of which he bequeathed to his son John. In 1732 he purchased a half interest in the Imlaystown mill property, after Peter Imlay had previously that year sold it to his brother William following his marriage to Lydia Biddle and his removal to Mansfield Township, Burlington County. When William Imlay died intestate some time before 1744, Robert's interest in the mill appears to have been the subject of legal dispute within the family, as was the title to the house that Patrick Imlay had built for his own use on what was then William's mill property. However, the heirs later agreed that Robert was to have the house for £46, plus a payment of £4 for the lot.[41]

Like his father before him, Robert Imlay combined a successful career as a planter and landowner with being a prominent Presbyterian and a leader in local church affairs. It was as trustees of the Allentown congregation that in December 1744 Robert Imlay and his friend Tobias Polhemus purchased from William Lawrence, a trader in Monmouth, for the consideration of five shillings proclamation money 'A Certain Lott of Land, containing one acre for the use of the Congregation'. A brick church was built on this lot in 1759. In the Royal Charter that was granted to the 'Presbyterians of Monmouth County' on 21 February

1770 by Governor Belcher, in the name of George II, Robert Imlay is named as one of the nine original trustrees.[42]

  Robert Imlay, who was already married by 1719 (when his son, John, was born), died in the latter half of 1754 – his will and inventory were dated 12 June and proved 10 December of that year.[43] The inventory of his estate made by his friends and neighbours Tobias and John Polhemus listed 425 acres of land, which were sold at vendue for £1749.7.6, household goods, a negro wench and

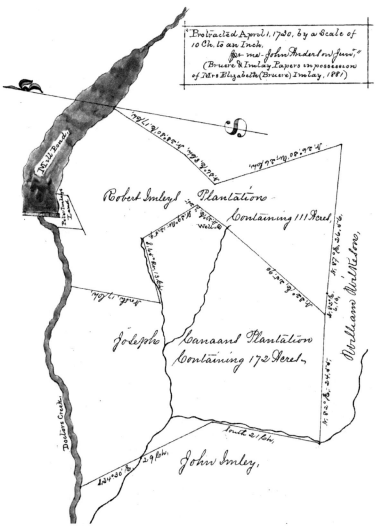

Figure 1. Plat of Robert Imlay's Plantation. Courtesy of the Collections of The New Jersey Historical Society, Newark, New Jersey.

child at £40, farm crops, live stock and equipment.[44] His total estate was valued at £2061.6.8 – a considerable sum at the time – which Robert left to his widow, Alice, and their five children: John, Peter, William, Elizabeth and Margaret. It was the second son, Peter, who, on 6 May 1756, acquired the Imlaystown homestead plantation, as well as the mill property, from Robert's executors (his son John and his son-in-law, Peter Tilton).[45] He apparently continued to do well, for as early as 1758 Peter was taxed for 380 acres of land. Since he was presumably well off, it is not immediately clear why in her 'Last Will & Testament', which was drawn up on 7 June 1761, his mother should leave only a token settlement to her oldest son (despite being her 'well beloved' John) and nothing at all to her three youngest children, yet bequeath all of her possessions to Peter, with smaller legacies to Peter's three minor children. Alice Imlay's will (which she signed as 'Allys Imlay') is a historically significant document because it contains the first known reference to Gilbert Imlay:

> I give and bequath my whole Estate to my Son Peter Imlay both Reail and personable whatsoever and wheresoever whome I do hereby Constitute and Appoint my only and sole Executor only leving him to pay two small Legasys – the first is to pay to my well beloved son John Imlay the sum of five shillings procklamation money & the second is to my grand child it name is Robert Imlay a son of my son Peter Imlay the sum of Ten pounds Procklamation money the money is to be put out at Intrest when the said child is Ten years old & at the age of Twenty one he is to have Both Principal & Intrest and if he Dies before he is that age then I order the said money to be Equally Devided Betwixt my son Peter Imlay two other Children Peggey Imlay & Gilbert Imlay.[46]

It is plausible to conjecture that Alice Imlay left all her worldly possessions to her second son and his children because Peter had recently been widowed and his young children had lost their mother. Information about Gilbert Imlay's father is scarce, but we do know that he married a Mary Holmes in 1762 and that they would have a daughter together, Elizabeth.[47] The mother of his first three children had therefore been another, unidentified woman (although some in the family have suggested that she was a Henderson).[48] Gilbert cannot have been much older than four or five when his mother died; by the time he was in his mid-teens, his stepmother had also passed away (although there is no record of Mary's death). On 13 April 1772 his father once again married, this time to a widow by the name of Euphemia Reading, née Reid.[49] This meant that when he was eighteen years old, Gilbert had acquired a second stepmother. What may have been more unsettling to an impressionable youth than this fact alone was that Euphemia brought no less than nine children into Peter Imlay's family (aged between four and seventeen) – being the children she had borne during the thirteen years she had previously been married to Daniel Reading, who had served as a county collector and captain in the militia before his death in October 1768.

By the end of 1773, Peter and Euphemia would have added another two children of their own (Peter and William) to what was already a bustling family.

It has often been assumed, on the basis of Alice Imlay's will, that Robert must have been the eldest of the three children, followed, in that order, by Peggy and Gilbert.[50] However, this is disproved by the records of Robert's death that appeared in two Philadelphia newspapers in 1827, both of which stated that Robert Imlay was 69 when he died on 11 September of that year.[51] Since Alice's will was probated on 17 August 1761, Robert would only have been three when his grandmother died: that would make it highly improbable that Peggy and Gilbert had been younger than their brother. Alice quite possibly left a bequest of £10 to Robert either because he was the youngest and therefore the most vulnerable or simply because he was named after his grandfather. If Robert was born in 1758, then it is possible that Peggy may have been born around 1756, and Gilbert around 1754 – or the other way around. However, what supports the earlier date as the year of Gilbert's birth is that it would be in line with the Parish register of St Brelade's Church on the Isle of Jersey, which states that Gilbert Imlay died on 20 November 1828, aged 74 (and was interred four days later).[52] This would make Gilbert, born on 9 February 1754, the oldest child; Robert, born in 1758, the youngest; and Peggy, born between 1754 and 1758, the middle child.

Gilbert Imlay grew up on the Imlay home plantation that had belonged to his great-grandfather Patrick, and which his father had acquired from the estate of his grandfather Robert Imlay in 1756. No details about his early years have come to light. It is tempting to speculate that the loss of his mother and grandmother at a tender age, and being raised through boyhood, adolescence and late teens by two stepmothers (who between them had given him twelve half-brothers and sisters), may have had a detrimental effect on his ability to foster emotionally stable bonds with women in later life. On the other hand, growing up in the domestic instability of Peter Imlay's household may have crucially shaped him in terms of his independence, self-sufficiency and adaptability – skills he would come to rely on in the peripatetic life he would lead and which are reflected most of all in the remarkable ease with which he could establish relations with people from all walks of life and could reinvent himself in an instant as the circumstances dictated. In one respect his father's example undoubtedly had a formative impact on Gilbert: he could not have had a better apprenticeship in the land-jobbing trade than Peter Imlay could offer him.

Peter Imlay quite successfully continued in the family trade of buying and selling landed property and steadily increased the acreage he owned in Imlaystown and the surrounding area. On 15 January 1766, for instance, Peter Imlay gave John and Mary Coward £500.2.0 for a tract of just over 90 acres adjoining land he already owned in Imlaystown.[53] While his father and grandfather had still been free-holding farmers who speculated in land to supplement their income, there is no evidence that Peter ever had any interest in being a tiller of the earth – nor does he seem to have shared the religious zeal of his forebears, or, indeed, of many of his relatives who came after him. It was especially after he got married to Euphemia Reading in 1772 that Peter Imlay's land transactions increased sharply in scale and number. It would appear that Euphemia had not only provided him with more stepchildren than he might have wished for but with substantial capital as well. Euphemia was connected to two very prominent New Jersey families. Her father, Colonel John Reid, was the youngest son of John Reid, who had been gardener to the Lord Advocate and author of *The Scotch Gardener* before being sent over to America as a surveyor by the proprietors of New Jersey in 1683, where, having settled at Freehold, he became a member of Assembly and was appointed Surveyor-General of New Jersey in 1702. Euphemia's father-in-law, John Reading, had been Governor of New Jersey from 1756 to 1758 – the first American-born Governor in the British colonies. Given her social background and apparent means, it is probably no coincidence that Euphemia was co-signatory to most of the deeds documenting Peter's transactions after 1772.

It is also evident that, following his marriage to Euphemia, Peter's social ambitions were quickly outgrowing the rural domesticity of Imlaystown and were gravitating more and more towards the urbanite gentility of Allentown, a few miles to the west. Significantly, nearly all of Peter Imlay's property deals in the 1770s involved the sale of land in and around Imlaystown. Thus, in 1772 Peter Imlay and his then business partner Abraham Hendricks were advertising the sale of one of the family's crown jewels, the Imlaystown mill property.[54] On 20 March the following year Peter and Euphemia sold twelve and a half acres of meadow to Aaron Ivins for £100.[55] On 4 September 1778 Peter advertised the sale of 'A Plantation in Upper Freehold, Monmouth County, about four miles from Allentown and twelve miles from Bordentown, containing about 400 acres of land'.[56] And by deed dated 27 May 1779, 'Peter Imlay of Upper Freehold, yeoman, & Euphemia his wife' sold to John Britton no less than seven tracts at Imlaystown totaling just under 410 acres for £20,000.[57] Having given up his position as 'freeholder' for Upper Freehold (as elected county officials are called in New Jersey to the present day), Peter finally uprooted himself and his family from the Imlay homestead plantation in May 1779, and he and Euphemia settled in Allentown.[58] Yet Peter Imlay by no means retired from the speculation trade. By deed dated 13 February 1782 Peter and Euphemia received £375 in gold and silver for the sale of a plantation in Shrewsbury to Arthur Donaldson of Mansfield.[59] Not long after they had settled in Allentown (by deed dated 2 March 1781), Peter bought the Allentown gristmill from Arthur Donaldson and his wife for £3,000.[60] In November 1784 Peter put the mill property back on the market again. Advertising the sale of the 'valuable Mills in Allen-town' in the

Pennsylvania Gazette, Peter stated that she would grind '20,000 bushels country work per year, and 10,000 bushels merchant work'. The mill was a prime piece of property, which included forty-two acres of land, fourteen acres of meadow and seven acres of woodland, as well as two dwelling-houses, a barn, a brick spring-house and twenty fruit-bearing apple trees.[61] However, the post-bellum economic slump had considerably slowed down the property market. Peter and Euphemia eventually managed to sell the Allentown mill at a loss on 22 January 1788 to Robert Pidgeon, who paid £2,500 for it.[62]

Gilbert Imlay's father must have been a very wealthy man at the time of his death. Unfortunately, we do not know when he died. Given the amount of property he owned and the number of dependent children he had, he must have left a will; if so, it has not survived. Hence there is no way of telling whether Peter Imlay left his son Gilbert any property or money, nor whether Gilbert was still around to leave anything to. Indeed, it seems more than likely that Gilbert had started to fend for himself not long after his father married Euphemia on the eve of the outbreak of hostilities between Britain and her colonies.

* * *

By and large, the Imlays were on the Revolutionary side in the dispute. Gilbert's father, Peter, for instance, was a signatory of the 'Petition for Stricter Militia Law' (31 May 1779) and sold produce to the Continental Army (May 1780).[63] During a meeting in Allentown in July 1782, a 'Mr. Peter Imlay, senior' (most likely Gilbert's father) was elected as an executive member of an association aimed at ending and preventing all trade and 'dishounorable intercourse and traffick with the enemy' by 'a great number of the whig inhabitants of the township of Upper Freehold'.[64] A 'Mr. Peter Imlay, jun.' was also elected as an executive member, whilst a 'John Imlay' (who may have been Peter's older brother, 'Judge John') was elected chairman of the association. The two brothers had not always seen eye to eye when it came to taking action against the Tories. Thus, while in May 1781 John Imlay been a signatory of a 'Petition Urging Action against the Disaffected & Favoring Retaliation', in December of that year Peter had signed a 'Petition against Association for Retaliation'.[65] Army records show that a large number of Imlays served in one capacity or another in the Continental Army, several of them holding officer's ranks.[66] One of the most distinguished soldiers was a Lieutenant Isaac Imlay, who served both at the battle of Germantown (4 October 1777), which the Americans lost, and at the battle of Monmouth (28 June 1778), which ended undecided.[67] Two Imlays, a David and a William Eugene, who had graduated from Princeton in 1773, made it to the rank of captain, while one – James Imlay – was a major.[68] At least one Imlay either was or was suspected of being a Loyalist: in 1777 the Whig authorities in Pennsylvania detained a William Imlay and sent him prisoner to Virginia.[69] A Samuel Imlay and another William Imlay, Ensign, were both taken prisoner in March 1777 for refusing to bear arms and were delivered at Haddonfield, the temporary home to New Jersey's Revolutionary War government, 'to await further directions by the Legislature'.[70] One Peter Imlay, a private in the Monmouth militia, was a prisoner of war in 1778 and was released in September of that year in a prisoner exchange.[71]

Gilbert Imlay was around twenty-two years old when the American Revolution broke out. He enlisted on 10 February 1777, the day after his twenty-third birthday, and was commissioned as a first lieutenant in Captain John Burrowes's company in Colonel David Forman's Additional Continental Regiment.[72] Both Imlay's commanding officers were staunch Patriots, and both were intensely hated by the Tories. Forman was a notorious retaliator, while Burrowes was a rich merchant who was known to supply large shipments of corn to the Continental Army and to allow the whale boat navy to hide in his mill pond and the local militia to train on his property. On account of his swarthy complexion, Forman was nicknamed 'Black David', whereupon the Tories gave Burrowes the sobriquet 'Black David's Devil'.[73] Forman's regiment had been organized in compliance with a resolution of Congress of 27 December 1776, which authorized General George Washington to raise, 'from any or all of these United states', sixteen battalions of infantry, in addition to those already voted by Congress.[74] The regiments were not numbered, but were known by the names of their respective colonels, and were raised at large. First formed in January 1771, Forman's regiment was never fully completed. On 1 July 1778 its enlisted men were incorporated into the New Jersey Line and on 1 April 1779 its officers, with what new recruits they had gathered, were merged with Spencer's Additional Regiment.[75]

Gilbert Imlay's name appears on copies of the company payrolls for the period 1 December 1777 through 31 May 1778, his pay rising during this time from $27 a month to $46. On his regiment's general pay abstracts for the months of June and July 1778 Imlay is listed as Regimental Pay Master, a position that we know from other documents he held from 1 December 1777.[76] It is not known whether Imlay saw any action during the time he was enlisted in Burrowes's company. He almost certainly was not present at the battle of Monmouth. A company muster roll indicates that on 12 June 1778 Burrowes's unit was located at Mount Holly and as far as can be ascertained Forman's regiment did not take part in the battle.[77] As for Imlay's activities during the time he was enlisted, all that has come to light is his interceding on behalf of a group of soldiers from his home county who had been detained for presumed Loyalist sympathies. Writing from Haddonfield, where, fleeing from the British, the New Jersey Assembly and Council of Safety had temporarily started to meet, Imlay sent a 'memorial' on 19 May 1777 to William Livingston, New Jersey's first Revolutionary governor, and to the Council of Safety of New Jersey, in which he requested that 'a Number of

[men] supposed to be dangerous and disaffected to the government', who had been arrested in January in Monmouth County and had since been imprisoned in Philadelphia, be released and permitted to join Colonel Burrowes's company of Colonel Forman's regiment.[78] On 21 May the Council granted Imlay's request and that same day William Livingston wrote to the Pennsylvania Board of War requesting the conditional release of the 'disaffected' New Jerseymen held in Philadelphia.[79] Two days later the prisoners arrived at Haddonfield, where they were interviewed by the Council to ascertain whether they would be willing to serve in the company in which they had enlisted. Imlay had asked for a total of sixteen soldiers to be pardoned and enlisted in Burrowes's company; in the end seven of them 'took & subscribed the Oaths to the State, enrolled themselves & were delivered to Lieut. Gilbert Imlay'.[80]

According to Forman's regiment's 'casualty book' Imlay was 'omitted' from the company payroll on 1 July 1778 – no doubt because the regiment had ceased to exist on this day. However, according to the general pay abstract for July 1778, Imlay 'resigned' from the army on 24 July. Since there is no record of his having enlisted in any other army unit, we may assume that Imlay's contribution to the American Revolution was over by the summer of 1778. Significantly, on the day he resigned from the army Imlay sought and obtained two statements vouching for his service record and character, notably his handling of the regiment's payroll. In the first, William Palfrey, Paymaster General of Washington's army, certified that Imlay received 'Six thousand Three hundred & thirty Six dollars in full for the pay of [Forman's] Regiment from the first of December 1777 to June 30, 1778 and that he ha[d] received no other money on Acc^t. of S^d. Regt'.[81] In a second document Major William Harrison, who had taken over from Forman as the regiment's commanding officer until its officers and men had been transferred to the regular army, declared that Imlay had 'conducted himself as a diligent and good officer' in the period he was under his command, and that as paymaster he had settled 'all regimental accounts with the detachment'.[82]

After the armies that traversed it and clashed in battle on its soil had left for other fields of glory and defeat, New Jersey was left in a dysfunctional state, with law and order in abeyance and its people divided and traumatized. State and local government was practically in suspension. The legislature finally met in the autumn of 1777 in Princeton, but was impotent. Although Governor Livingston and the Council for Safety now had full authority of the law, they had little power to enforce their mandates. The government was widely assumed to be corrupt and the courts were accused of being engaged in favouritism when it came to selling forfeited Tory property. Illegal trade, smuggling, racketeering and revenge kidnapping and hangings were the order of the day. In the west, one of Trenton's most zealous defenders of the Royal cause, Daniel Coxe III, had raised the 'West Jersey Volunteers' in the course of 1777–8, and during the

British occupation of Philadelphia acted as a self-appointed magistrate of police without emolument. In the south, bands of Tories and outlaws were engaged in widespread depredations and furnished the British in Philadelphia with provisions. Commenting on the situation in the south, the Swedish pastor Nicholas Collin wrote: 'Everywhere is distrust, fear, hatred, and abominable selfishness ... Parents and children, brothers and sisters, wife and husband, were enemies of one another.'[83] In the north, widespread disorder erupted as the militia and patriot bands tried to break up the movement of provisions from profiteers and Loyalists to the British on Staten Island, Paulus Hook and Perth Amboy.

Monmouth County, in particular, was a lawless place after the theatre of war had shifted to Pennsylvania and beyond. While military engagements had largely ceased elsewhere in the state, in Monmouth County the vicious internecine struggle between Loyalists and Patriots showed no sign of abating. Acting as a shadow government to the duly elected county representatives, David Forman's Association for Retaliation meted out brutal revenge on the relatives of Loyalist raiders and traders. The Loyalists retaliated in increasingly desperate ways. The most notorious case of Loyalist reprisal was the lynching of Joshua Huddy, a former captain of the Monmouth militia. In April 1782, months after the battle of Yorktown, the last major military engagement of the war, Loyalists captured Huddy at the surrender of the block-house at Tom's River and took him to New York. After William Franklin had ordered Huddy's execution, his captors dragged him from his cell and hanged him. Huddy's body was brought to Freehold and he was buried at Old Tennent Church. More than four hundred people gathered to protest his murder and a petition was sent to George Washington demanding retribution. Patriot outrage over the case almost scuttled the peace talks with the British and nearly cost the life of a young British officer, Captain Charles Asgill, whose hanging in retaliation was averted by last minute French diplomacy. Huddy became known as 'the hero martyr of old Monmouth', but the truth of the matter is that he was also a cold-blooded thug who operated a privateer, the 'Black Snake', seized Loyalist property and publicly boasted of his role in the hanging of Stephen Edwards, a Loyalist spy. Just punishment and retribution were two sides of the same coin in wartime New Jersey – and both were meted out by self-styled adjudicators of justice. More than any other act of vigilante retaliation, the murder of Joshua Huddy will have brought home to Imlay and other (former) officers of Monmouth militia how precarious their lives were, even though the war had effectively drawn to a close.

In economic terms, New Jersey fared little better in the wake of the American Revolution than it had following the French and Indian War. Profiteering, black marketing and clandestine trade with the enemy had gradually disappeared in the course of the war, but regular economic activity remained weak. Many thousands of Loyalists had fled the state and of those who had remained many had their property either destroyed or forfeited. Marked for life as traitors, Loyalists found it hard to re-establish themselves as merchants and shopkeepers. The agricultural sector, too, was in crisis. Foraging of farm produce, horses and livestock during the war was followed by a series of bad harvests after the war. Once more New Jersey's currency was in crisis. The government managed to stem the tide of inflation by replacing the worthless continental currency with new 'emission money', but as this money began to flow back into the state coffers as tax revenue, a currency shortage developed. Farmers and traders who could no longer pay their taxes, let alone their debts, were in dire distress. Government measures to consolidate the currency supply and pay off the state's wartime debt, including arrears to soldiers and suppliers, somewhat stabilized the economy, but it was not until 1787 that New Jersey would recover from the war.

Details of Gilbert Imlay's activities in New Jersey following the battle of Monmouth are few and far between, and for those, as so often in his life, we have to rely on surviving court records. In a litigious nation, court scribes are its most prolific chroniclers. The records tell us that after he resigned from the army in July 1778 it did not take long for Gilbert Imlay to be drawn into the maelstrom of wartime racketeering and rogue trading. Thus, on 29 January 1779 Monmouth County Court issued a 'capias writ' ordering the county sheriff to arrest Imlay and to detain him until he should appear before the Court of Common Pleas during the April session to answer Richard Robins's 'Plea of Trespass' for damages of £500.[84] At some point later Monmouth County Sheriff Nicholas Van Brunt signed the reverse of the writ 'cepi corpus' ('I have taken the body'), confirming that Imlay had now been detained. The outcome of this case is unknown.

In April 1780 another writ for Imlay's arrest was issued, this time by David Brearly, Chief Justice of the New Jersey Supreme Court at Trenton (which had replaced the West Jersey Supreme Court at Burlington and the East Jersey Supreme Court at Perth Amboy). This suit involved a case of debt for £4,400 'Current money of New Jersey' and had been brought against Imlay and his co-defendant Isaac Reckless by Daniel Hendrickson.[85] A rich mill owner, former member of the Provincial Congress and a colonel in the Monmouth County militia, Hendrickson belonged to one of the most prominent and powerful families in New Jersey. Interestingly, Hendrickson was well acquainted with Gilbert's Imlay father, Peter, along with whom in July of the following year he would be elected as executive member of the Allentown association against 'dishounorable intercourse and traffick with the enemy'.[86] Hendrickson was a formidable opponent to take on in court, and £4,400 proclamation money was a considerable sum (around $200,000 dollars in today's money). Unsurprisingly, in May 1780 Gilbert Imlay found himself in court – and 'in Custody' – again, this time before the judges of the New Jersey Supreme Court. The writ identifies Imlay as a resident of the township of Chesterfield, in Burlington County, approximately seven miles south-west of Imlaystown (which confirms that he had left his parental home by then). From the case notes it appears that on 25 December 1779 Imlay had given Hendrickson his bond for £4,400 'current money' but had since failed to make any repayments. Through his attorney, Bowes Reed, Hendrickson was demanding £2,000 in damages. In July Imlay appeared before another Supreme Court Judge, Isaac Smith, and was 'delivered to bail on the taking of his body unto Joseph Brown Gentleman of a plea of debt at the suit of Dan Hendrickson'.[87] The New Jersey Supreme Court minute books document Hendrickson's dogged efforts to reclaim his money from Imlay, who sometimes appears as the sole defendant, sometimes with his co-defendant Isaac Reckless.[88] In April 1781 the Supreme Court passed a preliminary judgement, the 'Defendant having neglected to plead pursuant to several Rules for that Purpose'.[89] The ultimate verdict is unknown.

In the same month that the Supreme Court at Trenton was passing sentence on Imlay in the Hendrickson case, the Monmouth County Court at Freehold was issuing another writ for his arrest. On 26 April 1781 Judge John Anderson ordered the county sheriff – none other than David Forman, the notorious Associator – to arrest Gilbert Imlay, along with Isaac Reckless, Anthony Taylor and Charles Adams, and to detain them until they could appear before the Court of Common Pleas during the July session to answer Daniel Griggs's plea of trespass for damages of £2,000.[90] On 25 July the court issued a second writ for the arrest of the four men, although this time the plea was for damages totalling £5,000.[91] At some point later David Forman endorsed the writ 'cepi corpus', suggesting that he had made one or more arrests in the case. During the October session of the Court of Common Pleas it appeared that it was Isaac Reckless who had first incurred the debt back in October 1779. Although it is not clear how Gilbert Imlay and the others got involved in the case, they were now collectively sued for £700 continental currency for 'Goods, Wares and Merchandize' which Griggs had supplied to Reckless but which he had not been paid for, as well as for £700 'for meat, drink, washing and lodging' and for 'money before that time advanced, paid, laid out and expended' by Griggs.[92] While the Monmouth County Court archives have yielded no clues as to the outcome of this particular case, a parallel case in which Daniel Griggs was suing the four men for £1,000 in damages was going through the Supreme Court at Trenton during the course of 1781, until the suit was finally discontinued by Griggs's attorney, William Willcocks, during the November session of the court. Griggs's attorney was back in the Supreme Court suing Imlay, Reckless, Taylor and Adams in May 1783. However, that case also had to be abandoned at the September session after the sheriff informed the court that the defendants were not in his bailiwick.[93]

With warrants out for his arrest in Monmouth and Burlington counties – the only counties in which he had any social networks he could turn to for support – it is more than likely that Imlay had decided not to await the outcome of Griggs's case against him and had left New Jersey for good some time before September 1783. This is corroborated by the fact that the New Jersey archives have produced no reference to Imlay after the collapse of Griggs's Supreme Court suit against him.[94] In fact, it is reasonable to conjecture that Imlay had been spending more and more time outside of his home state since his resignation from the army in July 1778, and that at least for some of that time he had been residing in Philadelphia.

The timing for such a move was propitious. Situated right across the Delaware from Haddonfield, where Imlay had been stationed during part of the war, Philadelphia had been evacuated by the British on 18 June 1778. The administrative and socioeconomic confusion following the handover of power from the Tories to the Whigs presented all kinds of trade opportunities – especially clandestine – for fortune seekers like Imlay: impecunious young veterans without any strong family ties or clear career prospects. On the one hand, hundreds of merchants who had been too close to the British were trying to leave the city, eager to dispose of their property; on the other hand, large numbers of fortune seekers were flocking into Philadelphia hoping to profit from the expected economic boom. The sudden influx of so many strangers into what was already a bustling urban centre would certainly have given Imlay the chance to reinvent himself. Nor was he the first Imlay to try his luck in Philadelphia. Following his marriage, his elder brother Robert had settled in Philadelphia, where he was a merchant in the firm of Imlay and Potts.[95] John Imlay, Gilbert's second cousin, had been a resident of Philadelphia since 1776. Following his marriage to Elizabeth DeBow in 1773, John had gone into shipping and had earned a fortune during the wartime trade, mainly with the West Indies. One of the first to take the June 1777 oath of allegiance to the state of Pennsylvania, John Imlay was a commissioner of the New Jersey Admiralty, in which capacity he was the presiding judge of the New Jersey Admiralty Court sitting in special session in Mount Holly on 5 and 6 August 1778 to decide the fate of the schooner the *Charming Nancy* – a case that would reveal the evidence for one of the six indictments for 'culpable action' brought against General Benedict Arnold during the court martial that was held in Morristown, New Jersey, in January 1780.[96] It is not known whether Gilbert Imlay was ever in touch with his second cousin, but there is a potentially very interesting, albeit tangential, connection between Imlay and the story of Benedict Arnold, which *may* put Imlay on the ground in Philadelphia in the second half of 1778.

When the British army evacuated Philadelphia in some haste in June 1778, society belles like Peggy Shippen, who was to marry Arnold in 1779, and her elder sister, Elizabeth, were all in a flurry. Their regular beaux, many of whom were drafted from the British officer corps, had left town almost overnight, and it was as yet unclear where suitable replacements were to be found. It was during this trying time that one of Philadelphia's leading belles, Rebecca ('Becky') Franks, the high-spirited, seventeen-year-old Loyalist daughter of David Franks – who had been aide-de-camp for General Benedict Arnold during the war and was now assistant to Arnold in his capacity as military governor of Philadelphia – wrote the following distressed note to her close friend Elizabeth Shippen:

> I heard Mr. Imlay say he intends paying you a Vis soon, so look out for him th first fine day. when the roads will permit my return God knows. I begin to grow Home sick tis very dull such Weather for I hant a soul to speak to except Aunt nor a Book to read. I'm determined to send to Imlay for one this Afternoon. I hant seen a Beau since the day before yesterday where can the Wretches keep ...[97]

Since Elizabeth Shippen married in December 1778, when she became Mrs Burd, the visits of the obliging 'Mr. Imlay' to her and Rebecca Franks must have taken place between July, when David Franks and his family arrived in town, and the end of the year. Unfortunately, there is no conclusive evidence to confirm that Gilbert Imlay is the beau in question. But, then, given the timing of the episode, the lack of any likely alternatives in the Imlay family (most of whom were devout Presbyterians) and his future gallivanting lifestyle, Gilbert Imlay could easily have fitted the bill.

2 LAND-JOBBER À LA MODE

I do not wish to depretiate Mr. Imlays stability or Character, he is unknown to me, it
is an undertaking of Great magnitude & very few gentlemen are equal to
Samuel Beall to John May, 14 February 1786[1]

It has been a matter of debate among scholars as to when exactly Imlay appeared
in the western territories of the Ohio Valley. According to his own account of
it in the *Topographical Description*, Imlay first crossed the Allegheny Mountains
'in March', and, finding Pittsburgh 'not [yet] recovered from the ravages of winter', immediately decided to leave for the balmy climate of Kentucky, arriving at
Limestone, near present-day Maysville, 'in less than five days'.[2] Unfortunately,
he does not give us the year. Pointing out that 'the long court record of the business and legal entanglements that marked his residence of not quite two years
in Kentucky' begins in 1784, Rusk infers that Imlay did not appear in Kentucky
before the spring of that year.[3] This date appears to be confirmed by the fact
that Imlay was sworn in at Louisville as a deputy surveyor of Jefferson County
under George May on 7 April 1784.[4] However, by that time Imlay had already
begun speculating in Kentucky lands. His earliest documented transaction was
with the veteran pioneer and land-jobber Daniel Boone. In March 1783 Boone
agreed to accept Imlay's promissory note for £2,000, to be paid in two instalments in exchange for a tract of 10,000 acres located on Hingston's Fork of the
Licking River in Fayette County, which Boone had entered on 26 December
the year before.[5] Also in March 1783 Imlay purchased another 20,000 acres of
land in Fayette in a transaction with Captain John Holder – a deal that, as we
shall see, would go horribly sour later.[6] On the 3 August 1783 Imlay concluded
another complicated land deal with Holder's business partner Matthew Walton;
this particular deal involved several thousand acres of land in Jefferson County,
and would lead to a legal battle that would continue until the early 1800s, long
after Imlay had left Kentucky and America.[7] On 11 November of that year Imlay
bought Elias Barber's treasury warrant 18,879, which authorized him to lay off
in one or more surveys a quantity of 18,176 acres of land; on the very same day
he entered four tracts of land in Fayette County.[8] In themselves these early land
deals do not prove that Imlay was actually in Kentucky in 1783; land was often

bought by absent speculators or prospective settlers in the East through the mediation of land-jobbers on site or from 'outlyers', men who made improvements to land with the sole purpose of selling it to others, not to settle. Yet the nature and scale of his earliest land acquisitions, as well as later correspondence and legal documentation relating to them, would suggest that Imlay was very much on the ground in Kentucky before 1784.

From his surviving letters and contemporary accounts of him, Imlay comes across as someone who possessed remarkable social skills and had a congenial, ingratiating disposition. It is therefore less surprising than it may appear that within a few months of being appointed as deputy surveyor in March 1784, Imlay was in intimate correspondence with and had gained the trust of such seasoned Kentucky pioneers and land speculators as John Holder, Matthew Walton, John Floyd, Christopher Greenup, Humphrey Marshall, and George and John May. Land grabbing was an eminently respectable pursuit among the district's founding settlers, and Imlay seems to have blended seamlessly into this fraternity of speculating friends. Although his 15 March 1783 contract with Boone identifies Imlay as a resident 'of the State of New Jersey',[9] it is unlikely that Boone would have parted with what his son Nathan later described as 'a splendid tract' to a complete stranger.[10] In fact, about two weeks before he signed his contract with Boone, Imlay had been making an offer on a large tract of land far exceeding his acquisition of Boone's tract, a transaction that almost certainly puts Imlay in Kentucky on or before 1 March 1783. The evidence for this is contained in a letter from Isaac Hite, dated 26 April 1783.

A native of Hampshire County, Virginia, Isaac Hite had first come down the Ohio River to Kentucky in the spring of 1773, having fallen in with Captain Thomas Bullitt's surveying party. In 1774 he was appointed a deputy surveyor for Fincastle County under Colonel William Preston, and was a member of the party sent out by Preston in that year to make surveys on military warrants at the Falls of the Ohio and elsewhere. Despite increasing Indian hostility, Hite returned to Kentucky in 1775, when he was chosen as a representative for the Boiling Spring settlement on the Transylvania Convention. A permanent resident of Kentucky County since that time, Hite was wounded with Boone, John Todd and Michael Stoner during the defence of Boonesborough in April 1777; he also served on General Rogers Clark's Indian campaigns of 1780 and 1782.[11] Locating, surveying and selling land was a major source of income for Hite, as it was for so many early Kentucky pioneers, and many of the surveys he made were for members of his own family. Writing from Fountainbleau (just south of Harrodsburg) to his father Abraham in South Branch, Hampshire County, Virginia, Hite revealed that he had 'in contemplation a Scheme' whereby, if his father should agree, he would sell off all of his interests the Salts Springs and instead buy tracts on Rough Creek, north of Green River, which, he had reason to believe, contained enough 'large Banks of Iron Ore' to begin an 'Iron Manu-factory' there.[12] Unlike some, Hite was a cautious speculator, and he did not want to commit himself to the new scheme before he had actually sold the Salts Springs, for which, he wrote, he had received many offers. He then outlined to his father the 'speculation' he had in mind:

> If it pleased God to spare me, till the time of my paym.^{ts} become Due; Mr Walker Daniel & myself have finish'd our contract with Mr Geo. May, and have four years from the 25.th Decr last to make the first paym.^t of £4800 and then £1200 P.^r annum till paid; Mr Daniel at the time of our giving our Bonds to Mr May in the first of March informed me Mr Emley ~~from~~ Agent for a company had offered £11.5 Pr C.^t for that part of our purchase in partnership of Messrs Jno & Geo. May & Jno Floyd inconsequence of his having purchased out Jno May & Jno Floyd[.] our proportion thereof amounted to 76000 and the Bargain Between Mr Daniel and Mr Emley at that time only was delayed for my approbation, which I gave and empower'd Mr Daniel to close the Bargain, which he expected to do upon better terms than was then proposed[,] being able to give Mr Emley longer time to make paym.^t and Mr Geo. May's agreeing to take Mr Emleys Bond for our first paym.^t and give up ours; in this situation I left it, and have not had an Opportunity to see Mr Daniel on the Subject Since, I expect to see him every day and by the first Oppert.^y will let you know what ~~I have~~ is done and endeavour to Transmit you copies of our contracts and Bonds; as the regulating the papers respecting that purchase, and some other Business I expect will be entered upon by Mr Daniel & myself at this place in a few Days: –[13]

It is reasonable to conjecture that the Mr Emley here introduced is in fact Gilbert Imlay. In an age when the spelling of words and names was still quite fluid and often rendered phonetically, Imlay's last name was more often than not spelled 'Emley' in contemporary correspondence, grants and other documents.[14] More importantly, we know from his deal with Boone that Imlay was in the market to buy large tracts of land in Kentucky and that it is likely that he was in the area in the spring of 1783. Also, if 'Emley' and Gilbert Imlay were one and the same person, it would make it a lot less puzzling why the principal surveyor for Jefferson, George May, would barely a year later (on 7 April 1784) appoint a greenhorn from the East, who had no apparent skills and certainly no relevant experience, as one of his deputies.[15] It would also explain why, as Hite reports, George May was apparently unconcerned about giving up the bonds of two well-established and well-to-do Kentucky settlers – Isaac Hite and Walker Daniel (who had laid out the town of Danville in 1781 and was appointed attorney general for the Kentucky District on 3 March 1783) – in exchange for Imlay's bond for £4,800. Again this suggests that by early 1783 Imlay had already gained a firm foothold in Kentucky and was doing business on an inside track.

What is intriguing in Hite's letter is the suggestion that Emley/Imlay was acting as an 'agent for a company'. It is not known what company this might have been, but it is hard to see what Imlay's creditworthiness was based on, other than on the financial backing – or the suggestion of such – of people he was representing. Since New Jersey did not have a western frontier, it did not have a bounty-land warrant policy for veterans of that state; someone like Imlay would therefore not have had any military warrants of his own. On the other hand, military (and even more so, treasury warrants) were traded on a massive scale in the East, as many Revolutionary veterans preferred whatever ready cash they could get over the right to survey land in the West. Philadelphia was a major centre for the trade in western land and land warrants, and it is therefore no surprise to see John May, one of the biggest wholesalers in Kentucky lands, turning up in Philadelphia in the course of 1781 to dispose of some of the land he had acquired in partnership with Samuel Beall.[16] It is thus conceivable that Imlay was in the employ of one of the several companies of land speculators that had been formed in Philadelphia and that, according to Humphrey Marshall, had 'disgorged their immense accumulations of paper money, or bills of credit, on Virginia Land warrants' and 'had their agents in Kentucky, for the purpose of realizing them by location'.[17] If Imlay was indeed such an agent, this would certainly explain why George May would be interested to close a deal with him. John and George May, along with their other partners, notably Samuel Beall, were quite anxious at this point in time to dispose of large chunks of their huge land acquisitions to recover some of their costs and cash in on their investments. John Floyd, their partner in the proposed deal with Imlay, also turns out to have been very eager in the spring of 1783 to sell off a large portion of his extensive land interests. In a letter to Colonel William Preston, dated 28 March 1783, Floyd writes:

> I have for some time past been endeavouring to bring my affairs into a small Compass in order to spend more of my time at home; & I have in some measure effected my purpose of disposing of my right to a large Quantity of Land which I am not even obliged to show. I am to receive seven pounds per hundred for locations. You may perhaps disapprove of my Bargain but I had more business of that sort on my Hands than I could possibly attend to, & if it is so that uncultivated Lands here are Taxed 4/ per hundred I have more yet than I can well pay for.[18]

Unfortunately, Floyd died on 10 April, less than two weeks after he wrote this letter, from injuries sustained during an Indian ambush; although there is no further information from him to corroborate this, the timing of his disposal of his 'right to a large Quantity of Land' would seem to correspond to Imlay's supposedly having taken over John May's and John Floyd's share in the deal with Hite, Daniel and George May, some time prior to 1 March 1783. It is not known how big May's and Floyd's interests were in the original partnership, but, given that both men frequently entered very large claims and held grants to many of them, it is unlikely to have been smaller than Hite's and Daniel's share of 76,000 acres.

This would suggest that even as early as 1783 Imlay was in the market – for himself, or as an agent for others – for well over 100,000 acres of Kentucky land.

What ultimately came of the whole transaction is unclear, but that Imlay had in some way acquired an interest in land formerly owned by Floyd is confirmed by Imlay's letters to Henry Lee. The founder of Lee's Station in Mason County, Lee presumably possessed the kind of local knowledge that Imlay lacked, and it was probably for that reason that Imlay began to engage Lee's services as a surveyor and agent in trying to locate some of the more elusive tracts.[19] The letters to Lee give us a detailed insight into Imlay's land-jobbing operations. Even this sketchy correspondence contradicts the familiar image of Imlay as a callous and treacherous land booster who cheated poor and unsuspecting settlers out of a few acres of Kentucky land. In fact, the image of Imlay that appears from the letters to Lee is that of an astute manager heading up a brisk and fairly extensive business network – indeed, as an agent acting for one or more large investors. Thus, Imlay initiates and brokers the deals, finds people to do the legwork – surveying and registering the claims, as well as sorting out legal entanglements – and coordinates and supervises their activities. A man who seized business opportunities when and where they offered themselves, he comes across in his correspondence as focused and very energetic – almost hyperactive. The handwriting – frequently illegible, the spelling sometimes phonetic and the punctuation often erratic – is that of a man who is always working to meet a deadline (the due date of a promissory note, or registering a claim at the surveyor's office), who has no time for details or decorum, and who is constantly on the move.

Thus, on 2 September 1784 he is writing to Lee from Beargrass, complaining that William Triplet, a deputy surveyor for Fayette County, whom Imlay had asked to survey some tracts he had bought from John Holder, had 'done nothing with [his] business' and urging Lee to 'do everything in [his] power to make a completion of it'. In passing he requests that Lee undertake to survey land entered in Bowdoin's name, and goes on to write:

> I have now to Request that you will survey all the land that is Entered in Col Floyd's Name that is not already survey'd. There is one or two tracts on the Ohio that I fear will give you some trouble to find, but I shall as in all other cases make you full Compensation for such trouble. You can get these Entries or orders of surveys on my account at the office.[20]

The 'office' would be George May's Jefferson county surveyor's office at Louisville, where, judging from the places he is writing from, Imlay can only have been a very infrequent visitor. Rather than doing much, or any, of the surveying himself, Imlay rather used his position as deputy surveyor to expedite the administrative process of his land transactions at the Surveyor's Office. On 14 September Imlay is writing from Lincoln, asking Lee again to survey the Holder tracts, as well as 'the Land or Entry of Mr Bowdoin's of 5,000 & off acres', as he will probably 'leave this Country sometime in October for the East'.[21] A week later he shoots off another hurried note to Lee, now from the Falls of the Ohio:

> Dear Sir,
>   I omitted mentioning in my last by M^r. Bullet that Capt Martin would survey the 2000 of Holder opposite the Little Miami. Also that Mr Hite will survey the 2000 on Hickman. You can know from Mr Triplet what he has done.
>   Success attend   Adieu
>   G. Imlay
>   Falls of Ohio 21st Spt 1784
>
> Pray do not fail writing to me or D^r. Skinner in my absence every opportunity.[22]

On 10 October Imlay was writing to Lee from Danville, impressing upon him again the importance to locate and survey the land that formerly belonged to Floyd: 'I wish you to do the whole of this Business with all possible dispatch ... Puting the highest confidence in your abilities & diligence I shall Rest assured that a completion of the Whole Business will be made'.[23] Having spent most of his time since he first arrived there in 1774 locating and surveying land, Floyd had owned some of the choicest tracts in Kentucky, and this may well explain Imlay's impatience in getting Floyd's land surveyed.[24]

A high transaction speed was vital to Imlay's operations. A speculator rather than a settler, Imlay acquired land to sell it, not to own it. In fact, few of the deals a speculator like Imlay would make involved the actual transfer of legal ownership of land. Since warrants, entries and surveys could be sold, traded or reassigned at any time during the patenting process, speculators would typically sell their interest at the earliest possibility of a profit. Frequently, surveyed land would be disposed of before the survey had been registered, thus passing the surveying fee on to the buyer. Another reason why speculators were inclined to resell tracts they had bought as quickly as possible was that often the land had been paid for by a bond drawn on the buyer. Cash-strapped speculators like Imlay would have to make sure they had found a buyer for their land before the first instalment of the bond was due – often disposing of their contracts or interests in a contract within days of the original purchase. For this very reason it is impossible to determine with any degree of accuracy how many acres of land Imlay accrued in total during his land-jobbing days in Kentucky, but on the basis of his documented transactions we know the number to have been at least 200,000 – although it may in reality have been closer to 500,000. Yet of all the land he ever bought, roughly only 30,000 acres went through all of the steps of the patenting process, with a grant issued by the Virginia Land Office and title transferred to Imlay as the legal owner.[25]

Since he was a short-term trader, Imlay was wary of investing time, effort and money in land that might become the subject of a legal challenge, and hence not give an immediate return on his investment. It is for this reason that he urges Lee 'to survey with caution to prevent litigious disputes with prior Claims' and always to check first with the Surveyor's Office whether a tract has already been entered or surveyed by someone else, before doing the actual survey.[26] Apparently in response to a query from Lee, Imlay explains a little later: 'What I mean by more than common trouble is that you will not survey the Entries implicitly but will first ascertain the state of the Entry previous to surveying Relative to its being prior or Junior to any in the same place, & in case they should be prior not to survey'. However, Imlay was by no means intimidated by the thought of having to go to court. Thus he insists that if Lee finds that a junior survey has been made of a tract he has surveyed before, he should immediately alert his attorney, Dr Alexander Skinner at the Falls of the Ohio, so 'that he may know how to Caveat'.[27] Hence, the Order Books of the Supreme Court of the District of Kentucky contain records of a string of caveat cases brought by Skinner on Imlay's behalf against competing land-jobbers who had encroached upon his turf.[28] Imlay's letters to Lee also reveal that Skinner acted as Imlay's paymaster for bills drawn upon him while he was in the East, so that even when he was not around to oversee business personally, operations would carry on as planned. On 27 September 1784 Imlay authorized Skinner to act for him with power of attorney in during his absence and represent him in his partnership with John Holder.[29] Exactly why he did this, is not known; but it was almost certainly related to a remark at the end of his 10 October 1784 letter to Lee, when he announced cryptically, 'Farewell. God bless you. On Wednesday morning I launch into the wilderness. Expect to see me by Christmas.'[30]

If Imlay, as it would appear, had fairly urgent reasons for taking the Wilderness Road towards Cumberland Gap and the East, they are not revealed to us. What *is* clear, however, is that Imlay at this point had plenty of legal reasons to lie low for a while. In fact, within a week after he had been sworn in as deputy surveyor, the Jefferson County Court had issued a writ commanding the sheriff to bring in Imlay and a certain William A. Lee to answer a plea of debt at the May term for refusal to repay Alexander Cleveland a bond for £200.[31] Imlay easily managed to give the sheriff and the court a wide berth, but in August of the same year an arrest warrant was issued against him on a charge of trespass from one David Standiford, who claimed damages of £60.[32] Since he had failed to obey the court order to answer Cleveland's plea of debt until then, the Louisville court on 9 December ruled that unless Imlay appeared in court at the next session, it would decide the case against him. Skinner's brief apparently went beyond looking after Imlay's business interests alone, for it was he who on 9 April 1785 supplied bail on Imlay's behalf. At the same time Benjamin Sebastian, acting as Imlay's attorney, entered a plea on his client's behalf to the effect that the bond to Cleveland had been bargained incorrectly.[33] This move slowed down the legal process with the effect that Imlay could carry on with his business activities unhampered.

One of the transactions in which Sebastian represented Imlay concerned a scheme Imlay had embarked upon some time late in 1785 with his old partner Isaac Hite. Hite's pet scheme to build an 'Iron Manufactory' on Rough Creek, just north of Green River, had not yet panned out towards the end of 1785. Perhaps it was the untimely death at the hands of Indians of his business partner Walker Daniel in August 1784 that made Hite look for other investors in the project. At any rate, on 2 November 1785 Hite entered into a contract with Gilbert Imlay and Amos Ogden to erect an ironworks on the upper or middle falls of Rough Creek (the exact spot was still to be determined), one of the tributaries of Green River. In the 'Articles of Agreement' that were drawn up and signed on 5 November, the three partners in what came to be known as the 'Green River Company' agreed to erect a 'Bloomery Forge', and subsequently, with the profits arising from operating this forge, to build a 'Furnace' as well.[34] The three also bound themselves to invest whatever future profits the venture would yield back into the company for a period of seven years. Amos Ogden was appointed to 'direct, superintend, manage and render proper Accounts to the person appointed by the company to keep their Books'. Whether Ogden seriously intended to stand by his contract is a matter of conjecture, but it is highly unlikely that Imlay, given the general nature of his business ventures, felt much commitment to such a long-term investment scheme as Hite was proposing. On the other hand, the terms that Hite was offering his partners were clearly too good to be refused: not only did Hite agree to sell to Imlay and Ogden two-thirds of a 200-acre prime location he owned on Rough Creek, but he also accepted their bonds for £150 each by way of payment.

The partnership was doomed from the start. Amos Ogden was last seen in Kentucky on 5 January, allegedly going East to procure workmen for the construction of the forge; the last Hite ever heard from him was through a letter that was sent from Baltimore on 28 July 1786, in which Ogden offered to be released from his interest in the contract with Hite provided the latter would cancel his bond of £150.[35] As for Imlay, he left Kentucky for Richmond almost immediately upon signing the contract with Hite. The deed confirming Imlay's one-third's share in the company was signed in Imlay's name by Sebastian, as his attorney, on 12 January 1786.[36] Only three days later Sebastian disposed of one third of Imlay's interest in the company to one Daniel Henry of Jefferson County, probably in order to pay off one of Imlay's outstanding debts.[37] Thus, the 'Green River Company' met the fate of scores of similar ventures during the Kentucky land bubble of the mid-1780s. The case left a long trail in the various

Kentucky county courts, as first Isaac Hite himself and then his heirs persistently but fruitlessly tried to recuperate their money and get compensation for lost revenue. At one stage, during a session of the Supreme Court sitting in Chancery on 9 June 1789, the court decided that since the two defendants were no longer residents in the state of Kentucky, orders for them to appear before the court on 4 November next were to be printed in the *Virginia Gazette* 'for two months successfully', as well as 'published at the meeting House near Bardstown ... on some Sunday immediately after Divine Service, and on the front Door of the Courthouse in the town of Danville'.[38] In the course of 1791, the Supreme Court was still ordering similar notices to be advertised.[39] Isaac Hite's heirs, represented by Harry Innes, finally gave up their suit against Imlay and Ogden in October 1799, when the original agreement was annulled and the absentee defendants were ordered to pay the litigation costs incurred by Hite's heirs.[40]

On the face of it, it would appear as if Imlay never intended to stand by his contract in the first place; yet there are reasons to believe that his intentions were in fact more honourable than has sometimes been suggested.[41] We know from the letter of attorney Imlay wrote to Sebastian from Beargrass on 26 October 1785 that he was relying on Isaac Hite to look into the state of an entry for 50,000 acres on Green River made in the name of John Lewis, on which apparently several other entries were depending.[42] Imlay urges Sebastian to constantly encourage Hite to forward to the Register's Office all surveys that might be near running out of date. He added that '[i]n order to facilitate the business', he would 'endeavor to procure a credit in the Surveyor's Books of Jefferson and Nelson and provide a fund for the Register's office'.[43] In the same letter Imlay empowers Sebastian, should John Lewis come to the country, to dispose of his part in the survey of 22,000 acres made in Lewis's name on Floyd's Fork 'in a manner as can be agreed upon' between him, Lewis and Isaac Hite.[44] All of this suggests that Imlay stood to lose significantly more than he might possibly gain from swindling Isaac Hite out of a few acres of land and absconding from Kentucky. In fact, if anything, the extensive credit arrangements Imlay makes with Sebastian in his letter of attorney indicate that Imlay very much intended to continue to do business in Kentucky and, presumably, to return there. He informs Sebastian that as soon as he arrives in Danville he will set up more 'remote funds' for Sebastian to draw on. Not only will he leave £50 in the hands of Colonel Isaac Shelby but he will also make available 2,500 acres of land purchased of Joseph Lewis at the mouth of Cave Creek to be disposed of as needed.[45] Apparently, a Mr Freeman of the Dutch Station had proposed to view it and, in case he should think it an eligible place to settle on, he would pay £300 for 2,000 acres, 'that is to say he will give a Negroe Wench and two Children one about three years old, the other about 10 months, and £20 in hand and his Bond for £150 payable in May 1790 with lawful Interest from Christmas next'. Should Mr Freeman confirm the bargain after having seen the land, Imlay continues, Sebastian is to sell the Negroes to Mr Bullitt or Colonel Christian. Even more than the detailed nature of these arrangements, and the fact that Imlay apparently had no problem with accepting a bond payable five years hence suggests that he was in no way contemplating turning his back on the Kentucky land business just yet.

It also has to be stated in his defence that Imlay had planned to leave Kentucky in the autumn of 1785 considerably before he signed the agreement with Hite. In a note he wrote from Danville to William Clark on 26 September, Imlay urged Clark to refund a sum of 'upwards of £30' which he had advanced 'on account of General [George Rogers] Clark' by 20 October at the latest, at which time he was planning to leave the country for Richmond.[46] When on 5 November he still had not received any payment, Imlay wrote to Clark again, informing him this time that Sebastian would be collecting the money from him.[47] Imlay's actual departure from Kentucky is confirmed in a letter from Colonel William Christian. Writing from Beargrass on 4 November, Christian informs his mother that 'Captain Imlay a near neighbour of ours ... went off to Virginia Yesterday', but that he would stop at Danville for a few days (most likely, as we now know, to meet with Hite and Ogden there and sign the contract for the ironworks).[48] Imlay was still in Danville on 6 November, since on that day he wrote a memorandum to James Marshall, a judge at the District Court at Danville, instructing him how to represent him in straightening out the legal entanglements arising from his contract with Holder.[49] Christian's detailed letter provides several good reasons why Imlay would want to leave Kentucky at this point. The Indians had been stepping up their bloody attacks on stations in Jefferson County and a general Indian war was expected. As a result, Christian writes to his mother on 12 December 1785, settlers were leaving the county in droves, while all during the autumn no new immigrants had come down the river. To make matters worse, Christian goes on to write, there was a crippling shortage of cash and virtually no credit to be had, while legal disputes over land claims were spiralling out of control. In short, the demand for land had collapsed, leaving the speculators desperate: 'The speculators are starving and can sell no Land. Every man is a seller & no purchasers.'[50] Imlay must therefore have realized that if he was to raise cash to meet his bonds or to find a seller for any of his interests and claims, he would have to find them in the East. In fact, it is reasonable to assume that he went to Richmond in order personally to collect the patents that were issued there in his name on 9 and 12 December, when Imlay became the legal owner of 18,971 acres of land in Jefferson County.[51]

When in early November 1785 Imlay made his precipitous departure from Kentucky for Richmond, he had a far more weighty and honourable reason than swindling Isaac Hite out of a couple of hundred pounds. In a letter written from Beargrass on 2 November 1785, Imlay informs John Helm, a surveyor whose services he had enlisted, that he is about to leave for the East, more particularly for Richmond, in order to meet a certain 'Mr. Bealle' and his partners there in connection with the sale of some land.[52] This 'Bealle' was in fact Samuel Beall, the wealthy Virginia entrepreneur and business partner of John May; and the sale of land was the deal that Beall at one point described as 'an undertaking of Great magnitude' and one that 'very few gentlemen [were] equal to' – a reference to an agreement between Imlay and John May drawn up on 28 February 1785, whereby Imlay acquired nearly 100,000 acres of land in Jefferson, Nelson and Fayette Counties in one single transaction.[53]

John May was one of the biggest players in the Kentucky land bubble of the early 1780s. May's land hunger was well-nigh insatiable, and in August 1779 he devised a grand scheme that would plunge him, his brothers Richard, William and George, and Samuel Beall into one of the biggest land speculation plots in Kentucky's history.[54] May's ingenious speculation scheme had its roots in the passing earlier that year of a number of land laws by the Virginia General Assembly. One of the provisions of the Virginia Land Law of May 1779 was the establishment of a general Land Office; another was the development of a land patenting process ostensibly aimed at protecting the rights of early Kentucky settlers over and against those of more recent settlers and speculators from elsewhere. All persons who had made an improvement and planted a crop in Kentucky prior to 1 January 1778 were entitled to a 400-acre 'certificate of settlement'. An additional 1,000 acres, adjacent to the 'certificate of settlement' tract, could be purchased under a 'preemption warrant'. Settlers who had moved in after January 1778 but before the passage of the act were to have a preemption right of 400 acres. The fatal weakness of the Land Law was that no similar provision was made for future settlers, not holding settlement or preemption rights. This would prove to have catastrophic consequences, as the May 1779 Land Law simultaneously authorized the selling of so-called 'treasury warrants', to be used for patenting 'waste and unappropriated land'.[55] After proof of payment was established, the Virginia Land Office provided a printed warrant specifying the quantity of land and the rights upon which it was due. No proof of prior military service or residency was required for purchasing a treasury warrant. The initial price was £40 for every hundred acres. Proceeds from the sale of the treasury warrants were used 'to create a sinking fund in aid of the annual taxes to discharge the public debt'.[56] Military warrants and settlement and preemption rights had precedence over treasury warrants, which made it hard to locate good lands which could be entered without conflicting with prior and better claims. Even so, Virginia Land Office treasury warrants were being bought in large numbers by speculators, and many of them were sold in Philadelphia. From 15 October 1779, the first date on which treasury warrants could be sold, to 24 December 1783, the final date in 'Treasury Warrants Register II', over 23,000 treasury warrants were purchased from the Virginia Land Office or authorized by the Virginia General Assembly by special act or resolution.

At the heart of John May's scheme was the shrewd – though not very patriotic – calculation that the escheator in the county of Kentucky responsible for the sale of the former British possessions would be forced to sell premium Kentucky land at a price much lower than the official state price. May's gamble depended on the fact that the law on escheats and forfeitures required the escheator to sell the land for *ready money*, and, moreover, to pay this money into the Treasury *within* twenty days, under the penalty of paying 2 per cent interest over the money from the time of receiving it. May figured that because of the chronic lack of cash money in Kentucky and because of the high security risk involved in transmitting the money to Virginia within twenty days, the Treasury in Richmond could be prevailed upon to accept ready money payments as if they had been paid to the escheator in Kentucky. This way the escheator would not run the risk of the money getting into the wrong hands, while May would be able to buy land in Kentucky without having to hand over any cash to the escheator – thereby at the same time cutting out his competitors on the ground in Kentucky, whose business was severely hampered by the lack of ready money. Yet the main benefit of May's scheme was that it allowed him to bargain a much better price for Kentucky land, knowing full well that both the escheator and the Treasury would prefer substantive sales at a reduced price to more modest sales at the official state price. Thus, instead of the official price of 32 shillings per acre, May was buying tracts in March 1780 at 10 shillings an acre – though prices were rising rapidly, and even at that time prime tracts on or near the Ohio were fetching up to £6 (or 120 shillings) per acre.[57]

Initially May's 'Land Scheme' proved to be a great success. While Beall was stationed in Virginia, where he made frequent trips to the Treasury in nearby Richmond to acquire the warrants (mainly paid in tobacco) and to the Land Office to make sure their claims were properly registered, Richard, William and George May were doing the actual surveying and laying out the lands in Kentucky; John May commuted up and down between Virginia and Kentucky, taking the warrants one way and the surveys the other. By June 1780 vast amounts of land had been thus been claimed and surveyed. Yet, as May's craving for more and more land turned into a regular addiction, Beall began to get increasingly impatient to cash in on some of his massive investments. Upbraiding May for having acquired 'more Land than one Man should possess', Beall finally decided to pull the plug on his partner and to cut off his supply of capital in November 1780.[58] Writing to May from Richmond, Beall announces that he has 'come to a determined resolution not to risque one shilling more in Land over the mountain, this resolution I cannot alter, I w.d rather wish to sell Land than to buy & no temptation however great will induce me to advance further, I am willing that you sell a part of your & my particular Land, & vest a part of the proceed in other Lands that you judge will be more for our Interest'.[59] Although in the course of 1781 and 1782 May grudgingly agreed to dispose of some of the land, he continued acquire more land, drawing all the while on Beall for surveying fees, land taxes and other expenses.[60] In December 1782 Beall commended May on having made a large sale, but encouraged him to sell more, fearing that the taxes and the sheer costs of surveying and patenting their claims would ruin them. But May continued to purchase more land. On 9 January 1783 he was writing to Beall to persuade him to underwrite a deal with Colonel John Floyd, who had offered more than 80,000 acres at a bargain price.[61] It is symptomatic of John May's severe *rabies agri* that on the very same day he entered into an agreement with his brother George and John Floyd for just over 220,000 acres of land in Jefferson County.[62] On 28 March 1783 'John May *et al*. entered a further 223,000 acres on a single day, with one tract on the Green and Ohio rivers measuring no less than 160,000 acres (41,178 acres of which were later withdrawn).[63]

Increased Indian hostility was only one of the reasons why veteran speculators like Floyd were dumping their land claims wholesale in the course of 1782 and 1783. The sharp drop in the demand for land led to what John May described as an 'amazing Fall of the Price of Kentucky Land', to as low as £30 per hundred acres (or 6 shillings per acre).[64] To make matters worse, the drop in the price of land was accompanied by rampant inflation, which put an enormous strain on the market and caused investors like Beall to panic. In September 1784 Beall threateningly urged May to come to Williamsburg 'as Expeditiously as Possible' in order to 'finally settle [their] Accounts'.[65] It was very much a buyer's market, and in the absence of any significant numbers of new settlers, those buyers were increasingly speculators. With the air rife with rumours of the creation of a new state, they were gambling on prices rising again spectacularly after Kentucky's entry into the union and hence were descending upon Kentucky in ever greater numbers. In January 1785 May complained in a letter to Beall that 'at this Time nine out of ten of the Inhabitants are large Speculators' – presumably as opposed to more honorable gentlemen entrepreneurs like himself and his partners.[66] Barely a month later, however, May would be forced to enter upon a contract involving just under 100,000 acres of land with precisely one of those land sharks eager for a quick profit in the murky waters of the Kentucky land market.

The actual contract between May and Gilbert Imlay has so far not come to light, but what do survive are copies of a 'Memorandum of the Lands comprehended in an agreement entered into between Gilbert Imlay & John May', dated 28 February 1785.[67] Listing each item individually, the 'Memorandum' clearly reflects the motley, wholesale nature of the 94,713⅓-acre deal. Some of the tracts had been surveyed for John May himself, others for Beall, and others again were jointly owned by May and Beall, or by them in partnership with William

May, David Meade, Robert Morris, William Booth and various other investors. Included in the deal were also several treasury warrants in the name of Booth and others, for land still to be located. It is obvious that Imlay had joined the major league of Kentucky speculators.

However, what is equally obvious is that, even though many of the surveyed tracts had been located on military warrants, which tended to be less vulnerable to rival claims than treasury warrants (the latter having been issued by the truck-load), Imlay had bought what amounted to a clearance inventory of odd bits and pieces of land and claims, which it would take a lot of time, effort and money to secure and sell on as individual items. At the same time, Imlay was contractually obliged to make sure that the entries were swiftly located, properly surveyed and accurately registered, and that adequate provisions were made for the payment of fees and expenses. In addition, given the complicated nature of the business and the high risk of litigation, resulting in the potential loss of claims, the contract stipulated that Imlay was personally to oversee all steps of the patenting process.[68] Finally, it also becomes apparent from the Beall-May correspondence that if Imlay were to fail to meet his financial obligations, the contract would become null and void, and the title to the land would revert back to May, Beall and their partners. Given all these conditions and stipulations, it is clear that only a high-risk speculator like Imlay could have signed the contract.

At a going rate at the time of anywhere between £20 and £50 per hunderd acres, depending on soil and situation, Imlay's contract potentially could have yielded a considerable sum of money. In the absence of the actual contract between John May and Imlay, it cannot be ascertained with absolute certainty how much Imlay agreed to pay for the land; however, the correspondence between May and Beall and an undated memorandum found among Samuel Beall's papers allow us to make a calculated guess. Apparently, Imlay was to pay for the land in five instalments: £1,500 by 15 June 1786; £2,000 by 15 May 1787; £2,500 by 15 May 1788; £2,000 by 15 November 1791, with interest thereon from 15 November 1789; and the balance on 15 November 1792, with interest from 15 November 1789.[69] We do not know for certain how much the price per acre was that Imlay was to pay and, hence, how much the last instalment would have been. However, from article 7 of the contract, which Beall copied in his memorandum, it can be deduced that the price Imlay paid was £15 per hundred acres. This would suggest that the negotiated price for the combined tracts, surveys, entries and warrants was around £14,000, plus interest over part of that amount. In a market of rapidly rising land prices, Imlay would have stood to earn a small fortune; but in a flat or a falling market, the agreement could soon become a strangulation contract. Seeing that at the time of his concluding the agreement with May he was not even able to meet bonds for only a few hundred pounds, it is obvious that Imlay only had two options: immediately sell on significant numbers of tracts, warrants and entries to others, or find partners who were willing to offer security to his bonds.

Perhaps it was because Beall had badgered him into concluding the deal with Imlay, but at any rate, it soon became apparent to May that he should have looked a little more carefully into Imlay's credentials and credit history. From 1780 onwards, his expanding business interests required him to spend a large part of the year in Kentucky – unlike Beall, who remained all year round in Williamsburg. May was therefore in a better position than was his partner to monitor the progress Imlay was making in carrying out his contract. By June 1785, May had heard from Imlay only once since the latter had arrived at the Falls of the Ohio (in a letter dated 30 May).[70] It did not take long for May to draw his conclusions from Imlay's elusiveness and that same month he extracted himself from the tripartite agreement with Imlay. In a letter to Beall dated 2 July 1785 May confirms that they had adjusted their business arrangements on 30 June 1783, to the effect that May had sold his interest in the contract to Beall.[71] What had concerned May in particular was that whereas Imlay was contractually bound personally to oversee the locating and surveying of tracts and to arrange for fees and expenses to be paid, he appeared to be doing no such thing. By the early autumn, apart from drawing on May for expenses and injudiciously entering tracts in his own name (which in some cases overlapped with claims entered earlier on military warrants by May himself!), Imlay seems to have made little headway towards fulfilling the terms of his contract.[72] Fearing that Imlay might default on his agreement with Beall, May told his partner in September that he should immediately annul the contract.[73]

In the meantime, however, Imlay had not been completely idle. Back in October of the previous year he had left detailed instructions with his attorney, Benjamin Sebastian, whom he appears to have appointed for the express purpose of assisting him in his mega-deal with May and Beall. In the memorandum Imlay urged Sebastian to advise and assist his chief surveyor, Richard Woolfolk, in whatever way he could in sorting out any legal entanglements that might ensue from his activities. Having left his book of locations with them, in July 1786 Imay had written to Richard Woolfolk and John Helm from Louisville, instructing them to 'proceed with all possible Dispatch' to survey the tracts that had been entered in the name of John May and company, but to 'take every Precaution concerning the Indians and in no Case to relax [their] Prudence in that respect'. At the very least the wording of the letter suggests that Imlay was confident he could sell some of the land on to someone else, for he urges Woolfolk and Helm to 'be sure to make Comments on all the surveys that you make for me Relative to its Situation, Soil or any Real Advantages it may have'.[74]

Since it had always been Samuel Beall's money – not John May's – that had financed their speculation scheme in Virginia treasury warrants, it does not come as a surprise that Beall would soon begin to increase the pressure on Imlay. In August 1785 Beall sent the following letter to Imlay:

W[illia]msburg, 26ᵗʰ, August, 1785

Mr. Gilbert Imlay

Sir,

I conclude Mʳ. John May hath fully communicated to you his late agreement with me wherein he has transferred to me the Purchase money arising on his part of land sold to you wherein I was formerly interested with Mʳ. May, consequently you will be pleased to consider yourself as accountable for the money arising due from you under your agreement with Mʳ. May dated the [space] so far as arises on the sales of Land before mentioned. I expect you will comply with the respective engagemᵗˢ that you made under said agreement, and that you will be pleased to consider me as representing Mʳ. May therein so far as respects the said Land –

Mʳ. May hath shewn me your Receipt for £100 currency to be employed toward the surveying and securing our Land, when this money is expended you will be pleased to render an Auᵗ. [audit] of such expenditures to my friend and agent Edmund Taylor Esq. whom I have empowered to receive & adjust the same, this being done Mʳ. Taylor will from time to time discharge my quota of Disbursmˢ. arising on Land as far as ~~far as~~ my share extends, and will also pay up Mʳ. Rogʳ. Morris's share of Charges and expenditures arising on his Land, it will be essentially necessary for you at all times to furnish Mʳ. Taylor with a clear Auᵗ. to shew for what purpose you have employed the money you have received, specifying as clear as possible the surveys made by you, & making the expenditures attending each survey as near as possible, this cannot be dispensed with, otherwise I cannot effect a settlement with those I am concerned with. I cannot draw on them for money untill I state the accounts and shew the sum due thereon.

I have advised Mʳ. Taylor to consult with you with respect to the sale of some of the land that is now held in Company between you and myself only – I much wish to sell as much as will raise ready money to defray charges on on [*sic*] all the land I am concerned in. I expect by selling it low it will command one third or one fourth Cash, or perhaps you may engage men to do this business and take land in payment. I submit this to Mʳ. Taylor and yourself – any thing in this way that he may come into, I will confirm. I hope sales may be made to save me from further advance, money is very scarce here, and I wish not to expend more money in the back Country. Should any land be sold, such part as is on credit, Bonds taken for the same should as well for your share as for my quota, be placed in the Lands of Mʳ. Taylor, p[aya]ble to me, untill you comply with the several Articles of Agreement stipulated between you and Mʳ. May & by Mʳ. May assigned to me. I am bound by agreement with Mʳ. May to attend minutely to you and his agreement – I cannot <u>admit longer credit</u>, on land sold, for any part, than the <u>1ˢᵗ. of Octᵇ. 1789</u>. I must earnestly request the favour of you to use every means in your power to have the surveys compleated as soon as possible – I am extremely anxious to have this business closed with all possible expedition, it has already been too long delayed. I wish you to consult with Mʳ. Taylor who will be proper assistants to employ, and also to advise with him on all occasions respecting his business – he is well acquainted with the different Characters over the mountain, & will I am sure at all times be serviceable to you and myself when in his power.

I have been some time anxious to visit Europe, this cannot take place for some time, and I hope before I go you'll have finished the surveys, and I have good reason to suppose I may dispose of land in Europe to great advantage – I shall readily if agreable to you dispose of your Interest with mine. M͏ʳ. May has no doubt pointed out to you M͏ʳ. Morris's <u>share</u> of the land transferred to you, and my Interest also – this will shew you the proportion of Expences that M͏ʳ. Taylor will have to pay. I shall be glad to hear from you by every good opportunity – Letters put into the Post Office any where on the Continent will reach me.

> I am very respectfully
> Sir,
> Yr mo Obst
> Sam. Beall

August 26ᵗʰ. 1785, to
Gilbert Imlay.
by Js. Breckenridge
under cover to Mr.
Edmund Taylor[75]

This letter is revealing in more than one way. It confirms, for instance, that Imlay's agreement with May and Beall was not so much a sales as a *lease* contract. In fact, Imlay was no more than a sub-contractor hired to survey and secure May's and Beall's land claims in exchange for a share in the profits on future sales. Yet it also becomes evident from the letter how desperate Virginia land tycoons like Beall and the May brothers had become to get out of the Kentucky land bubble, which was evidently about to burst. This was no doubt why they had decided to sell their land to an impecunious speculator like Imlay in the first place: in the bleak reality of the frontier economy, it was never quite clear who was preying on whom. What is clear is that as a gentleman speculator, Beall was considerably out of his depth in the turbid world of Kentucky land-jobbing. Since he had bought out John May, Beall depended on local agents like Edmund Taylor to look after his interests 'over the mountain'. But ultimately, he was at the mercy of business partners like Imlay, who, being all too aware of the predicament Beall was in and having nothing to lose, might – or might not – stick to the terms of their agreement and render proper accounts of their transactions. The archives of the county courts make abundantly clear that such partners were a rarity in Kentucky. It further testifies to Beall's inexperience – or his decency – that he was willing to extend credit to Imlay until as late as the autumn of 1789. But, in the light of Imlay's future career as a promoter of emigration to Kentucky, what is perhaps the most interesting aspect of Beall's letter is his remark that he was hoping to sell some of his land 'to great advantage' on the European market, and that he was quite prepared to dispose of Imlay's interest in the agreement in a similar manner. For all we know, Beall was inadvertently handing Imlay the exit strategy he would soon need.

In February 1786 Beall complained in a letter to John May that he was 'too great a Stranger to the Business for want of information' from both him or Imlay, and he urged May to return to 'back country' as soon as possible to find out what the state of affairs there was.[76] Even though Imlay had been 'many weeks at Richmond' during the winter (a mere fifty miles from Williamsburg), he had not contacted Beall once, nor had Beall so far received a single patent for any of his land. Although even then Beall did not 'wish to depreciate Mr. Imlays stability or Character', his continued silence 'surprised [him] exceedingly'. Beall was now getting seriously worried about Imlay's ability, though not his intention, to handle the job and meet the terms of their agreement. It 'is an undertaking of Great magnitude', he mused, that 'very few gentlemen are equal to'. Beall took some comfort from the fact that Imlay was apparently on an extensive sales trip to the north-east. In January Imlay was in Baltimore, in February in New Jersey, and in March he was in New York, where allegedly he had been making considerable sales of land.[77] However, disposing of his land may have proved a little harder than anticipated, for the following May he was expected back in Baltimore but by the end of July he had failed to arrive there.[78] We know he was in Philadelphia in early September, for on the 7th of that month he appeared in person before Edward Shippen – Peggy (Shippen) Arnold's father – and Plunkett Fleeson, justices of the Court of Common Pleas in that city, in order to acknowledge and confirm the written indentures by which he had some time prior to his appearance in court sold a total of 15,043 acres of his own land, all in Jefferson County, to the former Continental Navy privateer Colonel Silas Talbot, then of Philadelphia, for £750 Pennsylvania paper money and 12,771 silver Spanish milled dollars.[79] However, as we shall see, none of this money would end up in Beall's pocket.

By the spring of 1786 John May was back in Kentucky, but there was no sign of Imlay. In March Imlay had written to John May from New York to the effect that the sales he had been making there had made him confident that he would be able to execute the terms of their agreement.[80] He claimed that he had brought 'Col Lee & one Col Hindman of the Eastern State of Maryland' into the contract as partners, and that they would be good security. In the course of April it became clear to John May that Imlay had also let General Wilkinson and James Marshall of Fayette County in on the deal as partners, each for one-sixth part, and that he had accepted their bonds by way of payment. May was not impressed. Writing to Beall, he observed that, according to Imlay's agreement with them, Wilkinson and Marshall

> are answerable only to him [Imlay] and, each for himself only neither of them to us. [Imlay] has written to them to enter themselves as Security to me for their respective Shares, but they seem unwilling so to do because of their Bonds to him.
>
> I know Nothing of their Property, and therefore cannot say whether they would be good Security for the Land or not. The[y] do not appear to have much.[81]

To make matters worse, May reported that 'The Indians have been more troublesome this winter than I ever knew them, & have done more mischief than they ever did at the same Time of Year. Col. Christian & Col. Donaldson are amongst the slain: And they are dispersed through almost every Part of the Country where our Land lies it has been impossible to proceed in surveying for several Months past'. Under these circumstances it was very unlikely that Imlay would be able to carry out anywhere near the amount of surveying he would have to do to generate the level of sales he needed to meet the first instalment of his bond, which was due on 15 June. In May's assessment, Imlay's only hope lay in the potentially beneficial effect on land prices that might arise from discussions then underway in the Virginia Assembly to establish an independent State of Kentucky. 'I think his paying us will altogether depend on the Lands rising in Value', he wrote to Beall, adding, 'I do not by any Means think it advisable to suffer him to Speculate on our Property'.

But speculating was precisely what Imlay was doing, and in a big way, too, as becomes evident from the details of his arrangement with General James Wilkinson and James Marshall. When he appointed Benjamin Sebastian as his acting attorney in October 1785, Imlay in fact asked him to take care of two transactions. The 'first purchase' was his February 1785 contract with John May, but the memorandum hints at another, related, deal, this time involving Wilkinson, who had been Imlay's agent in Fayette County since May, and James Marshall, who had been acting as Imlay's attorney in his dispute with John Holder.[82] An entry dated 8 November 1785 in the Kentucky Supreme Court Deeds Book reveals the nature of this transaction. It appears that some time prior to 8 November Imlay had sold a third of the land he had bought from John May to Wilkinson and Marshall, and that on that day he gave his bond to his partners for the considerable sum of £40,000, which was to be annulled as soon as he conveyed the patents for the land to Wilkinson and Marshall, and on condition that the land would be equal in quality and situation to the other two-thirds.[83] It is not clear how much Wilkinson and Marshall would actually have been willing to pay Imlay for the land, but what *is* clear is that the deal with Wilkinson and Marshall, like the one with John May, left the burden of surveying and patenting the land firmly on Imlay's shoulders. In the cut-throat Kentucky land-jobbing market of the 1780s, there were sharks, and then there were bigger sharks.

Investing at most a few hundred pounds of real money to cover initial surveyors' fees and other expenses (and even this largely on credit), Imlay thus managed to construct an impressive but delicately balanced financial house of cards, made up of interdependent subcontracts and mutual bonds. This, he hoped, would fulfil the terms of his original agreement with John May. Though of anxious disposition, Beall saw no reason to fear that Imlay might fail to deliver. Writing to George May from Williamsburg on 23 May, Beall was still confident that 'Captn Imlay will be here the 15th of next Month' to render accounts.[84] On 13 June

Beall wrote to Imlay's agent Alexander Skinner, expressing his continued trust in Imlay's 'good Character' and intentions:

W^{msburg}, 13th June 1786

Dear Sir,

    I have this moment a letter from Mr George May's respect^s Mr John May's late Contract with Captn Gilbert Imlay. I have long since informed Captn Imlay, and the Hon^l Henry Lee Esq that I am Mr J. May's representative in this Continent, and they have written to me acknowledging such nature, and Captn Imlay promises to attend and Complete the Contract here. I have a letter from Mr John May to Captain Imlay informing him that powers are vested in me to Complete this Business, it is in my wish to conduct with candour & justice, and from the good Character I have of Captn Imlay, I trust no difficulty will attend it. I hope the favour a Line from You by return of Stage – please to advise me when I may certainly expect to see Captn Imlay but Southall will personally deliver this [illegible] I hope in time for your Answer tomorrow as I wish to go to Gloucester on hearing from you and in a few days I shall proceed to Sea for some Weeks for Mrs Beall's Health[85]

However, being on the ground in Kentucky and knowing many of the major players in the land-jobbing business there, John May was not so easily fooled by Imlay's assurances and financial consortiums. In letters he wrote to Beall in the course of May and June, May reported that Imlay had not been back in Kentucky all spring and that he had made no arrangements whatsoever with any of his agents and attorneys to carry out or oversee the surveying and patenting process. To make matters worse, Edmund Taylor, Beall's representative in his deal with Imlay, died suddenly in June. As a result, even though he no longer had a direct interest in the contract with Imlay, May found himself acting more and more on Beall's behalf. In late June, May complained to Beall that Imlay's continued absence had made it necessary for him 'to pay the same Attention to this Business as if [he] had not bargained with him'.[86] Apart from an increase in Indian attacks on settlers and surveying parties, what made it imperative that the surveys were done as quickly as possible was the sharp rise in the number of land disputes. Complex legal entanglements and endless law suits were threatening to shut down the entire land business in Kentucky. 'Our Lands turn out extremely well', May reported to Beall on 27 June, 'though we shall, as well as all other Adventurers, have many Disputes. The late Adventurers totally disregarded old Claims, most of which are again surveyed for several others, & in many Instances there have been from one to seven or eight Surveys made on the same Land; and as many Grants issued thereupon.'[87] The situation was beginning to look so grim that according to May even Wilkinson and Marshall 'would be glad to be clear of the Contract'. On 14 July John May informed Beall that Imlay had written to him some time in June, from somewhere in the East, to assure him that he would comply with the terms in the contract; it had also been 'intimated' to May that

Imlay had written to Wilkinson and Marshall that the first payment had been made on time, and that the whole venture was still on track.[88] Needless to say, no such payment had actually been made, and Imlay continued to give Kentucky and Williamsburg a wide berth.

In John May's assessment, all of this could only mean that Imlay was intending to enter into a legal dispute with them in order to delay payment. He also had a hunch what that dispute might involve. Article 7 of the original agreement between John May and Imlay – the only article that has survived, in a copy found among Beall's papers – stipulated how Imlay was to be compensated in case William May's interest in the transaction was sold before the contract was actually signed. According to the article, Imlay was to receive whatever the land fetched *in excess* of the agreed minimum price of £15 per hundred acres, and was to be extended credit towards payment of the first instalment to the amount the land sold *under* the agreed price.[89] Apparently, however, Imlay had been telling other people – though not May – that he was to have credit for the *entire* amount of sales at the rate of £15 per hundred acres.[90] Since William May had sold his land for considerably less than the agreed minimum rate, Imlay stood to gain a great deal if his interpretation of article 7 of the agreement with May was correct; indeed, the credit he thought he was entitled to would more than cover the first instalment of his payment.

But in this, the most critical, phase of their negotiations with Imlay, Beall's letters were not getting through to May any more, leaving the latter to second-guess whether Beall had ever met Imlay in June and, if so, what had emerged from that meeting. On 9 October May complained that he had 'written so many Letters to [Beall] without receiving an Answer that [he is] very much at a Loss to account for it' and that he urgently needed to hear from Beall 'for several Reasons of very considerable Consequence'.[91] Fully aware that the June deadline had passed but ignorant of the current status of the deal, May was anxious to communicate to Beall that 'there has been no Person here to act for Imlay since [he] came out, and not one Farthing of Money provided'. Apparently, Wilkinson and Marshall had paid some of the expenses, but, as May observed, had he not advanced most of the money himself, nothing would have been done and their business would have 'suffered exceedingly'.[92] By 27 October, at which time he would normally have returned to the East, May was still in Kentucky, desperately trying to complete the surveys for the Beall/Imlay contract before the winter set in. 'I am at present in a very disagreable State of Suspence', he wrote to Beall, 'of not knowing whether the Bargain [with Imlay] stands or not ... not having any Person to give me the least Assistance on Behalf of Imlay, nor one Farthing of Money to pay his Proportion of Expences. He has totally given up the Business and left no one to act for him or any Money to pay Expences'.[93] Even as late as November, May was still in Kentucky, frantically waiting for news from Beall:

I am still without any of your Letters since those dated some Time in the Spring
and know not how to act With Respect to the Contract with Imlay[,] not knowing
whether it is annulled or not; and being detained here on that Account much longer
than I expected; the Business requiring the Attention of some Person here and Imlay
having left no Person who can or will act for him.[94]

He continued, 'The Business of surveying, &c is nearly compleated and will
be finished this Fall before I leave the Country: But you ought to have some
Person here to act as your Attorney, as there are many Matters in which You
are interested in this Country wch make it necessary'. In the same letter to Beall,
May – now almost hysterical with anxiety – accused Imlay of having deliberately
undermined the terms of their agreement by appointing as his legal representative for registering surveys in Imlay's name (a 'Brother in Law') – viz. James
Marshall – 'who knew Nothing of the Situation of the Country', thus allowing
Imlay to 'make such Representations thereof as would deceive any Person who
had not some Knowledge of the Country'. As a result, May had spent the best
part of six months entering caveats against junior surveys and entries, and resur-
veying and re-registering the very tracts he had sold to Imlay back in February
1785. 'You will see by Imlays & my Agreement', May continued,

> that I was apprehensive of such Proceedings as these; & therefore bid him up to
> attend to the Surveys of all the Lands in Person w[hi]ch it was possible for him to
> attend to; and he was not to trust others except in Cases where there was a necessity
> for the Surveys being made before he could attend them himself; and his empowering
> Marshall to direct the Surveying of this Land, instead of attending thereto himself,
> was a manifest violation of the Agreement, and must subject him to the Paiment of
> all Damages that may be sustained thereby. He had no Power to give such Authority
> to Marshall; & therefore you ought to reject the Survey and have another Return of
> the Land, made agreeably to a Survey w[hi]ch I have ordered. This is not the only
> Instance in which Injustice has been done us by Imlays non attendance.[95]

May was so frustrated by the whole situation that he was now almost begging
Beall to terminate his contract with Imlay. By December, May still had not
received any letters from Beall. Writing to Beall from Danville on the 27th, May
said he would have declared the contract void with Imlay's attorney long since,
had he 'not been afraid of counteracting [Beall's] views'.[96] His position was indeed
far from enviable: whilst he was no longer formally a partner in the contract after
Beall had taken over his interest in it, he ultimately stood to gain from his new
agreement with Beall only if Imlay actually managed to survey, register and sell
what was now effectively Beall's land. Therefore he could not simply stand by
and watch as hordes of speculators piled new claim after claim on land that he
had already surveyed, whilst at the same time the value of his treasury warrants
was plummeting as vacant land was disappearing rapidly. Neither Imlay nor his
partners and attorneys having advanced as much as a farthing since last winter,

May had been forced to cover all the costs ensuing from the Imlay deal himself: 'It has Cost me since I came out upwards of £120 for amending the Locations on Cany, Surveying the Land in small Surveys & paying the Expences of the Deputy & Chain-carriers, besides Surveyors & Registers Fees; & Expences of other Land and all the Assistance wch I have had, has been the Credits before mentioned & a Credit on your Acc^t for the Registers Fees'.

Whether May ever heard from Beall before his planned return to Virginia in March 1787 is not known. But, as it turned out, he need not have been so worried about Beall's agreement with Imlay – at least not until the spring of 1787. May had known since September or early October 1786, through his brother George, that Beall had finally managed to have a meeting with Imlay in Rhode Island (although he presumed that Beall had 'got the Matter fixt before this Time').[97] Evidently, even as late as the autumn of 1786 Imlay had stayed well clear of both Virginia and Kentucky, so that it was in the end Beall himself who had to travel to the north-east to obtain an interview with his elusive partner. No record of their meeting has emerged, but Beall must have learnt enough from it to write to Imlay on 27 October 1786:

> Sir,
>   In consequence of Letters and from Mr John May empowering me to annul his Contract with you, bearing date the 28th Feby 1785, I hereby make the same null & void, as much so as if no such contract had been entered into –
>   I am &c
>   S Beall
>   Wmsburg, 27 Octr 1786

With this perfunctory note came a sudden and inglorious end to the most ambitious project in Imlay's career as a speculator and junk bond trader in the Kentucky land bubble of the 1780s. He had hoped to make a fortune by investing everything he had – which was virtually nothing; at the end of the day, virtually nothing was what he ended up with. For, as far as we can tell, the agreement with John May and Samuel Beall brought Imlay no significant financial gains, while the losses – mainly in surveying expenses, registration costs, legal fees and lost surveys – were for the most part borne by May and Beall.

Imlay's returns from three hectic years of trading in the 1780s Kentucky land bubble may have been modest, but they were by no means atypical. The Virginia system for distributing its public lands in Kentucky introduced in May 1779 was notorious for its wasteful inefficiency. Notably the introduction of treasury warrants, which authorized the purchaser to locate and lay off a specific quantity of unclaimed land wherever he could find it, had hugely boosted speculation by non-resident investors and absentee land owners. By 1784, when Kentucky District had only a few thousand widely scattered settlers, thousands more land warrants had been issued by Virginia than there was land available. The reckless piling of grant upon grant, crudely surveyed and marked, if at all, was further confused by disputes over settlement rights, tax titles and secondary ownership claims, cluttering up court dockets for decades to come and causing 'wide spread discontent and distress ... a litigious spirit, and in some instances, a disregard of legal right in general'.[98] As a result, even owners of large, often unsurveyed tracts of hundreds of thousands of acres of Kentucky land were frequently satisfied to sell only a few hundred acres, likewise unsurveyed. Others, like John May, were inclined to cut their losses and liquidate their holdings wholesale, offloading their dodgy claims onto speculators who were even greedier, and generally more desperate.

On the other hand, Imlay did not emerge from the land-jobbing business completely empty-handed. As the May-Beall deal was rapidly unravelling, he had still managed to acquire and sell the odd couple of thousand acres on the side all through 1786. Thus on 1 June he obtained a grant for 2,000 acres in Fayette County jointly with Matthew Walton, and on the same day Walton and John Holder assigned him another 1,000 acres in the same county.[99] On 10 July he secured the grant to two-thirds of a tract of 4,023 acres in Jefferson County (John Holder being grantee to the rest).[100] And on 14 November grants were issued in Imlay's name for four tracts in Fayette County totalling 3,400 acres.[101] However, in respect to what Imlay's plans and intentions were from the late summer of 1786 onwards, what is more interesting than these acquisitions were the *sales* that he was making in this period. Thus on 1 August he sold a tract of 2,148 acres in Fayette County to James Wilkinson for £500, which, significantly, was the first time that Imlay's name was recorded as a grantor, not a grantee.[102] Then, in early September, as we have seen, Imlay disposed of 15,043 acres in Jefferson County to Silas Talbot, and, finally, on 26 September he agreed to sell to Arthur Lee of Virginia the 4,023 acres in Jefferson County that had been granted to him, jointly with John Holder, on 10 July.[103] Two key things stand out in these transactions in comparison to land Imlay had sold before the middle of 1786. First, all of these sales concerned land to which he held legal title, as opposed to earlier transactions, which had involved the selling, trading or reassigning of warrants, surveys or entries, none of which transferred legal ownership of the land thus sold. Second, even though some of the payments he received in the transaction would have been in promissory notes, we know for certain from the Silas Talbot deal that Imlay was keen to assign his patents for cash payments. Thus cashing in on the few hard assets he had acquired during his career as a speculator – his patents – suggests that Imlay must have realized that it was time to bail out and move on to new adventures.

3 FRIENDS IN HIGH PLACES

[Imlay] is better acquainted than either you or me
Thomas Rutland to James Bagues, 11 December 1786[1]

By the time his most ambitious speculation scheme – his contract with John May and Samuel Beall – collapsed in late 1786, Imlay must have realized that his days as a land-jobber were well-nigh over. His curriculum vitae in general did not look too good at this point in his life. Since his early twenties, he had had a brief but undistinguished career in the Revolutionary army; he had emerged relatively unscathed from the breakdown of socioeconomic order in wartime New Jersey, though with little to boast about, either; and he had been an enterprising land-jobber in Kentucky, albeit a spectacularly unsuccessful one. Now at thirty-two, he was down and out, and had run out of obvious career options. Having defaulted on so many debts, cheated so many people out of their land and property, and ignored so many court summonses, there was virtually no place left in the union for him to hide, let alone to make an honest living. It is highly unlikely that he ever went back to Kentucky after he left the district in November 1785. There were no sightings of him there throughout the spring and summer of 1786, and, besides, the legal and financial fallout of the collapse of the deal with Beall and May in the autumn of that year rendered any thought of resuming trade in Kentucky impracticable. Nor does he seem to have visited Virginia again after December 1786, when he wrote his famous farewell note to Daniel Boone during a brief visit to Richmond. The prominent Virginia lawyer and Revolutionary-era diplomat Arthur Lee – who had every reason to find Imlay after the latter had first failed to deliver the patents to the 4,023 acres he had sold to Lee back in September and who had then reneged on his legal obligation to offer him land in as good a situation and of the same quality – could not find a trace of Imlay anywhere in Virginia despite his best efforts.[2] Writing to Arthur Lee on 5 March 1787 from Richmond, fellow-Virginian John Marshall reported that according to his brother James, who had acted as Imlay's attorney in Kentucky and who knew him well, Imlay either was or soon would be in New York – just about the only place outside of the western territory and the middle states where he *could* move around freely.[3]

Exactly how precarious the situation had become for Imlay is revealed in a letter from Captain James Bagues, who was acting as paymaster to Thomas Rutland, a merchant based at Annapolis. When he was in Kentucky in the course of 1785, Imlay had bought a quantity of goods from Rutland through the mediation of Daniel Henry, giving Rutland a bond for just over £300 by way of payment.[4] When it appeared that no payment was forthcoming, Rutland began to bombard Imlay with a string of increasingly strongly-worded letters. Under constant pressure in the late 1780s from aggressive creditors and delinquent debtors, Rutland was a relentless, even ruthless, opponent, whose relationship with his business associates was so extremely contentious in nature that he readily believed the truth of the rumour that an order had been issued to take him, dead or alive. But Imlay did not flinch. Writing to Rutland from New Jersey in the late spring of 1786, Imlay argued that since he had come to a prior arrangement with Daniel Henry, on whom allegedly he had a claim in connection with an earlier transaction, he felt he was under no obligation to honour his bond with him.[5] Determined to collect his money from Imlay, in July 1786 Rutland employed the services of James Bagues. Yet by the following February, Bagues had not managed to obtain a meeting with Imlay. By now more than a little tired of having been given the run-around, Bagues wrote to Imlay in February 1787:

> Agreeable to your promise to meet me in Baltimore on or about 20th November last, I went to that place, and waited several days, expecting your Arrival, but very much to my Disappointment, and Expence, I returned to Annapolis without seeing you. Since which I have even been at the Trouble of going to Richmond – hearing you was there – but unfortunate for me, you had left that Place, before my Arrival a few Days.
>
> You have already been informed by me and know how expensive it was for me to be continually following you, in the manner I have done, to and from New York down to Richmond in Virginia.
>
> For fear of Miscarriage, I have wrote you, (Copy) by way of Alexandria – Williamsburgh and Richmond – and hope it will be in your powers to determine whether and when I may expect to see you – It is out of my Power to wait longer than the reasonable time given for Answer to this, in a short time after which, if not satisfactory answered, I shall be obliged to transfer your Bill for what I can get, which I cannot conceive will be much to your Credit and I am certain to my Disadvantage – to prevent which, I hope you will arrange Matters, so as to releive [*sic*] me from my present Necessities and you from any further Trouble.[6]

Bagues's letter aptly illustrates that, by the early spring of 1787, Imlay had in effect become a fugitive in his own country. With Rutland, until his death in 1789, tenaciously calling upon his extensive network of business contacts for information concerning Imlay's whereabouts, people were on the lookout for Imlay in every major trading town up and down the east coast.[7] Yet the Rutland case also confirms that if it was Imlay's close relations with the rich and powerful that had given him the creditworthiness he had enjoyed throughout his career as land-jobber and entrepreneur, it was those same connections that, remarkably, continued to keep his creditors at bay and him out of jail. Significantly, although he had no reason to trust either Imlay's word or his credit, even Thomas Rutland – not a man easily swayed by reputation or social status – urged Bagues 'to take [Imlay's] Note of hand' instead of cash at any time, 'as he is better acquainted than either you or me'.[8] Rutland was particularly intrigued by Imlay's close connections with various members of the Lee family, one of the oldest and politically most influential families in Virginia. Thus, in March 1788, Rutland noted with evident interest that Arthur Lee, with whom Imlay had conducted business, had recently been made a commissioner for the Continental Congress to seek foreign aid. In January of that same year Rutland had written to Arthur Lee's elder brother, Richard Henry Lee, to ask him where he could find Imlay, with whom, he had been told, Lee was 'very well acquainted'.[9] As it happens, the 'Henry Lee' with whom Imlay was in cahoots was not Richard Henry Lee – a member of the Continental Congress (1774–9), sponsor of the Virginia independence resolution, signatory of the Declaration of Independence, and state delegate to Congress in 1777, 1780 and 1785 – but his cousin, Henry 'Light-Horse Harry' Lee.

It is, indeed, remarkable, not just how many influential men in Kentucky Imlay was on excellent terms with, but how many of them were willing to act on his behalf or vouch for his credit and reputation. Thus, during the period he was an active participant in the Kentucky land business, Imlay appointed a string of prominent citizens as attorneys, who would typically negotiate for extensions on bonds and contracts, keep creditors at bay, represent him in court or at the surveyor's office, and act as his proxy whilst he was away on business elsewhere in Kentucky or in the East. Imlay's attorneys included Dr Alexander Skinner, Judge James Marshall, Judge Benjamin Sebastian, General James Wilkinson and Colonel Henry ('Light-Horse Harry') Lee.

The Louisville-based physician Dr Alexander Skinner may not have been the best-connected man in Kentucky (although he knew and did business with General Wilkinson),[10] but James Marshall certainly was. Born in Fauquier County, Virginia, James Markham Marshall was the son of Colonel Thomas Marshall of Virginia. A veteran of both the French and Indian War (during which he served under General Braddock) and the Revolutionary War (during which he commanded the third Virginia Regiment), Thomas Marshall was a member of the Virginia Convention that declared independence. In 1783 he was appointed surveyor-general for the District of Kentucky, and established his office in Lexington. Having fought in the Revolutionary War in one of the companies of Alexander Hamilton's regiment, James Marshall had come to Kentucky when his father moved his family there in 1785. Not long after, he went to field to fight a duel with James Brown, a judge of the district court at Danville and Virginia delegate to Congress for the District of Kentucky. A district judge in his own right, James Marshall was the brother of John Marshall, a highly-regarded constitutional lawyer in Virginia, who would go on to become Secretary of State under President Adams and in 1801 would be appointed the fourth Chief Justice of the United States Supreme Court. James Marshall would return to Virginia in 1795, when he was to marry Hester, daughter of Robert Morris, the Revolutionary War financier, signatory of the Declaration of Independence and the Constitution. A witness to the unfolding of the Reign of Terror in Paris in 1793, James Marshall was sent by Washington as a special agent of the government to negotiate the release of Lafayette, first at the court of the King of Prussia in Berlin, and later at Olmutz, where the Austrians had imprisoned the general.[11]

Imlay must have been on relatively intimate terms with James Marshall by the end of 1785. In November of that year, James Marshall, in partnership with James Wilkinson, had taken on a sizeable share of Imlay's contract with Beall, presumably for no other reason than to hoodwink Beall into believing that Imlay had considerable financial backing in the scheme.[12] Similarly, the memorandum Imlay prepared for Marshall that very same month in connection with his acrimonious land dispute with Captain John Holder betrays a degree of openness and trust on Imlay's part rarely seen in any of his writings.[13]

Of all of Imlay's attorneys none intervened more often on behalf of his client than Benjamin Sebastian. Sebastian had been ordained a minister of the Episcopal Church by the Bishop of London in 1766 and the following year became rector of a church in Northumberland County, Virginia. Having studied law in Virginia, Sebastian settled in Kentucky in 1784, where he became a judge of the District Court. There he joined the forces that were bent on undermining the position of George Rogers Clark in the district, and appears to have been one of the earliest recruits into the James Wilkinson camp after the latter had settled in Louisville in early 1784. Soon Sebastian was one of the ringleaders of Wilkinson's secessionist plot against the United States, and a prominent member of the general's innermost circle of political advisers and associates, known as the 'Danville Group', which beside Sebastian included Harry Innes, who had given up his position as presiding judge of the District Court to become attorney general after the death of Walker Daniel; George Muter, like Sebastian a judge of the District Court; and John Brown, a nephew of William Preston who had studied law under Jefferson and had come west for adventure and profit. Sebastian and Wilkinson were members of the Kentucky conventions of 1785, 1786, 1787 and 1788.[14] In August 1787, whilst plotting to put Kentucky under vassalage of the Spanish King, Wilkinson was confident that the Convention would nominate Sebastian to be their agent to negotiate with Congress the terms of Kentucky's admission into the union.[15] Sebastian was also a key player in Wilkinson's 'Spanish Conspiracy'. Having been appointed a judge of the Court of Appeals in 1792, he was forced to resign from his post in December 1806 after it had emerged that he had been receiving an annual pension of $2,000 from Spain, in recognition of his efforts to broker a deal with the Spanish at New Orleans over import duties.

Imlay's documented involvement with Sebastian dates back to 26 October 1785, when Imlay sent a long letter to Sebastian, in which he asked him to act as his attorney: 'Expecting the complicated state of my business in this country will not only require the attention of a person acquainted in landed cases but will require much care and Judgment, I have to request that you will so far undertake it as to be my acting attorney in all cases'.[16] Sebastian represented Imlay during all of his major transactions. These included the founding of the 'Green River Company', the ill-fated joint venture Imlay entered upon in November 1785 with Isaac Hite and Amos Ogden; the after-sale management of his complex contract with Samuel Beall and John May; the transference of one-third interest in this contract to Wilkinson and Marshall; and, finally, the sale of nine tracts in Jefferson County to Silas Talbot.[17]

However, the most intriguing of all of Imlay's many partnerships during his Kentucky years was no doubt the one with General James Wilkinson. Indeed, their business activities in Kentucky were so entwined and the time of their arrival there so close that one commentator has speculated they may have travelled to Kentucky together.[18] It is quite possible that Imlay and Wilkinson had first met in Philadelphia not long after the British troops had evacuated the town in June 1778. Wilkinson, at any rate, had arrived there by the summer of 1778. Nor did it take long for him to renew his intimate friendship with Benedict Arnold, whose favourite aide he had been during the siege of Boston and at Montreal during the invasion of Canada in 1775. In November 1778 Wilkinson married Ann Biddle, a daughter of the prominent Philadelphia family. Ann was the younger sister of Clement Biddle, the prosperous merchant at whose home Wilkinson would spend much time with Aaron Burr in the course of 1804, while the two men developed the scheme to establish an independent empire in the south-west. From July 1779 to March 1781 Wilkinson served in the War Office in Philadelphia as clothier general of the Continental Army.

Wilkinson set off for Kentucky from Philadelphia some time in the autumn of 1783, crossing the Allegheny Mountains on horseback, and taking a Kentucky flat-boat down to the Falls of the Ohio.[19] He is known to have been in Lexington in February of the following year, but since ice and inclement weather made travel on the Ohio River quite hazardous during the winter months, it is likely that he came to Kentucky in late 1783, and spent some time elsewhere in the district. Given that the Ohio River trade was his first venture in the West, he may well have spent some time in Louisville, which, because of its position near the Falls, had become a major hub for trade up and down the Ohio.[20] John Filson's 1784 map of Kentucky puts Wilkinson's house on the south fork of the

Elkhorn River, a stone's throw from Colonel Thomas Marshall's surveyor's office in Fayette County.[21] Soon Wilkinson was on very friendly terms with surveyor Marshall and, indeed, with the local authorities and leading businessmen generally. For wherever he went, as Kentucky historian Humphrey Marshall observed, the general practised the 'arts of popularity ... with much assiduity, and success'.[22] As in the case of Imlay, it was particularly through his ingratiating personality and his social skills that Wilkinson quickly won people's trust. Marshall, who had settled in Kentucky in 1782 and who would become one of the general's most vociferous enemies, gives the following sketch of Wilkinson's character in his *History of Kentucky*:

> The presence, the manners, and conversation of this gentleman, were calculated to attract attention, excite curiosity, and produce interest ... He had been an officer in the regular army – was at the taking of Burgoyne – and lately, a member of the Pennsylvania legislature.
>
> Besides these circumstances, so well adapted to prepossess the feelings, and captivate the hearts, of the simple and rustic Kentuckians, – nature herself had gratuitously furnished Wilkinson, with a passport, which ensured his favourable reception, wherever he was seen and heard. A passport expressed in a language, which all mankind could read; whose influence everyone felt; and which none would suspect, scrutinize, on the first perusal ... A countenance, open, mild and facile; manners, bland, accommodating, and gracious; an address, easy, polite, and gracious; invited approach, gave access, ensured attention, cordiality, and ease. By these fair forms, he conciliated; by these, he captivated. The combined effect was greatly advantageous to the general, on a first acquaintance ...[23]

Given the similarities in their characters, it is not hard to see why Wilkinson and Imlay should gravitate towards each other on the western frontier, nor why Wilkinson would reappear in Imlay's novel *The Emigrants* as 'General James W—', the congenial society host and avuncular mentor of the hero and Imlay's alter ego, Captain James Arl—ton. Imlay's characterization of Wilkinson as someone who was as liberal with his wines as he was with his words – speaking often and at length about his sacred honour, his undying love for his country, and his vision of establishing an empire in the West that would overshadow that of ancient Rome – rings historically true and is confirmed by many contemporary accounts of him, most evocatively Humphrey Marshall's:

> Whatever truth there may be in the observation, that the way to ladies' hearts, is through the eyes; Wilkinson's experience had taught him, that the way to men's hearts, was *down their throats*. He lived freely, and entertained liberally. If he paid for his fare it was well for those who furnished it; if he did not, it was still well for himself and those who feasted on it. He surrounded himself with the idle young men, of both town and country, who loved him dearly; because they loved his beef, his pudding, and his wine. They served to propagate his opinions, blazon his fame, to promote

his popularity, and to serve him in elections; objects of primary consideration with him.[24]

Though far too busy to join the 'idle young men' who orbited the charismatic general, there is little doubt that Imlay spent considerable time in Wilkinson's company. Evidently a keen student of his lectures on the rise of the American empire in the West, Imlay would later put the general's teachings to good use in his *Topographical Description of the Western Territory of North America*, which was written at least in part to propagate Wilkinson's geopolitical ambitions for the western territory.

Before long, Wilkinson had become the nucleus of a group of like-minded men of independent spirit, many of them dissatisfied with Virginia's rule over the district and favouring early independence. A key common denominator among them was that many of them had served either in the militia or the Continental Army. It was the convergence upon Kentucky of large numbers of Revolutionary War veterans – some of them having come to claim land granted to them on military land warrants, many others, like Imlay, merely to speculate – that afforded Wilkinson the electoral platform from which he could launch his campaign for outright independence. While other men of his rank preferred a comfortable life in the East, by simply settling among them, Wilkinson won the respect and allegiance of many of Kentucky's military brethren.

Out on the trans-Alleghenian frontier, where everybody was from somewhere else and where hence very little social structure and cohesion existed, veterans would frequently use their Revolutionary War ranks, not merely as a badge of honour but as a mark of recognition and reliability, as well as of their creditworthiness. The higher the rank, the higher someone's trustworthiness and credit rating. Thus, it is not surprising that as he crossed the Allegheny Mountains, Imlay promoted himself from first lieutenant to captain – issuing himself a new passport to a new way of life. For if he ever was a 'Captain in the American Army during the War', as he claims on the title page of the *Topographical Description*, there is no evidence in the military records to confirm this. Although invariably signing his letters simply as 'G. Imlay', all of his acquaintances and business associates in Kentucky, and later in England and France, knew him as 'Captain Imlay', and that is how he is referred to in all contemporary correspondence, court records and other documents. As 'Captain Imlay', he won the confidence not only of other recent immigrants – often veterans, like himself – but especially of the 'old guard' – the generation of early settlers, speculators and 'Indian fighters' like Colonel Daniel Boone, Colonel John Floyd, Captain John Holder, Colonel Richard Henderson, Colonel William Christian, Colonel John Fleming, General Isaac Shelby and General Benjamin Logan – with most of whom Imlay did business. It was this fraternity of veterans that dominated the land business in Kentucky, and that would soon also dominate the local political agenda – at the top of which was separation from Virginia.

Wilkinson reported in his memoirs that the reason he had decided to emigrate to Kentucky was that, being but of modest means, it had become his 'duty to a young and beloved family, to endeavour, by all honourable means, to advance [his] fortune'.[25] But that was not the main reason why he urgently needed to 'advance his fortune'. Throughout his career in the Continental Army, Wilkinson had been suspected of having cheated his way to the top and of having been involved in a number of intrigues. One of these, the so-called 'Conway Cabal', was a conspiracy, devised in late 1777 and early 1778, aimed at ousting General Washington as commander-in-chief of the Continental Army and appointing Horatio Gates in his place. Although allegations had been made against him more than once, Wilkinson had always enjoyed a remarkable degree of confidence from his superiors, notably from Benedict Arnold and General Gates. Though not one of the principal conspirators, Wilkinson, supposedly drunk, blew the cover of the plot by revealing the content of an incriminating letter which General Thomas Conway had written to Gates. Because of his involvement in the Conway Cabal, Wilkinson was forced to resign his positions as brevet major general and secretary to the board of war, but he was allowed to serve as clothier general of the army. It was finally an incident of corruption in his capacity as clothier general that caused him to lose the support of his benefactors. Publicly denounced by General Washington, Wilkinson resigned from the army and headed for the western territory – hardly the reluctant choice of a caring pater familias, as Wilkinson suggests in his memoirs.

According to Humphrey Marshall, Wilkinson had come to the West at the head of 'a mercantile, or trading company' recently formed in Philadelphia.[26] In fact, when he arrived in Kentucky, Wilkinson was not only the accredited representative of the substantial firm of Barclay, Moylan & Co. of Philadelphia, but he had also set up his own trading company, in partnership with Major Isaac B. Dunn (who would later become one of the general's key associates in the Spanish Conspiracy).[27] It is evident from his correspondence with Dr Hugh Shiell, who lived at Crow's Station (near what is now Danville), that throughout 1784 and 1785 Wilkinson was involved in both the wholesale and retail trade in a wide range of articles, including cloths, tools, bacon, wine, or generally anything that came down the Ohio River to the Falls.[28] He also operated, in partnership with Walker Daniel, a salt works at Bullitt's Lick, and owned a grist mill in Lincoln County just south-east of Danville.[29] Yet it is equally evident that fairly soon after his arrival the trade in dry goods and salt was not Wilkinson's sole or even main business venture. By the spring of 1785 he was already deeply immersed in large-scale land acquisitions in Fayette County, where, with a number of different partners, Wilkinson was entering large tracts of land of sometimes over

40,000 acres each, which he would subsequently try to dispose of in the East with the help of agents there.[30]

One of Wilkinson's key associates in the East was Dr James Hutchinson of Philadelphia. On 20 June 1785 Wilkinson sent Hutchinson a deed and warrant for two surveys which he asked the latter to sell in Philadelphia on behalf of the owners. Promising Hutchinson 'the highest Commission that *ever* was given for doing Business', Wilkinson adds, 'if you could make more extensive sales, I could send you immediately several hundred thousand acres –'.[31] This turns out to have been more than idle talk, for by August 1786 he was writing to Hutchinson: 'I shall by next May have Patents for 100,000 Acres, which I shall be able to sell at 6d. per Acre'.[32] However, Wilkinson was by no means as solvent as the size of his land business suggests. Increasingly he had begun to rely on the Philadelphia trade in Kentucky lands to finance his ventures in the dry goods business. By the middle of 1786 he had piled up so much debt with various suppliers that he was on the verge of financial ruin. Writing to Hutchinson in August, he urged his partner immediately to sell the tracts he had patented in Hutchinson's name: 'I trust in God & in your exertions, that you will be able should the land not be sold, to fund upon it. The 32,000 Acre Tract is alienated to you & the patent will Issue in your name – it is clear of all dispute, & the Tract is realy valuable. The 20,000 & odd acres of J. H. Craigs which I put you in June, lies near the Big Bone & is really valuable.'[33] In the same letter Wilkinson informs Hutchinson that he has made him his legal attorney, granting him the authority to sell any of his land at the earliest possible opportunity.

Wilkinson's documented dealings with Imlay date back to the early autumn of 1784, but probably started considerably before that time. That the two men had established an intimate partnership of some sort prior to September 1784 can be inferred from a letter Wilkinson wrote to one Mathew Irvine on the 27th of that month:

> Dear Sir,
> Your affairs with Mr. Imlay remain in the same situation they did when I last wrote you – however I expect by my return that Mr. Imlay must have procured unequivocal Titles sufficient to take up his Bonds – if he has, the Business will be immediately closed, otherwise it will remain in its present situation – for were I to push or expose Imlay in his present critical situation, ruin would come upon him and you would lose your property, probably for ever – depend, Sir, on my fidelity and attention, and be assured I am Your obliged and obedient servant,
> James Wilkinson.[34]

It is not known what transactions the two had been involved in for Wilkinson to be in a position to decide on Imlay's financial fate, but that Imlay was in dire straits at the time becomes clear from existing letters and other documents relating to his ill-fated contract with Captain John Holder. In March 1783 Holder had promised to assign to Imlay by contract a total of 20,000 acres in Fayette and Jefferson counties.[35] If nothing else, this deal with Holder upsets the conventional myth of Imlay as the consummate conman who always got the better of anyone who crossed his path. For no sooner had they exchanged bonds (Imlay's by way of payment, and Holder's as penal bonds, which would become due in case of breach of contract), than it appeared that Holder had had no clear title to several of the tracts involved in the deal when he sold them to Imlay. Thus one tract, a settlement and preemption called Poplar Ridge, which was on the road from the Falls of the Ohio to Bullitt's Lick, Holder had sold to Imlay knowing that it was 'prior occupied'. In other cases, tracts turned out not to have been surveyed according to entry – which would effectively have made the claims invalid – or Holder could not or simply would not reveal where the entries were located. When in the autumn of 1783 Henry Green, deputy surveyor for Fayette County, was instructed by Imlay to call upon Holder to show him the entries so that they could be surveyed, Holder gave him such vague descriptions of the locations that Green and his two chain-men spent four weeks in vain searching for them.[36] On 15 July 1784 Imlay authorized William Triplet, deputy surveyor for Fayette County, to speak to Holder about the missing entries, but again to no avail.[37] As for the entries in Jefferson County, by November 1785 Holder had still failed to assign them to Imlay, by which time most of the claims would have been lost, even if they were ever located. Imlay had realized apparently too late that, as he writes to his attorney Alexander Skinner on 27 September 1784, 'there is no Law making valid or of any effect assignments made on Entries'.[38] It was the mistake of an absolute beginner. The letter to Skinner also reveals the true nature of Imlay's financial predicament: because he had not been able to capitalize on Holder's land, he was now not only unable to meet his bond to Holder but he was also unable to meet his financial obligations in other schemes, which he had underwritten with the expected sale of Holder's land. When he wrote to Irvine on the same day, Wilkinson was probably not exaggerating when he described Imlay's financial position in late September 1784 as 'critical'.[39]

Imlay and Wilkinson were steady business partners by the end of May 1785, when Imlay informed the surveyor Henry Lee that the general had 'undertaken' his business in Fayette County and thenceforward would be paying his surveying fees.[40] Wilkinson not only looked after Imlay's affairs during the latter's frequent perambulations, but he also relieved him from time to time of tracts that had got caught up in legal entanglements. As in the May/Beall deal, they appear to have operated in these transactions as conman and accomplice, the seller playing the role of the innocent victim of circumstances and the other that of the bona fide buyer. The most widely reported transaction that Imlay and Wilkinson were involved in during this time is the one involving Boone's 10,000 acres on Hingston's Fork in Fayette County. A popular legend like Daniel Boone being one of the nation's untouchables, the story is invariably cited to denounce the two men as unpatriotic scoundrels, yet their behaviour in the affair was by no means uncommon in the profiteering days of the frontier economy. Boone's tract was surveyed on 4 March 1785 by Thomas Marshall, surveyor, and Daniel Boone, deputy surveyor.[41] The contract between Imlay and Boone specified that Imlay was to pay his first instalment of £1,000 by 15 May of that year, and the second by 15 May 1786. Yet by December 1786 Imlay sent the following note to Boone from Richmond (see Figure 2):

> Dear Sir,
>
> I am exceedingly sorry it is not in my power to give you any assistance for such is the imbarrising state of affairs in this country, that I have not been able to recover a pound from all the engagements [assignments?] that have been made me. However I shall take every step in my power and will return in the spring. Judge Symmes has bought some Land of me and its probable as we have not fix'd upon the Tracts he may be induced to take the Land I purchased of you. I must therefore beg that you will shew him every attention in your power as his setteling among us will be a general benefit to the Country. I am sure I need add nothing more to make you more industrious in assisting him. I am with the greatest regard your most ob^d. servant
>
> Richmond   G. Imlay[42]
> 21st Decr. 1786

Since trying to stay one step ahead of his creditors was central to his operations, it is the kind of note Imlay must have written on many occasions. Having the classic stamp of a conman's suave discourse (a blend of self-exonerating excuse and seemingly constructive advice), it cleverly makes Boone himself ultimately responsible for recouping the money Imlay owed to him. While Imlay was not fibbing when he claimed that he had just entered into a contract with the prominent New Jersey jurist John Cleves Symmes, who had recently moved to the West, it was part of Imlay's familiar repertoire of tricks to suggest to his business partners that he was on intimate terms with public figures of more immaculate reputation than he himself could boast.[43] However, Imlay never told Boone the one piece of really bad news for him: he no longer actually owned Boone's tract, having sold it to Wilkinson well over a year before, on 26 September 1785 to be exact.[44] Treacherous as this is, what commentators have so far failed to note is that Imlay in all likelihood did in fact pay the first instalment of £1,000. For, although he had a knack for losing land and money to strangers, not even Boone would have assigned the land to Imlay when he did, on 18 August 1785, without having received at least part of the sales price.[45] What biographers of Boone tend to find most galling in the entire affair is that Wilkinson subsequently offered the land for sale, promoting it as having been 'located and surveyed by Col. Dan Boone'.[46] Indeed, adding insult to injury, Wilkinson even went so far as to sue Boone when he found out that Boone had lost part of the tract to older claims.[47]

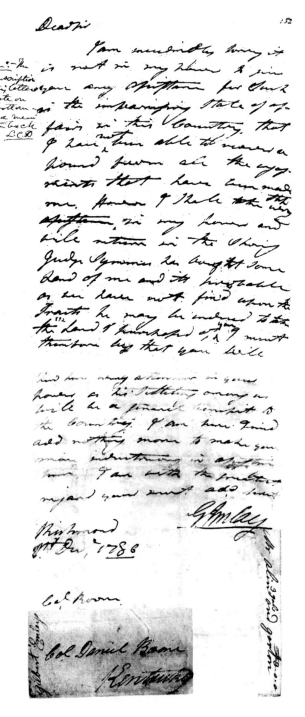

Figure 2. Letter from Gilbert Imlay to Daniel Boone, 21 December 1786. Courtesy of Wisconsin Historical Society, Madison, Wisconsin.

Imlay's Judas letter to Daniel Boone – his first and perhaps most illustrious victim – in a sense marks his farewell to the land-jobbing business. Thus, it was not a coincidence that shortly before, on 10 November 1786, exactly two weeks after Beall had annulled their contract, Imlay formally put all of his remaining business interests into the hands of a new attorney, Henry Lee. The fact is recorded in a Kentucky Court of Appeals Deed, the wording of which very much suggests that Imlay was not only planning to retire from business, but from the country as well:

> Gilbert Imley of Jefferson County, Virginia, nominates and appoints the Hon. Henry Lee, Jr., Esq., of Westmoreland County, Virginia, his true and lawful attorney in fact, to contract for, agree for, mortgage, or sell all his property, real and personal, and adjust all matters in regard to such estate or business, in the manner and form which the attorney may think proper, and upon sale to execute conveyances and receive considerations, and to appoint other attorneys under him if necessary for the same purposes. November 10, 1786.[48]

The 'Hon. Henry Lee, Jr., Esq.', Imlay's new attorney, was none other than the renowned Revolutionary war hero Colonel Henry 'Light-Horse Harry' Lee III, the father of the future general of the Confederate Army, Robert E. Lee. The eldest son of Henry Lee II, Henry Lee, Jr, grew up with a love for horses and horse riding, as well as an appreciation of art and literature. At fourteen he was sent to the College of New Jersey at Princeton, where one of his classmates was James Madison, while James Monroe and Aaron Burr were also in attendance at the time. He excelled academically, but was even as a college student known for his disputatious nature. Paul C. Nagel described Lee's disposition as 'arrogant, vain, imperious, ambitious to a fault, painfully sensitive'.[49] His planned legal education in England was interrupted by the threat of war between Britain and her colonies. Having obtained a commission in the Virginia Light Dragoons, Lee quickly made his mark with his knowledge of horses and his leadership talents, displaying his daring and ingenuity in several skirmishes with the enemy. His adroit horsemanship soon earned him the sobriquet 'Light-Horse Harry'. His reputation was such that in January 1778 the British sent out a company of more than 200 men to arrest him at Spread Eagle Tavern near Valley Forge, where he had been supplying Washington's troops with materials captured from the British. With only seven of his men Lee somehow managed to get away, killing five enemies. It was this feat that first brought Lee to Washington's attention, who promptly offered him a position on his staff. But Lee turned down this attractive assignment, saying he was 'wedded to [his] sword'.[50] Thereupon Washington made him commander of an independent corps of light dragoons with the rank of major. His most spectacular success in the war was the bold attack in August 1779 on the British fortification at Paulus Hoeck (Hook), New Jersey, across the Hudson River from the main British force in New York City. With an augmented force of 400 and acting under Washington's direct authority, Lee valiantly led his troops into the fortification, killing 50 and taking 159 prisoners. In a letter to Congress, Washington afterwards wrote that 'The Major displayed a remarkable degree of prudence, address and bravery upon this occasion, which does the highest honor to himself and to all the officers and men under his command. The situation of the fort rendered the attempt critical and the success brilliant.'[51] Lee was awarded a Congressional gold medal for bravery – the only one to be given to an officer of his rank.

Whether Imlay was still in New Jersey when the battle of Paulus Hook took place or in Philadelphia, Henry Lee's heroic victory can hardly have escaped him. If he was back in Monmouth County, Imlay is almost certain to have been aware of Henry Lee's presence in the area in the summer of 1780, when upon Washington's direct instructions Lee was collecting horses and cattle from British-occupied Monmouth County.[52] Given their different walks of life at this time, it is unlikely that he ever met Lee whilst he was still in New Jersey, but fate – helped along by the similarities in their personalities, their shared military background, and their craving for adventure and large fortunes – would quickly bring the two men together. In March 1780 Lee – now a lieutenant-colonel – was sent south under Nathanael Greene. As commander of what was known as 'Lee's Partisan Corps' or 'Lee's Legion', Lee was involved in skirmishes with Cornwallis's retreating army in the Carolinas. Then, in 1782, just after the British surrender at Yorktown, Lee for no clear reason suddenly resigned his commission. In April of that year he married his second cousin, the nineteen-year-old Matilda Lee. The 'divine Matilda', as she was known, was the daughter of Philip Ludwell Lee, and heiress to the family estate in Westmoreland County, Stratford Hall Plantation, a brick Georgian great house built between 1730 and 1738 by Thomas Lee, founder of the Ohio Company and quondam acting governor of Virginia.

It was from the comfort of Stratford Hall that Lee set out to expand his family fortune. Following the example of his revered general, Washington, he thought that fortune might be most readily won by speculating in western lands. From 1783 onwards Lee was investing heavily in several speculative schemes, some devised by others, some by himself. The plan that he was convinced would make his fortune was the building of a city near the Great Falls of the Potomac River, which he named 'Matildaville' after his beloved wife. A brilliant military strategist, Lee turned out to be a rather less talented businessman. The 'Matildaville' project soon became a financial disaster, in part because he failed to get clear title to the very land he was building his city on. Lee dealt with set-backs in business the way he had dealt with them in battle: always choosing to press ahead and trying fight his way out of a problem. However, his financial position eventually became so desperate that he was forced to resort to measures which were certainly immoral, if not simply illegal. Thus, like Imlay, Lee began to offer land for security which he no longer owned. At the nadir of his financial decline, he was reduced to appropriating the money for his daughter's dowry, and once even gave George Washington a bad cheque.

Imlay's dealings with Light-Horse Harry Lee have so far gone virtually unnoticed by historians and biographers. This is odd since Imlay knew Lee at least as early as 1783, when Imlay first came to Kentucky to speculate in land there. In fact, it seems quite likely that when Isaac Hite wrote to his father in April 1783 that Emlay/Imlay was acting as the 'Agent for a company' that was seeking to buy upwards of 76,000 acres of land he owned in a partnership with John and George May and John Floyd, it was Light-Horse Harry who was the silent investor on whose behalf Imlay was trying to acquire such vast quantities of land in Kentucky.[53] One of the reasons why many commentators on Imlay's land-jobbing days in Kentucky have missed or misconstrued the connection between Imlay and Harry Lee proceeds from a misreading of a letter that Imlay wrote on 28 May 1785 to Henry Lee, the surveyor and founder of Lee's Station in Mason County. In fact, this letter makes clear that Imlay was not dealing with just one but *two* Henry Lees. Having informed 'Lee' in his letter that General Wilkinson had 'undertaken' his business in Fayette County, Imlay goes on to write: 'I have got M[r] Lees survey of 4000 acres received with some difficulty. The fees was £2-15-7½.'[54] Evidently, Imlay was acting on behalf of a 'Mr. Lee' who was *not* the Lee that was doing his surveying for him in Fayette County – and who, apparently, was not even in Kentucky at the time Imlay wrote his letter. Since Light-Horse Harry is not known ever to have crossed the mountains into the Kentucky District, this would make it even more likely that it was his survey for 4,000 acres that Imlay was referring to. Indeed, it is quite possible that the warrant authorizing the 4,000-acre survey was the military warrant that had been granted to Lee on 31 October 1783 for having served seven years as lieutenant colonel in the Virginia line.[55]

It also appears that the 'Col Lee' mentioned in passing by John May in his letter to Beall in the spring of 1786 as one of those Imlay had 'admitted' into his contract, was in fact Light-Horse Harry. This is corroborated by Samuel Beall's 13 June 1786 letter to Imlay's attorney Dr Alexander Skinner, in which Beall informed Skinner that he had notified Imlay and 'the Hon[l] Henry Lee Esq' that he had become John May's representative.[56] This confirms that one of the transactions that Harry Lee and Imlay were involved in as business partners was in fact the contract for around 94,000 acres that Imlay had signed with John May in February 1785.[57] Apparently, Imlay had at some point sold Lee's part of the contract with May to John Cleves Symmes, a former associate justice of the Supreme Court in New Jersey. This is most likely to have taken place in February 1786, when Imlay was in New Jersey during his sales trip to the north-east. However, following Beall's annulment of the contract with Imlay in October 1786, Symmes had never received any of the land he had bought (and presumably paid for). Having contacted Lee for information concerning Imlay, Lee wrote to Symmes in April 1787, professing that his only involvement in Symmes's 'contract with Mr. Imlay was the burthening [himself] with the security to his bond'.[58] Lee went on to claim that he had done so out of 'friendship' to Imlay and, having full 'confidence in [Imlay's] punctuality & truth', asserted that Symmes's account of Imlay's behaviour was to him 'as distressing as unexpected'. It is not hard to see why Lee and Imlay should have become such good friends.

There is some evidence to suggest that Imlay and Lee were involved in additional deals with John May outside of the February 1785 contract. One of these transactions with May was not finalized until December 1787, which is confirmed by a copy of an indenture found among John May's papers:

> Recd. This 19th day of December 1787 from John May his bonds for the conveyance of twenty Thousand Acres of land in the district of Kentucky in full of all demands of Imlay, Skinner & Lee against the said J. May under the several Contracts entered into between them for Western Lands & expences attending them.

Witness	Henry Lee [seal]
James Wilkinson[59]	Attorney for G. Imlay
	Henry Lee [seal]
	Alexander Skinner

> All Contracts between the parties are hereby annulled & to be respectively delivered up.

Teste	Henry Lee
	attorney for G. Imlay
James Wilkinson	Henry Lee
David Stewart	Alex. Skinner
	John May[60]

Imlay had left the United States by December 1787, yet in absentia he would remain implicated in Henry Lee's entangled business arrangements for years to come. Indeed, one of Lee's and Imlay's botched joint ventures would still be going through the courts two decades after the original purchase was made. This is revealed in a long string of legal documents that survive in the archives of the various Kentucky courts regarding a suit from Matthew Walton against Imlay and Lee.

On 8 May 1797 Matthew Walton appeared before the Justice of the Peace for Washington County to lodge a complaint of fraud against Imlay and Lee. In the bill of complaint that was registered at the District Court for the Bardstown District on 11 May, Walton accuses Imlay and Lee of having broken a contract they had entered into on 3 August 1783 for the sale of a number of 'entries, plats and certificates' concerning a considerable (though unspecified) quantity of land in Jefferson County.[61] According to the document, Walton had sold the tracts to Imlay and Lee at a rate of £12.10.0 'for all first rate land' and £10 'for all other lands' (these would have been the rates per hundred acres). It further states that Walton had assigned all the entries, plats and certificates to Imlay and Lee in exchange for Imlay's bill for the total purchase money. The Jefferson County Entries Books reveal that several of the tracts involved in this transaction had been entered in Walton's name on 23 December 1782 and 28 March 1783, while the Virginia Land Office Grants Book identifies Gilbert Imlay and Henry Lee as joint assignees of Matthew Walton for one of these tracts – 1,200 acres on the south side of Little Clifty waters of Rough Creek, which had been entered on 23 December 1782 and surveyed on 1 February 1783 (treasury warrant 11,708).[62]

Walton had several reasons to be dissatisfied with the behaviour of his partners. Whereas Imlay had apparently made a small down payment upon signing the contract, by the time the remainder of his bill was to be redeemed, Walton had discovered that 'Imlay [had] left the united states some time about the year 1788 without having discharged [his] bond for the payment of the land'.[63] Upon learning about Imlay's alleged departure from the country, Walton turned to Imlay's partner and attorney, Henry Lee, and demanded that he honour the terms of the original agreement. On 15 February 1794 by way of payment Walton received Lee's bond on John May for 20,000 acres, and Lee also agreed to return half of the entries, plats and certificates. However, it soon became clear that when Lee gave Walton his bond on John May, that bond had already been discharged. Walton hereupon demanded that the contract be immediately annulled, which Lee 'utterly refused to do'. To his dismay, Walton subsequently learned that on 12 August 1796 Lee had sold his share of the entries, plats and certificates to Henry Banks. He would have been even more upset had he known that, over a year before, Lee had already sold Imlay's interest in the contract with Walton to the same Henry Banks. According to a deed drawn up on 5 May 1795, Henry Lee 'of the Commonwealth of Virginia as Attorney in fact for Gilbert Imley late of America' sold to Henry Banks of Virginia, for 5s., 'all the Lands lying and being in the state of Kentucky which was or is the Property of the said Gilbert Imley, or which the said Lee might be Intitled to as his Attorney in fact ... the Quantity and discription of which cannot at this time be ascertained, whether it be by Deed, Patent, Mortgage, Survey, Location, Contract, or otherwise'.[64] Ten days later, on 15 May 1795, Lee had also sold to Banks all the rights, titles and claims to land in Kentucky once held by the deceased Dr Alexander Skinner – Imlay's former attorney – whose heir and representative Lee was.[65]

But the deal did not bring Banks much satisfaction: as Imlay and Lee had never paid Walton for his land, Banks now found himself named the third defendant in Walton's case against Imlay and Lee. In consequence of Walton's 'Bill in Chancery', from July 1797 onwards the Supreme Court for Bardstown ordered the sheriff of Fayette County month after month to summon Imlay, Lee and Banks to appear in court at the next session, or risk a fine of £100 each.[66] On 2 December 1797 Banks finally responded to Walton's bill of complaint, when he issued a sworn statement in the presence of a justice of the peace in Philadelphia, which was acknowledged during a session of the Bardstown District Court on 11 May 1798.[67] Confirming that back in August 1796 he had paid 'General' Lee a 'large sum of Money' in excess of $20,000 for the 'sweeping purchase' of all the Kentucky lands once entered, claimed or owned by Lee, Imlay and Skinner jointly and individually, Banks denied any wrongdoing or malicious intent.[68] In a 'supplemental answer' to Walton's bill, dated 22 July 1799, Banks reiterated he had acted in good faith in his transaction with Lee, but now also demanded that the patents to the land he had bought immediately be issued in his name, and that Walton pay him damages for having been 'so long and so unjustly deprived of the use and enjoyment of his Property'.[69] However, the case continued to drag on in the Bardstown District Court until finally, on 21 July 1802, the Supreme Court, with the consent of both Walton's and Bank's attorneys, 'ordered that this suit be removed to the General Court' – the state's principal common law court.[70]

The ill-fated Walton deal was only a minor setback for Henry Lee in a land-jobbing career that was marked by boundless optimism and reckless investments, and that would end in his bankruptcy and incarceration for debt in 1809.[71] The main difference between Lee and Imlay was that Imlay knew when to quit, or perhaps, rather, that – being a Revolutionary War hero, the owner of 3,000 acre estate in Virginia and having many friends in high places – 'Swindling Harry Lee', as he was dubbed at the time,[72] could afford to go on speculating far beyond the point where an insolvent gambler like Imlay would simply have to cut his losses and move on to other places and other trades.

Light-Horse Harry Lee was by no means the only one of Imlay's well-connected friends and acquaintances to end up considerably out of pocket after their business partner had absconded. Harry Innes, Kentucky Supreme Court judge and – from 1784 onwards – attorney general, represented several of Imlay's plucked associates. Since his duties at court did not fill his days, Innes regularly offered his services in registering and investigating land claims, collecting debts, overseeing property and in litigation over land surveys. In several instances clients, some of them attorneys, gave him relevant correspondence and documents relating to their cases. The dossier Gilbert Imlay originally prepared for James Marshall in his dispute with John Holder over the 20,000 acres in Fayette County is one of the case files that thus ended up among Harry Innes's papers.[73] Evidently, Imlay's file had fallen into the hands of someone who had bought Imlay's claims on Holder, and had asked Innes to locate the tracts and obtain legal title to them.

Another prominent jurist who kept a file on Gilbert Imlay after he had bought land from him that never materialized was John Cleves Symmes, a former associate justice of the New Jersey Supreme Court (1777–3) and a member of the Continental Congress. It is possible that Imlay had known Symmes from his days in the New Jersey militia. Between 1776 and 1779, Symmes was commander of three regiments of the New Jersey militia and was in charge of the forts on the New Jersey frontier. He also fought at several battles, including the battle of Monmouth. Cherishing a dream of establishing a colony in the West, Symmes had gone down the Ohio River in the spring and summer of 1787 on a tour of inspection. Apparently he had also hoped to see Imlay in Kentucky, no doubt in connection with their contract from February 1786. Disappointed at not having found Imlay anywhere, he had sent requests for information concerning Imlay to a string of people, including Henry Lee, Colonel Brearly, the chief justice of New Jersey and Richard Clough Anderson, surveyor general for Virginia military lands in the western territory. Forwarding Lee's response to him, Symmes wrote to Anderson in June 1787: 'I beg you will preserve Col. Lees letter, as I shall like to be posesst of every document that has ever had existence on the subject of Imlay['s] contract with me in case I should ever be obliged to resort to the law for my demands –'.[74] Needless to say, Judge Symmes would never recover Imlay's tracts. However, this setback paled in comparison to the future fate of his western colony. Having found the ideal site north of the Ohio, between the Miami and Little Miami rivers, Symmes petitioned Congress in 1788 for a grant of two million acres of land, later to be reduced to one million acres. Due to inaccurate surveys, mismanagement and endless litigation over land claims, the 'Miami Purchase', as it was known, would end in a general debacle and personal bankruptcy for Judge Symmes.

Of all of Imlay's victims, none was more respectable than Arthur Lee. Brother of the Declaration of Independence signatory Richard Henry Lee, Arthur Lee was born in Virginia. He was educated at Eton and received a degree in medicine from the University of Edinburgh. He read law at the Temple in London and was admitted to the English bar. He also studied botany and was a fellow of the Royal Society. Having served as the London agent for Massachusetts in the early 1770s, Lee became a prolific pamphleteer for the patriots during the Revolutionary War. In 1776 Congress appointed him, along with Franklin and Silas Deane, commissioner to negotiate a treaty of alliance, amity and commerce with France, and also to negotiate with other European governments. Although he had had little involvement with the negotiations, in 1778 Lee signed, with Franklin and Deane, the treaty between the United States and France. After further unsuccessful diplomatic missions to Spain and Prussia, Lee was recalled to the United States in 1779. He was a member of the Virginia House of Delegates in 1781 and a delegate to the Continental Congress in 1782–5. From 1784 to 1789 he served on the Board of Treasury.

In September 1786 Arthur Lee had bought Imlay's tract of 4,023 acres in Jefferson County, on the north side of Beech Fork, opposite the mouth of Pleasant Run.[75] In May 1787, Henry Lee, acting as his attorney, sold four more of Imlay's tracts to Arthur Lee, all situated in Fayette County: three tracts, totalling 2,400 acres, on the longest fork of Huston's Fork, just north-east of Lexington, and one tract of 1,000 acres on Main Licking near the Upper Blue Licks salt spring.[76] Arthur Lee must have known – or thought he knew – what he was doing: not only were the tracts 'excellent Land & said to be most valuable in 1787',[77] but all five tracts had been patented to Imlay in July and November 1786, so Lee was actually acquiring legal title to the land. However, in the end Arthur Lee was to derive little pleasure from his purchase – nor, indeed, did Lee's brother and heir, Francis Lightfoot Lee, who became the new owner of Imlay's former tracts upon Arthur Lee's death in 1792. The first problem Francis Lee encountered in establishing his title to Imlay's tracts was that the original deed whereby Imlay had given power of attorney to Henry Lee on 10 November 1786 had gone missing.[78] This seriously compromised the legality of Henry Lee's conveyance of the four tracts in Fayette County to Arthur Lee. The problem was fixed when in 1810 Henry Lee executed a new deed in which he reconveyed Imlay's tracts to Francis Lee.[79] But this by no means spelled the end of Lee's worries.

Looking into the status of his surveys in 1812, Lee discovered that all four tracts were occupied by a large number of squatters and settlers, several of whom had competing claims on Lee's tracts under various settlement and preemption rights, as well as a multitude of military and treasury warrants. The situation of the three tracts on the longest fork of Huston's Fork was particularly complex. Overlapping land claims as a result of survey errors or disputed claims – a phenomenon known as 'shingling' – were commonplace in the buoyant Kentucky land market. The plat that Lee made at the time illustrates exactly how precarious claims of ownership for a piece of land in Kentucky often were (see Figure 3). In order to regulate the sale of vacant lands and to curb large-scale speculation, the Virginia Assembly in 1779 introduced a land act under which 'actual settlers' were offered the right to purchase 400 acres at a price below that available to non-residents (most of the latter being speculators). Those who had made improvements to the land, which entailed the building of a regulation-size cabin, were entitled to 'preempt' an additional 1,000-acre track adjoining to their 'settlement' at a slightly higher rate than the settlement rights. Lee's plat reveals that Imlay's 1,000-acre tract (treasury warrant 4342; marked 'E' in Figure 3) had been surveyed so that it actually overlapped with both his settlement of 400 acres (marked 'A') and his preemption of 1,000 acres (marked 'B') – along with no less than nine other tracts!

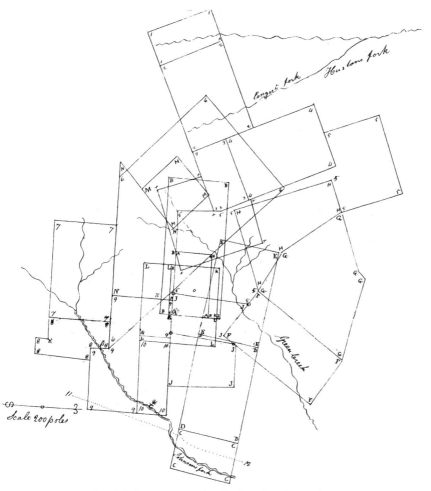

Figure 3. Shingled Plots near Huston's Fork of South Fork on Licking River, Kentucky. Courtesy of the Department of Rare Books and Special Collections, Princeton University Library, Princeton, New Jersey.

Overlapping land claims created endless and expensive litigation, with law suits often being dragged through the courts well into the nineteenth century – inevitably in many cases ending in the loss of some or all of a claimant's land grants. Advertisements of large tracts of Kentucky land for sale appearing in local newspapers in the 1820s and 1830s again and again illustrated the uncertainty and insecurity of titles. For instance, in a long advertisement in the Frankfort *Commentator* of 14 November 1821 Henry Banks listed twenty-one tracts, containing some 123,000 acres, which he had acquired from Gilbert Imlay and others and which he now sought to sell, openly conceding that some tracts had defective surveys, were involved in pending suits, or were claimed or occupied by others.[80] After inflation and Indian hostility, shingling was the single most important cause of the collapse of the Kentucky land bubble in the second half of the 1780s. But, while shingling had dire effects on all those seeking clear title to the land they thought they had acquired (settlers as well as speculators who were in it for the long haul, like Arthur Lee), nimble-footed operators like Imlay were hardly affected by the phenomenon – nor, indeed, by the currency crisis: the secret of their trade was to dispose as quickly as possible of land they had not paid for in the first place. However, it was a trade that could not be carried on forever. With his reputation in tatters, both among the powerful investors in the East and the speculating fraternity in the West, not even Imlay's friends in high places could keep him in business. Inexorably, Imlay was being drawn into a more desperate, and much darker, trade.

Postscript

It is possibly a mark of Imlay's relatively prominent status among the motley crowd of early Kentucky pioneers and settlers that his presence in the western territory was immortalized by John Filson on his famous 1784 map of the Kentucky District. Born in Chester County, PA, John Filson had drifted across the mountains in search of fortune in the promised land of Kentucky some time during the summer or early autumn of 1783 – not long after Imlay had arrived there. When he left the district over a year later, he had taught in a school at Lexington, worked as a surveyor, had claimed three large tracts of land for himself, and had written the first history of Kentucky.[81] Published in Wilmington, Delaware, in October 1784, *The Discovery, Settlement and Present State of Kentucky* included the first ever biography of pioneering legend Daniel Boone, as well as the 'Map of Kentucky'. Although he seems to have done considerable surveying along the Ohio River and in central Kentucky, the map was for the greater part not drawn from actual surveys. Instead, Filson relied mainly on accounts by some of Kentucky's most seasoned pioneer settlers, notably Daniel Boone, Levi Todd and James Harrod. Identifying the homes of many of his friends and acquaintances ('Col. Boone's', 'Col. Todd's', 'Gen. Wilkinson', 'Floyd's', 'Hites' and 'Col. Shelby's') and depicting a network of roads, mills, towns and villages, Filson's map reads very much like a picture postcard of an intimate, cosy community. Conveying an atmosphere of civilization and progress, Filson's map is in fact an idealized rendition of the region's rapid settlement and development, produced with the aim of encouraging settlement in the district.[82]

One of the homes depicted on the map is 'Emley's', situated at the fork of Mill Creek, which empties into the Kentucky River, about twenty miles from the Ohio River. Even though the map identifies 'Emley's' as a 'station' (usually denoting a cluster of cabin homes), this denomination was often used rather loosely – and may in any case have been an engraver's error. At any rate, it can hardly be a coincidence that a 'Captain Imlay' had a cabin built in precisely the same spot marked on Filson's map as 'Emley's' – just west of Drennon's Lick on the west fork of Mill Creek. The evidence for this is contained in an indenture dated 19 November 1796, by which Jesse Taylor and his wife, Elizabeth, of Alexandria (Fairfax County, Virginia) sold a number of tracts in Kentucky containing 20,000 acres to Augustine Jacqueline Smith and James Watson of the same town and county. According to the deed, the boundary of one of the tracts crossed 'several branches of Mill Creek [and] crossed the West fork of the said Creek on which Captain Imlay's Cabbin is built'.[83] If, as it would appear, Filson's 'Emley's' station was in fact Imlay's 'Cabbin', this would suggest that John Filson knew Gilbert Imlay, or at least knew of him. However, it should not be inferred from this that Imlay actually ever resided on his property on Mill Creek. Since anyone who, prior to March 1780, had built a cabin or had otherwise made any 'improvement' to a plot of land was entitled to a preemption right of 1,000 acres adjoining his settlement right, hundreds of cabins were erected in Kentucky on behalf of absentee landowners who never planned to occupy their frontier dwellings. Ironically, the image of Gilbert Imlay as the owner of a frontier cabin set on the banks of a babbling brook in the pristine Kentucky wilderness would soon become one of his most attractive assets.

4 SLAVE TRADER

The interests of nations are bartered by speculating merchants. My God! with what sang froid artful trains of corruption bring lucrative commissions into particular hands ... These men, like the owners of negro ships, never smell on their money the blood by which it has been gained, but sleep quietly in their beds, terming such occupations lawful callings ...

Mary Wollstonecraft to Gilbert Imlay, 22 September 1794[1]

In September 1786 Imlay appeared before Edward Shippen and Plunkett Fleeson, justices of the Court of Common Pleas in Philadelphia, in order to acknowledge and confirm the written indentures by which he had earlier agreed to sell nine tracts of land in Jefferson County, amounting to 15,043 acres, to the former Continental Navy privateer Colonel Silas Talbot, then of Philadelphia, for £750 Pennsylvania paper money and 12,771 Spanish silver milled dollars.[2] The Talbot transaction had been unusual for Imlay for at least two reasons: the bulk of the land involved in the deal exchanged hands for hard silver instead of the usual promissory notes, and Imlay actually held legal title to all of the lands for which he received the silver dollars. In fact, he had specifically travelled to Richmond in December 1785 to be able to collect the patents for the nine tracts in person.[3] Imlay must have had a very good reason for disposing of the bulk of his patents – the only real assets he ever got out of his land-jobbing activities – in a single transaction. Evidently, the opportunity had arisen to invest his nest-egg in a venture that was more lucrative and less risky than the land-jobbing business had been. That venture turns out to have been the triangular trade, and the man who introduced him to it was none other than the Revolutionary War hero Silas Talbot.

Congress having retired him from the Continental Navy as a lieutenant colonel without pay on 1 January 1782, Silas Talbot was eager get back into the world of business as soon as the Revolutionary War ended. His wartime privateering had brought handsome returns, which he had invested wisely in land, real estate and wharves in Providence. In late 1783, as trade with Virginia and the Carolinas was picking up again, Talbot bought the sloop *Peggy*, and began shipping agricultural produce from Rhode Island to the southern states, bringing back rice and especially tobacco.[4] The growth of the tobacco trade caused a sharp increase in the demand for land in the south, and hence in the demand for slave labour.[5] This surge in the trade in slaves was reflected in the shipping news columns and sales notices that appeared in the local newspapers in Charleston, which was a major hub in the triangular trade. Thus, in its issue of 14 September 1785 the *Charleston Evening Gazette* reported that between 17 March and 3 September of that year a total of 2,445 slaves had arrived in Charleston from Africa, the West Indies and other parts of the Americas. Like so many other investors from Providence and elsewhere in the north-east, Talbot could not resist the temptation of a windfall profit in the Guinea trade. The *Peggy* had already occasionally carried slaves to Charleston, and in August 1785 Talbot negotiated with Cyprian Sterry, Providence's largest African trader, for the purchase of a half interest in a slaver, the ninety-ton brigantine *Industry*, 'together with one half of her ... Tackle, Apparel &c. as she last came from Sea', for the sum of £450.[6]

Talbot and Imlay probably first met in the early spring of 1786, when Imlay was in the north-east trying to dispose some of the land he had acquired under the contract he had signed with John May and Samuel Beall in February 1785. Seemingly as eager to get into the Kentucky land bubble as Imlay was to get out of it, Talbot sold Imlay on or around 7 March a one-quarter interest in the *Industry* and her cargo to be paid for in 'land oppor[tunities]' – most likely a reference to the nine tracts of land that Imlay would transfer to Talbot in September.[7] No separate monetary transaction is recorded for Imlay's purchase of the first one-quarter interest in the *Industry*, which suggests either that Imlay paid for it using some of the cash he received from Talbot for the nine tracts or that the sale price for the brigantine was deducted from the sale price for Imlay's land. Because the value of the land clearly exceeded that of the ship, Talbot would still have owed Imlay a substantial amount of money.[8] On 9 March Talbot sold Imlay his remaining one-quarter share in the *Industry*, though this time without an interest in the cargo, accepting Imlay's promissory note for four prime slaves and £21.4.0 in cash by way of payment.[9]

Colonial America, just as much as the early republic, was constantly faced with a shortage of specie and paper money, and Imlay would have been quite familiar with the practice of using of slaves in lieu of cash money. Especially in the land trade out on the western frontier, slaves were the preferred 'currency' because of their relative 'liquidity', as opposed to Virginia and the Carolinas, where merchants would often use cumbersome commodities such as cured and baled tobacco leaves as tender. Having grown up in New Jersey, Imlay would have been equally familiar with both slave-owning and slave-trading. In fact, New Jersey had a higher slave population than any colony north of Maryland, with the exception of New York. Introduced in New Netherlands by the Dutch traders in the early 1600s, slavery initially increased only moderately in New Jersey after the British took control of the Dutch colony in 1644. However, slavery was encouraged in New Jersey under the proprietors' 1664 'Concessions and agreement', which offered sixty acres of land for every imported African slave (later reduced to thirty).[10] After the two Jerseys were united in 1702, the colony of New Jersey allowed the duty-free importation of African slaves, thus becoming the transit port for slave labour to other colonies. It has been estimated that by 1715, of a population of 21,000, 1,500 were blacks, most of whom were slaves.[11] The census of 1726 records 2,580 blacks, principally slaves, in a population of 32,442. By 1775, that number had risen to 10,000, comprising around 8 per cent of the total population of the state. The largest numbers of slaves were to be found in Bergen and Monmouth counties. Employed as farmhands or as domestic servants, slaves will have been a familiar sight to Gilbert Imlay as he grew up on his father's plantation. Thus, the archives of the Monmouth County Court record that, in 1758, Gilbert's father, Peter Imlay, sued one David Ketcham for damages because the latter had failed to pay in full the sale price of £65 Proclamation money for a slave called 'Peter', whom he had bought from the elder Imlay in 1750.[12] It is also known that Gilbert Imlay's second cousin, John Imlay, the wealthy and much-respected merchant of Allentown, owned slaves. As late as 1787 John Imlay purchased a slave named 'Caesar' for the sum of £90 from David Forman – the notorious patriot and commanding officer of the regiment Gilbert Imlay had served in during the Revolutionary War.[13] At a time when owning slaves and investing one's savings in the trade in human cargo was still distressingly ordinary, Imlay's venture into the triangular trade was by no means unusual.

When Imlay bought his 50 per cent stake in the slaver, the *Industry* had already been on the Gold Coast for several weeks. The brig had sailed from Providence on 15 October 1785 under captain Benjamin Hicks with a crew of 16.[14] By early January the *Industry* had arrived at the Dutch fort of Kormantine.[15] In a letter to Talbot dated 19 January 1786, Hicks reported that he had so far bought 30 slaves 'of the Blacks' for 30 gallons of rum a head and had sold 50 hogsheads of rum to the Dutch at the fort to be paid for in slaves, men at 150 gallons and women at 130 gallons. Ultimately he hoped to get a cargo of at least 150 ('if the Slaves don't rise') and expected to be able to sail by 1 May, provided he could get enough water. Hicks also observed that the vessel's upper deck was in bad order and was leaking considerably.[16] A month later the *Industry* was still anchored at Kormantine, by which time Hicks had bought 96 slaves and had sold the remainder of the rum to 'the Chief of the Castle'.[17] The *Industry* finally arrived in Charleston on 1 August 1786.[18] The next day the following advertisement appeared in the *Charleston Morning Post* and, with slight variation, in the 3 August *Columbian Herald*: 'Gold Coast NEGROES. Just arrived in the

Brigantine Industry, Benjamin Hicks, Master, from Africa, and to be sold on Tuesday next, August the 8th, A Cargo of prime, young NEGROES. The terms will be made known on the day of sale. Nathaniel Russell.' Similar announcements appeared in every daily issue of the *Columbian Herald* and the *Charleston Morning Post* until 8 August, the day of the sale.

Evidently, conditions for the slaves aboard the brig had been more severe than usual, and there had been massive loss of life.[19] This is confirmed by a letter from the Charleston firm of solicitors Murray, Mumford & Bower, which wrote to Talbot in early September to warn him that the *Industry*'s voyage was likely to be unprofitable: 'She bought we hear about One hundred & eighty Slaves off the Coast of Guinea, near half of which died before the brig arrived in Charleston where she now is'.[20] In fact, the sales bill drawn up on 9 September by Sterry's factor in Charleston, Nathaniel Russell, listed only sixty-seven slaves sold: thirty-four men, twenty-one women and twelve children (Figure 4).[21] It also listed expenses that suggest the slaves had been struck down by some deadly infectious disease: a doctor to attend sick slaves, nursing for them on shore, blankets and medicine.[22] Aside from the human cost, this circumstance meant that, at an average price of £42 per slave, the owners of the *Industry*'s cargo – Sterry, Imlay and Talbot – had sustained a joint loss of nearly £5,000 in potential profits on the voyage.[23] But the high mortality rate among the slaves would not be the only set-back for Imlay, nor indeed for Talbot.

Talbot would have done better to keep a personal eye on his interest in the *Industry*'s voyage; instead, almost immediately after he had sold his share of the ship to Imlay, he had departed for Kentucky.[24] A June 1786 letter from Sterry to Talbot reveals not only that the sale of the *Industry* had been negotiated hastily but also that Talbot had a very good reason for wanting to spend some time in 'the Western World'.[25] Like Imlay, Talbot was facing acute financial problems: 'Your friends here are all well', reported Sterry from Providence, '& your persicuters have been very quiet since you have been gone'. With Talbot's creditors apparently keen to strip him of his remaining assets, Sterry urged Talbot that if Imlay should wish to visit Providence, he should 'charge him to keep the matter of his purchase a secret as it may induce some of your enemies to trouble me'. While Talbot was in Kentucky in April and May gathering information about the logistics of the Mississippi River trade from New Orleans to the mouth of the Ohio (and possibly inspecting the tracts of land he had bought from Imlay), Cyprian Sterry was overseeing his business interests regarding the *Industry*. Not long after Captain Hicks had set course for America, Sterry discussed with Imlay where to sell their cargo. In May Sterry had instructed Hicks to sell the entire cargo in the West Indies and to return to Providence with a ballast of molasses.[26] But in June Sterry and Imlay agreed that it was no longer profitable to sell slaves in the Carolinas and Georgia, where inflation was on the rise after the

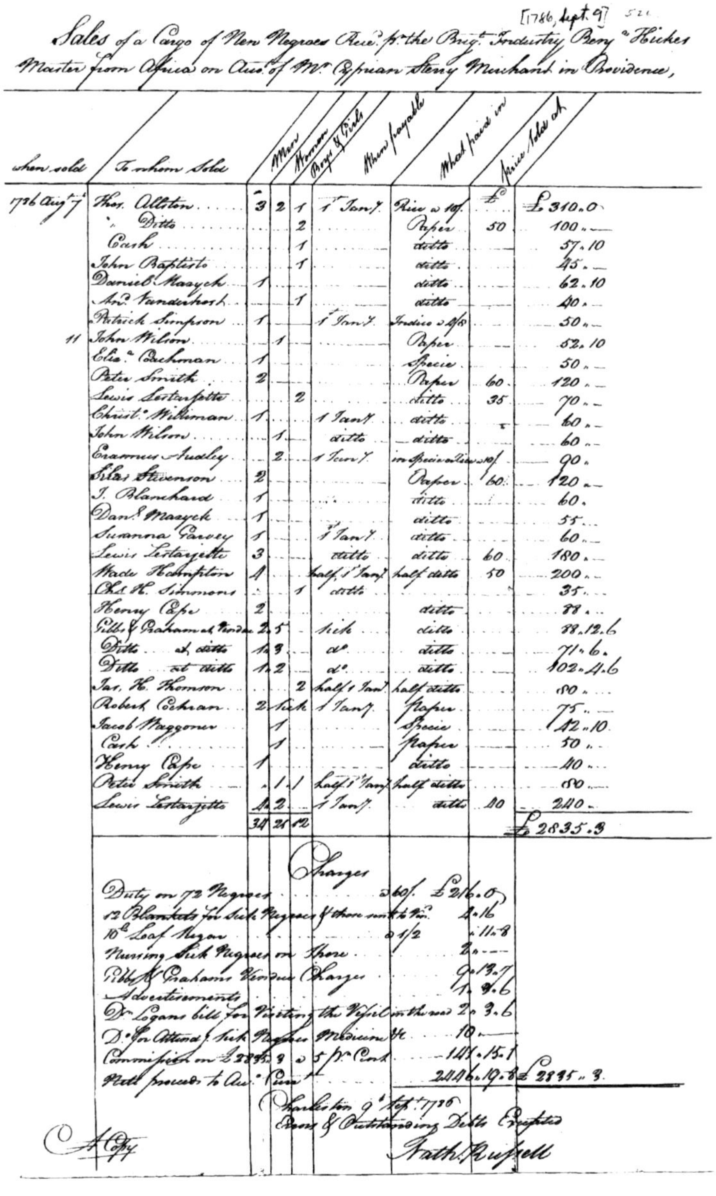
[1786, Sept. 9]

Sales of a Cargo of New Negroes Recd. pr. the Brigt. Industry Benja. Hicks Master from Africa on Acct. of Mr. Cyprian Sterry Merchant in Providence,

when sold	To whom Sold	Men	Women	Boys & Girls	When payable	What paid in	Price Sold at	
1786 Augt. 7	Thos. Allston	3	2	1	1st Jany.	Rice @ 10/.	£	£310.0
	Ditto			2		Paper	50	100.–
	Cash			1		ditto		57.10
	John Baptiste			1		ditto		45.–
	Daniel Mazyck	1				ditto		62.10
	Arn. Vanderhorst			1		ditto		40.–
	Patrick Simpson	1			1st Jany.	Indico @ 4/8		50.–
11	John Wilson		1			Paper		52.10
	Eliza. Coachman	1				Specie		50.–
	Peter Smith	2				Paper	60	120.–
	Lewis Lestarjette			2		ditto	35	70.–
	Christo. Williman	1			1 Jany.	ditto		60.–
	John Wilson		1		ditto	ditto		60.–
	Erasmus Audley		2		1 Jany.	in Specie or Rice @ 10/		90.
	Silas Stevenson	2				Paper	60	120.–
	J. Blanchard	1				ditto		60.
	Danl. Mazyck	1				ditto		55.
	Susanna Garvey	1			1st Jany.	ditto		60.–
	Lewis Lestarjette	3			ditto	ditto	60	180.–
	Wade Hampton	4			half 1st Jany.	half ditto	50	200.–
	Chs. H. Simmons			1	ditto			35.
	Henry Cape	2				ditto		88.
	Gibbs & Graham at Vendue	2	5		Sick	ditto		88.12.6
	Ditto at ditto	1	3		do.	ditto		71.6.
	Ditto at ditto	1	2		do.	ditto		102.4.6
	Jas. H. Thomson			2	half 1 Jany.	half ditto		80.
	Robert Cochran	2	Sick		1 Jany.	Paper		75.
	Jacob Waggoner		1			Specie		42.10
	Cash		1			Paper		50.
	Henry Cape	1				ditto		40.
	Peter Smith		1	1	half 1st Jany.	half ditto		80.
	Lewis Lestarjette	4	2		1 Jany.	ditto	40	240.
		34	21	12				£2835.3

Charges

Duty on 72 Negroes	@ 60/.	£216.0	
12 Blankets for Sick Negroes & those sent to Ven.		2.16	
10lb. Leaf Tobacco	@ 1/2	.11.8	
Nursing Sick Negroes on Shore		2.–	
Gibbs & Grahams Vendue Charges		9.13.7	
Advertisements		1.4.6	
Dr. Logans bill for Visiting the Vessel in the road		2.3.6	
Do. for Attend. Sick Negroes Medicine &c.		10.–	
Commission on £2835.3 @ 5 pr. Cent		141.15.1	
Nett proceeds to Acct. Curr.t		2446.19.8	£2835.3.

Charleston 9th Sept. 1786
Errors & Outstanding Debts Excepted
Nath. Russell

A Copy

Figure 4. Bill of Sale of Human Cargo. Courtesy of Mystic Seaport Museum, G. W. Blunt White Library Collection, Mystic Seaport, Connecticut.

recent introduction of paper money, and that the West Indies would be a better alternative.[27] However, at a time when markets and commodity prices were as changeable as the weather, ships' captains were virtually autonomous in deciding where to sell or trade their cargoes; in this case, Hicks decided to put in at Charleston.

Having staked his last assets in the venture, Imlay was clearly anxious to capitalize on his investment. By September, however, the deal had begun to unravel. On 6 September Sterry wrote to Talbot that, though Russell had so far sold twenty-three slaves, payable in rice, indigo and paper money, he had been unable to procure any 'hard Money'. Therefore Sterry urged Talbot to furnish him with the cash for his part of the portage bill, which came to about $300.[28] On 16 November Talbot forwarded Imlay's promissory note for four prime slaves and £21.4.0 in cash to Nathaniel Russell, asking the factor to advance to him the counter value of Imlay's bond out of the proceeds from the sale of the cargo of the *Industry*. 'My reason for sending the note on to you', Talbot explained, 'is that Capt. Imlay's circumstances are in all human probability much derang'd and unless I can git you to stop the contents in your hand, the debt will I fear be wholly lost to me'.[29] Since Imlay had apparently left the north-east and was not expected to return, Talbot suspected that he had renounced his claim to a quarter of the cargo of the *Industry* to his creditors. Were the creditors to lay their hands on Imlay's share of the cargo, Imlay's note to him would be worthless because Imlay's ability to meet his bond depended on his share of the profits from the voyage. Russell had some disappointing news for Talbot, informing him in early January 1787 that, since the bill of sale of half of the *Industry* from Sterry to Talbot made no mention of the brig's cargo, he was unable to forward Talbot any share of the proceeds from the cargo's sale. For the same reason, he also could not advance him any money against Imlay's note.[30]

In late February or early March 1787, Imlay arrived in Charleston, where he had meetings with Russell in an attempt to clear up his entangled deal with Talbot.[31] In a long and detailed letter to Talbot dated 5 March, Imlay afterwards expressed his dismay at not being able to collect his share of the proceeds because of Talbot's carelessly drafted contract with Sterry. He urged Talbot to seek legal assistance immediately, and recommended that he put the case in the hands of Peter Freneau, South Carolina Secretary of State, who also acted as attorney to Imlay.[32]

Once again Imlay demonstrated his talent in persuading well-placed attorneys to act on his behalf. Peter Freneau was the younger brother of Philip Freneau, known as 'the Poet of the American Revolution'. It is quite possible that Imlay became acquainted with Peter and Philip Freneau before he left his home state of New Jersey. The Freneau brothers' mother, Agnes Watson, was from Freehold, not far from where Imlay was born and raised, and Philip had attended the College of New Jersey at Princeton. If Imlay had known Philip before, he might have met him in Charleston through his acquaintance with Peter, since the poet visited his brother there in 1785, 1786 and possibly 1787. Peter Freneau settled in Charleston in December 1782. He became deputy secretary in 1784 and secretary of state in 1787, holding the latter position until 1794. Known as 'the Apollo of Charles Town', the handsome and dashing Peter Freneau was a prominent member of the Charleston beau monde, reputedly one of the most aristocratic of the South, with many of its inhabitants being members by birth of the French and English nobility.[33]

Two days after he penned his lengthy letter to Talbot on 5 March, Imlay added two separate postscripts which reveal why he was in dire need of a good attorney. His initial anxiety having turned into a slight panic, Imlay declared in the first postscript:

> As the contract has been carried in every Instance into execution on my part, and as I have suffered greatly from a variety of circumstances some of which prevented our carrying the contract for the 4 slaves and ¼ of the Brig into immediate execution, I wish particularly as I am so remote from M[r]. Sterry that you would impower M[r]. Russell to dissolve it[.] I think this request is fair and I presume you will not hesitate to comply with when you reflect on the many disappointments I have sustained. You will please open a correspondence with M[r]. Freneau as soon as possible.[34]

In the second postscript, Imlay pointed out to Talbot that since it would be crucial to their case against Sterry 'to prove the Handwriting of M[r]. Sterry', Freneau should be notified immediately that Imlay had 'absolutely got now in [his] possession' a letter from Sterry in which the latter stated that 'M[r]. Russell had no order from him to dispose of the Slaves'.[35]

Whatever action was undertaken, it was to no avail: both Imlay and Talbot ended up losing their investments in the *Industry*. Talbot eventually managed to get £30 from Russell against Imlay's note to him, but that was all. In November 1801, Talbot made one last, futile attempt to persuade Russell to extend him credit. By then Cyprian Sterry had gone bankrupt and Talbot had lost his last hope of reclaiming his quarter share in the sale of the *Industry*'s cargo and, equally, of redeeming Imlay's bond. 'Perhaps, Sir', Talbot wrote to Russell:

> there never was a Voyage that turned out more compleatly unfortunate to any Mortal than that performed by the Industry as it regarded myself, for out of one half of the Brig and her Cargo which I owned when she sailed, I now declare that I never received a shilling except the thirty pounds you allowed me to draw for towards Imlay's Note in my favor. Having sold half of the Brig and one quarter of her Cargo to Imlay and he having absconded, I lost the whol[e] of that Property except such sum as I have and may receive from you.[36]

As Talbot's letter intimates, it had proved to be considerably more difficult than expected to secure legal ownership of the nine tracts in Jefferson County that he had purchased from Imlay in September 1786, despite the fact that Talbot had not only recorded the nine patents in his name at the Nelson County Clerk's Office, but also put an attachment on Imlay's property in Kentucky. Learning about the cunning details of the contract from Judge John Cleves Symmes, Benjamin Sebastian (Imlay's attorney in Kentucky) was outraged that Talbot had somehow managed to 'recover the purchase money & hold the Lands too'.[37] Yet, in the final analysis, Imlay's duplicity was victorious over Talbot's cunning, for it soon emerged that Imlay's Kentucky tracts had already been heavily mortgaged at the time when he gained legal title to them and sold them to Talbot. As a result, Talbot was forced to take one of Imlay's creditors, Robert Johnston, to court because the latter had claimed title to at least one of the nine tracts (the 3,528 acres on Beech Fork), which Imlay had presumably offered him as collateral for a debt incurred some time prior to the sale to Talbot.[38]

The collapse of the *Industry* venture effectively closed the legal net around Imlay. Being sought by the sheriffs of Jefferson and Nelson counties and a posse of creditors chasing him up and down the east coast, a return to Kentucky, New York, Rhode Island or Virginia would almost certainly have led to his arrest for debt and fraud. In April 1787, when Talbot employed the services of Colonel D. Hart of Morristown, New Jersey, to put Imlay's bond before the auditors at the May session of the Trenton Supreme Court, his home state of New Jersey also became too hot for him.[39] Almost at the same time, another of Imlay's creditors, Oliver Pollock, started a suit against Imlay in Charleston for £400 in damages. Imlay had defaulted on a promissory note he had signed on 30 November 1786 for 934 Spanish milled silver dollars, which he was supposed to have paid back by 20 February 1787.[40] In March John Grimké, associate justice of the Charleston Court, issued a writ ordering South Carolina sheriffs to seize all of Imlay's assets and summoning Imlay to appear before the next Court of Common Pleas in July.[41] On 19 May Sheriff James Kennedy of the Charleston District Court seized all of Imlay's assets 'in the hands, Custody & Possession of Nathaniel Russell,' presumably Imlay's claim to a quarter of the net proceeds of the *Industry* venture.[42] Needless to say Imlay did not make an appearance in court, and in August a jury ruled in favour of Pollock, awarding him £240 in damages and interest.[43] In all likelihood Imlay had absconded well before then. As far as can be ascertained, Imlay was still the legal co-owner of the brig *Industry* when he left the United States. However, having defaulted on his financial obligations, Imlay's contract with Talbot was presumably declared null and void not long after he disappeared, after which his former attorney, Peter Freneau, became one of the *Industry*'s new owners.[44]

Historians have so far been unable to establish approximately when and from where Imlay left North America for Europe, but the Silas Talbot Papers appear to set the record straight on both of these issues. In a letter from Nathaniel Russell to Silas Talbot dated 15 December 1787, Russell, who as a well-connected factor in Charleston would certainly have been in a position to know, stated that Imlay had made his way south to St Augustine, the hub of the slave trade in Spanish colonial Florida, and from there sailed to England.[45] Although Russell does not give the exact date of Imlay's departure from North America, it can be inferred from his letter that it was in the late spring or early summer.[46] Assuming that he took a direct passage from St Augustine to England, this would put Imlay on British soil in or before the autumn of 1787, ironically the year in which the London Society for the Abolition of the Slave Trade was founded. Unsurprisingly, Imlay was allegedly already off on another mission: 'I am informed', Russell wrote, that Imlay 'obtain'd Letters of Credit & if he succeeds in getting goods intends to carry them into the Indian Nation'.

Though it may seem unlikely, it is certainly not implausible that someone would still have wanted to extend credit to a fraudulent entrepreneur like Imlay. Wherever he appeared, people seem to have entrusted him with their money, their ideas, and sometimes their dreams. Not all of these people will have done so out of greed, innocence or stupidity. Imlay's dealings with Talbot, Freneau and Russell confirm that even while a growing number of sheriffs and debt collectors were seeking urgent interviews with Imlay, his talent to ingratiate himself with prominent figures in business and genteel society clearly had not abandoned him. Though this talent had not brought him significant or lasting material gain, it did enable him after every fresh deception to tap into other social and professional networks and, like a chameleon, to adopt the *couleur locale* of his new environment. His social ease and intelligence and his ability to inspire confidence would stand him in good stead when he slipped out of the United States and re-emerged in Europe.

5 AUTHORITY ON THE AMERICAN WEST

> Printing and navigation have compleately changed the complexion of Europe; they
> must change that of the whole GLOBE
>
> Gilbert Imlay, *The Emigrants*[1]

At first sight it is hard to imagine that the Gilbert Imlay who had so quietly and
ignominiously departed from the United States in the course of 1787 was the
same Gilbert Imlay who appeared in the full public glare of London's periodical press in the late spring of 1792. He had left his native America a penniless
land-jobber and a bungling slave trader, but when we next hear from him he
is 'Captain' Imlay, a 'Commissioner for laying out Land in the Back Settlements' and the 'intelligent and lively author' of *A Topographical Description of
the Western Territory of North America*.[2] Having overnight become an authority
on America's western territory, by the time his novel *The Emigrants* appeared in
March 1793, Imlay was hailed by William Enfield in the *Monthly Review* as an
author who, on 'the general subject of politics', expressed himself 'with the freedom of an enlightened philosopher'.[3] Imlay's reincarnation as a Jacobin 'modern
philosopher' and a champion of social and political reform could not have come
at a more propitious moment. 'Bliss was it in that dawn to be alive', Wordsworth
famously wrote in *The Prelude*, describing the atmosphere of heady optimism
generated by the popular movement for social and political reform in England
in 1792:

> O times,
> In which the meager, stale, forbidding ways
> Of custom, law, and statute took at once
> The attraction of a Country in Romance;
> When Reason seem'd the most to assert her rights
> When most intent on making of herself
> A prime Enchanter to assist the work,
> Which then was going forwards in her name.[4]

Contrary to America and France, where the respective Revolutions had involved
widespread bloodshed and massive social disruption, the 'British Revolution' –
though certainly not free from violent upheaval – was largely fought in the pages

of various print media. Many of these texts were distributed, read and debated by a rapidly swelling audience of literate artisans, labourers and shopkeepers that frequented the nation's coffee-houses, ale-houses and reading clubs. The controversy over the causes of the French Revolution and the consequences it might or should have for the future make-up of Britain's society and political institutions had turned the British into 'an inquisitive, prying, doubting, and reading people'.[5] Book production and consumption in Britain had seen a fourfold increase since 1750, but the 'Revolutionary Debate' of the 1790s witnessed an unprecedented increase in the annual production of novels, pamphlets, sermons, poetry and periodical publications. The British Revolution was first and foremost a print revolution, as well as a revolution in print. Or, as H. N. Brailsford so aptly remarked, 'The history of the French Revolution in England begins with a sermon and ends with a poem'.[6] The sermon, 'A Discourse on the Love of our Country', was delivered in 1789 by the leading Dissenter and political pamphleteer Dr Richard Price; written not long after the sacking of the Bastille on 14 July 1789 – an event which marked the beginning of the populist uprising in France – Price's sermon identified the French Revolution as the natural and just successor of the Glorious Revolution of 1688–9, which had laid the foundation for Britain's parliamentary monarchy, and of the American Revolution, which had ushered in the independence of the American colonies as a sovereign nation. The poem Brailsford referred to was Percy Shelley's *Hellas* (1821), in which, inspired by the same revolutionary fire and hope that had moved Dr Price, the poet creates a glorious vision of the ideal republic, but, significantly, finds it beyond the perilous world of fact, in the timeless realm of the muses and the imagination.

It was ultimately less Price's plea for parliamentary reform than his passionate and unqualified glorification of the French Revolution as the dawn of a new age utopia and an example to Britain that set the nation aflame. Edmund Burke was quick to denounce Price's sermon in his *Reflections on the French Revolution* (1790) – his passionate rhetoric of declamatory rage clearly betraying that 'his mission was to spread panic because he felt it'.[7] Although Burke's book does not offer a sustained philosophical critique of the French Revolution but relies on superb rhetorical exaggerations instead, it did manage to put the main conservative arguments firmly on the political agenda: the rejection of the ideology of natural rights; the dismissal of a social contract theory; an insistence on institutional continuity (church, monarchy and common law); the preference of familial affection over reason, and practical experience over speculative rationality. Burke's *Reflections* struck an immediate chord with the political, social and religious establishment in the nation, and soon became conservative Britain's main answer to the Revolution in France and to its growing body of sympathizers at home. However, his eloquent rhetoric inspired his enemies as much as his supporters, thus triggering a 'mighty debate' that was to last for a decade and that was to determine the future of the British nation – or so the participants thought at the time.

Until France declared war on Britain on 1 February 1793, this national debate was still dominated by the friends of the French Revolution and others arguing for political and social reform at home. The reformists were encouraged in their campaign by a number of extraordinarily influential radical publications. Within months of the publication of Burke's *Reflections*, the writer, educator and radical feminist Mary Wollstonecraft published a first retort, *A Vindication of the Rights of Men*; this was followed in 1792 by her best-known work, and one of the founding texts of modern feminism, *A Vindication of the Rights of Woman*. A year before James Mackintosh had taken a forceful public stand against Burke in his *Vindiciae Gallicae*. Also in 1791 the pamphleteer and political activist Thomas Paine joined the fray, having first helped to stoke up the fire of revolution in America. His immensely popular *Rights of Man* (Part I) was in every way a direct answer to Burke's *Reflections*: it not only argues for natural rights, a written constitution and the right of every generation to govern its own affairs, but it does so in a discourse that is as abstract as it is uncompromising in its hard-hitting logic. Indignation at Burke's attack on his radical friend, Dr Price, and excitement over the French Revolution inspired Joel Barlow to write his wildly ambitious *Advice to the Privileged Orders in the Several States of Europe resulting from the Necessity and Property of a General Revolution in the Principle of Government*, which appeared in February 1792, only days before the second part of Paine's *Rights of Man*. 1792 also saw the publication of what has been described as 'the first full-blown revolutionary novel', *Anna St. Ives*,[8] written by Thomas Holcroft, one of London's leading radicals and a close friend of William Godwin.

Offered to the public in May 1792, Imlay's *Topographical Description* should first and foremost be read and interpreted within this wider intellectual context, and textual genealogy, of Britain's national debate of the early 1790s – rather than within the narrow confines of the genre of American travel writing and topography per se.[9] Crucially, Imlay's treatise reformulated the prevailing mode of topography/travel writing into an ideological discourse of space: although it still employs the language and format of topography, the *Topographical Description* was instrumental in the shift – which was both semantic and paradigmatic – from 'wilderness' into 'territory' and from the West as trans-Alleghenian 'land' into the West as the space for the establishment of an alternative, Jacobin American 'empire'. In the same way that in April 1791 Brissot de Warville had published his *Nouveau Voyage dans les États-Unis* in order to teach the French nation a lesson in preserving liberty once it had been acquired through revolution, Barlow published his translation of Brissot's *New Travels* in February 1792 with Paine's London publisher J. S. Jordan in order to promote the republican principles of France and the United States in Pitt's England. Similarly, Imlay wrote his *Topo-*

graphical Description to further the cause of liberty in Britain by praising the republican legacy of the earlier popular revolts in America and France – as well as offering the friends of reform a transatlantic asylum of perfect equality and pastoral bliss, should their aristocratic oppressors manage to remain in power.

* * *

British reformers in the early 1790s were quick to recognize their own anti-establishment agenda in Gilbert Imlay's radicalization of the American Revolution. When Imlay's *Topographical Description of the Western Territory of North America* was published on 21 May 1792, it was immediately enlisted on the Jacobin side in the print war that had erupted in the wake of the French Revolution. Imlay's publisher, John Debrett, was a London bookseller and stationer who was known for his sympathetic leanings towards the reformists' cause. His shop opposite Burlington House at 179 Piccadilly was a popular haunt for radical Whigs and a motley crowd of republican writers and activists.[10] Debrett had originally set up his business across the street at 178 Piccadilly, after the radical bookseller John Almon – a staunch friend of John Wilkes and a scourge of William Pitt and his government – had turned his business over to him in 1781.[11] Debrett's neighbour was the bookseller John Stockdale, who, in response to Almon's decision to retire in favour of Debrett, had set up a rival business at 181 Piccadilly. If Debrett's was frequented by Whigs, Stockdale's soon became a fashionable lounging place for the Pittites.[12] Unlike Debrett's, Stockdale's imprints included several topographical and cartographical items, which suggests it may ultimately have been its marketability as a reformist tract advocating emigration to America that attracted John Debrett to the *Topographical Description*. Although his name is nowadays associated almost exclusively with *Debrett's Peerage* (first published in 1802) and *Debrett's Baronetage* (first published in 1808), a list of 'New Publications printed for J. Debrett' for the year 1793 confirms that John Debrett was at the time firmly committed to publishing tracts promoting social and political reform in Britain, notably those invoking the enlightening examples of the Revolutions in America and France.[13]

　　Internal evidence suggests that the *Topographical Description* was specifically designed to participate in the 'mighty debate' then underway in Britain. Like Crèvecoeur's *Letters from an American Farmer*, which was likewise aimed at a British, not an American audience, Imlay's *Topographical Description* is offered to the reader as 'a series of letters to a friend in England'.[14] In part at least, Imlay's book taps into the European cultural heritage of transatlantic pastoralism and agrarian primitivism that was popularized, if not quite established, by Crèvecoeur's *Letters*. For instance, Imlay's alter ego is clearly based on Crèvecoeur's narrator, Farmer James, who also professes to be a simple 'farmer of feelings' – 'neither a philosopher, politician, divine, or naturalist' but a 'scribbling farmer'.[15]

For his part, the English 'editor' of Imlay's *Topographical Description* describes his American friend, the 'G. Imlay' mentioned on the title page, as a 'man who had lived until he was more than five-and-twenty years old, in the back parts of America', where he had become 'accustomed to that simplicity of manners natural to a people in a state of innocence'.[16] From the very outset Imlay juxtaposes the 'probable rise and grandeur of the American empire' and the flawed empires in Europe, where 'ignorance continue[s] to darken the horizon' and citizens live under the 'gothic tyranny' of corrupt power.[17] Having travelled extensively through Europe after his lengthy sojourn in the American back settlements, Imlay's narrator is 'powerfully stricken with the great difference between the simplicity of the one [i.e. America], and what is called *etiquette* and good breeding in the other [i.e. Europe]'.[18] Being a man of unspoiled manners and morals, the editor deems his American friend 'better calculated than ourselves to judge of our manners'. Besides being an eclectic account of the American Horn of Plenty and a practical 'How-to-emigrate-to-Kentucky' guide, Imlay's *Topographical Description* thus becomes a comparative analysis of, in the words of our Kentuckian Noble Savage, 'the simple manners, and rational life of the Americans, in these back settlements' and 'the distorted and unnatural habits of the Europeans', which the American narrator reminds us, 'have flowed no doubt from the universally bad laws which exist [in Europe], and from that pernicious system of blending religion with politics, which has been productive of universal depravity'.[19] Farmer James is ultimately unable to resolve the dilemma he faces of neither wanting to join the American bid for independence nor wanting to return to Europe – choosing instead the idealist, Rousseauesque opt-out of a life 'under the wigwham'.[20] Imlay's narrator, however, wants to carry the American Revolution to its radical extreme. For while Crèvecoeur emphatically dismisses the 'back settlers' on the western frontier as being 'ferocious, gloomy ... unsociable' and really little more than a regressive 'mongrel breed, half civilized, half savage',[21] Imlay depicts those very same western pioneers as the true inheritors of the American Revolution, and the wilderness frontier as the centre of a future American empire.[22] 'It is physically impossible for man to degenerate to barbarism',[23] the narrator observes in what appears to be a defiant sneer at the cultural pessimism evinced by Crèvecoeur, who had designated the back settlers as 'offcasts' and America's 'bad people'.[24]

Modern commentators on the *Topographical Description* have generally been sceptical of the editor's claim that 'no work of this kind has hitherto been published in this country'.[25] The texts that are most commonly cited as 'sources' for Imlay's *Topographical Description* are John Filson's *The Discovery, Settlement and Present State of Kentucky*, especially in connection with the topographical details of the western territory, and Crèvecoeur's *Letters*, notably because of the discourse of utopianism and sentimental agrarianism that both texts share. Neither

Filson's nor Crèvecoeur's text is mentioned in the *Topographical Description*, but given their wide dissemination and impact, it is inconceivable that Imlay was completely oblivious of their existence. Indeed, in the case of Filson's *Discovery* there are sufficient verbatim similarities between that text and the *Topographical Description* to suggest that Imlay consulted the earlier account of Kentucky while he was composing his own.[26] That said, considering that at the time plagiarism in topographical and travel writing was the norm rather than the exception, the *Topographical Description* remains a remarkably original text, which appears largely to have been written from the author's own observations and experience.[27] Certainly Imlay's topographical description of the western territory east of the Ohio is much more detailed and far more accurate than any previous account of the area – including Thomas Hutchins's *Topographical Description of Virginia ... Comprehending the Rivers Ohio, Kenhawa, Scioto ...* (1778), Filson's *Description* (1784), Daniel Boone's *Adventures* (1784) and Jedidiah Morse's (brief) description of the west in his *American Geography* (1789). For one thing, until the early 1780s, virtually all explorers, surveyors and topographers who produced accounts of their travels through the western territories had followed the courses of rivers and creeks, leaving the inland region between the Ohio and the Allegheny Mountains largely undocumented. In contrast to many of his predecessors, Imlay rarely fantasizes about what he has not witnessed or experienced himself.

On the contrary, Imlay's alter ego is quite willing to admit that he is unable to comment on the quality of the land south of the Cumberland Mountains because he had never travelled there; that he cannot confirm reports that there are 'black lead mines' upon the headwaters of the Kentucky River because he has not been able 'to procure any certain information respecting them'; and he apologizes for not be able to speak 'with more precision' about the exact northern limits of the state of Kentucky simply 'because these things have not been ascertained from observation'.[28] Nor does he have any problem acknowledging the authority of earlier writers in areas where he has no expertise, and he is careful to credit the appropriate authority in each case. Thus, he plainly states that, since he is 'too ignorant of botany', he has borrowed his details concerning the natural history of America in Letter X from 'Buffon, Kalm, D'Abenton, Catesby, and Pennant', while he respectfully yields to the higher authority of 'Croghan, Boquet, Carver, Hutchins, and Dodge' for details concerning the various Indian tribes (though noting in passing that based on what he gathered from local settlers, 'these authorities' sometimes report 'from hearsay, or proceed upon conjecture').[29] For information on the quality of the soil in the 'fork' of the Ohio and Mississippi rivers, Imlay gratefully acknowledges previous topographical observations made by 'Charlevoix, Hutchins, and Carver': 'These authorities have all considerable merit. They have written so agreeably, that their books have been generally read; which has tended to disseminate a knowledge of this country in a savage state.'[30] Imlay is particularly generous in his praise of his fellow New Jerseyan Thomas Hutchins (born and raised in Monmouth County, like Imlay), who had been appointed the first and only civil 'geographer of the United States' by Congress in May 1788, a little under a year before his death: 'I must now beg you travel with Hutchins from hence to Detroit ... His observations I have been told are considerably accurate, and as I have not had the advantage of travelling this route, I recommend you to read his book, which was originally published in England, and no doubt is still to be had.'[31] Imlay also respectfully acknowledges Jefferson's 'accurate' descriptions of 'the medicinal, inflammable, bituminous, and other springs' in Kentucky, adding that 'his account of the natural history of this country is generally to be depended upon, so that it is scarcely possible to make any improvement upon it, until further discoveries have arisen'.[32] However, in the final analysis the signal point here is not that Imlay knew and respected the various authorities on the western territory, but that he ultimately aspired to go *beyond* those authorities, and *beyond* their discourse of topography and natural history. Unlike its predecessors (with the exception of Jefferson's *Notes*), Imlay's *Topographical Description* constitutes a sustained geopolitical doctrine, in that it not merely describes the western territories in terms of a New Canaan for the prospective emigrant, but also provides the physiocratic rationale for the opening up and development of the western territories.

A doctrine of political economists developed in France in the eighteenth century, physiocracy is characterized chiefly by the belief that government policy should not interfere with the operation of natural economic laws and that land is the source of all wealth. In contrast to Enlightenment thought in general, liberty is considered not so much a precondition for universal prosperity as the *consequence* of prosperity. In other words: liberty follows trade and commerce, not the other way around. Accordingly, Imlay's attitude towards the natural environment of the western territories is not that of an idealist Pantisocrat seeking refuge from oppression and persecution or of a vapid 'lover of the meadows and the woods, and the mountains', but that of a staunchly utilitarian, pragmatic real estate developer. Thus, when he describes the 'delectable region' of Kentucky,[33] Imlay is not transported by Wordsworthian 'aching joys' and 'dizzy raptures', but is rather thinking of the richness of the soil, the navigability of the rivers and lakes, and the wholesomeness of the climate.

Of course, the key asset of the western territory of the United States is the land, the soil and situation of which Imlay depicts in the most exuberant colours. Although all of the land beyond the Allegheny Mountains is 'extremely fertile, well-watered, and abounding with all kinds of timber calculated for building houses, boats, cabinet work, &c. &c.', and while the tracts on the headwaters of the Scioto in particular are 'as fine a body of land as the imagination can paint', the genuinely 'fine lands of Kentucky' are first encountered at Limestone, where 'the champaign country' on the eastern side of the Ohio begins: 'Everything here assumes a dignity and splendour I have never seen in any other part of the world'.[34] From Limestone to Licking Creek the country is 'immensely rich', yet after 'passing the Blue Lick, the soil, if possible, increases in richness'.[35] Unsurprisingly, the area to the south of the Blue Lick – covering the greater part of Fayette County and the northern section of Jefferson County – was precisely where most Imlay's land transactions had taken place:

> From [the Blue Lick] to Danville is about fifty miles. Lexington lies about midway, and is nearly central of the finest and most luxuriant country, perhaps, on earth. From Lexington to Leesburg is about twenty miles; to Boonsbury it is about twenty; the Upper Blue Lick nearly thirty. This square which is nearly fifty miles, comprehends entirely what is called first rate land.[36]

The area around Louisville – another of Imlay's haunts – also comes in for a fair share of his praise. Thus, the tracts on Beargrass Creek are said to be 'beautiful and rich', while Louisville itself 'will soon become a flourishing town'.[37] The Rapids are described as 'truly delightful':

> The river is full a mile wide, and the fall of water, which is an eternal cascade, appears as if nature had designed it to show how inimitable and stupendous are her works. Its breadth contributes to its sublimity; and the continually rumbling noise tends to exhilarate the spirits, and gives a cheerfulness even to sluggards.[38]

Needless to say, provisions are both plentiful and cheap, while the country is richly endowed with natural resources. In addition, the orderly fashion in which Kentucky lands had been surveyed under the supervision of the Virginia Land Office and transactions had been duly registered at the Richmond Register's Office would make it safe to buy land in Kentucky for even the most inexperienced and genteel of British settlers. Indeed, 'the order and quiet, which prevailed [in Kentucky] in 1784, was sufficient to have induced a stranger to have believed that he was living under an old settled government'.[39]

But Imlay knew well enough that even a promised land was a worthless land if it was not easily accessible. The northern route to Kentucky – by wagon from either Philadelphia or Baltimore across the Alleghenies to Pittsburgh and then down the Ohio River on flat-bottomed barges – was an onerous and often dangerous one, and no matter how smooth Imlay makes the journey appear, it would continue to render produce dear in the western settlements, despite Imlay's claims to the contrary.[40] The key to reaching the back settlements lay in the navigability of the Mississippi and Ohio rivers, and it is not surprising that in his *Topographical Description*, Imlay (following earlier authors like Hutchins, Carver, Filson and Jefferson) dwells at length on the unique transportation potential of the West's interlocking rivers and lakes. And in those rare instances where Nature had failed to accommodate the commercial interests of the West,

science and technology would soon come to man's aid. Thus, Imlay is hopeful
that it will soon be possible to travel by water from the Chesapeake to the Great
Lakes, once 'the gentlemen from Virginia' – a covert reference to his friend Light-
Horse Harry and his partners in the Potomac Company – will have completed
the construction of the canals around the falls in the Potomac and removed
the obstructions in the Monongahela and Cheat rivers. This would reduce the
portage between the Potomac and Ohio to only about twenty miles.[41] As soon
as the problem of upstream navigation is resolved (and Imlay is confident that
this will only be a matter of time, given experiments with steam-powered boats
then being conducted by 'Mr. Rumsey of Virginia'),[42] dwellers on Kentucky's
green and fertile fields would be able to open up communications and trade with
the settlements on the Pacific coast and in Canada. Seeing that, '[a]ccording to
the present system, wealth is the source of power' and that 'the attainment of
wealth can only be brought about by a wise and happy attention to commerce',[43]
Imlay proudly concludes that the western regions, far from being an outpost of
civilization on the margins of America, were actually at the heart of the North
American experiment and mankind's best bet to realize even the wildest, most
extreme notions of physiocratic progress and Jacobin perfectibility:

> You will observe, that as far as this immense continent is known, the courses and
> extent of its rivers are extremely favourable to communication by water; a circum-
> stance which is highly important, whether we regard it in a social or commercial
> point of view. The intercourse of men has added no inconsiderable lustre to the polish
> of manners, and, perhaps, commerce has tended more to civilize and embellish the
> human mind, in two centuries, than war and chivalry would have done in five.[44]

In defiance of the widespread belief in the De Pauw-Buffon-Raynal theory of
inevitable physical, moral and cultural degradation in the New World, Imlay
has this message for his European readers: 'It is physically impossible for man
to degenerate to barbarism'. The western territory may still be in 'a wild state'
now, but its natural resources, along with liberty, 'cultivation' and 'the science
of government' will inevitably generate a state of perfection 'in arts, philosophy,
wisdom and science'. In the West's wildness lies the promise of its unstoppable
rise among the commonwealth of nations.

In the course of the letters considerable slippage occurs in Imlay's use and
meaning of certain key terms. Thus, when in the early letters he uses the word
'we', Imlay usually refers to the American people; however, gradually 'we' is used
to denote the settlers in the Ohio Valley and elsewhere in the West. Similarly, the
phrase 'our empire' is synonymous with 'the federal empire' and 'the American
empire' in passages in which Imlay is offsetting social and political conditions in
the United States against those in Europe; but the phrase increasingly acquires a
more specifically western connotation, notably in those passages in which Imlay

is extolling the merits and glorifying the future of Kentucky and the wider trans-Appalachian region. Thus, we are told that

> to comprehend the object of the commerce of this country, it is first necessary to contemplate it, abounding in all the comforts of life, limited in its variety of climate only by what is not desireable; with a soil so prolific, a navigation so extensive, and a security so permanent from being inland, that it seems this vast extent of empire is only to be equaled for its sublimity but by the object of its aggrandizement.[45]

In fact, it turns out there is a secessionist political agenda embedded in Imlay's ostensibly objective topographical discourse, which becomes more manifest in the course of the letters. The presence of this underlying separatist ideology is noticeable, for instance, in the way Imlay represents the Allegheny and Cumberland Mountains in his text.

The Cumberland and Allegheny Mountains, which until the 1760s caused the colonization of America to be contained within the relatively confined coastal strip bordering on the Atlantic, undergo a staggered, two-stage metamorphosis in the *Topographical Description*. Rather than the impregnable obstacle to further westward expansion described in many earlier accounts of America, the Cumberland and Allegheny mountain ranges are at first presented to us not so much as a physical, but a *moral* watershed, separating the 'delectable region' of pastoral innocence in Kentucky from 'prejudice', 'despotism' and 'paltry sophistry' prevalent in Virginia, notably as reflected in Jefferson's sympathetic stance towards slavery.[46] In sharp contrast to what he had seen in the East, Imlay's rendering of the Arcadian region of pastoral bliss that presents itself to the emigrant on first beholding the Ohio Valley pertinently invokes Moses's first view of the Promised Land from the top of Mount Pisgah, while it also picks up on Daniel Boone's similarly stupendous first glimpse of the 'inconceivable grandeur' of the Ohio Valley and Kentucky's 'uninterrupted scene of sylvan pleasures' from a vantage point in the Cumberland Mountains.[47] Imlay's mountaintop prospect of the New Canaan in the West moves him momentarily to suspend his otherwise rational discourse of topography and natural history, and to indulge in an uncharacteristic 'rhapsody' of Rousseauesque primitivism (a lapse for which he promptly apologizes to his English friend):

> Everything here assumes a dignity and splendour I have never seen in any part of the world. You ascend a considerable distance from the shore of the Ohio, and when you would suppose you had arrived at the summit of a mountain, you find yourself upon an extensive level. Here an eternal verdure reigns, and the brilliant sun of lat. 39°, piercing through the azure heavens, produces, in this prolific soil, an early maturity which is truly astonishing. Flowers full and perfect, as if they had been cultivated by the hand of a florist, with all their captivating odours, and with all the variegated charms which colour and nature can produce, here, in the lap of elegance and beauty, decorate the smiling groves. Soft zephyrs gently breathe on sweets, and the inhaled air gives a voluptuous glow of health and vigour, that seems to ravish the intoxicated

senses. The sweet songsters of the forest appear to feel the influence of this genial clime, and, in more soft and modulated tones, warble their tender notes in unison with love and nature. Every thing here gives delight; and, in that mild effulgence which beams around us, we feel a glow of gratitude for the elevation which our all bountiful Creator has bestowed upon us. Far from being disgusted with man for his turpitude or depravity, we feel that dignity which nature bestowed upon us at the creation; but which has been contaminated by the base alloy of meanness, the concomitant of European education, and what is more lamentable is, that it is the consequence of your [his English friend's] very laws and governments.[48]

Yet aside from highlighting an ethical and aesthetical East-West divide, the Allegheny and Cumberland Mountains also create a fundamental ideological schism between the Atlantic states and the transmontane regions in the West. By blending the western territory's rivers, mountains, soil, climate and natural resources into a physiocratic, geopolitical doctrine of progress and universal prosperity, Imlay may have created a prototype of the doctrine of Manifest Destiny, but it is fundamentally different from the popular nineteenth-century version of it. Crucially, Imlay's physiocratic millennium does not have its origin in the early colonial experiments in Virginia and New England, nor even in the ideological energy released by the American Revolution: instead, Imlay envisages the cradle of his physiocratic utopia to be in the West, more particularly in Kentucky, and the ideological forces that rock it to be generated by the French, rather than by the American Revolution. Indeed, underlying Imlay's dream of America is a fervent plea for a secessionist utopia across the Alleghenies, whereby 'the Mountain' (as he refers to them) creates an ideological dichotomy between two distinct Americas: between the eastern states, which he regards as an outpost of an earlier, Puritan exodus, whose original energy had petered out and had become permeated with the social evils of the Old World, and the 'true', trans-Alleghenian America in the West, which was radically discontinuous with the earlier, European colonization of North America. Imlay's separatist agenda leads him to reformulate the notion of a federal America as a nation whose political power is not centred in the East – not in the 'federal city' that has just been established in the District of Columbia – but in the West, where the Ohio River Valley would become the principal seat of empire:

The federal government regulating every thing commercial, must be productive of the greatest harmony, so that while we are likely to live in the regions of perpetual peace, our felicity will receive a zest from the activity and variety of our trade. We shall pass through the Mississippi to the sea – up the Ohio, Monongahala and Cheat rivers, by a small portage, into the Potowmac, which will bring us to the federal city on the line of Virginia and Maryland – through the federal rivers I have mentioned, and the lakes to New York and Quebec – from the northern lakes to the head branches of the rivers which run into Hudson's-bay into the Arctic regions – and from the sources of the Misouri [*sic*] into the Great South Sea. Thus in the centre of the earth, governing by the laws of reason and humanity, we seem calculated to become at once the emporium and protectors of the world.[49]

Imlay may at times wax a little lyrical when contemplating his geopolitical master plan, but he was nothing if not pragmatic as well. Thus, he was acutely aware that if Kentucky had the potential to become the centre of the New World – indeed, of a New World millennium – because of its strategic position at the junction of the waterways of the future, this commercial and geopolitical potential was at the same time what threatened to undermine its glorious future. Like many western settlers, Imlay was convinced that 'whoever are possessed of this river [the Mississippi], and of the vast tracts of fertile lands upon it, must in time command that continent, and the trade of it, as well as all the native in it'.[50] Free navigation of the Mississippi was an economic necessity for Kentucky and the larger Ohio Valley, since the river was the only possible outlet for produce from the region. In the early pages of the book, Imlay recounts with evident disgust the attempts by the French in the course of the seventeenth and eighteenth centuries to put a stranglehold on the western settlements by an 'insidious' plan first to occupy the mouths of the St Lawrence and Mississippi rivers and subsequently to secure the communication between Canada and Louisiana by erecting an elaborate network of fortresses. But this 'colossian plan' is very much attributed to the Ancien Régime, notably to Louis XIV ('that voracious tyrant'), and emphatically *not* to the new, Revolutionary administration in France (Letter I). Besides, by the time Imlay was composing his *Topographical Description*, the French sphere of influence on the North American continent had been drastically reduced at the close of the French and Indian Wars. By the Treaty of Paris of 1763 all of Louisiana below latitude 32° and control over the mouth of the Mississippi had been ceded to Spain. Although as part of the 1783 Treaty of Paris, the United States had formally retained the navigation rights of the Mississippi that had formerly belonged to the British, the Spanish had more or less blockaded the river as part of a containment strategy aimed at frustrating the westward expansion of the United States. With the federal government showing only little sympathy with the plight of the western settlers, it is not difficult to see why in the early 1790s the rebellious Kentuckians should be ready to make overtures to the French, whose territorial ambitions towards Louisiana and the Mississippi Valley had been rekindled by the Revolution of 1789. Nor is it hard to see how Imlay, as the author of one of the most recent, popular treatises on the western settlements, was about to start rubbing shoulders with prominent Girondist politicians in France and getting involved in French foreign affairs.

If the free navigation of the Mississippi dominated the political agenda in the Kentucky Conventions from late 1784 onwards, the issue was also central to Imlay's concerns regarding the future of the western territory. Indeed, the obstruction of the Mississippi by the Spanish is identified in the *Topographical Description* as the single most important threat to the 'calculated rise of the American empire'.[51] Significantly, almost the entire second half of the Introduction is taken up by the text of a petition from 'the people of Kentucky in convention, in the year 1788' addressed to the United States Congress, in which the legislators are urged to 'remonstrate with the Court of Spain' upon the subject of the free navigation of the Mississippi.[52] The editor believes that the document 'contains sentiments so pure, and so manly', that it deserves to be reprinted 'at full length'. Which is all the more interesting because, borrowing the language of the natural rights tradition, the petition constitutes nothing less that a declaration of independence for Kentucky. Although it opens with an appeal to the 'paternal affection' and 'justice' of the congressional 'Fathers, fellow-citizens, and Guardians of our rights', the document is in fact quite Machiavellian in spirit and intent. Thus, having rehearsed how the Kentuckians had managed to secure their liberty after years of hunger, Indian hostility and other hardship without support from the union, the petition goes on to claim audaciously that 'no human cause could controul that Providence which had destined this western country to be the seat of a civilized and happy people'.[53] In mischievous reference to Jefferson's *Declaration*, the petition then bluntly raises the issue of Kentucky's inherent and inalienable rights:

> Then we ask, can the GOD OF WISDOM AND NATURE have created that vast country in vain? Was it for nothing that he blessed it with a fertility so astonishing? Did he not provide those great streams which enter into the Mississippi, and by it communicate with the Atlantic, that other nations might enjoy with us the blessings of our prolific soil? View the country, and you will answer for yourselves. But can the presumptuous madness of man imagine a policy inconsistent with the immense designs of the DEITY? Americans cannot.[54]

The author stops short of declaring Kentucky a free and independent state, but as far as he is concerned, the truth is self-evident: 'As it is the natural right to the inhabitants of this country to navigate the Mississippi, so they have also a right derived from treaties and national compacts'.[55] What makes the inclusion of such an explicitly secessionist document in the *Topographical Description* all the more intriguing is that it is not only a historical document, but that its anonymous author turns out to have been none other than Imlay's friend and business associate General James Wilkinson.[56] Close analysis of the *Topographical Description* reveals that Imlay's geopolitical treatise is inextricably bound up with Wilkinson's secessionist schemes and ambitions for the western territory.

* * *

General Wilkinson's secessionist campaign in Kentucky in the course of 1787–90 has often been described as one of the most treacherous acts in American history; it certainly brought the United States to the verge of a constitutional crisis and caused serious political discord in Kentucky. His enemies – of which there were many – described Wilkinson as 'the disorganizing spirit of an unprin-

cipled demagogue' and a long-standing vassal of the Spanish court.[57] By nature
vain and megalomaniac, Wilkinson had come to the West looking 'forward to
Independence & the highest Reputation in this Western World',[58] but there is no
evidence that until late 1785 Wilkinson was anything more than a spirited campaigner for free navigation of the Mississippi, or that he had ever met a Spanish
official or even been within a thousand miles of the authorities in Louisiana.[59]
It was only because of Congress's lukewarm support for a free Mississippi that
Wilkinson began to develop a more explicitly separatist agenda in the course of
1786–7. At least, that is the spin Wilkinson put on his treacherous activities in
retrospect. 'I foresaw we had nothing to expect or to hope from the union', he
observed in January 1789, 'and therefore I considered it my duty to look elsewhere for that patronage & support which the prosperity & happiness of our
expanding settlements loudly demanded'.[60] A serial traitor who revelled in cloak-
and-dagger intrigue, Wilkinson habitually felt called upon to 'sacrifice' his own
interests in the service of some 'righteous' cause that would invariably involve a
plot against the federal authorities and the stability of the union.

Wilkinson's transformation into a popular leader and separatist statesman
came at a time of growing frustration among Kentuckians over the lack of access
to foreign markets and the slow pace of the process of the district's separation from
Virginia and its establishment as an independent state. Extreme factionalism and
tumult dominated the political scene. Both Wilkinson and Benjamin Sebastian
– Imlay's long-standing attorney – had been members of the third Kentucky convention, which had convened on 8 August 1785. Although the third convention,
unlike its predecessors, did agree to send a petition to the Virginia Assembly to
pass an enabling act at its next session, it failed to establish a procedure for drafting
a constitution. The Virginia Assembly passed the enabling act on 16 January 1786,
but the strict procedural conditions and timetable it attached to the act caused
deep resentment amongst many Kentuckians. An upsurge in Indian hostility and
General George Rogers Clark's expedition against a number of tribes north of the
Ohio River prevented the September 1786 constitutional convention from meeting for lack of a quorum. When the constitutional convention did finally meet in
January 1787, news arrived from Virginia that the Assembly had passed a second
enabling act, which set a new timetable for the separation process and called for
a new constitutional convention in September 1787. It also stipulated that separation would occur only if Congress agreed to admit Kentucky into the union
before 4 July 1788. The delegates to the convention resented what they regarded
as the Assembly's high-handed action, and some were openly calling for an immediate and complete separation from Virginia. Then, in the early spring of 1787,
a number of like-minded spirits came together in a Jacobin-style 'committee of
correspondence in the western part of Pennsylvania'. Their first move was to send
a communication to the people of Kentucky, the gist of which was that during his

lengthy and ongoing negotiations with the Spanish chargé d'affaires Don Diego de Gardoqui, the American secretary for foreign affairs, John Jay, had offered to surrender the United States' claim to the navigation of the Mississippi for a period of twenty-five or thirty years in exchange for certain commercial advantages to the New England states.[61] This communication was seized upon by a number of prominent Kentuckians equally concerned about the navigation of the Mississippi, who adroitly converted the petition's specific complaint against John Jay into a more general charge against Congress and, beyond that, into an argument for independence.

In their 'Circular Letter directed to the different Courts in the Western Country', dated 29 March, four of Wilkinson's closest allies – George Muter, Harry Innes, John Brown and Benjamin Sebastian (all of whom Imlay knew from his Kentucky days) – called upon the people in the West to meet in Danville the following May, 'to prepare a spirited, but decent remonstrance, against the cession [by Congress]; to appoint a committee of correspondence, and to communicate with one already established on the Monongahela ... to appoint delegates, to meet representatives from the several districts on the western waters, in convention ... and to adopt such measures as shall be most conducive to our happiness'.[62] Federalists like Humphrey Marshall were strongly dismissive of the contents of the circular letter. They pointed out, first, that the General Assembly of Virginia had already sent a petition to Congress about the issue of the free navigation of the Mississippi four months before; and, second, that the call to meet in convention was unconstitutional, for, the district of Kentucky being represented in the General Assembly of Virginia, any complaints about the way the settlers were treated could and should be raised by the Kentucky delegates to the assembly. The most serious point of criticism, however, was that the separatists had deliberately misinformed the people of Kentucky about John Jay's preliminary proposal to Congress, in order to get their support for the conspirators' ambition to take Kentucky out of the union. After all, as Marshall pointed out, the free navigation of the Mississippi below latitude 32° was not for John Jay to surrender to the Spanish, simply because when Britain lost her territory on the river to Spain, she lost with it her right of navigation.[63]

Then, in the midst of this turmoil over Kentucky's political future and the Spanish blockade of the Mississippi, General Wilkinson decided to go on a trade mission to New Orleans. In April he freighted some flatboats with a small cargo of flour, bacon, butter and tobacco, embarked on the Kentucky River, and sailed down the Ohio and the Mississippi, finally arriving at New Orleans on 2 July 1787. The timing and the motives for Wilkinson's venture into Spanish Louisiana have preoccupied historians ever since. Why did Wilkinson decide to undertake this mercantile trip down the Mississippi at this particular point in time? Was it an exclusively mercantile trip, or was it somehow connected to the separatist movement in Kentucky? Why would he risk losing his investment at a time when, according to some at least, he was bankrupt;[64] in the knowledge that that the safety of his fleet of flatboats would be under constant threat from the treacherous currents of the Mississippi and Indian attacks, and that the Spanish authorities seized all boats and cargoes coming down the Mississippi as contraband?

Wilkinson claimed in his *Memoirs* that he was a 'perfect stranger' in New Orleans when he first arrived there.[65] Even though there is no conclusive evidence to the contrary, it is highly unlikely that he had not had any prior correspondence with merchants in that city who were interested in the merchandise he was shipping down the Mississippi. Wilkinson's military experience had taught him the value of orderly systems and the delegation of tasks, and in the few years he had been out West he had managed to set up a dense and far-reaching network of agents and associates. New Orleans would certainly have been within the outer parameter of his mercantile empire. Besides, the general was playing for high stakes, and he could not afford to make any mistakes. Increasing crops of tobacco had been piling up in Kentucky over the past three years in quantities for which there was no domestic demand and no available foreign market. In the course of 1786, Wilkinson's agents had been travelling up and down the district buying up tobacco on option contracts, thus securing Wilkinson the right to acquire large amounts of tobacco at very low prices in the following spring. If he were to succeed in persuading the Spanish authorities at New Orleans to give him exclusive trading rights with Spanish Louisiana, Wilkinson stood to make a fortune – especially since the Spanish were at the time in the market to purchase more tobacco than Louisiana produced, and were willing to pay $9.50 for a hundredweight for tobacco that cost only $2 in Kentucky.[66] Was Wilkinson's trip to New Orleans then simply the calculated gamble of an over-confident adventurer with a thirst for intrigue and pecuniary gain?

Spanish colonial administrators were nothing if not diligent archivists who reported frequently and voluminously to their superiors on the state of affairs in the far-flung parts of the empire. It is from letters, dispatches and other documents sent to various administrative headquarters by the Spanish governor for West Florida and the Louisiana Territory, Esteban Miró, and the intendant of New Orleans, Martin Navarro, that we are able to reconstruct the details and background of Wilkinson's trip to New Orleans. When Wilkinson's fleet of flatboats arrived in the city, more than his reputation as a former brigadier general in the American forces must have preceded him, for he managed to manoeuvre his cargo past the various Spanish military and customs checkpoints without any apparent difficulty. Upon his arrival at New Orleans, orders were swiftly issued for the general's boats and cargo to be left alone, and Wilkinson was escorted to the 'Government House' for an urgent meeting with Miró and Navarro.[67]

Apparently under the impression that Wilkinson was the chief military officer of the United States in the western territory, the two Spaniards treated him with due consideration. Indeed, they seem to have taken quite a liking to the general, whose bearing and manners they took as a sign of an excellent education. Although trade between Kentucky and New Orleans was high on Wilkinson's agenda, Miró and Navarro's report to the minister of war and treasury of the Indies, Antonio Valdez y Bazan, leaves little doubt about the general's true motives.[68] Explaining the reasons for his surprise visit, Wilkinson offered his hosts an encouraging account of the political conditions in Kentucky, stating in effect that 'it was the intention of all to put themselves under the protection or vassalage of his Catholic Majesty'.[69]

It is not hard to see why Miró and Navarro would be eager to learn Wilkinson's thoughts on the bilateral political interests of the Spanish and the Kentuckians. The governor and the intendant were well aware that the settlers in the Ohio Valley were deeply frustrated over the issue of the navigation of the Mississippi. What they feared more than an intervention by Congress was that the western pioneers would become so exasperated at the Spanish blockade of the Mississippi that they would take matters into their own hands and secure navigation of the river by force. Initially, the Spanish adopted a two-fold strategy in the endeavour to stop the Americans from encroaching upon the Louisiana territory: first, by supplying arms to Indian tribes declared to be under Spanish protection so that they could oust trespassing backwoodsmen from their hunting grounds; and second, by encouraging Americans and other nationals to settle on land claimed by the Spanish, notably on the east bank of the Mississippi. But by early 1787, the Spanish were getting seriously concerned about the threat of an imminent incursion by an irregular force from Kentucky. Thus, in February, Navarro sent a dispatch to Spain saying that there was no time to be lost in strengthening the Spanish positions in Louisiana, reminding his superiors that 'Mexico is on the other side of the Mississippi, in the vicinity of the already formidable establishments of the Americans'.[70] In March, Miró entreated the President of the Council of the Indies, the Marquis La Sonora, to make available large sums of money for laying out fortifications.[71] It is more than likely that Wilkinson's account of the bellicose mood of the Kentuckians – many of them Revolutionary War veterans and skilful in the use of arms – contributed considerably to the inquietude felt by the governor and the intendant. For shortly after the general had left New Orleans in September, Navarro sent off another dispatch to Spain in which he pointed out that the riches of New Mexico and the mines in the Ouachita District (in what is now western Arkansas) were 'powerful motives for a nation restless, poor, ambitious, and capable of the most daring enterprises'.[72] Imlay's *Topographical Description* reflects the belligerent attitude of the Kentuckians towards Spanish Louisiana at this time. In a barely veiled

threat to the Spanish, Imlay observes: 'The Spaniards may put us to some inconveniences for a few years to come; but, in doing this, they will not only risk the
loss of New Orleans, but the whole of Louisiana, which they consider as the key
to Mexico'.[73] Regarded within the context of Jay's 'betrayal' of Kentucky to Gardoqui and of Wilkinson's petition to Congress cited in the Introduction, Imlay's
remark amounts to a deliberate flouting of Congress as well as a bold assertion
of Kentucky's self-reliance.

In the light of all this, Imlay's digression in Letter V of the *Topographical
Description* concerning experiments being conducted by James Rumsey in Virginia to develop steam-powered riverboats for the upstream navigation of rivers
takes on a new meaning. In fact, steam propulsion had become a politically
sensitive issue in the West. Thus, the Spanish were much disquieted by the rev-
elation that it might soon be possible to surmount the current of the mighty
Mississippi. Yet it was not through James Rumsey but John Fitch that they first
heard about the principles of steam navigation. After completing his early tests
with the technology on the Delaware, Fitch had gone to Kentucky in the early
1780s, where he had become a deputy surveyor, adding to his income by working in mill-building. It was the latter experience that in April 1785 gave him
the idea to apply the power of steam using paddle-wheels. In order to raise the
cash needed to develop his idea, Fitch returned to the East, where he quickly
produced his 'Map of the North West Parts of the United States of America'.
Supporting himself with the proceeds of the sale of his map (which he had himself engraved, and printed on a borrowed cider press), Fitch continued to work
on his design for a steam-powered boat. Either sales were poor, or his experiments absorbed more money than anticipated, for in the space of a few weeks
Fitch concurrently launched several new funding schemes. Thus, on 30 August,
he presented a memorial to Congress in which he proposed that the government
'encourage the sale' of his map 'to the amount of four thousand subscribers'; he
would then execute the steamboat scheme at his own expense.[74] This initiative
eventually came to naught, after Rumsey had begun a pamphlet campaign asserting that he had a prior claim to the invention of a steam-powered vessel, and that
his design was superior to that of Fitch.[75] In September Fitch presented to the
American Philosophical Society 'The Model, with a drawing and description of
a machine for working a boat against the stream by means of a steam engine',
and called upon a number of prominent Americans for support – among them
Benjamin Franklin.[76] Again, the response was disappointing. Probably some
time in late August or early September 1785, Fitch next approached the Spanish
chargé d'affaires, Gardoqui, who was then in Philadelphia for his negotiations
with John Jay concerning the navigation of the Mississippi. Unlike Congress,
Gardoqui was immediately interested in Fitch's idea of navigation by power
applied to paddle wheels, as he was in Fitch's 'accurate' map of the north-western

United States. It is obvious why he would be: apart from providing reliable topographical details, Fitch's map is really a blueprint for the laying out of ten new states in the fork of the Ohio and Mississippi rivers, while his design for a steam-propelled Mississippi riverboat promised easy access to these new states – that is to say, access through Spanish controlled New Orleans. In his next dispatch Gardoqui sent a description of Fitch's invention and two copies of the map to the Spanish government.[77] One of the two copies of Fitch's map and Gardoqui's dispatch were promptly forwarded to Count Galvez, who had just taken over as Viceroy of Madrid and Captain General of Louisiana and the Floridas.[78] Galvez was so impressed with Fitch's invention that he immediately sent word about it to the governor and intendant of New Orleans. Thus, by the time Wilkinson arrived in that city, Miró and Navarro were well aware that the Mississippi could before long be navigable upstream as well as downstream, and that this might well shift the balance of power in the entire trans-Alleghenian region. They will also have realized that the Kentuckians would soon be clamouring even louder than before to be released from their commercial stranglehold.[79]

In his first meeting with Miró and Navarro, Wilkinson volunteered to elaborate his ideas about the future relations between Kentucky and the Spanish territory into a 'memorial'. He finished this document in the course of August and formally submitted it on 5 September.[80] The memorial makes it absolutely clear that it was Wilkinson, not Miró, who first proposed the Spanish Conspiracy. In the first part of his memorial he gives an outline of the general political situation in Kentucky, arguing that the dissatisfaction of the Kentuckians with Congress and the rapid growth of the population in the West will inevitably lead to 'a distinct confederation of the western inhabitants'. But he warns the Spanish that upon gaining independence, the Kentuckians will resort to any means to gain the free navigation of the Mississippi – even if that meant calling upon the British for assistance and putting themselves under their protection. He then plunges into a discussion of 'what ought to be the policy of the Spanish court at this critical juncture'. Most crucially, he says, Gardoqui should 'without hesitation peremptorily and absolutely refuse to Congress the Navigation of the Mississippi'. Seeing that the settlers in the Ohio Valley would 'continue subordinate and look up for protection to that power which secures them this most precious privilege', Spain would help itself by helping the western settlers if they withheld access to the Mississippi from the United States and gave it to Kentucky and other American western settlements instead. A confederation of viable, independent western states would in effect create a buffer between the Louisiana territory and the United States – thus ensuring that the Atlantic United States would remain just that. It would also prevent Kentucky from allying itself to Great Britain – which, were that to occur, would inevitably mean that Spain would lose the Louisiana territory to Britain, and probably Mexico as well. In a key passage in the memorial Wilkinson states that, since the 'leading characters of Kentucky' have 'urged and intreated' him to undertake this mission to New Orleans in order 'to discover, if practicable, whether [Spain] would be willing to open a negociation for [their] admission to her protection as subjects', he is 'persuaded the People of this District, so soon as they have organized a Government of their own, will make a formal application to the court of Spain'. Wilkinson would not be Wilkinson if he did not conclude his memorial by requesting a small personal favour in exchange for exerting his political weight in Kentucky in support of the proposed plan, that is, whether he could get permission to appoint an agent in the city who might receive and sell on his behalf cargoes of 'Negroes, live Stock, tobacco, Flour, Bacon, Lard, Butter, Cheese tallow, [and] Apples', to the amount of $50–60,000.

A day after they received the general's memorial, Miró and Navarro sent him a formal reply. They had already permitted him to land and sell the cargo he had brought into New Orleans in July and return home with the proceeds of $35,000, and now granted him permission to send a consignment of goods for sale in the city, albeit only up to half the sum he had suggested. They also stipulated that the proceeds of the transaction were to remain in the provincial treasury until the King of Spain should have ratified their plan.[81] Having agreed to stay in touch with his new Spanish friends in 'one of the most incomprehensible of ciphers', Wilkinson left New Orleans for the Ohio Valley by way of Charleston and Philadelphia on 16 September.[82] Returning to Kentucky 'in a chariot, with four horses, and several slaves', Wilkinson was welcomed like a general after a successful campaign and was hailed by many as a hero who had single-handedly opened up the Mississippi to his countrymen.[83] For even though the permit to trade with New Orleans was a personal privilege to the general, few doubted but that a more general permit would soon follow. Humphrey Marshall was among those who suspected from the start that Wilkinson and the Spanish authorities in New Orleans had agreed on a 'double plot', whereby an ostensibly commercial scheme that gave Wilkinson and his friends the exclusive privilege to trade with Spanish Louisiana concealed a political plot aimed at severing the West from the union and turning it into a Spanish protectorate.[84] Miró and Navarro's report confirms that Marshall's conjecture about a double plot was correct. Marshall was also right to surmise that the same double plot would allow Wilkinson to carry on his political intrigue for many years and finally escape punishment – all the while enriching himself and his associates. Even if Wilkinson's double plot had really been designed to delude the Spanish with 'grandiose undertakings as a means of realizing a profitable commercial speculation', as Miró conjectured at one point,[85] the general's reputation among the majority of Kentuckians would have suffered a fatal blow had they known that a few days before he submitted his memorial to Miró and Navarro, Wilkinson formally renounced his American citizenship. Pointing out in a separate statement that self-interest 'regulates the passions of nations as well as of individuals', Wilkinson concluded that no one could accuse him of breaking 'any law of nature or of nations, of conscience or of honor, in transferring [his] allegiance, from the United States to his Catholic Majesty'.[86]

When Wilkinson returned to Kentucky in February 1788, the ratification process for the federal constitution was in full swing. The separatists were strongly opposed to the new constitution because it was incompatible with their ambition to establish closer ties with Spanish Louisiana. A large majority of the people supported this view, and the April general election for the Kentucky convention was a landslide victory for the anti-federalists. The fact that the Virginia convention ratified the constitution on 25 June did not stop the 'Spaniardized republicans' – in Marshall's colourful language – from carrying on with their campaign for independence from the union.[87] On the contrary, the Kentucky convention met in July in a rebellious mood. When word arrived that Congress had just abandoned the process of admitting the District of Kentucky into the union as a separate state on the grounds that this was a decision to be taken by the new Congress under the new constitution, the convention in a defiant move decided to adjourn the session and meet again in November, after fresh elections, and with the express aim to obtain separation from the United States. In the intervening time, the 'Spanish Party' stepped up their campaign to organize public opinion in favour of separation, making the most of the Mississippi trade argument. Despite the fact that Virginia had ratified the new constitution, John Brown, Kentucky's only delegate to Congress, was having private meetings in New York with Gardoqui, during which the latter assured him 'that if Kentucky [would] declare her independence, and empower some proper person to negotiate with him, that he ha[d] authority, and [would] engage to open the navigation of the Mississippi, for the exportation of their produce, on terms of mutual advantage'.[88] All the while, Harry Innes, attorney general for the District, was in frequent communication with the Spanish authorities at Natchez, using a network of trusted agents going up and down the Mississippi delivering secret messages.[89]

At the start of the November convention, the scene was set for the separatist coup d'état. The Spanish party was now openly calling for a declaration of independence, the immediate introduction of an independent government, and a treaty with Spain for the navigation of the Mississippi; the Federalists were screaming 'high treason'. Evidently feeling certain of victory, Wilkinson read the full text of his address to the intendant of Louisiana to the delegates at the convention; on 10 November he submitted the address to Congress that Imlay later reprinted in his *Topographical Description*. It was ultimately their overconfidence that made the separatists overshoot their mark. For, once it became clear to the people of Kentucky that Wilkinson and his associates were about to take the district out of the union and into an uncertain future connection with Spain, public opinion began to shift and turned against the general's party. Fearing a popular uprising against any formal proposal to establish an independent government in Kentucky, Wilkinson decided to back down. The convention eventually agreed on a watered down petition addressed to the Virginia General Assembly – not Congress – in which the representatives once more requested to be admitted into the union as an independent state.

Although an immediate constitutional crisis had been averted, this was by no means the end of foreign intrigue in Kentucky. In fact, Spain, France and Britain were all actively involved in shaping the political future of the West in the autumn of 1788. In the course of 1788, Pierre d'Argès had come to Kentucky on a secret mission from Gardoqui, the main purpose of which was to colonize the Lower Mississippi by tempting settler families to leave Kentucky in exchange for liberal grants of land and other benefits.[90] At the Falls of the Ohio D'Argès formed an acquaintance with Pierre Tardiveau, a wealthy French trader who two years before had put before his own government a scheme for the seizure of New Orleans and Louisiana.[91] And in October 1788 Colonel John Connolly arrived in Kentucky from Detroit on a secret mission to turn Kentucky into a British protectorate. Under the guise of trying to locate lands he once owned near the Falls of the Ohio, Connolly was to assist the western settlers in obtaining navigation of the Mississippi by equipping and arming a force of ten thousand men to move down the river against New Orleans, where they were to receive support from a British fleet. These foreign intrigues would continue for a few years and only finally peter out after the July 1789 Kentucky convention – during what has been described as 'a fortunate and most opportune lull of personal enmities and political bitternesses' – finally managed to send an unequivocal request to the Virginia general assembly to become an independent state.[92] The Virginia Assembly thereupon swiftly passed the final Act of Separation on 18 December 1789, thereby establishing relative political stability in the Kentucky District.[93]

Yet even this did not deter Wilkinson and his 'zealous partizans of Spain' from making fresh efforts to separate Kentucky from the United States.[94] Thus, after his first memorial had elicited only a lukewarm response from the Council of State in Spain, Wilkinson produced a second 'memorial' in September 1789, in which he proposes a scheme for the encouragement of emigration from the American settlements in the Ohio Valley to Louisiana.[95] The aim was to spread the Spanish influence in the Ohio Valley, so that, after they had separated themselves from Virginia, the American settlers would readily agree to establish closer ties Spain, first through a commercial treaty with that nation, and then, by converting Kentucky, and possibly Tennessee, into a Spanish province.[96] In order to make the annexation of Kentucky by Spain go as smoothly as possible, he devised a detailed plan for the wholesale bribery of prominent men ('nota-bles') in the Kentucky and Tennessee region, and, for full measure, added a list of suitable pensioners and the sums of money to be paid to those who should be 'pledged to the interests of His Catholic Majesty'.[97] Having been offered $100,000 to distribute for the good cause and drawing a personal pension of $2,000 a year, Wilkinson was involved in further attempts to revolutionize the West in 1795 and 1797–8. His separatist activities were to culminate, of course, in the extraordinary 'Burr Conspiracy' of 1806, which, had it not been for the fact that Wilkinson, at the time commanding general of the United States Army, defected and turned state witness against Burr, might well have caused the entire western part of the United States to separate from the East and be united to Spanish Louisiana.

* * *

It is very tempting to speculate – as, indeed, earlier commentators have done with some abandon – that Gilbert Imlay was somehow actively involved with General Wilkinson in the Spanish plot.[98] Since he had been closely associated with some of the leading figures in Kentucky's secessionist intrigues – notably James Wilkinson, Benjamin Sebastian and Harry Innes – and had known several others connected with it, there can be little doubt that Imlay was fully abreast of the secessionist scheme that was being hatched by Wilkinson and his cronies. However, at the end of the day, no conclusive evidence – indeed, no evidence of any kind – has come to light to suggest that Imlay was one of Wilkinson's aides, agents or spies in the Spanish plot of the latter part of the 1780s. If they were in communication during this time, it would have to have been by mail or messen-ger, for there is no indication that Imlay ever returned to Kentucky after he left the district some time in the autumn of 1785; for his part, Wilkinson never left Kentucky except for his trip down to New Orleans, from April 1787 to Febru-ary 1788. However, extensive scrutiny of Wilkinson's letters and other papers has not yielded any indication that the two men were in correspondence with each other in the 1780s, nor, indeed, after that period.[99] What can be stated with considerable confidence is that Imlay's *Topographical Description* was crucially informed by the geopolitical ambitions and intrigues that had held Kentucky in its sway in the late 1780s and that its author was entirely sympathetic towards the secessionists' endeavours to keep Kentucky and the West out of the union. In that sense, the ghost of General Wilkinson is felt in almost every aspect of Imlay's topography of the western territory.

In contrast to the majority of American and European topographers (with the exception of John Fitch), it is therefore with some authority that Imlay in Letter IV offers us a plan for the 'partition the country west of the Ohio into sep-arate States'.[100] Ignoring Hutchins's rectangular system of land platting, whereby land was divided into squares of one mile with meridian lines, Imlay maps out the 'imaginary boundaries of six new States' on the basis of a combination of topographical and economical data, notably the courses of the region's major rivers and its mountain systems, and the quality of the soil.[101] Interestingly, Imlay's projection of the six new states (an area now roughly covered by three states – Ohio, Indiana and Illinois) turned out to have more prognostic value than Fitch's grid-like partitioning of the north-west (Fitch, following Jefferson's ordinance of 1784, projected ten new states in the area). Imlay was also right in his conjecture that even though it was considered as belonging to 'the empire of Spain', the country in the fork of the Mississippi and Missouri rivers would be settled before the north-western part of what is now Illinois: the Louisiana-Missouri territory was created in 1805, that of Illinois in 1809. Evidently aware of the contemporary geopolitical sensitivities in the area, Imlay refrains from making any territorial claims west of the Mississippi: 'I will not be so indecorous as to parcel out the territories of other nations: it is sufficiently presumptuous to have gone so far as I have'.[102]

Imlay may have disagreed with Fitch in his assessment of how the north-western lands would ultimately be partitioned into new states, but he certainly shared Fitch's view that 'in one century, the west would be the centre and the Atlantic States the suburbs of the nation'.[103] The key contributing factor to development of the region would be the rapid growth of the population in the West, which, Imlay claims, 'has not only astonished America itself, but it must amaze Europe, when they enter in the views and increase of this growing empire'.[104] Kentucky, in particular, he goes on to observe, has shown a spectacular growth of its population. Although it had not been permanently settled until 1780, by 1792 the district contained at least 100,000 inhabitants, and the whole of the western region around 400,000.[105] If the population of Virginia was to double every 27¼ years, as Jefferson had calculated in his *Notes*, Imlay is convinced that the rate of doubling in Kentucky would be closer to 15 years. Whereas it would take 96 years for the population of Virginia to grow to between 6 and 7 million, the population in the west would be 6.4 million within 60 years. The reasons for this were obvious, according to Imlay. In the East, wars and foreign migration were a constant constraint on population growth. At the same time, slavery had rendered white men dissolute and idle, causing marriages to be 'less early, and less frequent'.[106] Being protected by the Allegheny Mountains, the western territory was free from these evils: 'Thus secured from wars, and the inland navigation of the country not subjecting us to material losses in that business; with the propensity to early marriages, produced by the simplicity and innocence of youth, tutored under the pure maxims of virtue and reason; it cannot be considered as a sanguine calculation, when we add the additional consideration of the probable number of emigrants we may receive, that our population will double once in fifteen years'.[107]

Imlay may claim that it was his primary aim in the *Topographical Description* to 'convey information' rather than to be 'agreeable' or otherwise biased,[108] yet it is obvious that his discussion of the relative population growth rates in the eastern states and the western territory takes on a significant ideological dimension. In this sense his handling of the population theme does not differ materially from the way in which Jefferson enlisted the duplication rate of Virginia's population in his rebuttal of Buffon's theory of American degeneracy.[109] 'It has been universally remarked', Thomas Robert Malthus similarly reflected on the earlier transatlantic population debates in *An Essay on the Principle of Population*, 'that all new colonies settled in healthy countries, where there was plenty of room and food, have constantly increased with astonishing rapidity in their population ... A plenty of rich land, to be had for little or nothing, is so powerful a cause of population as to overcome all other obstacles.'[110] However, Imlay goes beyond the population debate per se by establishing a link between Kentucky's remarkable population growth and the contemporaneous debate in Britain between the advocates for the perfectibility of man and society and those wanting to maintain the present order or things. Thus, his geopolitical vision of the western territory as an inland utopia in which the remarkable ratio of population growth is a measure of that society's idealist system of equality, moral purity and enlightened thought predates similar, albeit more ambitious and more radical claims regarding the organic perfectibility of man in society propounded by William Godwin in his *Enquiry Concerning Political Justice* (1793) and by Condorcet in his *Esquisse d'un tableau historique des progrès de l'esprit humain* (1795). Malthus's *Essay* was one of the most consistently argued denunciations of the 'perfectibility' thesis, according to which, as Malthus put it, 'population increases exactly in the proportion, that the two great checks to it, misery and vice, are removed; and that there is therefore no truer criterion of the happiness and innocence of a people, than the rapidity of their increase.'[111] On the basis of this argument, perfectibilism maintained that it was within the power of mankind to eradicate social evil by creating a society in which there is absolute equality among its members in terms of property, wealth and subsistence. Malthus famously retorted by arguing that 'the power of population is indefinitely greater than the power in the earth to produce subsistence for man' – the former increasing in a geometrical ratio (by multiplication), and the latter in an arithmetical ratio (by addition).[112] Accordingly, Malthus dismissed Godwin's and Condorcet's 'system of equality' as 'little better than a dream, a beautiful phantom of the imagination. These "gorgeous palaces" of happiness and immortality, these "solemn temples" of truth and virtue will dissolve, "like the baseless fabric of a vision", when we awaken to real life, and contemplate the true and genuine situation of man on earth'.[113] There can be little doubt that Malthus would have dismissed Imlay's perfectible American Arcadia with equal vigour.

The socially progressive agenda of the *Topographical Description* is reflected amongst other things in its emphatic condemnation of slavery. Imlay devotes an entire letter to the plight of the slaves in the Atlantic American states (Letter IX), although his late involvement in the triangular trade suggests he did so less from conviction than from expediency. While there had been a groundswell of support for the abolition of the slave trade before 1789, the French Revolution had given the abolition movement added impetus. Under the banner of the rights of man ideology, the issues of black freedom and Jacobin levelling and political reform began to blur in the minds of many plebeian radicals, causing the abolition movement to adopt elements of popular agitation. Thus Letter IX opens by praising the 'virtue and humanity' of all those in England who were participating in the boycott of West Indian sugar out of protest against Parliament's refusal to pass legislation abolishing the slave trade.[114] It singles out for special praise the unnamed author of a 'little pamphlet' that had instigated the sugar boycott. William Fox's 1791 pamphlet *An Address to the People of Great Britain on the Propriety of Abstaining from West India Sugar and Rum* had created quite a stir among reformist circles in Britain. Imlay was therefore by no means alone in identifying the sugar boycott as an act of Jacobin civil disobedience, on the grounds that the consumption of West Indian sugar and rum – both heavily excised by the state – had helped finance 'the tyranny of [Pitt's] ministry'.[115]

In addition, the slavery issue allowed Imlay to dissociate his western utopia even further from the (allegedly) illiberal laws and immoral practices in the slave-owning states in 'Old' America, notably in Jefferson's Virginia. Thinly veiled as 'the narrator', Imlay informs his 'friend in England' that 'in contending for the birthright of freedom, we [the Americans] have learned to feel for the bondage of others; and, in the libations we offer to the bright goddess of liberty, we contemplate an emancipation of the slaves in this country, as honourable to themselves as it will be glorious to us'.[116] And just to make sure his English friend will not mistake Virginia's stance on slavery for that of America as a whole, he reminds him that slavery is 'contrary to our bill of rights, as well as repugnant to the code of nature'.[117] The narrator subsequently embarks on a lengthy and scathing attack on Jefferson's views on slavery as expressed in his *Notes on the State of Virginia*. Dismissing Jefferson's assessment that a complete emancipation of slaves in Virginia would be impractical for both 'political' and 'physical and moral' reasons, he accuses the statesman of entertaining 'disgraceful prejudices ... against the unfortunate negroes'.[118] According to the narrator, Jefferson's 'mind is so warped by education and the habit of thinking, that he has attempted to make it appear that the African is a being between the human species and the oran-outang'.[119] With evident disgust Imlay's spokesman dismisses Jefferson's quasi-biological hypotheses about the physiological reasons why the African's skin should be black, or whether blacks 'secrete less by the kidneys, and more by the glands of the skin'.[120] For his part, the narrator professes always to have admired the African's 'proportion, muscular strength, and athletic powers'. He punctuates his critique of what amounts to Jefferson's racial profiling by deriding Jefferson's remarks that 'Religion has ... produced a Phyllis Whately [Wheatley], but it could not produce a poet'.[121] The narrator defiantly deems Wheatley's poetic genius to be much superior to Jefferson's rational judgement.

In a final salute to his Jacobin British readership, Imlay ends Letter IX by expressing his devout wish that the 'dazzling rays of philanthropy' which are currently shining forth from Britain may expose Jefferson's 'paltry sophistry and non-sense' and that they will 'give a stab to the principles of domestic tyranny, and fix an odium upon those leachers of human blood, as flagrant as they are contemptible'.[122] Those enlightened citizens of Britain would presumably feel perfectly at home in the projected State of Kentucky, which, we are told in Letter VIII, is governed on purely Jacobin principles. Indeed, the chapter opens with a proclamation that is drawn verbatim from Articles II, IV and VI of the 'Declaration of the Rights of Man and of Citizens' which had been adopted by the French National Assembly on 26 August 1789 and which had subsequently been reprinted in Paine's *Rights of Man*: 'Our laws and government have for their basis the natural and imprescriptible rights of man. Liberty, security of person and property, resistance against oppression, doing whatever does not injure another, a right to concur, either personally or by our representatives in the formation of laws, and an equal chance of arriving to places of honour, reward, or employment, according to our virtues or talents, constitute those rights.'[123] Letter VIII contains a comprehensive statement on the Jacobin principles of government on which Kentucky's perfectible society has been – or will be – built. It is important to realize that when the narrator talks about the 'collected sentiments of the people upon the subject of law and government', he is talking about the people of Kentucky – *not* the people of the Atlantic United States; and that when he referring to 'the principles of our constitution', he is *not* referring to the constitution of the United States, nor even that of Kentucky (which was only framed in April 1792), but to the French constitution of 1791, and indirectly to the 'Declaration of the Rights of Man', on which it was founded and which it invokes in its preamble.[124]

Letter VIII constitutes Imlay's most explicit contribution to the 'mighty debate' then underway in Britain – with the difference that Imlay not only takes on Burke ('whose paradoxical book has found its way out here'), but also Jefferson's *Notes on the State of Virginia*.[125] Whilst he respects Jefferson for his 'cardinal virtues, as well as for the career he bore in the glorious struggles for American independence', he takes him to task for his elitist principles of government, which he attributes to Jefferson having been educated 'when aristocratical opinions were common'.[126] Imlay is particularly dismissive of Jefferson's critique of popular governments and of his clinging to the 'despotic' idea that a nation's political leaders should be chosen from a natural aristocracy. It is 'lamentable', he observes, that Jefferson and other 'men of talents and genius, who have acquired celebrity among the friends of freedom, should, by vainly circulating their crude sentiments, retard the progress of reason'.[127] According to Imlay, men like Jefferson just go to prove the validity of Paine's observation that 'the age of aristocracy, like that of chivalry, should fall'.[128] It is evident from the text that Imlay had carefully read Paine's *Rights of Man*, which had appeared in March 1791. Not only does he fully subscribe to Paine's notion of the natural and inalienable rights of man, but he is also a strong supporter of the idea of the social contract: 'Government is a compact entered into by every community for the security of the happiness and prosperity of the State; every member of which is one of the aggregate body of that State; therefore laws ought to emanate from the sentiments of the people'.[129] Whereas Jefferson had argued that the General Assembly of Virginia should assume 'all the powers legislative, executive, and judiciary', the fabric of government in Imlay's Western democracy is characterized most of all by the strict division of legislative, executive and judiciary powers. In order for them to 'be a mutual check upon each other', Kentucky's Assembly will have 'two houses of representatives' (a house of delegates and a senate), which will annually elect a 'President of the State'.[130] But it was Imlay's manifesto on Kentucky's remarkably progressive system of laws and its independent judiciary that was particularly controversial in the political climate of the day. Coming on the heels of the Lafayette's 1789 'Declaration' and the 1791 constitution, Imlay's levelling proposal for a democratized judiciary would have been highly controversial in Britain in 1792:

> The judiciary power the people never parted with entirely, and the executive by the agents of the representatives, qualified to judge of the laws and nature of our particular constitution, is not only a custom, but forms a part of the government. It is one of the springs by which the harmony of the system is preserved; and should it at any time be destroyed, it is the people who are to rectify the abuse. They are the potential fountain of all power; and it is only necessary for them and their agents to know this, in order to prevent every danger of the wheels of government being clogged and impeded by the destruction of any one of its essential springs.[131]

Claiming that in Europe '[p]risons and dungeons have been perverted into both asylums for rapine and fraud', Imlay is equally opposed to a criminal code that turns mere offenders into hardened criminals. In Imlay's democratic republic of Kentucky, however, the 'State is the tutelary guardian of its citizens, the protector of innocence, the promoter of felicity and prosperity, the avenger of wrongs; and not the spoiler of comfort, and the tyrant of humanity'. Rather than being merely punitive, the laws in Kentucky will therefore be 'calculated to prevent distress from intemperance and folly, and the commission of crimes, as much

as possible'. In fact, he envisions a legal regime in which 'prisons are unneces-
sary, except for homicides and traitors'. Nor will in Kentucky the law allow the
authorities to 'rob the family of the property of the offender, by forfeiture of
lands and goods to the State', no matter how serious the crime.[132]

* * *

The first edition of the *Topographical Description* was widely reviewed in Britain,
with four reviews appearing in major British periodicals within five months of its
publication, and another two in the following year.[133] In America, no reviews as
such appeared, although both Matthew Carey's *American Museum; or, Universal Magazine* and William Young's *Universal Asylum and Columbian Magazine*
printed extracts from Letter V of Imlay's text in November 1792, while the *New
York Magazine; or, Literary Repository* published all but one paragraph of Letter
VII in September 1793.[134] The British reviews confirm that the first edition of
the *Topographical Description* appeared in what in retrospect can be described as
the onset of the 'Revolutionary Debate' that would soon come to dominate the
1790s. At a time when the French Revolution was for many in Britain still the
beacon of a new social and political order, accounts of the enlightened republic
that the Americans had established following their own Revolution were generally well received in the British press at the time. Thus, Brissot de Warville's
strong endorsement of American liberty in his *Nouveau Voyage dans les Etats-
Unis* had been warmly welcomed by Mary Wollstonecraft in her review of the
book for the *Analytical Review* in September 1791.[135] Appearing in the wake
of Joel Barlow's translation of Brissot's *Nouveau Voyage*, which had been published in February 1792, Imlay's *Topographical Description* also elicited generally
positive comments from the press. According to the reviewer for the *European
Magazine*, Imlay's book was 'of considerable importance to the Philosopher, the
Politician, and the Moralist'. He went on the say: 'It discloses a variety of facts
which astonish a mind unaccustomed to contemplate the laws of nature, of civil
polity, and the sublime system of Christian morality: it unfolds some principles
which, from their speciousness and novelty, are well worthy the consideration of
all classes of men'.[136] Enthused by Imlay's sanguine account of American society,
the *Critical Review* comments that 'On the other side of the Atlantic ... [m]en
possessing the knowledge of this enlightened æra, availing themselves of the
experience of ages, of the benefits and misfortunes attending different political
systems, have united without the ties which continue to interrupt, without the
difficulties which have perplexed Europeans, without the impediments, which
in their progress to improvement, *they* must have felt. As a political system, in
a new and untried situation, the Americans will afford to future ages, an example to guard from error, or a lesson of instruction'. The reviewer praises Imlay
as an author whose 'language is bold and clear; pointed, and often elegant. It

is the language of a man whose ideas are not confused, and whose opinions are matured by reflection.' And while he notes that the narrative sometimes 'rises to a degree of elevation' that must be described as 'suspicious', the reviewer deems this 'a slight, a pardonable exaggeration', concluding that '[o]n the whole, the facts in this work are highly valuable'.[137]

As may be expected from what was then the most radical of British periodicals, in a lengthy account the *Analytical Review* praises Imlay's book for its socially progressive agenda. The reviewer was particularly impressed with its description of America's liberal laws: 'While perusing this publication, we were forcibly struck with the great respect paid in America to personal liberty; the extreme care and attention in criminal cases towards the life of a citizen, and that happy and advantageous simplification of the laws, which precludes the vexatious delays, and expensive and ruinous litigations, that disgrace European governments in general, and that of England in particular'.[138] If the *Analytical Review* was Britain's leading shaper of public opinion, the *Monthly Review* aspired to be a guardian of conventional taste and opinion: hence it took a slightly more critical view of publications advocating social and political liberalism, especially when these could be construed to be anti-British. While the reviewer grants that the author's 'intimate knowledge of the interior parts of North America appears in every page of his work', he censures Imlay for depicting 'uncultivated nature' as a pastoral Arcadia, much in the same way as 'the ancient poets' of the 'golden age' did. The reviewer was savvy enough to see that, like Crèvecoeur's *Letters of an American Farmer*, Imlay's American letters were ultimately intended 'to invite emigrants' to settle in America. While the reviewer for the *Monthly Review* also praises Imlay's 'system of jurisdiction' as reflecting 'the dictates of sound sense and salutary policy, uninfluenced by old mistaken habits, and unfettered by precedents', he adds this warning note: 'however correct certain principles may appear on an abstract view, yet, in reducing them to practice, the conflict of interests and passions, which cannot be sufficiently known while we are framing general systems, will cause speculative plans to operate to a disadvantage on comparison with a constitution, which, however it originated, has grown with a people, as peculiar situations and exigencies dictated'.[139] The clash between 'system' and 'constitution', between the ideology of the Old and the New World would soon come to dominate the Revolutionary Debate in Britain.

6 JACOBIN NOVELIST AND DEFENDER
OF THE RIGHTS OF WOMAN

There is no reciprocality in the laws respecting matrimony

Gilbert Imlay, *The Emigrants*[1]

If the transformation from a hapless Kentucky land-jobber to a best-selling London topographer had been an unlikely change of fortune, Imlay's reinventing himself as a writer of political-sentimental fiction was at first sight an even more startling metamorphosis. Yet, in the experimental and highly politicized print culture of the 1790s, such genre crossing was by no means exceptional. Indeed, to the utmost chagrin of their conservative opponents, generic fluidity became something of a conscious discursive strategy among many radical authors. These Jacobin literati had recently discovered that aesthetic eclecticism allowed them to break up conventional moulds and modes of thinking, while it at the same time rendered their ideas less susceptible to anti-Jacobin satire and diatribe. The best-known cross-genre political writer was William Godwin. In his novel *Things As They Are; or, The Adventures of Caleb Williams* (1794), Godwin notoriously blended the discourses of political thought with various modes of popular fiction to create that 'diabolical' fabrication which the anti-Jacobins referred as a 'political novel' – an oxymoronic novelty they believed was aesthetically disgusting, morally revolting and ideologically suspect. Thus, Henry James Pye in his anti-Jacobin novel *The Aristocrat*:

> Such are the arts of the poet to interest his readers, and commendable is such art when used to inculcate virtuous principles, or even to afford innocent amusement. But diabolical is the attempt to collect and connect every possible event in such a manner, as to produce a probable series of incidents that shall make mankind dissatisfied with their natural or political situation, or plead an excuse for the breach of fidelity and chastity.[2]

Sympathizers of the radical school hailed the generic and ideological promiscuity of the 'political romance' as a radical modernization of the literary discourse. William Enfield was quick to note the potential of Godwin's *Caleb Williams* as a tool to popularize political debate in a sympathetic review for the Jacobin *Monthly Review*:

> Between fiction and philosophy there seems to be no natural alliance: – yet philoso-
> phers, in order to obtain for their dogmata a more ready reception, have often judged
> it expedient to introduce them to the world in the captivating dress of fable ... [*Caleb
> Williams*] is singularly entitled to be characterized as a work in which the powers of
> genius and philosophy are strongly united.[3]

However, though by no means a novelist and literary innovator of the stature of Godwin, the accolade for being the first novelist to cross the divide between political treatise and sentimental romance has to go to Gilbert Imlay and his Jacobin novel *The Emigrants*.

Imlay's *The Emigrants* was published on 12 March 1793, only days after William Godwin's magnum opus *Enquiry Concerning Political Justice* had gone on sale – a fact that was not lost upon contemporary readers of the novel.[4] Reviewers of both Jacobin and anti-Jacobin persuasion quickly picked up on the novel's double-barrelled political message of republican-style government and equal rights for women: two issues that also lay at the heart of Godwin's treatise on political justice – at least in the popular perception of it. While clearly not in the same league as Godwin's *Enquiry*, Imlay's novel catered for the same radical audience and aspired to a similar utopian ideal of a post-revolutionary paradise.

The chief exponent of British radicalism, Godwin single-handedly and almost overnight lifted the Revolutionary Debate to a philosophical level not seen before in British political discourse and whose impact on the age was so dramatic that it nearly pitched Britain into civil war. 'No work in our time gave such a blow to the philosophical mind of the country as the celebrated *Enquiry Concerning Political Justice*', William Hazlitt observed retrospectively in 1825; 'Tom Paine was considered for the time as a Tom Fool to him, Paley an old woman, Edmund Burke a flashy sophist. Truth, moral truth, it was supposed, had here taken up its abode; and these were the oracles of thought.'[5] Without any compromise to 'natural and generous feelings', Godwin unfolded his principles of Reason and Truth. The *Enquiry* took abstract reason 'for the rule of conduct', Hazlitt remarked, 'and abstract good for its end'. The 'narrow ties of sense, custom, authority, private and local attachment' were sacrificed in the 'boundless pursuit of universal benevolence'. 'Gratitude, promises, friendship and family affection' had to give way, and the void was to be 'filled up by the disinterested love of good and the dictates of inflexible justice, which is "the law of laws and the sovereign of sovereigns"'.[6]

Godwin's manifesto of rational anarchism could not have appeared at a more critical time. Between the fall of the Bastille and the publication of the *Enquiry*, the political situation had gone through a rapid development from democratization and social reform to renewed repression and public violence. The National Assembly, which formed France's effective national government between 1789 and 1791, had adopted the 'Declaration of the Rights of Men' and drafted a new constitution creating a limited monarchy. After Louis XVI had accepted the new constitution in October 1791, the new legislative body, the Constituent Assembly, pushed through major legislative reforms, including administrative and church reform, the abolition of feudalism and economic liberalization. Increasingly, however, the Assembly was marked by a bitter struggle between two factions: the moderate Girondists, mainly backed by the emergent middle class and led by Brissot; and the more radical Jacobins, who represented the vindictive lower classes and were headed by Robespierre, Marat and Danton. The Jacobins gradually succeeded in getting the upper hand over their opponents and soon violence once more erupted. In September 1792 the people invaded the prisons and slaughtered over twelve hundred aristocratic prisoners (the September Massacres), on the pretext that the inmates had been plotting a reactionary counter-revolution. Shortly afterwards, the Jacobins abolished the monarchy and put the king on trial for treason. The beheading of Louis XVI on 21 January 1793 sent shudders down the spine of the British establishment; it was followed almost immediately by France declaring war on Britain and the Dutch Republic on 1 February.

Imlay's Jacobin novel *The Emigrants* was immediately drawn into the maelstrom of political controversy that erupted in the wake of the Anglo-French war. Reflecting the growing spirit of nationalism in Britain, conservative readers and reviewers described the novel's political agenda as 'foreign' – a pernicious blend of American popular democracy and French sexual mores. Thus, while it had been lavish in its praise of the *Topographical Description*, the Tory *Critical Review* commented disapprovingly on *The Emigrants* along xenophobic lines: 'This work has two objects professedly in view, the one to recommend the government and manners of America, in preference to those of our own country – the other, to recommend divorces'.[7] The reviewer decidedly rejects the former proposal as an insult to British liberty and morality, and labels the latter as 'insidious' and a threat to English marriage laws, arguing that the introduction of more liberal divorce laws would 'inevitably degrade the [female] sex from the honourable companions of men, to the instruments of their looser pleasures, and slaves of their transient liking'.[8] The Whiggish *Monthly Review*, on the other hand, believed that Imlay's novel 'advances sentiments which will be generally approved by those, who are capable of divesting themselves of the powerful prejudices arising from self interest'.[9]

The Emigrants, or The History of an Expatriated Family is set partly in post-Revolutionary America – the action extends from September 1783 to July or September 1785 – and partly in 'pre-Revolutionary' Britain. It is an epistolary novel that combines a sentimental plot of impeded love with episodes of travel and adventure. The heroine, Caroline, is the daughter of an English merchant who takes his family to America following the loss of his fortune. Here she meets Captain James Arl—ton, a youthful veteran of the American Revolution, during the trip across the Allegheny Mountains into the Ohio Valley. Misunderstandings separate the lovers, and while Caroline remains in Pittsburgh, Arl—ton sets off down the Ohio to Louisville in 'a fit of expansionist pique'.[10] Arl—ton's wise friend G. Il—ray helps to sort things out, and the couple are reunited when Arl—ton rescues Caroline from a brief spell of Indian captivity. In the meantime, Caroline has also encountered an old man, who turns out to be her long-lost uncle, P. P—, who tells a harrowing tale of an unhappy marriage in England. Meanwhile, back in England, all is not well with the marriage of Caroline's sister Eliza, and towards the end of the novel we hear the sensational story of her separation from her brutal and dissolute British husband. In terms of geography, the course of the book moves from east to west, like the *Topographical Description* taking the emigrants from Philadelphia to Pittsburgh and down the Ohio to Louisville – the Allegheny mountains forming a topographical and moral watershed, with the 'chaste regions of innocence and joy' to the west while vice runs rife in Bristol and the east.[11] The symbolic geography mimics the transatlantic distinction the novel makes between European depravity and American innocence. Providing a utopian vision of the new world, the novel concludes with the marriage of the beleaguered couple, Caroline and Captain Arl—ton, who become the nucleus of a settler community on the banks of the Ohio, which is organized along radical, Godwinian notions of social justice. To complete the tale's felicitous denouement, Eliza joins the Bellefont community, having been whisked back across the Atlantic by the obliging Il—ray.

The Emigrants in many respects puts into fictional form the ideological concerns of the *Topographical Description*, although its underlying ideology of reform is more radical, and its geopolitical agenda more explicit. Thus, while downplaying any hint of personal interest and political ambition, the plot emphasizes the ease with which the emigrant may travel west and how an elaborate infrastructure of roads and waterways will be at his disposal once he arrives there. With its sentimental interest frequently being put to the service of its geopolitics, it is therefore no coincidence that *The Emigrants* at times reads more like a travelogue than a novel. Thus, the opening letters make much of the heroine's insistence to walk much of the way across the Allegheny Mountains, in sharp contrast to her lethargic brother, George, who prefers to be moved around on a wagon, along with the old people in the company. Even though Caroline's captivity by the Indians forces Arl—ton prematurely to abandon his frantic wilderness trip, the reader gets the distinct impression that moving across vast tracts of the rugged American landscape is not more arduous, and only slightly more risky, than a journey in rural England or a promenade in London, and certainly much more thrilling – sublime or picturesque sights presenting themselves at every twist and turn of the emigrant's tour. Coming across as a picturesque tourist rather than a hardy pioneer, Caroline muses, 'here is a continual feast for the mind'.[12]

Even more impressive than Caroline's rambles is Captain James Arl—ton's unstoppable wanderlust, which first takes him from Pittsburgh down the Ohio River to Louisville, and later further west, via St Vincent's (Vincennes) towards St Anthony's Falls and the sources of the Mississippi, from where he plans to travel down the river to Kaskaskia, then up the Missouri, back again to Kaskaskia, down the Mississippi to New Orleans, and from there back to Baltimore. What is more interesting than the extent and course of his western travels is the reason he sets out for the frontier in the first place. Initially, he mentions his intention of going down the Ohio after he has just received a coldly-worded note – ostensibly from Caroline, but in reality written by her jealous sister Mary – even though he has no idea what such a trip would involve. But it is only after a lengthy after-dinner private conversation with General W—, during which the two drink the best part of three bottles of old Madeira, that Arl—ton decides he should leave for the West 'without delay'.[13] Like Caroline, contemporary British readers may not have been able to interpret the coded discourse which Imlay uses to describe the communications between the general and his protégé. However, knowing what we now know about General Wilkinson's adventures in the West, it is obvious that Imlay's account of the episode of the two men's hour-and-a-half tête-à-tête is but a thinly-veiled reference to Wilkinson's trans-Alleghenian schemes. Thus, we learn that the general had 'in contemplation to remove to Louisiana in the spring', and that he wished 'to have an account of the country from a person' whom he could 'depend on'.[14] That the general had in mind a scheme far beyond merely making his fortune in trade becomes clear when he goes on to expatiate, 'in his usual way, upon what would be the brilliancy and extent of the empire which is forming in this part of the world [Kentucky]; which he said would eclipse the grandeur of the Roman dominion in the zenith of their glory'. If there is already a suggestion in the language used here of Wilkinson's geopolitical ambitions for the western territory (not to mention his verbosity and grandiloquence), we get a further hint that General W—'s 'empire' involves a strategic alliance with Spanish Louisiana. Puzzled as to why a man who had been so full of 'animated pleasure' had suddenly become so taciturn and distant (as well as half-way down the Ohio),[15] Caroline can only conclude that

> Something has intervened ... that made it necessary he should not repeat any thing
> upon the subject; for it is most likely, under the existing circumstances that governed
> his conduct, and to which it was his duty to attend, it would have been incompatible
> with his honour, and the object of his noble pursuits; – for I have understood, from

a casual conversation with General W—, that his object of visiting Louisiana is of the most patriotic kind.[16]

It is hard enough to imagine why a purely commercial mission to the western territory could possibly compromise Arl—ton's 'honour' as a veteran officer of the Revolutionary army, but it is even harder to see why General W— should want to point out to Caroline that Arl—ton's visit to Louisiana would be 'of the most patriotic kind'. Unless, of course, it was not quite so patriotic – from the union's point of view, that is.

Imlay's physiocratic, agrarian dream of an independent western state governed by the laws of reason and humanity is fulfilled in the utopian community founded by Arl—ton towards the end of *The Emigrants*. The unspoiled western territory affording 'an opportunity to its citizens of establishing a system conformable to reason and humanity', Arl—ton is confident that his 'model of a society' will be the nucleus of 'every civilized commonwealth' in the world.[17] For this purpose Arl—ton has purchased 'a tract of country lying upon the Ohio from the rapids of Louisville, and extending above Diamond Island [present-day Twelve Mile Island] to a point sixteen miles from its beginning, and running back an equal distance, which will constitute an area of two hundred and fifty-six square miles, or nearly, making an allowance for the bends of the river'.[18] This tract he will divided into 256 lots, each of which is to be settled by men who served with Arl—ton in the Revolutionary War (presumably because they are most likely to be men of honour and common sense). These men and their families will live in an idyllic, enchanting spot, against the background of the impetuous Ohio River, fertile meadows, whispering breezes and warbling birds. Having reserved six lots for himself and his closest friends, Arl—ton is to name his own estate 'Bellefont', after the gushing fountain that is at the centre of one of the lots. The days are to follow a regular routine of agricultural cultivation and rural relaxation, including much dancing to rustic music.

In socio-political terms, Arl—ton's riverside Arcadia is to be organized along radical, Godwinian notions of social and political justice. To guarantee absolute equality and liberty, each man owns the section of land that he occupies. All males over the age of twenty-one are entitled to vote for members of a house of representatives, who, in turn, elect a president. The latter is to hold office for only one year, and then has to remain out of office for at least seven years; thus 'every expectation of aggrandizement will fall to the ground, and love and harmony, must consequently be productive of every generous advantage; and the respectability of every citizen be established upon that broad basis – the dignity of man'.[19] A special assembly hall is to be built for the representatives, where they are to meet every Sunday throughout the year to discuss issues of agriculture, arts, government and jurisprudence. The Jacobin, anti-ecclesiastical Sunday meetings will have the added advantage that the members of the assembly will be 'prevented from listening to those itinerant preachers who travel about the country under the pretence of propagating the pure christian religion, but who are, in truth, the disturbers of domestic felicity, – the harbingers of hypocrisy, and whose incoherent sermons are a cloud of ignorance that too often spreads a gloom over the understanding of the uninformed, which nothing but the rays of reason can dispel, and which have too long darkened the intellect of mankind, and produced an obscurity of ideas that is truly lamentable'.[20] The constitutional arrangements and the separation of state and church advocated by Arl—ton confirm that his American Arcadia is to be a secessionist state, independent of the government of the United States, rooted in a tradition of French physiocratic thought, and turning south (*not* east), towards Louisiana, and beyond, towards Revolutionary France, for guidance and support. For if land and land ownership are key to the ideological aspirations of both the independent state of Kentucky and the western pioneer settler, that landed interest is never presented in terms of any Burkean notion of 'property'. Imlay's 'land' is first and foremost the mark and guarantee of republican liberty, equality and political justice. Unlike in Europe, where '[l]iberty, and the rights of men have been shamelessly profaned under the crude idea of the aggrandizement of commerce',[21] Imlay's radicals are essentially sustenance farmers, who, in the Marxist sense, by producing the crops that feed them, produce an idea – or ideal – of themselves, as well as the values that shape their society and give meaning to their lives.

It is within this radical economy of liberty and the rights of man that the novel develops its second major theme. Enthusiastically, *The Emigrants* 'espouse[s] the cause of oppressed women', especially the rights of women in marriage, which it ties to an anti-colonial agenda.[22] As it claims on the title page, the novel is 'A Delineation of English Manners'; it exposes marriage in England as a type of cultural captivity for women, and makes a plea for more liberal divorce laws. The treatment of women provides the most affecting example of the difference between Britain and America, and Imlay uses the issue of domestic politics to construct a utopian vision of American national character. The plot focuses particularly on two episodes of cultural captivity, both of which take place in Britain, which demonstrate the novel's key theme that 'There is no reciprocality in the laws respecting matrimony':[23] viz. the inset narrative of Caroline's uncle and his relationship with the married Juliana, and the story of Eliza.

The first of these stories runs for almost a fifth of the novel and has a complicated plot: set in England, the gist of it is that Caroline's uncle, P. P— Esq., is smitten with the tender Juliana, Lady B—, a 'beauty ... in tears', 'a victim to matrimonial tyranny', who constantly suffers 'violations of [her] dignity',[24] including the raucous behaviour of her husband's friends, the insolence of the domestic servants, and, not least, Lord B—'s predilection for drunken sex. During a

particularly moving rendition of Othello's 'put out the light' speech, Lady B—
faints into P. P—'s arms in a secluded alcove in the garden, as witnessed by the
footman. In what turns out to be a set-up (for financial and procreative reasons,
Lord B— wants to divorce his wife and marry someone else), Lord B— takes
out an action against Caroline's uncle for 'a criminal connection' with his wife.[25]
Refused entry to her parental home, Juliana takes refuge with her old nurse in
London; a jury awards damages of £10,000 against P—, which he cannot pay,
and thus spends the following decade in prison,[26] soothed only by the 'consola-
tion of [his] charming Juliana',[27] whom he marries after her divorce and by whom
he has seven children. Lord B—, his fortune gratifyingly dissipated by his new
wife, finally makes a settlement for damages of £500 and P— is released.

This narrative speaks to the ongoing cultural debates about the status of
women, and about the relation between gender and national identity. A number
of overlapping contemporary discourses foster Imlay's critique of sexual power
relations, especially the language of abolition, of Enlightenment rationalism,
and debates about the nature of political authority. Thus, Imlay makes use of
the familiar, emotive analogy between enslavement and the position of women,
whereby marriage is represented, in the words of the anonymous author of *The
Hardships of the English Laws in relation to Wives*, as 'a *State* of *Captivity*'.[28]
According to eighteenth-century British law, 'the very being or legal existence
of the woman is suspended during the marriage, or at least incorporated and
consolidated into that of the husband'.[29] Many writers, especially in the revolutionary 1790s, inveighed against the ignominy and injustice of this legal situation
which protected the right of property and male primogeniture at the expense of
female agency. Mary Wollstonecraft considered that woman was 'reduced to a
mere cypher' by this law. She alludes to 'the slavery of marriage' and cites 'matrimonial despotism of heart and conduct' as 'the peculiar Wrongs of Woman'. In
a general attack on established politics, Wollstonecraft also refers to the 'abominable traffick' of the slave trade, adding, in relation to the legal status of women,
that a 'more specious slavery ... chains the very soul of woman, keeping her forever under the bondage of ignorance'.[30] In Imlay's novel, Lady B— considers
herself '*bound* to my Lord by the ties of matrimony', despite the fact that Lord
B— thinks of women as 'a domestic machine'.[31] Observing their marriage, P.
P— has an insight into the 'state of degradation and misery' to which 'thousands
of amiable and sensible beings' are 'reduced',[32] using the vocabulary of abolition
to denounce marital tyranny. As in Wollstonecraft's writing, the attack on gender oppression is bolstered by a parallel attack on the slave trade: the father of
Miss R— (who is herself captured by a marriage plot), speaks out against slavery,
using the familiar trope of the disruption of family, and his daughter concurs
with his condemnation of the traffic in slaves, and hopes that an 'enlightened
government' will punish such 'Monsters'.[33]

The Emigrants also strategically adapts the language of political libertarianism and rationalist philosophy for a feminist position; like the rhetoric of enslavement and enlightenment, these debates provided a conceptual language from which to attack the tyranny of 'Custom', or what we would now call the ideological construction of gender. As Mary Robinson puts it in her *Letter to the Women of England on the Injustice of Subordination* (1799), 'The barbarity of custom's law in this *enlightened* country, has long been exercised to the prejudice of woman'.[34] The novel privileges a discourse of natural rights, what Caroline's uncle, in one of his explanatory, exculpatory letters to her about the Juliana affair, calls 'those absolute rights' which are 'antecedent to the formation of states' and which justify resistance to inhuman laws.[35] Caroline replies with the Burkean argument that in order to enter society men 'gave up part of their liberty ... to secure their more important rights'.[36] She initially presents the anti-divorce case, arguing that 'the laws respecting matrimony' may transgress 'the codes of nature', but that on them 'the tranquillity, safety, and happiness of society' depend. She argues that any liberalization of these laws would be tantamount 'to offering prizes to adultery, and instituting asylums for the incontinent'.[37] Thus, she describes her uncle's 'principles' as 'dangerous' (or revolutionary), they 'strike at the root of domestic quiet';[38] this is an argument that will be used again and again by conservative writers after 1793 when the fears engendered by the French Revolution retarded reform in any field for over three decades (by the time of Wollstonecraft's *Wrongs of Woman* (1798), such principles were explicitly described as 'French'). Yet, the reprehensible Lord B— argues, in almost identical language, that the '*tranquillity of society*' rests on the control of women, or what he calls '*tyranny*',[39] so that the reader is invited to make the link between individual and institutional oppression, between the beastly husbands of Il—ray's impassioned indictment of marital inequity and the sexual double standard, and the 'brutish legislators' of Arl—ton's reply to Il—ray's letter, both of which invite rational resistance.[40] To clinch the case, the specific historical moment of Juliana and P—'s bid for transatlantic liberty (they emigrate to America after P—'s release) coincides with the outbreak of the war between Britain and the colonies. The 'impolitic ... institutions' that drive patriotic Englishmen abroad, pursue the family to the back settlements where 'ferocious savages', the phrase comprehending both 'the authors of that unnatural war' and a literal band of Indians, kill Juliana and her seven children.[41]

Sympathizing with the sufferings of Juliana and her uncle, Caroline is won over from custom, or prejudice, to a belief in those 'principles' based on 'unalienable rights', figuring this change in terms of enlightenment, a movement from darkness to illumination of 'the region between prejudice and reason'.[42] She reflects on the institutions and laws which 'support the present practices respecting women and matrimony', and her thoughts dwell on the fate of Princess

Matilda of Denmark, the 'victim of political tyranny' and gender oppression.[43] The reader, like Caroline, is presumably similarly enlightened by Imlay's radical 'moral instruction'.[44]

Imlay thus capitalizes on a range of available sentimental and political discourses to expose the oppression of women. The novel's second story of an unhappy marriage, that of Caroline's sister Eliza, recapitulates many of the ideological points raised by the first story: this twice-told tale confirms the connection between Britain and gender oppression. Eliza is disgusted that, while living in a state of 'voluptuous richness', her husband Mr F— withholds any financial assistance from her impoverished family.[45] She 'contrast[s] the simple and sincere manners of the people of your hemisphere, with the studied ceremony of European customs' and laments that she, too, is not in 'those Arcadian regions' inhabited by her sister.[46] Eliza's husband neglects her, indulging in all sorts of extravagences (by implication, sexual as well as financial), until his finances are, as Il—ray puts it, completely 'deranged'.[47] Writing to Arl—ton, Il—ray describes Mr F—'s iniquitous behaviour:

> However he still flattered himself, that he had a resource in the charms of Mrs. F—, equal to redeem his ruined fortune, and give him permanent respectability; and as he had no belief there could be any dishonour in the proposal he meant to make, particularly as he had the example of many honourable gentlemen, he did not hesitate in consequence of an overture made him, by a nobleman in power, (who had only to charge cash expended in that way to secret service,) to propose to Mrs. F— the prostitution of her person.[48]

Like George Venables in Wollstonecraft's *Wrongs of Woman*, Mr F— attempts to barter his wife's body.[49] Mr F—'s attempt to prostitute his wife stands as the most despicable example in what is a more general critique of the economic basis of marriage and sexuality. We are reminded that in British law women are 'considered in the light of property' and that a separated wife may 'be subject to lose the very fortune she may have carried to her husband'.[50] Both Mr F—'s proposed sexual/financial transaction and Juliana's husband's action for criminal conversation are markers of a commercial society that contrasts with the chivalric one that the text supports.[51] The novel explicitly collates (British) marriage and prostitution: early in the novel, Miss Laura R— worries that she may have to marry Mr S—, a man who turns out to be tainted with all the vices of the Old World, because of the 'pecuniary distresses' of her father, and she fears the 'prostitution' of her feelings; Juliana refuses the 'most ignominious prostitution' of continuing to sleep with her brutal husband.[52] Ultimately, what is indicted is '[t]he prostitution of principle' in British political life, a public prostitution that poisons private life.[53] By implication, the American legislative system 'prevents the prostitution of principle'.[54] Apparently motivated only by commercial desires, the British body politic is enervated.[55] What turns out to be at stake is Britain's gender identity; the 'unmanly' behaviour of Mr F— and his supposed impotence parallel the emasculated state of his country.[56] Britain's commercial interests have 'contaminated' British hearts, producing '[e]very species of luxury' and '[e]ffeminacy has triumphed'.[57] P. P— 'blush[es] for the degeneracy of [his] countrymen', calling Mr F— 'a being' not '*a man*'.[58]

The Eliza episode includes a long disquisition on the difficulties of separation or divorce: Sir Thomas Morley informs Il—ray that Eliza 'could not be intitled to a bill of divorce, without she could either prove Mr. F—'s impotence or infidelity', which as Il—ray observes would be 'mortifying to a woman of sensibility'.[59] This case substantiates Imlay's prefatorial assertion about the great difficulty of obtaining a divorce in England, and one, as the novel makes clear, substantially more difficult for women than for men because of the sexual double standard. In fact, male infidelity would not have been grounds for a divorce and proving impotence in order to obtain a nullity was almost unheard of: in his table of cases at the London Consistory Court, Lawrence Stone records only seven cases between 1701 and 1720 and none between 1726 and 1857.[60] Stone also notes the exclusion of wives as petitioners, 'Between 1700 and 1800, no wife even attempted to break the male monopoly of Parliamentary divorce', and between 1827 and 1857 only three female petitions were successful: all involved either incest or bigamy as well as adultery.[61]

Imlay exploits the analogies between familial and international politics that pertained during the revolutionary period: as Jay Fliegelman argues, there was a close ideological connection between easier divorce laws and the political separation of the United States from Great Britain, institutionalized in the Declaration of Independence.[62] Certainly, to some people, the freedom to pursue life, liberty and happiness seemed to involve the right to be liberated by divorce from an unhappy marriage. Moreover, the belief in contractual relationships – by definition, open to dissolution – was '[c]entral to the rationalist ideology of the American Revolution'.[63] Divorce statutes passed by colonial assemblies had been contrary to the laws of England, and liable to veto; in 1773 such an act, passed by Pennsylvania, was disallowed by the Privy Council, and so came to play a modest part in the constitutional conflict. In the years after the war, the sentimental rhetoric of affectional and voluntaristic marriage was crucial to the affirmation of national character, and many texts, such as Royal Tyler's popular play *The Contrast* (1787), combine antipatriarchal and patriotic sentiment. Like Imlay's novel, the play contrasts 'a corrupt and luxurious England and a virtuous and hearty America'.[64] Perhaps most relevant here is the rhetoric of a pamphlet published in Philadelphia in 1788, *An Essay on Marriage or the Lawfulness of Divorce* (apparently the first such pamphlet in America). The writer defends divorce and permission for remarriage, quotes John Milton on 'domestic liberty' and draws an analogy between an unhappy marriage and slavery. America's (self-promoting) reputation as a freedom-loving land means that it should extend the 'same spirit of indulgence' to those constrained by marital 'bondage'.[65] Readerly sympathy for the distressed (the occasion of the essay was the suicide of an unhappily married woman) is conjoined with republican sympathy. *The Emigrants* explicitly offers emigration as the solution to marital inequity and as a means of validating sentimental experience that has no outlet in Britain: 'Put yourself under the protection of Mr. Il—ray', Caroline advises Eliza, 'and fly immediately from bondage to a land of freedom and love'.[66]

The novel proposes that the present British administration's resistance to reform may hasten its destruction, and that a third revolution may follow that of 1688 and the more recent American Revolution.[67] Conspicuously absent from this revolutionary genealogy is the French Revolution, which, of course, postdates the period in which the novel is set but not the period in which it was written and published, and which marks the novel's imbrication of national and gender discourses. The critique of British 'effeminacy' and impotence, both personal and political, is bound up with a triangulated set of national relations between Britain, France and America. Especially in the years after 1789, Britain defined itself as a manly nation, and broad attempts were made to emphasize the masculinity of English identity in opposition to that of the French, who were seen as the enemy and as effeminate. The French were regarded by the British as emotional, sensual, preoccupied with fashion and fancy food, and their country overrun by 'improper' women, either sexually promiscuous or 'manning' the barricades; the French Revolution itself could be seen, as Linda Colley puts it, as 'a grim demonstration of the dangers that ensued when women were allowed to stray outside of their proper sphere'.[68] National identity was frequently figured in terms of gender identity in the period, and both were fundamentally insecure in a hysterical political climate, as the defensive conservative reactions to pro-Revolutionary texts, especially those by British women, demonstrate. For example, writing republican history in her *Letters from France* (1790–6), Helen Maria Williams violated sexual and generic decorum and offended national political sensibilities, and she is castigated by Richard Polwhele as 'an intemperate advocate for Gallic licentiousness', taking her place with the other significantly 'unsex'd females' of his poem's title.[69] However, Britain's own status as an 'enlightened', rational and 'manly' nation is represented as compromised, in *The Emigrants* (and elsewhere), by the institutional oppression of women within marriage. Imlay imports other racial stereotypes, notably references to the East which bring with them hints of sexual ambiguity (along with the more obvious reference to irrational and unprogressive social practices), to characterize British corruption; thus, 'the tyranny of [its] laws' are analogous to those of 'a Turkish despotism [designed] to produce fidelity among women'.[70] By contrast, the 'Arcadian regions' of America offer a model of civil society, by implication one in which gender differences are more secure than in Britain or France. The 'more manly progeny' of the new world are indignant at the 'gothic tyranny' of British legislation, and offer a haven for oppressed women.[71] Thus, Imlay both inverts and transfers the gender paradigm promoted by conservative Britain from a cross-Channel (Britain/France: masculine/feminine) to a transatlantic one (America/Britain: masculine/feminine). Thus, America demonstrates a superior manliness while Britain languishes in a state of effeminate impotence.

However, alongside what should rightly be seen as a feminist critique of gender and national identities, the sexual-political agenda remains somewhat limited, the point being that, in Il—ray's words, 'the charms of fine women can only be relished by men who have not been enervated by luxury and debauchery'.[72] The novel's revolutionary critique of Britain's marriage and divorce laws rests on a potentially conservative (indeed, Burkean) rhetoric of chivalry, that is, the manly protection of beauty and virtue in distress.[73] Thus, while the novel may be said to pursue that strand of Enlightenment history that linked cultural progress with female emancipation, the emancipatory trajectory is oddly compromised, as is shown by a brief comparison with William Alexander's *History of Women* (1779). Alexander calibrates the condition of women and a country's place in the scale of civil society, and he compares what he regards as the 'privileges and immunities' of British women, which are secured by British laws, with the condition of European women, 'complimented and chained' by the codes of chivalry.[74] Imlay redresses the *dis*privileges of British women with a good dose of chivalry. A chivalric attitude characterizes Il—ray's theoretical indictment of marital oppression, which he puts into practice in his treatment of Eliza, and which motivates P—'s response to Juliana (as well as his outrage at the sacrifice of 'the most lovely woman in the world [Princess Matilda] to state politics');[75] the community established at the end of the novel is made up solely of military men who served in the Revolution, and who are idealized in order to serve this paradigm of gender relations. There are constant references to women's 'delicacy' and 'sensibility', they are 'helpless beings ... whose weakness demands [men's] most liberal support'.[76] There is a slippage between women's civil 'weakness' and other forms of cultural debility; the novel enlists support for a 'liberal system' that would give 'reciprocity to conjugal engagements',[77] but such a system would be predicated on male protection of women, a protection enacted most dramatically in Arl—ton's rescue of Caroline from her native Indian captors.[78]

While Arl—ton, suffering the pangs of disappointed love, dashes off into the wild zone west of Louisville, Caroline makes her own unintentional wilderness trip: attempting to view the falls at Louisville, she crosses the Ohio into Indian country and is carried off by a band of marauding Indians. Il—ray anxiously envisions the palpitations of Caroline's 'sensible heart', wondering 'How will her tender limbs support the fatigue of being hurried through briary thickets? How will her lovely frame be able to rest, without other covering, than the cloud deformed canopy of the heavens?'[79] Remarkably well, one is compelled to answer. Though she marches nearly 400 miles before Arl—ton, having come coincidentally upon Caroline and her captors on the Illinois River, rescues her, her tender limbs are positively enhanced by her experience and her wounds eroticized (the lacerations make her 'more lovely than ever').[80] Arl—ton describes how he finds 'the most divine woman upon earth, torn into shatters by the bushes and briars, with scarcely covering left to hide the transcendency of her beauty':[81] beauty in a state of distress and undress is surely the most affecting beauty. The text allows for a kind of Gothic voyeurism, Caroline being represented as an erotic spectacle, especially in the moment when Arl—ton hangs over her sleeping body quite 'distracted' by the sight of her 'half naked' bosom (eventually, in an ironic reversal of Enlightenment rhetoric, he is 'obliged to extinguish the light, to preserve [his] reason').[82] In other words, when the text shifts from a metaphor of captivity to a literal one, the bedrock of essentialism that lies beneath the novel's support for oppressed women is exposed. Thus, the female body is reified in precisely the way that the novel critiques elsewhere. Indeed, we might note that the captivity narrative codifies Caroline's status as a possession: Il—ray refers to the Indians' act of 'robbery', there is much talk of Arl—ton 'retaking' Caroline and much play with the notion that Caroline is now his 'fair captive',[83] this vocabulary suggesting that the female other continues to be seen as a possession. Asserting the 'extraordinary' circumstance that '[t]he Indians treated her with the most distant respect, and scrupulous delicacy',[84] the text interestingly resists a lurid depiction of the captors as a threat to white female innocence, but it re-inscribes the dominant, and problematic, chivalric code: Caroline simply circulates between men. The sexualization of the captive's vulnerability takes place *after* she has been recaptured, explicitly a symptom of white male control of women's bodies.[85]

The captivity narrative points to the limits of the rhetoric of revolution; read against the grain, the novel demonstrates how the American Revolution ultimately failed women. The novel proposes that the unhappy marriages produced by English inequality will be countered by the conjugal happiness that it makes central to America's destiny. By the end of the novel, all unsatisfactory husbands have been disposed of (the dastardly Mr F— shoots himself, and the duplicitous Mr S— succumbs to his drinking habits), and, in good sentimental form, everyone is with their proper partner (Caroline with Arl—ton, Il—ray with Eliza, and the sisters' wayward brother, George, is likely to be united with Mrs S—). But these happy marriages sublimate the questions about the oppression of women that have preoccupied the novel. We know that in the history of the new republic, the language of natural rights proved less powerful than the republican conception of womanhood which privileged woman's place in the home. As Linda Kerber has documented, though '[t]he rhetoric of revolution, which emphasized the right to separate from dictatorial masters, implicitly offered an ideological validation for divorce ... few in power recognized it', and post-Revolutionary America retained most features of British laws on domestic relations.[86] Only in Pennsylvania was a new divorce law adopted as a part of republican renovation. In 1785 the Pennsylvania Assembly claimed the right to regulate divorce for itself. Elsewhere, divorce required a private bill in the state legislature, requiring both financial and political clout. America contrasts with other modern revolutionary governments which prioritized divorce reform; thus, the French system of civil divorce, instituted in 1792, was an explicit part of the Jacobin programme (the Code Napoleon of 1804 restricted this system, but it was not eliminated until the Bourbon Restoration). Women in America remained disenfranchised while being assured that 'The solidity and stability of the liberties of your country rest with you',[87] a pattern that replicates the post-war experience of Native Americans, which has been described as 'rhetorical liberation and political subjection'.[88] Likewise, the novel concludes with a vision of woman's subaltern role in civil society: while Arl—ton is sorting out the government of his secessionist utopia (in which every *male* over twenty-one is entitled to vote),[89] Caroline is in a separate domestic sphere, visiting the wives and 'instruct[ing] them in various and useful employments, which must tend not a little to promote their comfort'.[90] As well as domestic instructress, she is a civilizing force in the wilderness – she does a lot of gardening – and a symbol of the virgin land she inhabits.

Mary Wollstonecraft argued that 'the laws of her country – if women have a country – afford her no protection or redress from the oppressor'.[91] *The Emigrants*, for all its critique of British laws, shows that the new nation did not necessarily offer women a country of their own. If the cultural captivity endured by women in Britain threatened to unmoor the fixities of gender, the new nation secured its difference from Britain by re-securing gender differences. The novel's espousal of the rights of women is predicated on the stereotype of feminine weakness, of a natural (essential) 'delicacy that is peculiar to the softness of [the female] sex', which thrives in the strong manly arms of America.[92] Thus, Imlay's celebration of national difference – the superiority of America against England (and, more generally, Europe) – continues to reify the female other as (European) possession or spectacle. In this sense *The Emigrants* points up a fundamental contradiction in the American revolutionary rhetoric of personal liberty. On 31 March 1776, Abigail Adams wrote to her husband John of her longing to hear about 'independency' and her hope that the rejection of British rule might entail the rejection of gender subjection. John Adams not only laughs at this thought, but even more disastrously for women's rights strategically exalts women's confinement: 'We [men] are obliged to go fair, and softly, and in Practice you know We are Subjects'.[93] In the *Topographical Description*'s libertarian empire across the Allegheny Mountains, 'women are permitted to enjoy all the privileges, and all that protection, to which reason and delicacy entitle them'.[94] Similarly, in *The Emigrants*, Arl—ton, the gentle colonialist entrepreneur, who feels life on his pulses, goes softly with women, granting them 'home rule', but not independence.

* * *

Imlay's publisher, Alexander Hamilton, was eager to cash in on the popularity of the *Topographical Description*. In London's buoyant and cut-throat market for popular fiction, in which many new novels only received only scant critical attention in the periodical press, *The Emigrants* would probably not have attracted the three reviews that it did if Hamilton had not identified Imlay on the title page as the 'Author of the Topographical Description of [America's] Western Territory'. Even so, sales must have been disappointing. Hamilton in all probability post-dated the novel on the title page as having been published in 1793, for it had already been advertised as published in the *St James's Chronicle* and the *London Chronicle* in early December 1792. Post-dating was a common stratagem used by printers to artificially extend the shelf-life of ephemeral fiction.[95] However, neither the publisher's ruse nor the relatively wide exposure in the periodical press at the end of the day contributed much to the novel's dissemination: Alexander Hamilton's business went bankrupt before the first review appeared in the *British Critic* in July 1793.[96] The 1794 Dublin reprint of *The Emigrants* seems to have gone unnoticed entirely in the periodical press.

The highly politicized print market of the 1790s in Britain was a primal scene of rivalry in which new titles were received and reviewed strictly along partisan lines. Within this context, *The Emigrants'* provocative twin message of Jacobin governance and reciprocality in divorce laws immediately attracted the vitriolic wrath of the conservative periodical press. The reviewer for the Tory *British Critic* was so put off by Imlay's stilted style of writing that he abandoned the novel after only a few pages. After citing a passage from the 'Introduction' to the novel and remarking on the novel's 'flowing and easy style', he ended his review by observing, 'There are readers to whom this style will, no doubt, appear irresistibly graceful: there are others to whom it will be altogether intolerable. To the former we leave the further perusal of these three volumes.'[97] The reviewer for another Tory magazine, the *Critical Review*, found sporadic 'strokes of local description which are interesting', but in the final analysis also dismissed the style of the novel as 'intolerably inflated, and at the same time very incorrect'.[98] However, the reviewer was a lot more censorious of Imlay's republican 'schemes' of recommending America's manners and constitutional arrangements over those in England, and of recommending a relaxation of existing English divorce laws.[99]

By contrast, reviewing the novel for the Whig *Monthly Review*, William Enfield was considerably more sanguine about Imlay's novelistic talents, guaranteeing that the magazine's readers would 'find in these volumes many things which are not commonly to be perceived in writings of this class'.[100] Enfield hails

Imlay as an 'intelligent and lively author', who on contemporary political issues expresses himself 'with the freedom of an enlightened philosopher'. He praises Imlay for pouring forth 'high and almost idolatrous encomiums on the fair sex' and for depicting 'the rise and progress of love with all the ardour of youthful sensibility'. Yet the novel's ambitions far outstrip those of the conventional senti-mental romance, Enfield claims, pointing out that *The Emigrants* offers frequent 'reflections' on 'the present state of society with regard to marriage' that 'discover a mind inured to philosophical speculation'. Enfield is particularly impressed with Imlay's thesis 'that the female world is at present, in consequence of the rigour of matrimonial institutions, in a state of oppressive vassalage'.[101] However, Enfield disagrees with Imlay's conclusion that 'it would greatly increase the hap-piness of society, if divorces could be more easily obtained'. According to Enfield, 'the inconveniences, which have flowed from the existing laws respecting mar-riage, have proceeded more from the depraved manners of the age, than from the nature of the institutions themselves', and he therefore concludes that 'the per-petuity and inviolability of the marriage contract contribute essentially toward the virtue and the general happiness of society'. Nevertheless, Enfield concludes that Imlay's novel is 'so perfectly consonant to the present state of manners, that we can easily credit the writer's assertion, that the principal part of his story is founded on facts'.[102]

Imlay's assertion that the 'principal part of the story is founded upon facts' and that he was 'only induced to give the work in the style of a novel, from believing it would prove more acceptable to the generality of readers' has almost univer-sally been dismissed in the past as little more than a trite literary convention.[103] However, there are several reasons for assuming that there is more substance to Imlay's claim than has so far been recognized. In making their way to Kentucky, first via Braddock's Road across the Allegheny Mountains to Pittsburgh and then by flat-bottomed barges down the Ohio River to Louisville, the T—ns and their escorts retrace the journey that Imlay himself made when he first ventured into the western territory in the spring of 1783. The employment of local lore (notably details concerning soil conditions) and of settlers' appellations for for-mal topographical names (such as 'the Mountain' for the Allegheny Mountains and 'Diamond Island' for Twelve Mile Island – in the Ohio River, twelve miles north of Louisville) confirms that the author had spent considerable time in the western territory.[104] It is also evident that much of the geopolitical content of the novel – notably the notion of a rising empire in the West – is directly derived from the *Topographical Description*, which in itself was based in part on authen-tic documents and original observations.

While it is undoubtedly not the case that 'in every particular [Imlay] had a real character for [his] model', we have also seen that some of the colourful detail in the novel's rendering of James Wilkinson as General W— reveals a familiarity with Wilkinson's background, personality and covert political schemes that only a friend or close associate could have acquired. Even the novel's stock sentimental heroine, Caroline T—n, appears to be based on a historical figure. When in the early part of the nineteenth century Lyman Draper and John D. Shane were making their extensive collections of records and interviews with early Kentucky settlers, two of these pioneers recalled that Gilbert Imlay had written a book about a 'Caroline Grayson',[105] whose maiden name was Caroline Matilda Taylor. Caroline Taylor has been described as 'an English lady of great beauty and accomplishments', who had emigrated to Kentucky with her parents, William Thomas and Mariah Taylor.[106] Both Caroline and her sister Mary (rendered as 'Margaret' in the Jefferson County Marriage Register but, interestingly, as 'Mary' in *The Emigrants*) were married in 1785, when William Davenport executed a bond to marry Mary and Benjamin Grayson a bond to marry Caroline.[107] After their marriage, Caroline and Benjamin Grayson settled in Bardstown, Nelson County, where Benjamin became clerk of the Supreme Court for the Bardstown District, in which capacity he signed several summonses for Imlay (along with Henry Lee and Henry Banks) to appear in the next session of the court in connection with the Matthew Walton case.[108] While nothing will satisfy those bent on 'proving' that the novel was, in fact, ghost-written by Mary Wollstonecraft, the hard evidence suggests overwhelmingly that *The Emigrants* was indeed written by Gilbert Imlay and 'founded on facts'.[109] Perhaps Wollstonecraft should have the final word on the issue. Writing from Paris in February 1795 to Imlay, who was then being detained in London on business – though comforted by the attentions of a young actress from a strolling theatre company – Wollstonecraft observed sarcastically: 'Reading what you have written relative to the desertion of women, I have often wondered how theory and practice could be so different, till I recollected, that the sentiments of passion, and the resolves of reason, are very distinct'.[110]

7 EXPAT RADICAL AND CONSPIRATOR

To the Eighteenth Century – May the revolutions, which it has given birth to, know no limits but the utmost boundaries of the earth, and its close be the end of despotism

Philadelphia Festival, 17 April 1795, celebrating the revolutions in
America, France and the Netherlands; in *New Jersey Chronicle*, 2 May 1795

Gilbert Imlay's *Topographical Description* and *The Emigrants* continued to reverberate through Britain's print culture for a decade or more after they first appeared. In the print war that erupted in the course of the 1790s between the reformist and conservative factions in British society, Imlay's writings featured as seminal texts on both sides of the ideological divide. While the treatises of Carver, Crèvecoeur, Brissot, Cooper and others were certainly prominent catalysts in the Revolutionary Debate, Imlay's American Arcadia became an absolute cornucopia, mined indiscriminately by Jacobins and anti-Jacobins alike in an increasingly contentious wrangle over Britain's socio-political future. Nor was Imlay's reputation restricted to Britain. In Germany, where the Revolutionary War had awakened a keen and sustained interest in America, Eberhard August Wilhelm Zimmermann's translation of Imlay's *Topographical Description* appeared only a year after the first British publication.[1] Many other German Americanists were familiar with the original English edition of Imlay's *Topographical Description*, among them Joel Barlow's friend Christoph Daniel Ebeling, a keen collector of Americana and author of the expansive *Geography and History of America* (1793–1816).[2] In the United States itself Imlay quickly became established as an authority on the western territory following Samuel Campbell's publication in 1793 of the first American edition of the *Topographical Description* – an adaptation of Debrett's second, expanded English edition of the same year. In November 1796 George Washington bought a copy of Imlay's 'History of Kentucky' as a present for his wife – thereby tacitly lending presidential recognition to the canonical status of *A Topographical Description* in America.[3]

Having successfully jumped the genre divide between the geopolitical treatise and the novel, and between topography and fiction, *The Emigrants* contributed significantly to the popularization of the doctrine of utopian agrarianism contained in Imlay's *Topographical Description*. As evidenced by William Enfield's partisan review in the *Monthly Review*, the novel's progressive, pro-American political agenda struck a sympathetic cord with many British reformers. For their part, hack-writers catering for Britain's growing plebeian radical readership were eager to jump on the bandwagon of the Jacobin novel and began to churn out a string of clones. Frances Jacson's *Disobedience* (1797) and the anonymous *Henry Willoughby* (1798) were among the more elaborate and ingenious imitators of Imlay's plot and setting. However, as the counter-revolutionary movement began to gain momentum, *The Emigrants* – as well as the *Topographical Description*, for that matter – came under fire from an increasingly vitriolic anti-Jacobin press. The conservative reaction against Imlay's radical utopianism produced two of the most consummate exponents of the anti-Jacobin satirical novel, viz. the anonymous *Berkeley Hall* (1796) and George Walker's *The Vagabond* (1799).[4] *The Emigrants* and its immediate literary disciples and detractors were at the vanguard of a larger host of British novels in the 1790s that recycled and refashioned the familiar themes and scenes of American travel accounts and treatises, either celebrating or subverting the notion of an American Arcadia.[5] They included Eliza Parsons's *The Voluntary Exile* (1795), Henry James Pye's *The Democrat* (1795), Robert Bage's *Hermsprong; or, Man As He Is Not* (1796) and Charlotte Smith's *The Young Philosopher* (1798) – to mention only those with significant American content. However, though a one-volume pirated reprint of the novel appeared in Dublin in 1794, *The Emigrants* itself suffered the fate of most popular fiction in the buoyant print market of the 1790s: it was not reprinted during the author's lifetime.[6]

By contrast, editions of Imlay's *Topographical Description* continued to proliferate, with Imlay's 1792 *Ur-text* in subsequent editions becoming the gravitational centre of a steadily expanding textual universe of appendices, footnotes, citations, maps, charts, statistics and indexes. Thus, the second Debrett edition of the *Topographical Description* adds no fewer than six appendices, as well as maps of the western territory of the United States and of the state of Kentucky, a plan of the Rapids of the Ohio, a table of distances between Pittsburgh and the mouth of the Ohio, and a comprehensive index. In addition to a reprint of Jefferson's 1791 'Report ... of the Quantity and Situation of the Lands not Claimed by the Indians, Nor Granted to, Nor Claimed by any Citizens, within the Territory of the United States', the 1793 Debrett edition attaches five 'appendices', which, collectively, turn out to be a pirated edition of John Filson's 1784 *Discovery, Settlement and Present State of Kentucky* – now broken up into self-contained items. Aside from Filson's own *Kentucky*, these texts are: 'The Adventures of Daniel Boon', 'The Minutes of the Piankashaw Council', 'An Account of the Indian Nations inhabiting within the Limits of the Thirteen United States', and a chart of the distances by road from Philadelphia to the Falls of the Ohio. Alexander

Fitzroy's sketchy plagiarization of Filson's text from 1786 had appeared without the Boone narrative, which made the 1793 edition of Imlay's *Topographial Description* not only the first full-text publication of Filson's *Kentucky* in Britain, but also the British reading public's first acquaintance with the adventures of America's ultimate pioneer legend, Daniel Boone.[7]

According to the 'editor', the inclusion of these 'considerable additions' was warranted by the first edition 'having excited a general curiosity respecting the Western country of the United States of America, but more particularly that of the state of Kentucky'.[8] Judging from the sharp increase in the number of publications on the subject, British readers had indeed developed a keen interest in, or, in case of the anti-Jacobins, an intense dislike for, what augured to be the irrevocable 'rise of the American empire'; however, it is evident that the additions to the *Topographical Description* were chosen particularly with an eye to encouraging emigration to the western territory. Thus, the 'Minutes of the Piankashaw Council' and 'An Account of the Indian Nations' are to convince the reader of the peaceable intentions of the Piankashaws and other Indian tribes on the Wabash River following the 1791 expeditions against them under the command of Generals Charles Scott and James Wilkinson. For its part, Jefferson's report on the disposal of public lands wants to highlight the availability of vast tracts of western lands and their well-managed and risk-free disposal by the federal government; the distance chart and the two maps were no doubt included to underprop the author's claims about the superb accessibility of the western territories, being allegedly at the centre of an intricate network of transcontinental roads and navigable rivers.

Of all the new material included in the second edition of the *Topographical Description*, the map of the western territories of the United States was perhaps the most significant addition (Figure 5). Several of the reviewers of the first edition had complained about the absence of a map.[9] The reviewer for the *Monthly*

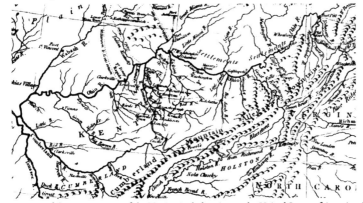

Figure 5. Map of the Western Part of the Territories belonging to the United States of America. From G. Imlay, *A Topographical Description of the Western Territory of North America* (1793), cropped.

Review was most outspoken, commenting that although Imlay's book contained 'a great variety of geographical and other interesting information', it 'require[d] a map, to render the author's course of travelling, his descriptions, and his reasoning, clear to the untravelled reader'.[10] Maps had always been an integral part of topographical descriptions of the New World; while they had never been free from geopolitical bias, from 1783 onwards maps of the United States had developed into ideological critiques of the nation's likely rise to sovereignty in a circumatlantic world still dominated by Europe's colonial powers. By the early 1790s maps of North America produced in Britain had gained a geopolitical status not seen before. Notably among British radicals critical of Pitt's administration, maps of America – especially those of the western territory – came to be regarded by actual and armchair emigrants alike as iconographic representations of a transatlantic utopia grounded in liberty, perfectibility and social justice. The popular success of the first edition of the *Topographical Description* therefore more than justified John Debrett's decision to commission a new large-format map of the United States for the second edition.

According to the legend, 'A Map of the Western Part of the Territories belonging to the United States of America' was 'Drawn from the best Authorities'. Although it identifies the engraver as Thomas Conder, it is unclear whether he also actually drew the map. This raises the question whether Imlay himself may have contributed to the design and production of the map. After all, he was evidently exceptionally well read in the topography of America in general, and that of Kentucky in particular. And although there is no evidence that he ever did much surveying under George May, his frantic land-jobbing activities on the ground in Kentucky and his constant trekking up and down the east coast and across the Allegheny Mountains had undoubtedly given him an excellent sense of the lay of the land. At any rate, the experience would have made him a positive expert on American topography in comparison to all those British geographers and map designers who had never actually been to North America (such as Thomas Conder). The received opinion among critics is that simply because the author of the second edition of the *Topographical Description* is identified on the title page as 'George Imlay', it is unlikely that he had any hand in producing the edition.[11] All it really suggests, however, is that Imlay had not been shown, or bothered to check, the reset title page before it was printed: in actual fact, he may very well have collaborated with Conder on some of the details of the map of the western territory. And there is no reason to assume that this was not the case with the map of Kentucky and the plan of the Falls of the Ohio; for although the features of the former are rather sketchy and those of the latter somewhat naive, they are both accurate enough in topographical detail to suggest that these are not mere artist's impressions (Figure 6). Even if, as is generally assumed, Imlay left London some time in or shortly after February 1793, the

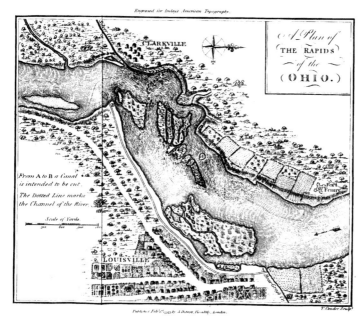

Figure 6. Plan of the Rapids of the Ohio. From G. Imlay, *A Topographical Description of the Western Territory of North America* (1793).

chronology of events would have allowed him to work with Conder on the two maps and plan, for all three explicitly state that they were published by Debrett on 1 February (and registered on that day at Stationer's Hall).[12]

Hence it is entirely possible that when Imlay's 'editor' claims in his 'Post-script' that he has drawn a map Kentucky 'from the best authorities', he was actually being sincere.[13] The map of Kentucky is almost certainly an updated version of Filson's 1784 map. Thus, it leaves out most of the old pioneer stations and adds towns and counties that had been formed in the intervening years, as well as the forts that had been built in response to the Indian Wars of the late 1780s and early 1790s. The two maps that are most likely to have inspired Conder's creation of the map of the western territories are Thomas Hutchins's 'New Map of the Western Parts of Virginia, Pennsylvania, Maryland and North Carolina' (published in London in 1778) and John Fitch's 'Map of the North West Parts of the United States' (1785). Although it incorporates some of the artistic and topographical features of both maps, Conder's representation of the western territories distinguishes itself from its sources in that it puts topographical detail to the service of Imlay's geopolitical agenda. This is most apparent from the way in which the major rivers and the Allegheny Mountains are featured in the three maps. Drawn in a perfunctory manner as so many random lines of decorative molehills, the mountains in Hutchins's and Fitch's maps are in no apparent topographical relation to the course of the rivers in the Ohio River Valley. In Conder's map, however, the mountain ranges and watersheds much more harmoniously blend in with the waterways of the West, offering a geophysical account for the direction in which they flow – west and south. It is as if the map wants to suggest that the creation of America's natural environment and Kentucky's unstoppable rise to empire were inextricably bound up with God's Plan and Providence.

The doctrine of manifest destiny also pervades the editorial footnotes added to the second edition of the *Topographical Description*. With most of them providing further details about the length, width and navigability of the western territory's rivers, the new footnotes collectively invigorate the geopolitical agenda that dominated the first edition of Imlay's book. Thus, a long footnote to Letter V outlines how via the Mississippi and New Orleans, the Ohio Valley has unimpeded access to markets in East and West Florida, the Spanish settlements in the Bay of Mexico, the West Indies, and Europe.[14] Another note in the same letter informs the reader that the Kentucky Assembly passed a law in July 1792 aimed at 'removing all the obstructions between Hudson's river and Lake Ontario' (including cutting a canal around the Rapids of the Ohio), thereby putting Kentucky at the centre of 'an inland navigation' stretching nearly 2,000 miles.[15]

The most extensive new footnote to the second edition, also in Letter V, is at the same time the most ambitiously geopolitical. Shifting its focus from the Ohio River Valley to the Mississippi River Valley, the note draws attention to the unique 'channels of communication' that will one day be opened up once the headwaters of the Mississippi are connected with the rivers that empty themselves into the Gulf of California and the Pacific Ocean in the west, and the Hudson Bay in the north. The editor goes on to point out that the 'great valley' that is formed by the 'Shining Mountains' (i.e. the Rocky Mountains) in the west and the Allegheny Mountains in the east 'constitutes what is called the Western Country of America, and is nearly in the centre of this vast continent'.[16] In contrast to the western territory, the eastern states are confined to a relatively narrow coastal strip, which seriously constrains the growth of its population. Worse than that, the revolutionary spirit of social justice and enlightened rationalism has all but petered out in the east. Invoking the authority of 'the most enlightened philosophers, particularly Dr. Adam Smith', the editor calls upon the federal government to abandon the 'system of aggrandizing commerce' that has become so deeply rooted in the east as to 'militate [against] philosophy, and the happiness of mankind'.[17] By contrast, the editor goes on to say, it is 'not only probable, but morally certain, that the present strength of the settlements west of the Allegheny mountains, must in the course of a very few years secure them from all invasion [by Indian bands]'.[18] For this reason the editor argues that the seat of the federal government be transplanted as soon as possible from the eastern United States to the rising empire of the great western valley, a move 'upon which the perfection of their political system depends':[19]

> In reflecting upon the object of the federal government, and the rapid strides it is making, it appears rather puerile in the United States thinking to make the seat of government permanent upon the Powtomac; or at least it would be so, to run the country to heavy expences, when it is obvious that posterity will, in the course of a century at farthest, remove it to the Mississippi, which is the most central, and consequently the proper place. By that means the efficiency of the federal government will act like the vital fluid which is propelled from the heart, and give motion and energy to every extremity of the empire.[20]

The rhetoric of General Wilkinson's geopolitical grandiosity unmistakably resounds in the materials that were added to the second edition of the *Topographical Description* – making it even more likely that Gilbert Imlay, who had been completing *The Emigrants* as the other text was being prepared for the press, was actively involved in producing the 1793 edition.

This certainly cannot be said for the third English edition of the *Topographical Description*, which appeared with John Debrett in 1797. In fact, the third edition of the *Topographical Description* is best regarded as entirely new publication altogether. A massively expanded edition, with the appended material covering well over half of the book's 600 pages, the third edition is a highly eclectic encyclopedia of North America, which virtually reduces Imlay's *Topographical Description* to only one of its constitutive parts, and Kentucky to merely one among several destinations recommended to prospective settlers. Indeed, although the reprint of the *Topographical Description* itself ostensibly covers the first 305 pages of the volume, 40 per cent of this section of the text actually consists of borrowed material that was neither in the 1792 nor 1793 editions of Imlay's topography. Among the inserted texts are extracts from Thomas Pownall's *A Topographical Description of the Dominions of ... North America* (1776) on the British middle colonies; from Tench Coxe's *A View of the United States of America* (reprinted in London in 1795) on the state of learning and civil and religious liberty; from a letter from Benjamin Rush to the American Philosophical Society on the maple tree and sugar making; and a letter from Major Jonathan Heart to Benjamin Smith on Native American culture.[21] The clearest indication that Imlay had not been involved in the production of the third edition of the *Topographical Description* is that wedged between Letter VII (Imlay's concise 'How-to-emigrate-to-Kentucky Guide') and Letter VIII (a celebration of Kentucky's enlightened form of government and superior legal code) is a lengthy extract of Thomas Cooper's *Some Information Respecting America* (1794). The *Topographical Description*'s main rival in the discursive tussle over America's preferred ideological space, *Some Information* had delivered a withering critique of Imlay's *Topographical Description* and had presented forceful arguments for prospective emigrants to settle in Pennsylvania, instead. The inclusion of an extract from Cooper's topography was probably the decision of the edition's somewhat cantankerous editor, who had also surreptitiously slipped an extract from a speech extolling the remarkable progress in the manufacturing industry in Pennsylvania into Imlay's 'Introduction'.[22] In several of the new footnotes to the third edition the editor also expresses himself in sceptical, sometimes even sarcastic terms about some of Imlay's claims. Thus, he flatly dismisses Imlay's assertion that settlements would have reached the Pacific in less than a century, and ridicules his observation that in Louisiana wine was produced for exportation.[23] However, the salient point here is not that Imlay's status as an authority on the western territory was waning, but, quite on the contrary, that by the late 1790s the Gilbert Imlay brand name was still powerful enough to make it commercially viable to publish what was in Britain at the time the most comprehensive treatise on the topography of North America.

Imlay's *Topographical Description* made a great impression on all those radical minds in Britain who considered their society to be hopelessly corrupt and their civil rights under serious threat from an outdated and despotic government. First published at a time when tensions were rising between the French and the British (with war between them eventually breaking out in February 1793) and when British opinion was becoming rapidly less favourable to revolution, Imlay's book was seized upon by many as the promise for a Rousseauesque return to nature in the pristine wilderness of the New World. The decision in 1794 of the Dissenting scientist and philosopher Joseph Priestley to settle in America and build an agrarian utopia there, triggered a widespread interest in emigration to America among progressive idealists in the 1790s, many of whom were thrilled by Imlay's description of the Kentucky paradise. This emigration movement among British radicals gained further momentum following the Pitt administration's crack-down on radicals, which culminated in the treason trials of 1794 and the introduction of the two 'Gagging Acts' in 1795. By the middle of the decade emigration to the New World had become so popular in radical circles that 'America' had become a byword for an asylum for radical emigrants. Thus, in his *A Political Dictionary* Charles Pigott defined the word 'emigrant' as 'one who, like Dr. Priestley or Thomas Cooper, is compelled to fly from persecution, and explore liberty in a far distant land, probably America'; the word 'refugees' Pigott annotated as 'English Patriots, as Dr. Priestley and his family, Mr. Cooper, of Manchester, &c. &c. who ... were obliged to quit a country pregnant with bigotry and persecution'.[24] Writing in 1795 in his journal *The Tribune*, John Thelwall claimed that the 'political and natural calamities' that had recently hit the country had triggered what he described as a 'rage of emigration'; he estimated that in the summer of 1794 alone some 80,000 people had emigrated to

America.[25] This figure is almost certainly inflated and would in any case have included only a relatively small number of radical activists. Even so, emigration to America was very much part of the spirit of the age and hence became a widely discussed topic in the Jacobin/anti-Jacobin debate. Generally speaking, the Jacobin writers tended to depict America as the ideal republic where Godwinian ideals of liberty, democracy, emancipation and the perfectibility of mankind could be realized; however, fearing massive shortages of skilled labour and dire social and economic disruption, the anti-Jacobins vehemently attacked the emigration movement, dismissing emigrants in pamphlets and broadsides as anti-patriotic traitors and vagabonds.[26] In the print war that thus erupted, 'America' became a crucial site of contestation where supporters of the 'new philosophy' and detractors of Jacobinism met in discursive battle over Britain's cultural capital – staging, in effect, in America's imagined 'backwoods' a British version of the French Revolution, which the increasingly repressive political climate at home prevented from taking place.

By far the best known of the 1790s' utopian emigration schemes was Samuel Coleridge's 'Pantisocracy'. His experiment in human perfectibility was to be created in pastoral seclusion in America and would promote equality of property, labour and self-government among its adult members, both men and women. The idea of a Pantisocracy was conceived by Coleridge and his friend Robert Southey in mid-1794, when the two poets were still undergraduates at Cambridge. Trying to decide on a site for the Pantisocracy, Coleridge and Southey thoroughly researched their 'American Plan'. In September 1794 Coleridge had daily meetings in the 'Salutation & Cat' coffee-house in Newgate Street with 'a most intelligent young Man' of their 'School', who 'ha[d] spent the last 5 years of his Life in America – and ha[d] lately come from thence as an Agent to sell Land'.[27] They also enthusiastically read several of the recent reports on the country's topography, including Brissot de Warville's *New Travels in the United States* (1792), Imlay's *Topographical Description* and Thomas Cooper's *Some Information Respecting America* (1794). The two latter texts were in fierce competition with each other, with Imlay tempting prospective emigrants to settle in Kentucky and the reformer and abolitionist Cooper arguing instead for settlement in the idyllic Pennsylvanian hinterland on the banks of the picturesque Susquehanna River, which was the region where Cooper and his business associate Joseph Priestley, Jr, were planning to found a utopian community (near Loyalsock Creek). Unsurprisingly, the rival emigration schemes promoted by Imlay's and Cooper's books were treated with contempt by the conservative press. Thus, in January 1795 the *British Critic* referred to 'Messrs. Imlay and Cooper as two rival auctioneers, or rather two show-men, stationed for the allurement of incautious passengers: "Pray ladies and gentlemen, walk in and admire the wonders of Kentucky". – "Pray stop and see the incomparable beauties of the Susque-hanna".[28]

Yet, it is important to realize that it was ultimately the French Revolution, rather than American land speculation per se, that motivated Imlay to write the *Topographical Description* and his follow-up sentimental novel *The Emigrants* and that shaped the central body of thought contained in them. Contrary to what is still widely assumed, there is no evidence that Imlay held title to a single acre of land in Kentucky when he arrived in England. But what he did find upon his arrival in England was that as an *ideological space*, America and American land were at the centre of contemporary political discourse, and increasingly so in the wake of the popular revolt in France. However, if Imlay's familiarity with the western territory of America was a highly-prized commodity in England's Revolutionary Debate, at least among those reformers campaigning for a radical shake-up of British society, the value of that commodity rapidly began to decline after France declared war on Britain in February 1793. Imlay's move to Paris in the course of the same month was therefore probably well-considered. In England harbouring any sympathetic thoughts towards the former colonies, let alone contemplating emigration to America, was increasingly regarded as a mark of one's Jacobin principles and hence of one's disloyalty to Britain; yet in France, where the dominant Girondist party had an ambitious geopolitical agenda vis-à-vis the American West, a man with Imlay's knowledge of the Ohio region and his contacts among prominent Kentuckians was still held in high esteem.

When Imlay arrived in Paris in the course of February 1793, the French Revolution was still young and scores of English, Irish, Scottish and American radicals, poets, literati and government agents had converged upon Paris, along with strings of adventurers, entrepreneurs and land-jobbers, including William Playfair, Colonel Blackden, James Swan and Joel Barlow.[29] Mary Wollstonecraft had been in Paris since December, while Thomas Paine had arrived there on 19 September 1792. Paine had been on friendly terms with a number of prominent British visitors, and although some of these left Paris after the declaration of war, a constant stream of Revolution tourists, as well as British spies, would come to get a hearing with the notorious guru of radicalism. Indeed, Paine was so overrun with visitors that he had been forced to hold levees twice a week at the Hotel Philadelphia (formerly White's Hotel) to deal with their sheer numbers. The constant stream of visitors became such a strain on him, that in January 1793 Paine went into 'internal exile' to the village of Saint-Denis, nine miles north of Paris, where he occupied part of an old hotel which had once been the residence of Madame de Pompadour.[30] It was here, surrounded by only half a dozen or so English disciples – including Thomas Christie and his wife Rebecca, Thomas Clio Rickman, William Choppin and William Johnson – that

Paine would continue to entertain visitors, although now by prior arrangement only. Among his renowned guests were prominent members of the Girondist administration, including Jacques-Pierre Brissot de Warville, Jean-Henri Bançal des Issarts, Jean-Marie Roland and his wife Marie-Jeanne, as well as a motley crowd of Revolution tourists, among them the South American freedom fighter General Francisco Miranda and a number of British and American republicans, including Mary Wollstonecraft, Joel Barlow, John Hurford Stone, Helen Maria Williams, and Gilbert Imlay.[31] Imlay's *Topographical Description* was undoubtedly his passport into the inner circle of Paine's radical friends and associates, many of whom were enthusiastic supporters of the American republican model. Perhaps the most influential of Paine's regular visitors was Brissot, leader of the Girondists, or Brissotins, who formed the dominant faction in both the Legislative Assembly (which had replaced the National Constituent Assembly on 1 October 1791) and the National Convention (which held its first session on 20 September 1792).[32]

Before leaving London, Imlay had received a letter of introduction to Brissot from Thomas Cooper. A lawyer, scientist and philosopher, Cooper was a prominent campaigner against the slave trade and, with Thomas Walker, one of the leading spirits of the Manchester Constitutional Society.[33] Along with his friend James Watt (son of the inventor of the steam ship), Cooper had visited Paris in the spring of 1792 in his capacity as deputy of the Manchester Constitutional Society. His brief was to establish contacts with patriotic societies in France for the benefit of the universal rights of man. Although they had maintained respectful communications with the Jacobin leader Robespierre, the two Manchester delegates appear to have had a much stronger rapport with the Brissotins. While their association with the advocates of moderate reform had apparently made it expedient for them to return in some haste to England in May, Cooper's acquaintance with Brissot will have added considerable weight to his recommendation of Imlay.[34]

Quite possibly it was Thomas Cooper – son-in-law of Joseph Priestley, who had recently become 'Citoyen de France' – who suggested to Imlay that he talk to Brissot about the plan to oust the Spanish from Louisiana and hand it back to the Republic. It would not have escaped Cooper's notice that Brissot was a warm admirer of America and that he held a keen interest in the geopolitical situation in the western territory and the lower Mississippi Valley. Before he had become a successful pamphleteer, editor of the Paris paper *Patriote Français* and populist campaigner for liberal causes, including the emancipation of slaves in the West Indies,[35] Brissot had made an extensive tour through the eastern United States in the course of 1788. His account of his travels, *Nouveau Voyage dans les États-Unis*, had appeared in Paris in 1791. English readers had become familiar with the lavish praise Brissot had heaped upon the United States through Barlow's translation of Brissot's travel account. In *New Travels* Brissot had claimed that 'The present state of independent America, will, perhaps, give us a glance at the highest perfection of human life that we are permitted to hope for'.[36] More importantly, in the brief final chapter of *New Travels*, entitled 'The Western Territory', Brissot had underlined the geopolitical tensions that were building up in the Ohio Valley. The western settlers, he wrote, 'all expect that the navigation of the Mississippi becoming free, will soon open to them the markets of the islands, and the Spanish colonies, for the productions with which their country overflows. But the question to be resolved is, whether the Spaniards will open this navigation willingly, or whether the Americans will force it.'[37] Brissot also reported on the anger felt by many in Kentucky over Congress allegedly having agreed with the Spanish minister, Gardoqui, 'that Spain should shut up the navigation for twenty-five years, on condition that the Americans should have a free commerce with Spain'.[38] Yet, most significant of all, even as early as 1788 Brissot had paid more than passing attention to precisely those schemes to bring about a separation of the West from the Atlantic states that General Wilkinson, Colonel John Connolly and others were involved in at the time – the very same that would later be at the heart of the covert political agenda of Imlay's Topographical Description. Brissot wrote:

> A degree of diffidence, which the inhabitants of the West have shewn relative to the secret designs of Congress, has induced many people to believe, that the union would not exist a long time between the old and new States; and this probability of a rupture they say, is strengthened by some endeavours of the English in Canada, to attach the Western settlers to the English government ...
> The Western inhabitants are convinced that this navigation cannot remain a long time closed. They are determined to open it by good will or by force; and it would not be in the power of Congress to moderate their ardour. Men who have shook off the yoke of Great-Britain, and who are masters of the Ohio and the Mississippi, cannot conceive the insolence of a handful of Spaniards can think of shutting rivers and seas against a hundred thousand free Americans. The slightest quarrel will be sufficient to throw them into flame; and if ever the Americans shall march towards New Orleans, it will infallibly fall into their hands.[39]

If Brissot's analysis was accurate, the French had everything to play for. With the Spanish lacking the military strength to withstand an attack on Louisiana and with the Atlantic Unites States prioritizing their own commercial interests over those of the western territory, all it would take to ignite the Ohio Valley into 'flame' was 'the slightest quarrel' – after which the Kentuckians would secure their much-coveted access to world markets and the French would regain New Orleans and Louisiana.

Imlay's arrival in Paris in February 1793 could not have been better timed. The retaking of Louisiana was high on the agenda of the National Convention.

Thus, on 25 January 1793, the Comité de Défense Génerale (which became the Comité de Salut Public on 6 April 1793) had asked Brissot to present a report on the possibility of an expedition against the Spanish dependencies.[40] Brissot had been at the centre of France's territorial ambitions in America even before the Convention held its first session in September 1792. He had lobbied energetically to gain the support of his party members, and had been instrumental in appointing Charles François Lebrun as Minister of Foreign Affairs in August 1792. In the second half of that year Brissot had tried to persuade Lebrun to enlist the services of General de Miranda, who had visited the United States soon after the War of Independence, to launch an attack on the Spanish colonies. At one point the plan involved the deployment of 30,000 San Domingo troops.[41] However, Lebrun deemed this plan too ambitious and decided instead to send Charles-Edmond Genet to the United States, with a secret mission to foment a revolution in Louisiana and the Floridas. It is generally accepted that Genet's appointment as Minister Plenipotentiary of the French Republic to the United States in January 1793 was at least in part the result of Brissot's intervention.[42] Brissot also proposed withdrawing General de Miranda from his post under Dumouriez during the latter's ill-fated expedition against the Netherlands in the early spring of 1793, and deploying him instead in the plot against Spanish Louisiana.[43] The Convention's ambitions vis-à-vis the Spanish possessions in America became all too plain when it declared war on Spain on 7 March.

What Imlay's objective had been in coming to the French capital – and that Brissot took it seriously – becomes evident from the letter of introduction that the Girondist leader sent to the head of the political division of the Department of Foreign Affairs, Louis Guillaume Otto, on 26 March 1793:[44]

> Je vous adresse le Capitaine Imlay Americain de l'Létat de Kentucky, qui m'a été recommandé par L'estimable Cooper du Manchester, il desiroit s'entretenir avec moi de L'expedition du Mississipi. Il me paroit très proper à vour donner Les renseignemens sur Le maniere de mettre ce plan à execution. Lorsque vous L'aurez entretenu, nous fixerons un jour avec Le Ministre pour avoir une Conference generele sur cet objet.[45]

The archives of the Ministry of Foreign Affairs contain two documents in which Imlay unfolds his plans for an attack on Spanish Louisiana. Internal evidence indicates that the first document, 'Observations du Cap. Imlay, Traduites de L'Anglais', was submitted some time after France had declared war on Spain on 7 March – presumably not long after Brissot's letter of recommendation to Otto.[46] Whether it was addressed to the Comité de Défense Générale or to its successor, the Comité du Salut Public, is not absolutely clear. Yet a reference in the second, much longer document, entitled 'Mémoire sur la Louisiane, présenté au Comité de Salut Public par un Citoyen Américain', seems to suggests that both were addressed to the Committee of Public Safety.⁴⁷ Writing in the third person, Imlay observes in the 'Mémoire': 'il craint d'ailleurs que les papiers présentés sur ce subjet à votre Comité par le Ministre le Brun n'ayent pas encore pu être examines dans en temps où vos travaux continuels suffisent à peine pour tout ce qu'exige de vous le Salut public'.⁴⁸

Imlay opens his 'Observations' by reminding the French authorities that Louisiana may be far removed from the wars France is currently involved in against 'the tyrants of Europe', but that Spain regards New Orleans as 'the key to its American possessions and its mines'.⁴⁹ Conquering this 'jewel in the crown' of Spain, he argues, would not only liberate 'millions of miserable inhabitants', but would have a number of other benefits as well. First, as that nation would have to build up its military presence in Louisiana, an attack on the region would sap Spain's finances, and hence considerably strengthen France's position in any ensuing peace talks with Spain – especially if such an attack had the support of the settlers in the western territory, with whose 'resources and intrepidness', he adds, Don Diego de Gardoqui, 'erstwhile Chargé des Affaires of Spain in New York and currently Finance Minister', was only too familiar. Second, once the Mississippi delta was occupied, French commerce would enjoy immense benefits from 'the abundance of goods of all sorts that the Ohio and the Mississippi would furnish as soon as their chains were broken'. Third, since 'it would be easy to arm Corsairs [privateers] at New Orleans', these lighter vessels could wreak much havoc on the Spanish ships, which, because they were heavier, could not gain access to the harbour. Fourth, because the plan would be carried out by American citizens, it had the ancillary advantage of eventually drawing the United States into the conflict, which was bound to happen as the 'free' Americans were certain to support 'the generous struggle' of France to establish 'universal liberty' and root out 'universal despotism'. Fifth, the plan could be executed at very little expense and would not in any way compromise France's other schemes.

Imlay may have had the ear of Brissot, but it is not surprising that he got no response from the Committee of Public Safety: it had far more serious schemes to consider than Imlay's rather inchoate proposal to take New Orleans. Not only had the Committee recently dispatched Citizen Genet to the United States on a special mission to 'free' Spanish America, but with a war with Spain generally expected to be declared within weeks, a string of similar plans to conquer Louisiana had been submitted to the French authorities during February and early March. The most far-reaching of these was General George Rogers Clark's plan of an expedition against Louisiana. Disgruntled over the rejection by the Virginia legislature of his land claims on the Indiana side of the Falls of the Ohio, Clark had first offered his services to the French authorities during the latter months of 1792. His detailed plan for an attack on Louisiana, which had been relayed through Jean-Baptiste Ternant, Minister Plenipotentiary of the French

Republic to the United States, had reached Paris by early February. According to Tom Paine, it had been received by the Provisional Executive Council of the Republic 'with satisfaction'.[50] At the time a member of the Convention, Paine wrote to Clark's brother-in-law, Dr James O'Fallon, on 17 February to confirm that Jefferson had been privately sounded about the general's suitability as commander of an invading force, and that the French Republic would want to have the first claim to any Spanish possessions that were conquered.[51] It is also clear from Paine's letter to O'Fallon that his 'sincere friend' Genet knew about Clark's Louisiana scheme and O'Fallon's involvement in it before he set off for America later that same month.[52]

It is likely that Genet was also familiar with the plan formally submitted in early March to the French authorities by Pierre Lyonnet, a French Creole and former resident of New Orleans. In his 'Considerations sur la Louisiane', Lyonnet proposed that seven or eight hundred men should be put on land in a port in the United States, and subsequently travel to the western territory in small groups, under the pretence of intending to settle on the banks of the Ohio. In the meantime, French agents at Fort Pitt and in Kentucky would have gathered a fleet of barges, and, once everyone was in place, the entire armada would sail down the Ohio and Mississippi rivers, pick up arms on the way, and take New Orleans under the cover of darkness. If this sounded too ambitious, Lyonnet went on to say, the authorities should at the very least send 'a few fearless and enterprising men' to Kentucky in order to mobilize a small insurgent force from among the American and French settlers there.[53] Not having had any response to either these suggestions (or his additional considerations) by early April, Lyonnet fired off an urgent letter to Lebrun, reminding him of his plan, which Otto and Brissot had put before him, as well as the names of the three agents who had been selected to travel to America to carry out 'this grand enterprise'.[54] The identity of the three 'agents' is not revealed in the letter itself, but another document in the archives of the Ministry of Foreign Affairs reveals that Lyonnet was referring to Joel Barlow, now released from his land-jobbing activities after the collapse of the Scioto Company; Stephen Sayre, a Princeton graduate who had become a banker and sheriff in London, and subsequently acted as an attaché to Franklin and Arthur Lee; and Beaupoil, a French officer who had formerly served in Poland.[55] Together with one Pereyat, Sayre and Beaupoil had in early March submitted a plan of their own to take New Orleans for the French government for the sum of 280,000 *livres*.[56] It is evident from further letters from Lyonnet to Otto in April and May that Lebrun had continued to ignore his plan to retake Louisiana.[57]

With so many schemers and soldiers of fortune offering Lebrun their services to deliver the Spanish colonies in America into the hands of the French government, it is not surprising that several of the plans began to blend into each other

and the personnel involved in one scheme reappear in another. Thus, in his letter
to Otto of 22 May, Lyonnet reported that Imlay had written to him to say that,
although more than two months had gone by without any response from the
minister, there had been 'no change [of plan]' and that he was still confident the
plot would ultimately succeed: but which plot he was referring to – Lyonnet's or
his own – was at this point entirely unclear.[58]

If Lebrun did not take Imlay's proposals seriously, Brissot evidently did. On
22 April he sent Imlay to the Minister of Foreign Affairs with the following letter:

> Paris ce 22 Avril 1793.
>
> CITOYEN MINISTRE,
>   Le Capitaine Imlay qui vous remettre cette letter m'apprend qu'il n'y a encore
> rien d'arreté pour l'expedition du Mississipi. Je vous avoue que cette lenteur me parait
> très prejudiciable pour la chose publique. Si ce Capitaine et les autres personnes ne
> partent pas sous 15 jours, il faudra renoncer a l'entreprise, et certes La Republique
> aurait des reproches très fondés à faire pour y avoir renounce, hatez vous donc de
> prendre un parti décisif. L'argent ne doit pas vous arreter maintenant. Avez vous
> besoin de l'avis du Conseil je suis prêt à y aller, pour y developer les avantages du plan
> mais de grace ne perdez pas un moment.
>   J. P. Brissot.[59]

To be fair to Imlay, his 'Mémoire sur Louisiana' deserved a better fate. With the
exception of Clark's proposal, Imlay's 'Mémoire' distinguishes itself from similar
plans then before the French government in its analysis of the geopolitical situation on the ground, notably in Kentucky. Thus, apart from revisiting the familiar
themes of the despotic rule of the Spanish authorities in Louisiana and the weakness of the Spanish defences in New Orleans, the 'Mémoire' centrally argues that
France's best chance of successfully launching a campaign against the Spanish
possessions in Louisiana is to tap into the frustrations and ambitions of the settlers in the western territory. Of the 400,000 people that lived on the shores of
the Mississippi and the Ohio, at least 40,000, Imlay claims, were as capable of
bearing arms as the 'most experienced veterans', because many of them have been
engaged for more than a decade in fighting the Indians. 'Ce sont des hommes
brulans du Feu de la liberté, et vivement aigris contre l'Espagne qui ne cesse de
violer leurs privileges, d'apporter des entraves au cours natural de leur prospérité,
et de paralyser pour eux la main active de l'industrie et de l'émulation'.[60] Given
the presence of such a large body of well-motivated fighting men in Kentucky,
Imlay estimates that the entire campaign against New Orleans and Spanish Louisiana would not cost the French Republic more than 750,000 *livres*. However,
should the Committee deem this sum too high, Imlay recommends that they
give Genet carte blanche to carry out his plan with the assistance of the western

settlers, who would be more than willing to undertake the expedition against Spain at their own risk and cost.

In the end, of course, none of what Imlay proposed to the Comité de Salut Public would come to pass. This was caused as much by the diplomatic row over Genet's mission in the United States as by political developments in France.[61] Although Jefferson and the Republicans initially welcomed Genet's mission to America, the ardent revolutionary zeal with which the new Minister Plenipotentiary began to carry out his instructions from the Comité immediately upon his arrival in Charleston on 8 April soon began to irritate Washington and the Federalists. Within days of arriving in Charleston, Genet had commissioned four privateers (appropriately christened *Republican*, *Anti-George*, *Sans-Culotte* and *Citizen Genet*), which before long were sending British ships captured as prizes into Charleston.[62] Genet's slow, triumphal procession up the east coast towards Philadelphia, to which he had been accredited, was marked by repeated public appeals to American enthusiasm for the French Revolution. This further increased the annoyance felt by the Federalists. By the time Genet arrived in the capital on 16 May, the Girondists had all but lost their grip on power, with the National Guard finally purging the Convention of all Girondists on 2 June. Brissot initially managed to escape from Robespierre's henchmen, but was, after a show trial, guillotined on 31 October, along with twenty other Girondist deputies. Although neither Genet nor Washington's administration learned of these developments until the end of 1793, the fall of the Girondists had effectively ended Genet's mission. On 11 October 1793, the Comité de Salut Public acceded to the American request for the recall of Genet, and ordered four new commissioners to replace him. With the demise of the Girondists, the French Republic's campaign for the conquest of Spanish Louisiana and the separation of the western territory from the United States had also effectively come to an end.

8 PURVEYOR TO THE FRENCH REVOLUTION

> Such are the effects of war, that it saps the vitals even of the neutral countries, who,
> obtaining a sudden influx of wealth, appear to be rendered flourishing by the destruc-
> tion which ravages the hapless nations who are sacrificed to the ambition of their
> governors.
>
> Mary Wollstonecraft, *Letters Written during a Short Residence*
> *in Sweden, Norway, and Denmark* (1796), Letter 3[1]

The new French administration's change of policy vis-à-vis the United States and
the Spanish possessions did not immediately deter individual Americans from
offering their services to the cause of the liberation of the Spanish American
colonies. Thus, on 23 November 1793 Joel Barlow and Mark Leavenworth submitted to Robespierre's government a detailed plan to take Louisiana and hand
it over to the French authorities. In their 'Plan pour prendre la Louisiane, sans
couter rien à la nation', Barlow and Leavenworth proposed to equip, arm and pay
an army of two thousand men at their own expense and lead them against Louisiana 'au nom de la République française'.[2] Coming on the heels of the adoption
of the Law of Suspects, which allowed for the creation of Revolutionary tribunals that sent thousands of 'traitors' to be guillotined, and in the midst of the
brutal suppression of the counter-revolutionary uprising in the Vendée (which
lasted from October to December), Barlow and Leavenworth's plan to establish a form of government in Louisiana 'founded on the republican principles of
the French constitution' suggests that Thomas Jefferson and the members of the
Democratic and Republican Societies were not the only Americans to continue
'worshipping the French Revolution' beyond the point where, in retrospect,
such support for 'the fanatical cult of Liberty' had become synonymous with
colluding with genocide.[3] Indeed, in a footnote to the reissue of his 'Letter to the
People of Piedmont', which appeared in 1796, Barlow still defended the establishment of the Revolutionary tribunal in March 1793, observing that it was 'to
be regretted that that institution was deferred to so late a period; as it was calculated to prevent a more tumultuous mode of exercising popular vengeance'.[4]

If Americans like Barlow, Leavenworth and Imlay could still move around
freely in France after the Jacobin coup d'état of June 1792 and even to some extent

continue to be engaged in the public political debate during the early stages of
the Reign of Terror, peddling schemes for the sacking of Spanish Louisiana was
no longer a viable, let alone a lucrative activity in Paris during the ascendancy of
Robespierre and the later Directory. The American expatriates in France needed
to diversify their business strategies, and that is exactly what many of them did.
Shipping and international trade became their new contribution to the French
Revolution – and to their own pocket books. When France declared war on England and The Netherlands on 1 February 1793, French émigrés almost overnight
lost their property, while Dutch and British traders lost their Continental markets.
From the middle of 1793 onwards, the British government began to implement a
series of blockades and other restrictive measures upon neutral trade aimed at bringing the French economy to a complete standstill. In order to put further pressure
on the National Convention, the British war measures were specifically targeted
at breaking the morale of the French people by hitting them where it would hurt
the most – in their stomachs. Thus the British Order of June 1793 had instructed
commanders of Her Majesty's ships of war and privateers that vessels carrying cargoes of corn, meal and other foodstuffs destined for France were to be seized and
the supplies to be taken to England. The Order of November of that year dictated
the detention of neutral ships laden with French colonial produce. As a measure
of the effectiveness of the British hunger blockade, in less than five months after
the November 1793 orders, over six hundred vessels had been detained in British
ports.[5] The effects of the blockade were exacerbated by France's maritime weakness.
To make matters worse, the harvest of 1792 had been poor in France. Soon the
French government was finding it hard to feed, equip and arm its swelling revolutionary armies, engaged in 'liberating' the nations of Europe. At home, increasingly
vociferous crowds were assembling in the streets of Paris and other cities clamoring
for the barest necessities of life, 'du pain et du savon' – bread and soap.

In this situation, fortunes were to be made by Americans trading in Paris
and elsewhere under the shield of America's neutrality.[6] Barlow was particularly
well placed to build up an extensive business emporium. With the exception
of Paine – who was about to be arrested – Barlow was the only American in
Europe to hold French citizenship. This gave him virtually unlimited access to
the corridors of power in the Jacobin administration. Thus, when Robespierre
set up a three-man purchasing commission late in 1793, Barlow was able to deal
directly with the commissioners. In December 1793, the month in which Paine
was arrested, Barlow won a contract with Robespierre's government to import
goods into France not affected by any explicit ban, and to export produce for
which there was no market in France. While Barlow was negotiating with the
purchasing agents in Paris, his associates were handling incoming and outgoing shipments at Le Havre. Soon Barlow and his partners were working with
Elias Backman, a merchant of Finnish extraction who had spent much time in

England and France representing his family's business interests before setting up his headquarters in Gothenburg in 1794. Backman carried on an extensive international shipping business with England, Spain and France, dealing in such commodities as grain, steel, wood, naval stores and potash – an ingredient used in the production of soap. This trade had become significantly more risky following the British naval blockade of French ports, but also considerably more profitable, as long as the Americans managed to get the shipments through. This typically involved chartering a British-registered vessel, or one sailing under neutral colours, ostensibly bound for Spain or Scandinavia and surreptitiously diverting its cargo to a French port. Prominent among Barlow's associates in his blockade-running activities were Colonel Benjamin Hichborn, Daniel Parker, Mark Leavenworth and Gilbert Imlay.

Although there is no dearth of manuscript material (the most significant Barlow collections being held at Harvard University, the Huntington Library and Yale University), Barlow's commercial activities – like Imlay's – are hard to reconstruct. No doubt this lack of documented evidence concerning Barlow's business dealings, particularly relating to the wartime trade with France, has to do with the illegal nature of that trade. Those involved in the trade avoided epistolary correspondence because the risk of letters being intercepted by either the British or the French authorities was simply too great. Instead, traders like Barlow and Imlay tended to rely on a network of trusted personal contacts. This is presumably one of the reasons why American traders moved across the Channel and over the European continent with such frequency and, travelling under the protection of their neutral passports, apparently without serious restrictions. It is therefore less surprising than it may appear that even though his name is mentioned only once in Barlow's business papers, Imlay became one of Barlow's closest associates in the course of 1794–5.[7] Indeed, working in close partnership and sharing friends, business contacts and trade secrets, the two men effectively 'operated almost as one'.[8] This makes Barlow one of the most likely candidates for the American business associate whom Mary Wollstonecraft would come to regard as her enemy and rival for control over Imlay, and whose name William Godwin systematically cut out of her letters before publishing them (and then destroying the originals). Being in many ways 'Barlow's shadow', as John Seelye put it, it is possible to retrace vicariously much of Imlay's life as a blockade runner during the French Revolution in the vicissitudes of Barlow's eventful career as a trusted purveyor to France's revolutionary government.

* * *

In fact, there are so many extraordinary similarities in the details and the chronology of their biographies that Imlay and Barlow can be said to have led parallel lives for much of their adult years prior to the mid 1790s. Born in the same year as Imlay, 1754, Joel Barlow grew up in a respectable Connecticut farming family. Having graduated from Yale College in 1778, Barlow in quick succession tried a variety of occupations that might have been an outlet for some of his restless energy. After serving as an army chaplain during the Revolutionary War, Barlow worked as a lawyer, journalist, printer, shopkeeper and attorney for disgruntled veteran officers. In 1786 he associated himself with a number of aspiring literati known as the Hartford Wits, all of whom were Yale graduates and of Federalist persuasion. In the course of 1786–7 Barlow was persuaded to contribute some half-hearted verse to the serialized satirical epic *The Anarchiad*, an arch conservative attack on French philosophy, paper money, Shay's Rebellion and European prejudice towards Americans. Much closer to his heart and ambitions was his poem *The Vision of Columbus*, which appeared in 1787. In this epic poem Barlow portrayed the great future and progress of the American experiment as part of God's plan of making 'the spirit of commerce' the civilizing agent of the world. Appearing with an authorized dedication to Louis XVI and an impressive list of subscribers, including George Washington, the poem attested to Barlow's diplomatic, if not so much his poetic talents. Though it did not bring him much pecuniary reward, *The Vision of Columbus*, and its British edition, gained him a reputation both in America and Europe as a poet with a keen eye for transatlantic political and economic relations.

It was these talents that would soon be brought to the attention of Colonel William Duer, one of America's greatest financiers and speculators of the day. Whilst serving under Alexander Hamilton as secretary to the board of the Treasury, Duer was closely involved in the disposal of unclaimed western lands – the only way in which Congress could hope to replenish the depleted finances of the new republic. When in 1787 the Ohio Company's inspirational director, the Reverend Manasseh Cutler, came to New York to petition Congress for a compact body of land of one-and-a-half million acres in the north-west territory, Duer quickly saw how he could serve the impoverished administration and in the process line his own pockets. Arguing that it would dispose Congress to accept a lower price per acre and more liberal credit terms, Duer persuaded Cutler to increase his application to five million acres, but with the secret proviso that the Ohio Company act as a cover for 'another company' – in fact Duer's own covert speculation scheme along the Scioto River in south-east Ohio.[9] Using his position at the Treasury to grant the Ohio Company's request for land, Duer thus unobtrusively – and illegally – managed to obtain a pre-emption right of three-and-a half million acres of western land, at a reduced rate of 66⅔ cents per acre in specie or in the heavily depreciated continental certificates of debt at par.[10] Cutler's Ohio Company was primarily a genuine colonizing scheme, but Duer's Scioto plan was a recklessly audacious land gamble of staggering proportions. Not only was the venture never chartered as a legitimate company, but the whole affair was conducted in such an underhand manner – without officers, minutes, formal correspondence, records or proceedings – that even today the identity of the majority of the original thirty shareholders remains unknown.

Unable and unwilling to invest any serious money into the scheme, Duer and his obscure 'Scioto Associates' were planning to pay for the land by selling chunks of it on to wealthy Europeans before the specified payment instalments became due in America – a practice speculators at the time referred to as 'dodging'.[11] All they now needed was a bright, energetic and versatile young man of solid background and unsoiled reputation who could represent their interests in Europe – preferably someone with an international public profile who inspired respect and confidence on both sides of the Atlantic. Manasseh Cutler knew just the man for the job. Joel Barlow was a minor agent for the Ohio Company peddling a small portfolio of company shares in Connecticut when Cutler recommended him to Duer as the Scioto Association's agent in Europe. Duer was at first sceptical but allowed himself to be persuaded. As for Barlow, the opportunity to see the wider world beyond his small Hartford law practice was enough to convince him that reselling the Scioto lands to prospective French émigrés was an assignment well worth taking on. Duer's offer of one sixtieth share of the Scioto tract by way of remuneration removed any lingering doubts he might have had.

Barlow arrived in Paris in June 1788, carrying a bundle of blank contracts and a stack of letters of recommendation. While he may have been unapprised of the dubious details of the venture, George Washington was obviously well aware of the precise nature of Barlow's mission to France and the beneficial effect a successful completion of the Scioto project would have on the precarious financial position of the republic. Barely a month after he had become the first President of the United States, Washington supplied no fewer than four letters of recommendation for a young man whom he ostensibly only knew as the author of *The Vision of Columbus*: one to Thomas Jefferson, then American minister to France, one to Comte de Rochambeau, one to Marquis de la Luzerne and one to General Lafayette – to whom Washington described Barlow as 'a genius of the first magnitude' and 'one of the Bards who hold the keys of the gate by which Patriots, Sages and Heroes are admitted to immortality'.[12] Thanks to Washington's endorsement Barlow was soon a regular guest at the salons of the Paris socialites. Getting large investors interested in the Scioto plan proved to be a lot harder. Facing stiff competition from rival land speculation schemes, the wholesale trade in western land was very slow. A year had gone by and Barlow was disheartened and ready to return to America when he met Colonel Samuel Blackden (or 'Blagden') of Massachusetts. Blackden had come to Paris as the agent for Henry Banks and Richard Claiborne, who were the owners of a vast tract of uncleared wilderness in Kentucky bordering on the Ohio River. The tract was to be the future site – or so they claimed – of an idyllic utopian community that was to be named after the renowned Chickasaw chief Piomingo, and was hence marketed under the captivating name of 'Ohiopiomingo'.[13] It was Blackden who introduced Barlow to William Playfair, a Scottish engineer and political economist who had come to France with the plan to establish a steam-powered rolling mill there. However, despite encouragement from Louis XVI himself, nothing came of the plan and Playfair abandoned engineering for the world of commerce. Soon after Playfair became Barlow's partner in the Scioto scheme, they decided to change their business strategy.

An unflagging optimist, Barlow even managed to turn the fall of the Bastille into a new business opportunity. Who could be more eager to resettle on an idyllic farm in Ohio than the persecuted émigrés from the Ancien Régime? In the autumn of 1789 Barlow, Playfair and six prominent Paris merchants founded the Compagnie du Scioto, a paper company set up to persuade French families to buy individual lots in the Scioto tract. Shortly afterwards they published a promotional 'Prospectus pour l'établissement sur les rivières d'Ohio et de Scioto, en Amérique'. Largely composed by William Playfair, the prospectus advertised the Ohio country as an earthly paradise, the crops bountiful, the climate excellent and the government beneficent.[14] By November Barlow reported that business was going well and that he had been concluding his first successful land transactions.[15] Although Barlow had repeatedly implored Duer to come to a firm settlement with Congress respecting legal title to the land, no news had arrived from his employers to confirm that the Scioto lands had actually been surveyed and patented.[16] Even so, Barlow continued to offer and sell land, and to disseminate glowing accounts of the infinite beauties, fertility and other blessings of the Scioto tracts. Perhaps for this reason, the scheme attracted primarily affluent urbanites, many of them members of the nobility, middle-class professionals and well-to-do artisans – all poorly equipped to clear land and to fend for themselves in the western wilderness.

When the first group of six hundred emigrants set out for the Scioto lands in January 1790, Barlow was still desperately urging Duer to provide the money to secure the lands. He pointed out to Duer that the entire Scioto venture depended on the appropriate reception and successful settlement of the first group of emigrants. Thousands of Frenchmen were interested in emigrating but were waiting to find out how the first settlers had fared. After many hardships the unfortunate emigrants arrived in the Ohio country, only to find that the famed city of Galliopolis was in fact a log cabin village, the climate extremely inclement, and the marauding Indian tribes equally unforgiving. Worst of all was that the land that they thought they had bought was not even owned by the Scioto Associates: since Duer and his backers had failed to pay the Ohio Company for their pre-emption right of three-and-a-half million acres, the land had reverted to the Ohio Company. In total around 150,000 acres of land were sold to prospective settlers at around $15 an acre, yet they found themselves stranded on an uninhabitable wilderness plot they did not own. In the meantime, despite his buoyant optimism, Barlow began to realize the venture was beginning to collapse. In the summer of 1790, when Duer attempted to cash a bill for 100,000 *livres* drawn on the Paris operation, Barlow did not have the funds to meet it. Rumours that the Scioto Company was insolvent caused the trickle of funds that had been coming in to dry up well nigh completely. Barlow made a desperate attempt to avert disaster by selling the right to dispose of the Scioto lands to the firm of DeBarth, Coquet and Company but at terms so unfavourable that neither he nor the original Scioto speculators stood to gain anything from it. Duer's bankruptcy in 1792 frustrated any hope his fellow shareholders and the hapless French colonists in and around Galliopolis might have had to recoup their losses.[17] The surviving emigrants were eventually bailed out by Congress in 1795, which granted them by way of compensation a 24,000-acre tract on the Ohio near Galliopolis, known as the 'French Grant'.

Visiting Galliopolis in 1796, Constantin Volney found only about eighty thin, pale and sickly survivors of the original six hundred French settlers; the rest had drifted elsewhere, died, or had never reached the Ohio.[18] Duer and his associates had never been interested in getting title to the land in the first place and only wanted to speculate on the resale and pre-emption rights. In fact, they had been dismayed to learn that Barlow had actually been selling land they did not own and had been recruiting settlers. Although they had given him carte blanche, they had not expected him to turn the speculation scheme into a legitimate land settlement plan. For his part, Barlow does appear to have been sincere in his dream to people the western country, but he was simply not up to the job. He certainly left too much of the daily business to Playfair, a man motivated by ambitions distinctly less honourable than Barlow's. The latter made some provision for the reception for the first batch of emigrants, but since the scheme was disastrously underfunded, the Scioto settlers were largely left to their own devices. When reports of disease, disaster and Indian scalpings began to reach relatives in Paris, Barlow was threatened with assassination and feared an attack on his hotel. To escape further embarrassment and, indeed, danger to his life, Barlow left Paris for London in the spring of 1791.

When he had first visited London in July 1788, Barlow had been carrying Jefferson's letter of introduction to the leading Dissenter and political pamphleteer Dr Richard Price, with whom he was soon on intimate terms. Having in the interim kept up a correspondence with several leading English radicals and writers, Barlow had been warming up to political and economic liberalism. Initially, he had been less than sanguine about the chances of establishing liberal government on the European continent. Yet days after the fall of the Bastille he wrote to his wife Ruth that 'however horrible, however cruel, however just, however noble, memorable, and important in their consequences' the events were he was witnessing in Paris, 'it was really no small gratification' to him 'to have seen two complete revolutions in favor of liberty'.[19] By the time he visited the National Assembly on 10 July 1790 along with eleven other United States citizens to offer his congratulations to the nation on the upcoming first anniversary of the sacking of the Bastille, Barlow had become a zealous convert to the French Revolution. In his speech to the delegates he enthused: 'The western star which is shedding its light from distant shores unites its rays with those of the glorious sun which is pouring floods of light on the French Empire, to enlighten, eventually, the universe'.[20]

Back in London Barlow quickly joined a motley group of reformers, including several American citizens who, for commercial or political reasons, or both, sometimes resided in England and sometimes in France. Soon he was on friendly terms with international radicals such as John Horne Tooke, a prominent member of the Society for Constitutional Information; Thomas Hardy, founder and early leader of the London Corresponding Society; Helen Maria Williams, the poet, novelist and chronicler of the French Revolution; John Hurford Stone, member of the London Revolution Society and printer of Barlow's *The Vision of Columbus*; and Mary Wollstonecraft, who was working on the manuscript of her *Vindication of the Rights of Woman*. Barlow described Wollstonecraft as 'a woman of great original genius', while she and Ruth became close friends.[21] William Godwin, who was drafting the *Enquiry Concerning Political Justice*, the ultimate manifesto in rational anarchy, stopped at the Barlows' one day in 1792 for tea and a discussion of 'self-love, sympathy, and perfectibility, individual and general'.[22] Barlow also met James Mackintosh, author of *Vindiciae Gallicae*; Joseph Priestley, the Dissenting scientist and staunch supporter of the French Revolution; the radical novelist and playwright Thomas Holcroft; and John Thelwall, a prominent ideologue in reform societies such as the Friends of the People, the Society of Constitutional Information and the London Corresponding Society. But the person that made the deepest impression on Barlow was Thomas Paine, whose *Rights of Man* caused a furore shortly after the Barlows arrived in London in the spring of 1791. Barlow would later refer to Paine as 'a luminary of the age, and one of the greatest benefactors of mankind'.[23]

Although he seems to have planned some sort of business venture with the ship and cargo broker Henry Bromfield, Barlow was almost immediately drawn into the Revolutionary Debate between the supporters and detractors of the French Revolution.[24] Before he knew it, he had become one of the Jacobin voices clamouring for radical political change and a new social order. Barlow had only half hoped to find a publisher for his haphazard translation of Brissot's *Nouveau Voyage dans les États-Unis*, but he was in the right place at the right time. Radical publishers were eager to satisfy the growing demand for progressive texts, in particular those presenting idealized views of America, and it was not long before Paine's publisher, J. S. Jordan, brought out an edition of Barlow's translation as *New Travels in the United States of America* (in February 1792). Barlow's *Travels* is a curious text, which is in many ways typical of the period of the 'great debate', during which Jacobins and anti-Jacobins would often put existing texts into the service of their side of the argument almost irrespective of what the original author had intended to say. Despite the fact that Barlow takes earlier writers on America to task for having been 'uniformly superficial, often scurrilous ... and huddling together ... a parcel of unfinished images',[25] it is not entirely inappropriate to consider the *Travels* Barlow's rather than Brissot's creation. Not only is the *Travels* an unfaithful, careless and inaccurate translation, it is also incomplete, containing only about 55 per cent of the original text. Worse still, Barlow apparently felt it was his duty to correct his author's errors and biases, notably deleting most of the passages in Brissot's text which he believed were too critical of the United States. The end result is a bizarre reversal of perspective and authorial intent. Whereas Brissot's original text had invoked the example of the American Revolution to teach the French people how preserve the achievements of their own, Barlow turns the spotlight on the Girondist leader, praising him as a 'courageous defender of the rights of mankind' and recommending the Frenchman's observations to his English and American readers because they could teach them 'the effects of habitual liberty on man in society'.[26] Nor could Barlow resist using a reference in Brissot's text to the Scioto Company to launch a lengthy defence of the company's credentials, aims and practices, and implicitly clear his name in the process. The only emigrants that had any reason to be disappointed in the Scioto affair, he boldly asserts, were aristocrats who had fled France in the hope of setting up a Bourbon monarchy on the banks of the Ohio River.[27]

Despite his interventions – or because of them – Barlow's *Travels* was a huge popular success. Immediately after its publication it was pirated in New York and Dublin, and again in Boston in 1797. In 1794 Jordan brought out a 'corrected' second edition, which was reprinted twice. There were five editions in German (four in 1792 alone, and a fifth in 1796), one in Dutch (in 1794) and one in Swedish (in 1797). Encouraged by the reception of his *Travels*, Barlow was persuaded to abandon the world of business for a while and to add his bit to the revolutionary campaign and accelerate the progress of truth and liberty in Europe. Sharing the radical community's indignation at Edmund Burke's attack on Richard Price, Barlow furiously set to work on his own vindication of the French Revolution. 'I have such a flood of indignation & such a store of argument accumilated in my guts on this subject', Barlow wrote to his brother-in-law, 'that I can hold it no longer; & I think the nurslings of abuse are cut more to the quick than they have yet been by all the diffusions to which the French revolution has given occasion.'[28] Written between October 1791 and January 1792,

Advice to the Privileged Orders in the Several States of Europe appeared in February 1792, a few days before the second part of Paine's *Rights of Man* came out.

Barlow was by no means an original or systematic thinker, but, then, nor were William Godwin or Thomas Paine, to mention only two of the most prominent radicals whose writings set the Revolutionary Decade ablaze. The discourse of late eighteenth-century reform and radicalism was very much the reflection of 'the spirit of the age', itself the product of a century of intellectual history and political and religious dissent. Barlow had become familiar with the work of William Blackstone, Locke, Montesquieu and Adam Smith before he had come to Europe; in France he had dipped into the *philosophes*, including Rousseau, Voltaire, Volney, Holbach and Condorcet; and in England he had profited from talking to Price, Paine and Priestley. Yet Barlow possessed the talent to represent a broad range of eclectic political and economic ideas with new clarity and vigour. With fierce attacks on oppressive government, the monarchy, primogeniture, standing armies, chivalry, and the all-pervasive influence of the Christian church on society, Barlow's *Advice* was considered by many to be as much of a threat to the established order of society as Paine's *Rights of Man*. Thus, in his summing up at the end of the treason trial against members of the London Corresponding Society, Chief Justice Eyre accused the Society's founder, Thomas Hardy, of having wholly approved of 'the works of two celebrated writers, Thomas Paine and Joel Barlow', who sowed 'prejudices against the Monarchy' and dared 'to strike at the Orders of this Country to which the public had a devoted attachment.'[29] And Edmund Burke himself was brought to complain during a debate in the House of Commons that he was constantly reviled over the issue of the French Revolution by radicals like 'Prophet Joel', who 'threatened to lay our capital and constitution to ruin.'[30] However, even though Paine's *Rights of Man* and *Advice to the Privileged Orders* have been described as 'complementary works',[31] Barlow's *Advice* was never banned, as *Rights of Man* was, its author was never convicted for writing it, as Paine was, and Joseph Johnson was never indicted for printing it, as Jordan was for printing *Rights of Man*.

With a new edition issued in June 1792 and other editions appearing in England and the United States, the *Advice to the Privileged Orders* firmly established Barlow's reputation in the public mind as a dedicated campaigner for socio-political reform, or an enemy of the state – depending on people's political convictions. Back in February, Mary Wollstonecraft had praised Barlow's *Advice to the Privileged Orders* as 'a sensible political pamphlet' which had 'prejudised [her] in his favour.'[32] In March John Horne Tooke recommended Barlow to be awarded an honorary membership of the Society for Constitutional Information, whose meetings Barlow had been attending. In October of the same year Barlow followed up on his *Advice* with *A Letter to the National Convention of France, on the Defects in the Constitution of 1791, and the Extent of the Amend-*

ments which Ought to be Applied, which presented his strongest arguments yet for a republic in which there was no room for a limited monarchy. The *Letter* was well received by the Society for Constitutional Information, which in November asked Barlow to be on the committee that was to draw up an address to the National Convention on behalf of the Society. Barlow's address to the Convention on 28 November was met with thunderclaps of approval from the delegates, but the British government is said to have been so alarmed by it that it may have prompted the treason trials of 1794.[33] Barlow even became embroiled in the cross-Channel propaganda war that erupted between France and Britain following the formal declaration of hostilities on 1 February. By a decree of 17 February 1793 the National Convention made the American an honorary citizen of France; at about the same time Barlow was forced to write to his wife in London under the alias of 'Mrs. Brownlow' after the British authorities had started to open his letters, while a friend, Colonel Hichborn, who had set out for London with letters for Ruth, had been stopped at Calais.[34]

However, domestic political developments in France would soon put an end to Barlow's role on the international political scene. By February 1793 the bitter power struggle between Girondists and Jacobins which had been slumbering for almost a year was coming to a head. When Robespierre's party finally ousted the Girondists from the Convention in June 1793, Barlow, like most Americans and Britons who had been active supporters of the Revolution under the Girondists, was almost overnight purged from the halls of power and fame. He gave up his political activities and quietly withdrew with Ruth into anonymity in the Parisian suburb of Mendon in June 1793. His letters of this period are virtually silent about the carnage that was spilling out over the streets of Paris during the Terror. In October he was an eyewitness to the execution of Brissot and other Girondist leaders, an account of which he included in the biographical sketch prefacing his translation of Brissot's *The Commerce of America with Europe; Particularly with France and Great Britain; Comparatively Stated and Explained* (1797). With the collapse of the fledgling French Republic and the suspension of the constitution in the autumn of 1793, Barlow lost both his mission in life and his extensive network of friends. Historical events once more forced him to reinvent himself.

Although he had become one of the most prominent Americans in Europe, Barlow was living in daily fear of his life during the Reign of Terror; since the collapse of the Scioto project, he had been virtually destitute as well. However, by 1796, at his own estimation, he was worth $120,000.[35] The general state of war in Europe had brought misery and distress to many, but had evidently brought windfall profits to a few. While Thomas Paine had fallen out of grace with the revolutionary government for opposing the execution of Louis XVI and had barely escaped the guillotine, Barlow managed to avoid political controversy and hence continued to enjoy the protection and benefits of his double citizenship.

Delicately treading the high wire between loyalty to the republican principles of
1792 and his early ambition to make his fortune, Barlow was fortunate enough
that Robespierre's government needed his services as an American trader in
France at least as much as he needed their business.

Barlow was by no means loath to go into the trading business. Immediately
after he had first arrived at Le Havre back in June 1788, he had been fascinated
by the intense spirit of entrepreneurship that pervaded the port town and by
the sheer volume of trade going on there. 'Havre is the principal entreport for
the province of Normandie, & and I believe for the Isle of France', he noted in
his diary. 'The African trade, the Baltic trade & the West India trade flourish
here'.[36] He was amazed to find that the town was absolutely packed with people.
Estimating that at least 30,000 people were living within its walls, he reported
that the town was about to be expanded. In the light of his own future career as
a merchant, it is interesting that Barlow was quick to note how war could boost
international trade. Writing in his diary, he observed:

> The town is enclosed with high walls, which in the days of ancient fortification were
> necessary against invasion, and are now as necessary against smuggling. This is gener-
> ally the case thro' Europe; that wars of conquest are turned into wars of revenue, &
> the contests between sovereign princes or states, are now contests between the prince
> and his people. For this purpose every considerable town in France is honoured with
> a regiment of soldiers, whose business is not so much to keep the peace, as to assist in
> collecting duties.[37]

Based on data he collected, he made an estimate of the duties collected annually
at Le Havre: 40 million *livres* on tobacco, 50 million on salt, and 37 million on
all other goods. He also kept a record of the provenance of the ships arriving at
Le Havre and of the cargoes they carried. He was particularly surprised to learn
about the significance of the trade with Scandinavia. A Swedish merchant by the
name of Jacobson told him that Gothenburg, although a considerably smaller
town, had a bigger trade going on than New York, mainly in whale oil, mackerel
and iron.

However, Barlow's commercial relations with Robespierre's repressive administration were less opportunistic than they may appear. The French Revolution
might have slid into tyranny, but Barlow was hopeful that in due course the
butchers would soon fall by their own knives. At the same time he was frustrated
to see France's bid for liberty, equality and fraternity undermined by the international coalition of hostile powers. He was convinced that Britain's economic
blockade was ultimately aimed at reinstating the absolute rule of the Bourbons
in France. The best hope for republicanism and natural rights to regain force in
France was to help the nation hold its own against its despotic enemies. Britain's interference with neutral American shipping was in his eyes not merely an

attack on the freedom of trade but on civil liberty itself. By running the British blockade and, indeed, on occasion flouting some of the French government's own trade restrictions, Barlow was striking a blow for freedom.[38]

Barlow's involvement in the risky but highly lucrative wartime import and export trade had started in the spring of 1793, when he responded to an invitation from Colonel Benjamin Hichborn of Massachusetts to act as a shipping broker and agent. A prominent Boston lawyer and ardent republican, Hichborn had come to Europe to make his fortune in the trade between France and the United States. By the time he approached Barlow, Hichborn had already taken two fellow Americans into his business, Mark Leavenworth and Daniel Parker, a banker who had briefly been involved in the Scioto scheme. In the late spring of 1793, Hichborn travelled to London to charter a suitable English vessel for the trade with the continent. He signed a contract with Henry Bromfield, a London merchant, leasing the *Cumberland* to the four Americans. The ship was laden with flour and rice, ostensibly destined for Bilbao in Spain, but it never got there. As it reached the mouth of the Gironde, the ship suddenly tacked to Bordeaux, where everything was in readiness to receive the cargo.[39]

Chartering English vessels or sailing a neutral vessel under an English flag was one way for the blockade runners to get around the orders of June and November 1793, by which the British had given themselves the right to seize enemy goods or goods destined for France in neutral vessels. But the profits that could be made in the trade with wartime France were such that many hundreds of American ship owners and merchants did not even bother to go to such lengths. American shipping to Europe expanded furiously during the Revolutionary wars and France was teeming with American opportunists of all walks of life eager to make a quick dollar where they saw a chance. When James Monroe took over from Gouverneur Morris as American ambassador to France in 1794, he was shocked that 'the only Americans whom [he] found [t]here were a set of New England men connected with Britain who upon British capital were trading to this country'.[40] Monroe singled out James Swan as 'a corrupt unprincipled rasca[l] who, 'by virtue of being the agent of France' and 'the only or most creditable resident American' in France at a time when America had no minister in that country, 'had a monopoly of the trade of both countries'. That 'unprincipled rascal' happened to be Joel Barlow's closest business partner.

A Boston merchant and financier, Colonel James Swan was a veteran of the American Revolutionary War. Yet his most memorable contribution to American independence had taken place in the run up to the war. On 16 December 1773, Swan and other members of the patriot brotherhood known as the 'sons of liberty' dressed up as Mohawks, stormed aboard three unsuspecting British ships in Boston harbour and dumped 342 crates of tea overboard. Like Barlow, Swan arrived in Le Havre in the early weeks of 1788. Having cultivated the acquaintance of the prominent merchants at Le Havre and Rouen and published a memorial stimulating trade between France and America, Swan, in partnership with Colonel Samuel Blackden, submitted a plan to the Ancien Régime in September 1788 aimed at alleviating the dire shortage of the population's essential food – bread – by importing American grains and cereals.[41] However, the plan expired amidst the ministerial jealousies of the dying regime. In 1791 Swan entered into a partnership with a French firm.[42] Initially, Dallarde, Swan & Company, as the new company was called, did most of its business with the ministry of the navy. But it was only when the British blockade was beginning to have an impact on the supply of food and war materials that Swan's business with the free-trading Girondists picked up dramatically. In order to deal with the problem of supplies, the Committee for Public Safety under Robespierre's leadership in October 1793 established the Commission des Subsistances. One of the Commission's main aims was to combat speculation and racketeering by individual merchants. Although the Jacobins scorned the merchant class in general for being anti-republican, the Commission knew only too well that the French army could not be armed and the people fed without merchants – particularly those involved in international shipping. No doubt making the most of his part in America's own struggle against the British, Swan was soon on excellent terms with the members of the Commission.

Having set up his headquarters at 63, rue de la Réunion (formerly the rue Montmorency), during the winter of 1793–4 Swan drew up a number of memoranda addressed to the Commission in which he outlined ways in which the Republic might benefit from the trade with neutral states in general and with his own company in particular.[43] According to Swan, the United States and other neutral countries would be willing to supply France with such commodities as wheat, rice, tobacco, indigo, salt meats, leather, naval stores, dried peas and beans, potash, pearl ash and saltpeter, provided that an acceptable method of payment could be agreed upon. Since the Republic could ill afford to export specie or draw upon whatever credit it had left abroad, the only way France could obtain the commodities it so desperately needed, Swan suggested, was to barter them against the goods it could part with without harming the war effort – that is, non-essential or 'luxury' goods. Well-to-do Americans, Swan maintained, would be eager to lay their hands on fine furniture, statues, clocks, mirrors and other luxury objects that had formerly adorned the palaces of the Bourbons and the mansions of the aristocracy.[44] Silks, taffetas, satins, laces and other 'anti-republican' materials would be equally sought after by affluent Americans – not to mention fine wines and brandies.[45] Swan also recommended that the Commission buy cargoes straight from ships' captains in the ports, ask no questions about the provenance of the goods and pay immediately and handsomely. Under these conditions, Swan assured the Commission, vessels flying the English flag would even allow themselves to be captured by the French off Dieppe, Le Havre or Saint-Valéry. Overseeing an extensive network of agents in Le Havre, London, Hamburg and Spain and having dealings with a large number of American captains, Swan's own company was excellently placed to oversee such and other activities to 'neutralize' cargoes, at a modest commission of 2 per cent, clear of all charges.[46]

Despite their reservations about mercantilism, Robespierre's government adopted Swan's proposal as their procurement model. A Commission report of February 1794 confirms that Swan's company had shipped a wide variety of commodities worth upwards of 20 million *livres* into France from ports in America, Portugal, the Netherlands and the Baltic.[47] The Thermidorian coup of July 1794 put an end to Robespierre's rule and, effectively, terminated the work of the Commission des Subsistances; however, Swan fared even better under its successor, the Commission du Commerce et Approvisionnements. Under the new Commission's direction, the procurement system of individual traders and special agents was revoked and the trade with neutral countries was placed in the hands of four commercial firms known for their commitment to the republican cause. The company that won the exclusive contract for the trade with the United States was 'James Swan & Johann Schweizer' – disguised in official correspondence under the code name of 'Jones & Gaspard'.[48] In the late autumn of 1794 James Swan set off for his native America after an absence of nearly seven years. From December 1794 to January 1796, 'Agence Swan' would be the official purchasing agent of the French government in the United States.[49] During the first seven months of 1795 alone, Swan managed to send over a hundred shiploads of provisions to France. All shipments were so expertly 'neutralized' – being sent in the name of American merchants, on American vessels, under American captains – that only seventeen were taken by the British (who in most cases were eventually forced to pay restitution).[50]

Although Swan had warned the Commission des Subsistances that the entire operation should be carried out under the utmost secrecy, the Commission's records contain details of transactions with a number of Americans, including Joel Barlow, Benjamin Jarvis, Mark Leavenworth, Michael O'Mealy, Benjamin Hichborn and George Meade.[51] Of these, Joel Barlow probably had the most extensive dealings with the Commission, with the exception of James Swan. By late 1793 he was dealing directly with the Commissioners.[52] His international reputation as a staunch supporter of the republican ideal, not to mention his dual citizenship, undoubtedly gave him an edge over most other competitors bidding for government procurement contracts. Like Swan, Barlow had a knack for weathering the Revolution's political storms, successively winning the confidence of Brissot's Girondist administration and Robespierre's Jacobin regime, as well as the Directory. Operating from the same business premises as Swan's, at 63 rue de la Réunion, Barlow was soon at the head of an extensive network of agents, sub-agents and captains that spanned much of Europe. His business correspondence, diaries and notebooks report the many business trips he made to Antwerp, Amsterdam, Hamburg and its neighbour town, the Danish enclave of Altona. Barlow conducted a particularly brisk trade with Scandinavia, where the Gothenburg based merchant Elias Backman was his main contact. Thus, in January 1794 Barlow sold an entire shipload of potash, 4,000 quintals, to the French government. Even though the Commission had complained about the exorbitant price Barlow was asking for it, they bought the cargo for 440,000 *livres* (or about $88,000).[53] Between France's need and the merchants' greed, handsome profits were to be made. Most of the 'neutralized' cargoes that Barlow managed to bring through the British blockade and into France were received by his trusted associates at Le Havre. One of his most loyal agents there was Gilbert Imlay.

When he arrived in Paris in February 1793, Imlay was vacillating between business and politics. Thomas Cooper's letter of recommendation to Brissot de Warville and his reputation as an expert on the western territory of North America had gained Imlay access to the inner circle of Thomas Paine's powerful political allies and associates. Rubbing shoulders at Paine's political salons with the likes of the Girondist leader Brissot, his interior minister Roland and the Venezuelan revolutionary General Francisco de Miranda, Imlay soon sniffed the wind of the regime's politics vis-à-vis the Spanish possessions in America. Within weeks of arriving in the French capital he produced the two memoranda in which he unfolded his plans to oust the Spanish from the Louisiana territory and hand back control to the French government. However, their ambitions being already inclined in that direction, the French ministers hardly needed encouragement. Indeed, the Committee of Public Safety had recently dispatched Citizen Genet to America with the secret brief to 'liberate' Spanish America. Besides, the increasingly bitter tussle between the Girondists and the Jacobins over the question of whether to execute Louis XVI or to dispose of him by imprisonment or banishment, and the subsequent radicalization of France's domestic political agenda, soon put an end to the Girondists' dream of reconquering New Orleans and Spanish Louisiana. Imlay's role as an agent provocateur ended with it.

One of Imlay's earliest business associates in Paris was Thomas Christie. Christie was in Paris as the agent for the London firm of Turnbull, Forbes & Company, which by 1792 still had a contract with the city of Paris to deliver corn. Imlay also had an agreement with this firm, as well as with another firm established in London, Chalmers & Cowie.[54] Like Imlay, Christie seamlessly combined a career in business with a life of letters and an active involvement in the republican movement in Britain. A nephew of the radical scientist Joseph

Priestley, Christie co-founded the highly influential *Analytical Review* with Joseph Johnson in 1788. In 1790 he spent six months in Paris, during which time he met many leading French revolutionaries, including the Comte de Mirabeau, president of the National Assembly, and Jacques Necker, the new regime's minister of finance. Having become a loyal supporter of the Revolution, upon his return to England Christie was one of many who participated in the Revolutionary Debate that erupted following the publication in 1790 of Edmund Burke's *Reflections on the Revolution in France*. In his *Letters on the Revolution of France and on the New Constitution Established by the National Assembly*, Christie refuted Burke's attack on the French Revolution as being lawless and violent.[55] In September 1792 Christie married a Miss Thomson and joined her grandfather, Mr Moore, as a partner in the latter's carpet manufacturing business at Finsbury Square. Imlay may well have known the Christies in London; at any rate, he quickly became a regular guest at their residence in Paris. It was there that he first met Mary Wollstonecraft, who was a close friend of Joseph Johnson and a regular reviewer for the *Analytical*. Imlay had always adhered to the principle that business and love did not 'chime together'; he was about to put his principle to the test.

9 BLOCKADE RUNNER AND INFAMOUS LOVER

I just now received one of your hasty notes; for business so entirely occupies you, that
you have not time, or sufficient command of thought, to write letters. Beware! you
seem to be got into a whirl of projects and schemes, which are drawing you into a gulf,
that, if it do not absorb your happiness, will infallibly destroy mine
Mary Wollstonecraft to Gilbert Imlay, 9 January 1795[1]

Gilbert Imlay's tempestuous but ill-fated relationship with Mary Wollstonecraft
has been recounted and picked over so often in the past two centuries that it
has become one of the most notorious causes célèbres in British literary history.[2] Wollstonecraft's collected letters to Imlay offer a poignant and revealing
insight into the ups and downs of their affair, and literary history owes a significant debt to William Godwin, Imlay's successor, for deciding not to destroy
the letters after his wife's death in 1797. Posterity would have been even more
appreciative had Godwin not interfered with Wollstonecraft's letters. As it is,
he not only expunged all proper names from the letters but particularly cut
those sections from her letters to Imlay that might otherwise have detracted
from the image he was trying to create of Wollstonecraft as a woman of great
sensibility and deep emotions.[3] Yet, heart-rending as the edited letters are,
Wollstonecraft's correspondence with Imlay inevitably represents her side of
the story; indeed, the entire sad tale of Wollstonecraft's affair with Imlay is
very much part of *her* biography, rather than his. If Imlay's treatment of Wollstonecraft has become one of literary history's most notorious sagas of a lover's
betrayal and abandonment, this is only because it has always been assumed and
expected that both partners were from the beginning equally committed to
their relationship. They were not.

Wollstonecraft's state of mind prior to when she first met Imlay has been well
documented. On the eve of her projected six-week trip to France, Wollstonecraft
joked in a letter to William Roscoe that she was 'still a spinster on the wing' who
might in Paris 'take a husband of the time being'.[4] She was putting a thin veil over
the fact that she was actually quite eager to settle into a long-lasting relationship,
if not immediately into marriage. At thirty-four, she would have been regarded
by most people at the time as too old for the marriage market.[5] The journey to

France had been undertaken in the first place to escape from the fiasco of the platonic relationship she had in desperation tried to set up with the artist Henry Fuseli and his wife. It was evident that by late 1792, Wollstonecraft, in Godwin's words, 'felt herself formed for domestic affection, and all those tender charities, which men of sensibility have constantly treated as the dearest band of human society'.[6]

'Domestic affection', however, was an alien concept to Imlay. He had never experienced it before, neither as a child nor as an adult, and, frankly, it made him feel quite uncomfortable. He told Wollstonecraft that he preferred the 'zest of life' to settling down into sympathetic domesticity with her.[7] She, of course, scoffed at his 'zest of life', which she thought amounted to merely a vulgar appetite for 'crooked business' and 'sensual pleasure' – or, in plainer language, 'eating, drinking, and women'.[8] Imlay admitted that he had lived with other women, that he was, in fact, still smarting from a recent liaison with a 'cunning woman' and, presumably, that he was hence not ready to commit himself at that point.[9] And marriage, of course, was entirely out of the question; he had made abundantly clear in *The Emigrants* that he considered it to be a corrupt institution. It also needs to be emphasized that during the three years, roughly, that Wollstonecraft was romantically involved with Imlay, the couple barely lived together for twelve months; even during this period Imlay spent most of his time away on some frantic business errand or other. The fact of the matter is, then, that although the figure of Gilbert Imlay loomed large in Mary Wollstonecraft's life between March 1793 and March 1796, she existed only on the margins of his.

When she first met him at the Christies', presumably some time in March, Imlay instilled such a feeling of 'dislike' in her that 'for some time' Wollstonecraft 'shunned all occasions of meeting him'.[10] It is quite conceivable that she took offence at 'Captain' Imlay's demeanour towards her: she regarded the kind of 'gallantry' with which officers tended to approach women as a particularly degrading form of sexual and moral enslavement.[11] She may have 'secretly panted' for her ideal male companion, but she was not about to be 'bribed into the love of slavery'.[12] Yet by the middle of April she and Imlay were in the throes of a passionate relationship. Her early letters to Imlay evince how Wollstonecraft, in Godwin's words, 'nourished an affection, which she saw no necessity of subjecting to restraint; and a heart like hers was not formed to nourish affection by halves. Her confidence was entire. Now, for the first time in her life, she gave a loose to all the sensibilities of her nature.'[13] There is nothing odd about a very attractive, intelligent, independent and passionate thirty-four-year-old woman with long wavy auburn hair falling head-over-heels in love with a tall, lithe, charming and handsome thirty-nine-year-old veteran of the American Revolution. Yet beyond their mutual physical attraction, Wollstonecraft and Imlay were above all brought together by the historical conditions dictated by the French

Revolution. Both had been drawn into the maelstrom of political controversy in England generated by the French Revolution, and it was on the wings of their contributions to the Revolutionary Debate – notably *A Vindication of the Rights of Woman* and *A Topographical Description* – that both had been carried across the Channel to Paris, quickly to be subsumed there into the close-knit expatriate community of British and American Revolution tourists.

The first contemporary account of their relationship is contained in a 19 April letter from Joel Barlow to his wife Ruth, who was then in London (Figure 7). Barlow, who had evidently been concerned about her as a single British woman amidst the political turmoil of the French Revolution, was relieved to discover that Wollstonecraft had finally found love – and protection:

> Mary is exceedingly distressed at your last letter – 26 March – to think that you are not to come here. She writes you today, she wrote a long letter before which it seems you have not got. Between you and me – you must not hint it to her nor to J[ohnso]n nor to anyone else – I believe she has got a Sweetheart – and that she will finish by going with him to A[meric]a a wife. he is of Kentucky & a very sensible man. Mum – I will tell you more when I know more.[14]

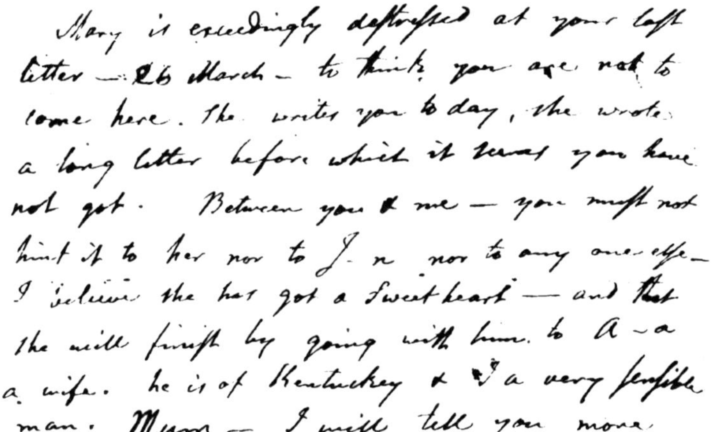
Mary is exceedingly distressed at your last
letter — 26 March — to think you are not to
come here. She writes you to day, she wrote
a long letter before which it seems you have
not got. Between you & me — you must not
hint it to her nor to J— n nor to any one else —
I believe she has got a Sweetheart — and that
she will finish by going with him to A — a
a wife. he is of Kentuckey & a very sensible
man. Mum — I will tell you more
when I know more..

Figure 7. Letter from Joel Barlow to Ruth Barlow, 19 April 1793. Courtesy of Houghton Library, Harvard College Library, Harvard University, Cambridge, Massachusetts.

Intellectually speaking, it is not hard to see why Wollstonecraft, the outspoken feminist and celebrated author of *A Vindication of the Rights of Woman*, might be attracted Imlay, the smooth-talking expert on the western territory of North America and best-selling author of the *Topographical Description*. Imlay's account of the western territory as the future site of a socially-just utopia had made a strong impression on many progressive minds in Britain who considered their society to be hopelessly corrupt and their civil and natural rights increasingly under threat from an outdated and despotic government. Offering both a blueprint for an American Arcadia and a practical 'How-to-emigrate-to-Kentucky' guide, Imlay's book convinced many that a Rousseauesque return to an original state of nature in the pristine wilderness of the New World was more than a dream. Throughout her adult life Wollstonecraft had been in dialogue with Jean-Jacques Rousseau's philosophy, notably his concept of natural education. In his fullest treatment of the subject, his novel *Émile, ou l'Education* (1762), Rousseau describes the story of a boy's upbringing in a natural state. While she applauded Rousseau's general principle of natural education, Wollstonecraft deplored his projected education of Sophie, the young woman intended for Émile's wife. For Rousseau, a woman's unique purpose is to please men, and to be charming, modest, virtuous and submissive. Wollstonecraft's disappointment in Rousseau stimulated her to articulate her own ideas on female education in the *Vindication*. She argued that if women constituted 'a frivolous sex', being superficial, silly and wanton or a combination thereof, it was because they were raised and educated to be so.[15] Educate girls as rational human beings, alongside boys, she proposed, and they will become not only as rational as their male counterparts, but useful members of society as well: 'Would men but generously snap our chains, and be content with rational fellowship instead of slavish obedience, they would find us more observant daughters, more affectionate sisters, more faithful wives, more reasonable mothers – in a word, better citizens'.[16] No matter how self-evident it may sound today, Wollstonecraft's vindication of the rights of woman was perceived by the British establishment to be as much of a threat to the social order as the French Revolution itself. Wollstonecraft knew that her feminist manifesto was light years removed from being implemented in Britain; by the spring of 1793 she had seen enough of the daily reality of the French Revolution to realize that gender relations were not going to change there any time soon, either.

Wollstonecraft had been fantasizing about an idyllic life on a farm in America for some time. Such a life of agrarian simplicity far removed from the corrupting impact of conventional society could be the ideal setting for an experiment in social utopianism based on her ideas concerning pastoral domesticity, egalitarianism, virtue and sympathetic affection. More practically, an independent, freeholding family farm would provide a safe haven for her impoverished sisters Eliza and Everina, whom she had been supporting financially as best she could. Before coming to France, Wollstonecraft had been asking the help of Joel Barlow to set her drifting younger brother Charles up on a farm in America. Indeed, she had arranged that the Barlows would chaperone Charles en route to America after the collapse of the Scioto debacle. This plan had fallen through by September 1792, after Joel Barlow had decided to stay in Europe in order to pursue a career as a radical writer and political activist. Charles had finally set off for America on his own, carrying a letter from Barlow to his Yale friend James Watson, in which he recommended Charles Wollstonecraft as 'a young gentleman of singular merit ... on his way to the Ohio, where he goes to be an American farmer'.[17] It was only after she had started seeing Imlay that her dream of emigrating to America and reuniting her dispersed siblings on a farm there suddenly looked like it might become a reality. In June she wrote to Eliza: 'I will venture to *promise* that brighter days are in store for you. I cannot explain myself excepting just to tell you that I have a plan in my head, it may prove abortive, in which you and Everina are included, if you find it good, that I contemplate with pleasure as a mode of bringing us all together again.'[18] Getting into business around this time, Imlay had apparently told Wollstonecraft that his aim was to gain £1,000, which would have been 'sufficient to have procured a farm in America, which would have been an independence'.[19] And who was more informed about the feasibility of such a scheme than the author of *A Topographical Description of the Western Territory of North America*, a former 'Commissioner for laying out Land in the Back Settlements'? Not only was her lover an expert on settlement in the western territory, his soul and being had been moulded by the very life of modest rural simplicity she was hankering after. Imlay was a 'most worthy man', she wrote to Everina, 'who joins to uncommon tenderness of heart and quickness of feeling, a soundness of understanding, and reasonableness of temper, rarely to be met with – Having also been brought up in the interior parts of America, he is a most natural, unaffected creature'.[20] Her excitement at having found this American incarnation of Rousseau's Émile was only matched by her anticipation of a life of domestic harmony and bliss on an American farm.[21]

Wollstonecraft may have loved him for his 'honest sympathy' and his 'frankness of heart', but Imlay was no unspoiled child of nature.[22] The last thing on his mind was to transplant himself to some desolate spot in the howling wilderness on the western frontier of America. He had seen too many poor emigrants harvest a meagre income from stony fields, pine away from hunger or disease, be scalped by marauding Indian bands, or, indeed, swindled out of their money or their land by land-jobbers like himself. It must have been quite bewildering, even daunting to him to see an idealized image of himself take complete control over the mind and the imagination of a passionate and emotionally vulnerable woman. Perhaps that is why he could never bring himself to tell her about his racketeering days in wartime New Jersey and his land-jobbing activities in Kentucky – not to mention his brief encounter with the triangular trade. Even Wollstonecraft's early letters to Imlay reveal a woman who was capable of quite dramatic mood swings, from the heights of heady infatuation to the deepest ravines of gloom, melancholy and depression. Was it reprehensible or merely faint hearted – or was it perhaps considerate – that Imlay concealed his unsavoury past from the woman who had decided that not just her happiness but her very sanity depended on his probity and his love for her? 'I will be *good*', wrote Wollstonecraft to her lover, 'that I may deserve to be happy; and whilst you love me, I cannot again fall into the miserable state, which rendered life a burthen almost too heavy to be borne ... I not only wonder how I can find fault with you – but how I can doubt your affection ... I assure you, that you are the friend of my bosom, and the prop of my heart'.[23]

Needless to say, Imlay and Wollstonecraft never made it to their farm in America. The closest they got to living the pastoral idyll was after Wollstonecraft left her lodgings with the Fillietaz family in rue Melée (Meslay) and relocated to a house in Neuilly-sur-Seine, then a village just north of the Bois de Boulogne. Following the Jacobin coup of 31 May 1793, Robespierre had proposed that all foreigners should be expelled; since, like most British expatriates, she had been close to the ousted Girondists, Wollstonecraft thought it was expedient to leave Paris. An additional reason may have been that, except for the Fillietaz's old gardener who looked after the house and garden in Neuilly, she had the place to herself, which made it a lot more convenient to organize rendezvous with Imlay. As an American citizen, Imlay could remain in Paris, where he had an apartment in Saint-Germain-des-Prés. The couple would meet at the barrièrre de Neuilly, one of the fifty-four tollgates in the city wall. Skirting the guillotine in the place de la Révolution, Imlay would bring her the latest news, along with the newspapers. She later recalled how she would occasionally set out to meet him crossing the fields of waving corn and carrying her basket of grapes, enacting the pastoral image she had created in her mind.[24] Every time she would leave the cottage to go to meet Imlay at the barrier, the old gardener would express his concern, for, to get to the barrier, Wollstonecraft had to cross the Bois de Boulogne, which was teeming with dangerous characters. But she would brush aside his concerns, saying that the great love she felt made her immune from all danger.[25] Far from being threatening, the Bois de Boulogne became their lovers' nest. When their daughter Fanny, who was named for Mary's dear friend Fanny Blood, was born in May of the following year, Wollstonecraft would fondly refer to her as 'my barrier-girl'.[26]

However, storm clouds were gathering over their idyll. On 27 August the moderate republicans in Toulon, who had been holding out against the forces of the Jacobins, opened the harbour and city to the British fleet commanded by General Hood. When the news reached Paris, the National Convention responded in xenophobic outrage and on 17 September 1793 passed the Law of Suspects. Under the new law anyone who was merely suspected of treason against the Republic could be arrested and incarcerated indefinitely, while so-called revolutionary tribunals were authorized to convict those found guilty and sentence them to death by the guillotine. Though the law was formally aimed at all 'enemies of liberty', foreigners were automatically treated as 'suspects'. Because of the war between the two countries, British expatriates in France were particularly vulnerable to random arrest. Imlay knew he had to act swiftly. In order to provide diplomatic protection for her, he registered Wollstonecraft as his wife at the American Embassy.[27] While they were not formally married, the certificate issued by the American ambassador, Gouverneur Morris, effectively extended Imlay's American citizenship to Wollstonecraft.[28] She could now safely leave Neuilly and return to Paris, where she moved into Imlay's apartment in Saint-Germain. Imlay's intervention had been both judicious and timely, for between 10 and 14 October about 250 British subjects were arrested and imprisoned in the Luxembourg, among them Wollstonecraft's friends Helen Maria Williams and Count von Schlabrendorf.

Now living openly with Imlay in Paris, and possibly having realized that she was pregnant, Wollstonecraft took Imlay's name – occasionally signing her letters 'Mary Imlay' or 'Mrs. Imlay'.[29] However, their 'honeymoon' was of short duration. About two months after they had started to live together, Imlay left for Le Havre on urgent business. His sudden departure, probably in the early days of November, was undoubtedly related to Committee for Public Safety in the preceding month having established a Commission des Subsistances, which was to regulate the import and export of food supplies and other goods vital to the Republic.[30] Since they had direct access to Robespierre's purchasing Commission, it was probably either Joel Barlow or his close associate Benjamin Hichborn who had sent Imlay to Le Havre as their logistics manager. It is more than likely that James Swan was also in one way or another involved in the venture.[31] While Barlow and his associates negotiated with the Commission about prices and ways of payment, Imlay handled the incoming and outgoing shipments, dealing with ships' captains, customs and accounts. Since secrecy was at the heart of all operations, Mark Leavenworth and Samuel Blackden acted as liaison officers, carrying messages back and forth between Joel Barlow's headquarters in the rue de la Réunion and Imlay's outfit in Le Havre (along with Imlay and Wollstonecraft's private correspondence).

Imlay left Paris shortly after what would turn out to be one of the most dramatic and historic stages in the evolution of the French Revolution. The Jacobin coup of June was coming to its period of reckoning and the guillotine was working overtime. First, Marie Antoinette was beheaded on 16 October. Then, on 31 October, Imlay was the first to bring Wollstonecraft the shocking news that Brissot, along with twenty other Girondist leaders, had been guillotined that same day.[32] On 8 November, only days after Imlay's departure for Le Havre, Madame Roland was conveyed to the guillotine. Before placing her head on the block, she bowed before the clay statue of Liberty in the Place de la Révolution, uttering the famous remark for which she is remembered: 'O Liberté, que de crimes on commet en ton nom!' ('Oh Liberty, what crimes are committed in thy name!'). With Imlay back at Le Havre frantically looking after his and Barlow's business interests, Wollstonecraft remained in Paris, trying to stay composed yet fully aware that she was 'nourishing a creature who [would] soon be sensitive of [her] care', even as Robespierre's blood-letting was at a frenzy.[33]

Inevitably, strains soon appeared in their relationship. Without any other obvious source of income at his disposal, Imlay was eager to make the best of the trade opportunities that were suddenly opening up under Robespierre's new purchasing regime. A self-confessed hater of commerce, Wollstonecraft became increasingly frustrated at Imlay evidently preferring doing business to spending his time with her and their unborn child.[34] Interpreting his continued stay at Le Havre as a sure sign that he had stopped loving her as before, Wollstonecraft began to show signs of delusion and depression. Directing a barrage of letters at him, she now upbraided him for his mercantilism, then apologized for adding to his worries; now telling him she was 'hurt' because he did not write, then crying tears of happiness when he did. Though Wollstonecraft's position was far from enviable, it must have been quite disconcerting to have been the recipient of some of her letters. The longer the separation lasted, the more intense her feeling for Imlay became, to the point where she began to suffer from erotomania. Sometimes she appeared to be possessed by Imlay and would then be obsequiously submissive towards him; at other times she could be almost aggressively possessive and would be imperious towards him. In January 1794, she wrote to Imlay:

> You have, by your tenderness and worth, twisted yourself more artfully round my heart, than I supposed possible. – Let me indulge the thought, that I have thrown out some tendrils to cling to the elm by which I wish to be supported ... But, knowing that I am not a parasite-plant, I am willing to receive the proofs of affection, that every pulse replies to, when I think of being once more in the same house with you.[35]

When one of Imlay's business associates, probably Blackden (a man who liked his drink), inadvertently confirmed what she had already suspected – that Imlay would have to remain in Le Havre for another couple of months – Wollstonecraft's melancholy turned into despair. At that point Imlay thought it expedient to invite her to come to Le Havre.

When she arrived at Le Havre on 25 January, both Wollstonecraft and Imlay registered with the police. Imlay registered as 'négociant', while Wollstonecraft, keeping up the fiction her of American citizenship, signed the register as 'Marie Imlay – Citoiene des Etas Unis', stating as her place of residence, 'Virginia'.[36] Imlay had rented a spacious house for them owned by an English soap manufacturer, John Wheatcroft, Jr, located conveniently close to the harbour, on the rue de Corderie in the Section des Sans-Culottes. Keeping several servants and regularly entertaining guests, the Imlays for a while led the conventional life of a bourgeois married couple. The birth of their daughter, Fanny, on 14 May 1794, completed the scene of conjugal domesticity. The child was duly regis-

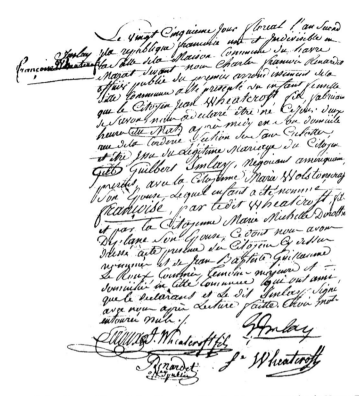

Figure 8. Birth Certificate of Fanny Imlay. Courtesy of the Archives municipales du Havre, France.

tered that same day in the Maison Commune of Havre-Marat (as Le Havre was now called) as 'Françoise', born in the 'legitimate marriage' of 'Citoyen Guilbert Imlay, Négotiant américain' and 'Citoyenne Marie Wollstonecraft son épouse' (Figure 8).[37] John Wheatcroft, Jr, and his wife were the witnesses. Wollstonecraft was soon engrossed in the pleasures and challenges of motherhood. As for Imlay, parenting does not appear to have come naturally to him. In fact, he seems to have been slightly embarrassed by the sudden intrusion into his private space of the new mother-daughter alliance: 'My little Girl begins to suck so *manfully*', Wollstonecraft wrote to Ruth Barlow, 'that her father reckons saucily on her writing the second part of the R—ts of Woman'.[38] Fortunately, a major trading venture was about to demand all of his time and energy and would require him to be out of doors a lot. The venture would soon snowball out of control and take over their lives.

It all started rather innocuously with what amounts to an act of kindness. Earlier in the spring of 1794, Imlay had bought a ship from an American captain.[39] There was nothing remarkable about this in itself, since it was one of the regular tasks in his partnership with Barlow to find vessels that could pick up cargoes in neutral counties, notably Sweden and Denmark, and then, hopefully, run the shipments through the British blockade into Le Havre. The American captain had previously hired as his master the twenty-five-year-old Norwegian Peder Ellefsen, who not only lost his employment when the ship was sold, but also found himself marooned at Le Havre. Imlay was evidently struck by the young man's distress. He initially slipped Ellefsen some money to support himself and hired him to do odd jobs. Soon Imlay began to entrust weightier tasks to the Norwegian, who came from an old established family of wealthy ironmasters and ship owners in the seafaring town of Arendal. Perhaps it was because of Ellefsen's respectable background or perhaps he simply had little choice: at any rate, in the late spring Imlay on two or three occasions dispatched Ellefsen to Paris to collect shipments of silverware and silver bullion (the product of the melting of ecclesiastical ornaments and other confiscated objects). In all likelihood these concerned advance payments from the Commission des Subsistances for goods they wished to purchase through the Barlow consortium. Wollstonecraft tacitly recorded two of Ellefsen's Paris pick-ups in letters to Ruth Barlow of 27 April and 8 July, when she referred to the person delivering her letters as a 'Danish Cap' (this might well have been a deliberate 'mistake' for 'Norwegian', given that the ship would formally sail under Danish papers and a Danish flag and that letters – especially those to and from foreigners – would often go astray or be opened).[40] The dating and wording of the letters suggest that the silver shipments arrived in Le Havre in May and June, respectively. It is possible that other associates of Imlay's, such as Blackden and Leavenworth, had made similar collections.

The hoard of silver, later estimated to be worth £3,500,[41] was kept in the room Imlay had rented for Ellefsen in a local merchant's house – probably Wheatcroft's. By now apparently fully cognizant of Imlay's secret plan, Ellefsen some time between his trips to Paris pointed out a French vessel at Le Havre that could be bought cheaply and that would fit the purpose. On 18 June Imlay purchased the three-master *La Liberté* from its French owners, the Laent brothers. The ship was subsequently certified by the Danish Consulate in Le Havre (which dealt with all Scandinavian shipping) as a Norwegian vessel, based in Kristiansand and renamed *Maria and Margaretha*.[42] Although in reality owned by Imlay, the ship's papers named Ellefsen as her owner. The papers also indicated that the ship was ostensibly destined for a port in neutral Denmark, carrying only ballast.[43] The ship's mate was a New Englander called Thomas Coleman. On 13 August, Ellefsen and Coleman quietly transferred the silver to the ship. The crew, largely made up of sailors from Holstein in northern Germany, was in the dark about the ship's concealed cargo.

The metamorphosis of *La Liberté* into the *Maria and Margaretha* was a classic example of 'neutralizing' a ship and its cargo – except in this case the aim was not to sneak a cargo past the British blockade and into France but to smuggle one *out* of the country and dodge the blockade, as well as any of the Algerian pirates that since the start of the war had begun cruising the waters off the Danish coast with the connivance of the British.[44] Yet as long as the ship's paperwork presented a convincing case, a successful appeal could be launched at the Admiralty Court in London for the return of a neutral ship and cargo if captured. Imlay had clearly devised an ingenious strategy which he must have thought would cover all eventualities. Should the *Maria and Margaretha* be captured, the British would find that just about everything about the ship – flag, cargo, crew and papers – was 'neutral' or at least not what it really was. Prior to his sailing, for instance, Ellefsen was asked to sign a bill of parcels 'in which the articles he took were not specified'. In a separate document, signed on 13 August, Imlay instructed Ellefsen to set course for Gothenburg and deliver the 'articles' to Elias Backman, from whom he would receive further instructions.[45] In Gothenburg the vessel was to undergo repairs and take on cargo from Backman. To cover the costs of the repairs and the purchase of the cargo, Backman was to receive thirty-one of thirty-two bars of silver and thirty silver dishes and plates from Imlay.[46] In order to avoid the British navy and their privateering Barbary allies, Ellefsen was to take a northerly course, following the Norwegian coast, and then make his way south towards Gothenburg along the coast of Sweden. Both Wollstonecraft and Wheatcroft double checked the documents before Ellefsen signed them. Ellefsen also signed a receipt for the silver, with Wheatcroft witnessing Ellefsen's signature. This receipt was then enclosed in a letter dated 13 August, which was addressed to Elias Backman and to be opened only by him. It was ostensibly a letter of recommendation from the United States Vice-Consul at Le Havre, Francis Delamotte, who was writing on behalf of Gilbert Imlay. The opening courtesies suggest that Delamotte and Backman knew each other quite well, presumably from the days Backman was a merchant at Le Havre.[47] Delamotte goes on to introduce and recommend Gilbert Imlay, 'a citizen of the United States'. He assures Backman that he can fully trust Imlay and that he may expect 'significant commissions' from him if he does what Imlay asks of him. If this is a genuine letter of recommendation, Delamotte is curiously vague about the exact relationship between Backman and Imlay. For one thing, if Backman and Imlay were previously unknown to each other, as the letter suggests, it is highly unlikely that Backman would have been the intended recipient of the unspecified 'articles' on board the *Maria and Margaretha* – which we now know to have been £3,500 worth of silver bullion and plates. Presumably Delamotte couched his letter in such vague terms to throw the British off the scent in case the ship was stopped and searched.[48] Should the letter get through to Backman, he would know precisely why the silver had been sent to him and what he was supposed to do with it. All Backman would need to see in the letter was Imlay's original signature, 'G. Imlay', at the bottom of the letter, next to Delamotte's.[49]

But in the end, none of Imlay's precautions and ruses made any difference. After many frustrating delays caused by the endless formalities and complicated procedures involved in dealing with the Commission de Subsistances, the *Maria and Margaretha* finally sailed on either 14 or 15 August. Imlay had dashed off to Paris on urgent business as soon as the silver was safe on board the vessel, and it was actually Wollstonecraft – a self-proclaimed enemy of all things commercial – who gave Ellefsen his last orders. The ship safely reached Norway after a journey of nine or ten days, around 24 August. Then it vanished. Norwegian shipping records show that she put in at one of the small ports near Arendal, but that she never reached her destination port of Gothenburg.

Her involvement in what they tend to refer to as Imlay's 'silver ship' or, better still, his 'treasure ship', has tickled the imagination of many a Wollstonecraft biographer; indeed, one has her surreptitiously inspecting the forbidden fleur-de-lis gleaming on the Bourbon plates hidden in Ellefsen's room before they were carried onto the *Maria and Margaretha*.[50] In reality, however, the *Maria and Margaretha* episode gave little occasion for romantic titillation. It was not in any way unique, either. The number of similar transactions carried out under the new purchasing regime introduced by the Commission des Subsistances and its successor, the Commission du Commerce et Approvisionnements, must have run into the hundreds. Nor was this a particularly large shipment of silver – assuming that Imlay's estimate of its value (£3,500) was accurate. Also, it was not, as has been suggested, Imlay's 'plan' in the first place to import grain, alum and potash from Scandinavia in exchange for silver bullion.[51] If any foreign individual is to be credited with having devised the foreign purveyance system it would have to be James Swan, as we have seen. Besides, the value of the bullion involved in the transaction paled in comparison to the total value of the massive stocks of confiscated luxury goods stored in the national warehouses. It has been estimated that French commissioners could extend credit to traders of up to 60 million *livres* raised from the sale of luxury goods.[52] In the late summer and early autumn of 1794, when Swan's company, code-named 'Jones & Gaspard', received its instructions from the Commission du Commerce et Approvisionnements, they were authorized to purchase for the French Republic vast quantities of food supplies, gunpowder and raw materials in the United States, including up to 5.6 million barrels of flour and 400,000 hundredweight of rice.[53]

The *Maria and Margaretha* episode was not the first of the bullion exports in which Imlay had been involved. In March of 1794 a similar operation had taken place, this time involving an English vessel called the *Rambler*, and there may well have been others. Given that secrecy was at the heart of all wartime trading with and inside the French Republic, it is impossible to provide a detailed picture, yet looking at the timing of events and the movements of key figures, it is possible to reconstruct the general pattern of the plan. In early 1794, Elias Backman left the booming trading centre of Le Havre to set up a new business in Gothenburg. In March of that year he petitioned the Swedish Crown for permission to import gold and silver worth 172 million *riksdaler*.[54] The bullion was to be carried in the usually nimble English cutter the *Rambler*, a French prize secretly obtained by a French consul in Sweden and sold to Backman. Although Backman was the formal owner, the real owner could have been anywhere – even in France. Permission was granted and in May the *Rambler* set sail from Gothenburg under a neutral Swedish flag to pick up its cargo in France. However, the ship was captured en route by the British, who questioned its neutrality. Imlay's agent in London, Mr Cowie, reported the case to the Swedish authorities. The captain of the *Rambler* not carrying any papers, the British could not substantiate their claim, but it would take months before the ship was released. In the autumn it continued its journey to France, arriving back in Gothenburg with its precious cargo on 25 October. On the way home it, had briefly dropped anchor at Glückstadt, a small port on the Elbe, not far from Hamburg.[55]

In March 1794, when Backman requested permission to import bullion into Sweden, the Barlows left Paris for Hamburg. Trade opportunities in Hamburg and the adjacent Danish enclave of Altona, where the Barlows took up residence, turned out to be even better than in France. Barlow made more money during his year's stay in Hamburg than he had ever done previously or would subsequently. After the French army drove the British out of the Netherlands in December 1794, a significant share of Dutch trade and capital migrated to Hamburg, which as a result doubled its business. More than two thousand ships annually dropped anchor in the Elbe, many hundreds of which were American. When she visited Hamburg in September 1795 on her way back from her fruitless trip to Scandinavia to retrieve Imlay's silver, Wollstonecraft could not obtain lodgings as the town was 'swarming with inhabitants'. 'Mushroom fortunes', she said, were being made by merchants in Hamburg during the war.[56] While commissions were 'nominally only two and a half' per cent, they had now mounted to 'eight or ten at least' thanks to the 'secret *manoeuvres* of trade'. But those trading at their own risk could gain as much as 'cent per cent' – or a 100 per cent return on their investment.[57] In 'this whirlpool of gain' the 'interests of nations are bartered by speculating merchants', Wollstonecraft reported disparagingly; 'My God! with what *sang froid* artful trains of corruption bring lucrative commissions into particular hands, disregarding the relative situation of different countries – and can much common honesty be expected in the discharge of trusts obtained by fraud?'[58] Much of the transit trade Barlow was handling was carried on 'neutral' vessels, including many under an American flag. It was his task to make sure that cargoes from places like Copenhagen and Gothenburg, ostensibly destined for 'Lisbon', ended up in a French port, more often than not Le Havre.

Gilbert Imlay had been in Le Havre since the previous September, where he was receiving the incoming goods from Barlow and other American and Scandinavian merchants. Meanwhile, Benjamin Hichborn and James Swan, the chief American merchant in Paris, continued to deal with the Commission and arrange for credit and payments in bullion and luxury articles. Judging from Mary Wollstonecraft's letters to Imlay, Samuel Blackden and Mark Leavenworth were going up and down between Paris and Le Havre at frequent intervals, one presumes carrying more than her and Imlay's private mail.

This is not to suggest that Backman, Barlow, Imlay, Swan, Hichborn, Leavenworth, Blackden and probably one or two others were continually in cahoots with each other. Members of the consortium would be involved in different transactions with different associates. Some would work only on commission, others – like Swan – would head up their own company and deal directly with the Commission. And each of them, of course, would pursue their own projects whenever an opportunity arose. Yet most of the business in which this particular group of merchants was involved would be conducted within the northern trade network which had emerged in the wake of the British economic blockade of France and which was firmly established by late 1794. The major hubs in the network were: Paris (where the capital and the orders originated); Le Havre (the gateway harbour to France); 'Lisbon', 'Bilbao' (and other ghost destinations of ships bound for France); London (where legal challenges were mounted at the Admiralty Courts and the High Court); Amsterdam (where the banks cleared French payments and commissions); Hamburg (the chief transit harbour of the North German plain and one of the largest in the world); and Gothenburg (storehouse of the Scandinavian mainland and transit port for the Baltic). On the tide of this wartime mercantile order, capital would flow out of France, food supplies and raw materials would flow into it.

Given their complex nature and the high risk of fraud, transactions involving the export of bullion could only be undertaken by companies or joint ventures of some standing and with the right political connections. Following the decree of October 1793, all foreign trade was concentrated in the hands of the Commission des Subsistances. Agents of the Commission in the ports were not authorized to deal directly for cargoes with individual captains but had to wait for instructions from Paris, where endless formalities could delay contracts and payments for months on end. It is therefore highly unlikely that the Commission would have come to a private deal with a single merchant like Imlay – let alone when such a large amount of silver was at stake. The plans for both the *Rambler* and the *Maria and Margarethe* deals were probably hatched by Swan and Barlow not long after the Jacobins had come to power, possibly around the time Brissot and the other Girondist leaders were led to the guillotine in October 1793. Swan and Barlow, as well as anyone else involved in the plan – including Imlay – knew all too well where the silver was coming from that the Jacobins were melting into bars. They may have deplored the Terror – indeed, were horrified by it – but they steadied their nerves and assuaged their qualms by reminding themselves that the aristocracy's exorbitant wealth and the Church's splendour had been gained at the expense of the poor. If the people were suffering from hunger and deprivation as a result of the British blockade, it was legitimate, indeed, it was morally just, they persuaded themselves, to assist the republican government in feeding the people. Hence they were willing to do business with Robespierre's purchasing Commission, even as they were waiting and hoping for Robespierre and his regime to be toppled. When the guillotine did finally claim Robespierre's life on 28 July 1794, many of the expatriates rejoiced and felt a deep sense of relief – but few changed their ways.

Mary Wollstonecraft has traditionally been represented by biographers and literary historians as a fierce opponent of commerce and much is made of her frequent and often vitriolic attacks on Imlay's commercial activities. Indeed, it is still often assumed that to be a British radical in the 1790s was to be a utopian agrarian. However, radicalism in general and certainly Wollstonecraft's personal creed was slightly more nuanced than that. In fact, British radicalism in the late eighteenth century consisted of two main ideological tendencies which existed side by side: agrarian utopianism and commercial utopianism. What was known as 'speculation commerce', defined by John Thelwall as commerce based on mercantilism, was flatly rejected by radicals because it encouraged a global trade that was dominated by a small number of monopolists who, by accumulating commodities 'in the hope of exciting artificial wants', manipulated the marketplace to their own advantage.[59] Speculation commerce was also rejected by the commercial radicals because it encouraged governments to lend support to such artificial trade by introducing a system of excises and duties and by maintaining a naval force to defend the interests of the merchant marine trade.

However, 'commission commerce', which was understood to mean commerce based on countries exchanging abundant commodities for scarce but desired ones, *was* allowed as a valid contribution to the radical cause. Agrarian radicalism sought to offer solutions to moral and political decay by blending the ideas of 'the self-sufficient village community and the independent freeholder' with 'classical republican ideals of equality, simplicity and virtue'; commercial radicalism 'emphasised material progress and connected it with private property, self-interest and commercial society'.[60] Commercial radicals such as Thomas Paine and Joseph Priestley argued that the ideals of agrarian utopianism were 'antithetical to real human needs and aspirations' and were instead convinced that commerce 'expanded and humanized the mind by way of increased contact and the encouragement of mutual interdependence'.[61] 'Commerce', Paine observed in the second part of *Rights of Man*, 'is no other than the traffic of two individuals, multiplied on a scale of numbers; and by the same rule that nature intended the intercourse of two, she intended that of all'.[62] Since in this system the state had no role to play, the interests of individuals were guaranteed and trade was free and open to all. Like Adam Smith and the physiocrats, whose ideas on political economy they absorbed, commercial radicals believed that in a 'natural' economic world, trade would be based on the exportation of agricultural products and the importation of manufactured ones.[63]

Wollstonecraft was intuitively drawn towards agrarian utopianism, yet she does not appear to have been entirely unsympathetic towards commission commerce. She may have felt that while all commerce was detrimental to the faculty of the imagination, commission commerce at least satisfied real human needs without depriving people of essential commodities and could even foster harmonious relations between individuals and nations. Hence, morality and trade need not always be incompatible, according to Wollstonecraft, although often it was: 'Mr. Imlay has not been well for some weeks past', she told Ruth Barlow in July 1794, 'and during the last few days he has [been] seriously feverish. His mind has been harass[ed] by continual disappointments – Sh[ips] do not return, and the government is perpetually throwing impediments in the way of business. I cannot help sharing his disquietude, because the fulfilling of engagements appears to me of more importance than the making a fortune.'[64] In fact, contrary to what is commonly thought, Wollstonecraft was quite actively involved in the *Maria and Margaretha* saga: not just during the aftermath – her journey to Scandinavia in an attempt to retrieve the shipment after it had disappeared – but through much of the planning stage as well. Initially, she may have taken an interest in the scheme because she saw the man she loved driven to distraction by lengthy delays and financial worries which constantly frustrated business. But the arrival of Fanny had made it all the more expedient to obtain the kind of financial stability that would enable them to lead a life of self-sufficient interdependence – possibly in some idyllic wilderness setting in America.

Apparently Imlay had urged Godwin to cut any references in Wollstonecraft's letters relating to his business practices before publishing them. However, enough clues remain in the letters to reconstruct Wollstonecraft's involvement in the *Maria and Margaretha* scheme. By March, business was already vying with love for her attention, for writing to Imlay, who had gone to Paris for a brief visit, Wollstonecraft observes: 'Do not call me stupid, for leaving on the table the little bit of paper I was to inclose. – *This comes of being in love at the fag-end of a letter of business.* – You know, you say, they will not chime together'.[65] If there were any doubt what the nature of this 'business' might be, by the end of April it was evident that Wollstonecraft was fully abreast of the plans regarding the envisaged silver shipment; more than that, she had been working alongside Imlay in getting it organized in close co-operation with the Barlows – both Ruth *and* Joel:

> I wrote to Mr. B. by post the other day telling him that *I indulge the expectation of success, in which you are included, with great pleasure* – and I do hope that he will not suffer his sore mind to be hurt, sufficiently to damp his exertions, by any impediments or disappointments, which may, at first cloud his views or darken his prospect – Teasing hindrance of one kind or other continually occur to *us* here – you perceive that I am acquiring the matrimonial phraseology without having clogged my soul by promising obedience &c &c – Still we do not despair – *Let but the first ground be secured – and in the course of the summer we may, perhaps celebrate our good luck, not forgetting good management, together.* – There has been some plague about *the shipping of the goods*, which Mr. Imlay will doubtless fully explain – but the delay is not of much consequence as *I hope to hear that Mr. B. enters fully into the whole interest.* You will be civil to *the Danish Capt.*, who will take charge of this, he is a worthy unassuming man …[66]

It is important to remember that while Ruth was still in Paris at this point, Joel Barlow had been in Hamburg since March. Wollstonecraft had never written to Joel Barlow before, so why was she writing to him now, and specifically about the *Maria and Margaretha* venture? Whatever Imlay was doing, it is clear that Wollstonecraft had been discussing the shipment of the silver with Joel Barlow; it is also clear that she was a little concerned that Barlow might not be wholly committed to the project. On 23 May, ten days after she had given birth to Fanny, Wollstonecraft reported to Ruth Barlow that 'The vessel' was still 'detained' – apparently assuming Ruth would know what vessel she meant.[67] A further letter to Ruth from 8 July reveals that she had written to her and to Joel 'several times' and that she had finally received an answer from him the day before 'by the Dane'.[68] Fully involved in the intrigue, Wollstonecraft adhered to the agreed security protocol – as Barlow apparently did. Private correspondence might be sent by regular mail, but anything relating to the silver shipment was 'going by other conveyances' – that is, personal couriers.[69]

Quite soon after the *Maria and Margaretha* had set sail for Scandinavia, the plan for some reason began to go wrong. When it did, it again emerged that Wollstonecraft had been deeply involved in setting it up in the first place and that she very much wanted it to succeed. 'I want to know', she insisted in a letter to Imlay on 20 August, about a week after he had left for Paris on urgent business, 'what steps you have taken respecting —. Knavery always rouses my indignation – I should be gratified to hear that the law had chastised — severely; but I do not wish you to see him, because the business does not now admit of peaceful discussion, and I do not exactly know how you would express your contempt.'[70] Unfortunately, it cannot be ascertained with absolute certainty who the knave was because Godwin suppressed his name. It cannot have been Ellefsen, who had been at sea for about a week. If by 'seeing' the knave Wollstonecraft meant seeing him at Paris (as it appears she did), then that rules out Barlow, even though she had before evinced her irritation with his lackadaisical performance in her letter to Ruth in April: he was in Hamburg, where he had been since March.[71] Of the other likely suspects, Samuel Blackden, who had been drowning his homesickness in alcohol, had returned to America in late May (when he was so drunk, he had to be carried on board the ship he was sailing on).[72] Mark Leavenworth may have been a knave – he was struggling to stay solvent in business but eventually went bankrupt some time in late 1795 – but he was not high enough in the pecking order to be in a position to undermine the outcome of the entire operation.[73] It might have been a reference to James Swan, albeit that the confidant of French government and co-director of the Swan & Schweizer purveyance company would hardly qualify as a 'knave', even by Wollstonecraft's standards. Besides, if – as the wording of Wollstonecraft's letters suggests – this 'knave' is identical to the callous cad who would soon order Imlay around and on whose loans she came to depend to maintain herself, then it cannot have been Swan because he returned to the Unites States by the end of the year to become purchasing agent of the French government there. However, there was one member of the silver export consortium who was close enough to Barlow and hence to the purchasing committee to be familiar with the ins-and-outs of the secret bullion and luxury goods exports; who had worked with Barlow ever since the latter started out in business and was presumably for that reason left in charge in Paris when Barlow temporarily moved to Hamburg: Colonel Benjamin Hichborn, the Revolutionary War hero who had come to Europe to make his fortune. Whoever the knave was, somebody had seriously betrayed Wollstonecraft's and Imlay's trust and she was not going to let it pass. For at the end of September, she was still as peeved as before with whoever it was that compromised the scheme in which she now had a vested interest: 'I have received, for you, letters from —. I want to hear how that affair finishes, though I do not know whether I have most contempt for his folly or knavery.'[74]

By then rumours had begun to circulate about the *Maria and Margaretha's* ill-fated voyage. Captain Ellefsen was said to be back home at Risør, having transferred the command to the mate, Coleman. Ellefsen denied that there had been any silver on board the ship, which was reported to have been sunk near Arendal, off the Norwegian coast. Having been briefly back at Le Havre at the end of August, Imlay almost immediately set out for London – presumably to investigate the possibility of undertaking legal action in the courts. With Imlay unlikely to return any time soon and there being nothing left for her to do in Le Havre, Wollstonecraft returned to Paris with her baby in September. Many of her former friends had either left Paris or been guillotined, and she soon felt lonely and abandoned. Only her 'barrier-girl' gave her any solace. Understandably, she began to lose interest in the *Maria and Margaretha*, longing to see Imlay's former 'barrier-face' again – not that 'commercial face' of a man 'embruted by trade and the vulgar enjoyments of life'.[75] By the end of October she was begging him to return and 'not be so immersed in business, as during the last three or four months past'.[76] But it would not be until April 1795 that Wollstonecraft would see her 'husband' again.

In the interim, Wollstonecraft resorted to her former strategy of sending a barrage of sharply worded letters Imlay's way. In them she took Imlay severely to task for squandering his natural talents and virtue on trade and for failing to return to Paris. Yet she simultaneously tended to gloss over Imlay's shortcomings and present him instead as the helpless victim of the treacherous machinations of some mercantile will-o'-the-wisp – let us assume Benjamin Hichborn – who was leading him further and further into the quicksands of embruting speculation – and hence away from her and Fanny:

> [Hichborn], I know, urges you to stay, and is continually branching out into new projects, because he has the idle desire to amass a large fortune, rather than an immense one, merely to have the credit of having made it. But we who are governed by other principles, ought not to be led by him. When we meet, we will discuss this subject.[77]

She later confessed to Imlay, 'I did not think, when I complained of [Hichborn's] contemptible avidity to accumulate money, that he would have dragged you into his schemes'.[78] But he did. Soon a dispute erupted between Wollstonecraft and her rival that got more and more personal:

> [Hichborn] and I have not been on good terms a long time. Yesterday he very unmanly exulted over me, on account of your determination to stay. I had provoked it, it is true, by some asperities against commerce, which have dropped from me, when we have argued about the propriety of your remaining where you are.[79]

What made the situation all the more galling to Wollstonecraft was that, with Imlay away in London for an extended period of time and a baby to care for, she was 'left dependent' for money on Hichborn (with whom Imlay had made an arrangement): a man 'whose avidity to acquire a fortune ha[d] rendered him callous to every sentiment connected with social or affectionate emotions' and who could not help 'displaying the pleasure [Imlay's] determination to stay [gave] him', despite the visible effect it was having on her.[80] She had gone up to Hichborn's house half a dozen times to ask for her allowance, but she resented the man so much, that she would rather borrow the money she needed from someone else – someone not associated with Imlay's American business partners. 'I shall entirely give up the acquaintance of the Americans', she told Imlay.

'The agonies of such a separation', Godwin would later comment, 'great as Mary would have found them upon every supposition, were vastly increased, by the lingering method in which it was effected, and the ambiguity that, for a long time, hung upon it'.[81] One moment Wollstonecraft felt that she could beat her rival and persuade Imlay to 'listen to reason' and to agree to 'pursue some sober plan, which may demand more time, and still enable [him] to arrive at the same end'.[82] At another moment she was 'really tormented by the desire which [Hichborn] manifests to have [Imlay] remain where [he was]' and feared she might be losing him: 'Beware! you seem to be got into a whirl of projects and schemes, which are drawing you into a gulf, that, if it do not absorb your happiness, will infallibly destroy mine'.[83]

Increasingly, it became clear that Wollstonecraft had projected so much of what she held dear in life onto Imlay that the conflict with her rival was as much about saving her own soul as it was about saving her lover's. Yet, the key issue that was at stake for her had begun to shift from sensibility and affection to the imagination. Less concerned with his materialism and pursuit of sensual pleasures, she now believed that the merchant in Imlay, as opposed to the natural man in him, had 'not sufficient respect for the imagination'.[84] Imagination, she lectured him, 'is the mother of sentiment, the great distinction of our nature, the only purifier of the passions – animals have a portion of reason, and equal, if not more exquisite, senses; but no trace of imagination, or her offspring taste, appears in any of their actions'. Her observation that the imagination was 'the true fire, stolen from heaven, to animate this cold creature of clay, producing all those fine sympathies that lead to rapture', Imlay apparently summarily dismissed as 'romantic'. If anything, the gap between them was widening rather than closing, but Wollstonecraft continued to remonstrate with him. He had been urging her to come to England, but she had resisted, wanting him to return to France instead. 'What! is our life then only to be made up of separations? and am I only to return to a country, that has not merely lost all charms for me, but for which I feel a repugnance that almost amounts to horror.'[85]

The rest of the harrowing saga of the affair between Imlay and Wollstonecraft is well known and has been recounted in detail by generations of Wollstonecraft biographers. In April 1795, after eight months of separation, Wollstonecraft finally overcame her principles and her repugnance and accepted Imlay's offer of a servant to help her make the journey from Paris to London.[86] They briefly tried to live together in a furnished house he had taken for her and Fanny in Charlotte Street. But when Wollstonecraft wanted to renew their intimate relationship, Imlay moved out. Wollstonecraft never knew that her rival was a young actress of a strolling company of players, but it hardly mattered. Her bond of affection with Imlay was broken, whereupon she 'formed a desperate purpose to die', as Godwin put it.[87] 'It was perhaps owing to ['Imlay's] activity and representations',

Godwin went on to observe, 'that her life was, at this time, saved. She determined to continue to exist.' Evidently, Imlay had more empathy than he is often given credit for. Wollstonecraft sensed it and responded accordingly: 'I have just received your affectionate letter', she wrote to him shortly after the crisis was over, 'and am stressed to think that I have added to your embarrassments at this troublesome juncture, when the exertion of all the faculties of your mind appears to be necessary, to extricate you out of your pecuniary difficulties'.[88]

Imlay's 'embarrassments' and 'pecuniary difficulties' were undoubtedly related to the disappearance of the silver. For the next thing we hear, Wollstonecraft is off with her child and her French maid Marguerite on 'a mercantile adventure in Norway'.[89] Evidently determined to sort out what was for her very much unfinished business, the power of attorney by which Imlay named her his agent was executed on 19 May, only days after she had attempted to take her own life. Godwin reported that she undertook what was, by any standards, an arduous and challenging journey to Scandinavia because

> it seemed to require the presence of some very judicious agent, to conduct the business to its desired termination. Mary determined to make the voyage, and take the business into her own hands. Such a voyage seemed the most desirable thing to recruit her health, and, if possible, her spirits, in the present crisis.[90]

While Wollstonecraft no doubt needed the distraction and wanted to get away from London and Imlay's mistress(es) there, she would only have undertaken the mission if she had felt confident that it would reunite her and Imlay at the end of it – that is, by providing them with enough financial security for Imlay to be able to abandon his life of speculative trade. Wollstonecraft biographers have speculated endlessly about the question why Imlay did not go to Scandinavia himself to try to retrieve the silver or reach a settlement with Ellefsen. The simple answer is that he *had* tried and had concluded early on that the chance of recovering the silver was nil and that criminal proceedings might drag on forever. If Wollstonecraft wanted to have a stab at it, who was he to stop her? At the very least, it would take her mind off things.

Having been a serial defendant and plaintiff in the legal jungle of the Kentucky land bubble, Imlay had probably been involved in more litigation than the entire British radical fraternity in London taken together. Imlay would sue if there were any realistic chance of success, and he would immediately abandon any legal action the moment there was not. It must have been clear to him from the start that, legally speaking, the *Maria and Margaretha* had entered into extremely choppy waters since it had left Le Havre. Imlay having expertly 'neutralized' the vessel and its cargo, French law had no jurisdiction in the case. Under the orders of June and November 1793, British law would probably have regarded both parties as criminal. Norway being part of Denmark at the time,

Imlay's only chance of legal redress was to launch an appeal at the Danish courts. He had therefore instructed Elias Backman in the summer of 1794 to apply to Copenhagen, in an attempt to bring some sort of pressure to bear on the merchant community in Norway.

That autumn, in accordance with Danish legal protocol, a preliminary board of inquiry was appointed. It consisted of three commissioners drawn from the leading members of the regional business community. These were a merchant, Christoffer Nordberg, and A. J. Unger, a district judge, both from Strömstad, just north of Gothenburg, and Jacob Wulfsberg, a judge from Tönsberg in southern Norway. Having interviewed Ellefsen, the board of inquiry established that both the ship and its cargo had belonged to Imlay. However, Ellefsen denied having any knowledge of the fate of the ship or the silver after he had transferred the command of the *Maria and Margaretha* to Coleman. Far from satisfied with the outcome of the inquiry, Backman turned to his extensive network of contacts in the worlds of business, high finance and politics. By the end of 1794 the Swedish minister in Copenhagen made representations about the incident to the Danish government. Barely a month later a Royal Commission had been set up to hear the case and pass judgement. The Commission set to work at the end of January 1795 and in February ordered the arrest of Captain Ellefsen. Wielding considerable financial and legal power, the Ellefsens soon managed to have him released on bail, after which their lawyers exerted themselves in trying to slow down the case in legal chicaneries. Thus they successfully challenged the appointment of Judge Wulfsberg as one of the the Commissioners, on the grounds that he had been Backman's agent before and might therefore not be entirely impartial. By the time Wollstonecraft arrived in Scandinavia, the case had been kicked well into the long grass – as Imlay had surmised it would be.

The power of attorney which he had executed in May confirms that Imlay was eager to settle the case against Ellefsen out of court and to come away with whatever reasonable amount of damages Wollstonecraft would manage to squeeze out of Ellefsen or his affluent relatives. The convoluted letter needs to be read in full if one is to appreciate the complexity and delicacy of the task that awaited Wollstonecraft in Scandinavia:

> Know all men by these presents that I Gilbert Imlay citizen of the United States of America residing at present in London do nominate constitute and appoint Mary Imlay my best friend and wife to take the sole management and direction of all my affairs and business which I had placed in the hands of Mr. Elias Backman negotiant Gothenburg or in those of Messrs Ryberg & Co Copenhagen; desiring that she will manage and direct such concerns in such manner as she deem most wise & prudent. For which this letter shall be a sufficient power enabling her to receive all the money or sums of money that may be recovered from Peter Ellefsen or his connections whenever the issue of the tryal now carrying on against him, instituted by Mr

Elias Backman at my request, for the violation of the trust which I had reposed in his integrity.

Considering the aggravated distresses, the accumulated losses and damages sustained in consequence of the said Ellefsen's disobedience of my instructions I desire the said Mary Imlay will clearly ascertain the amount of such damages, taking first the advice of persons qualified to judge of the probabity of obtaining satisfaction, or the means the said Ellefsen, or his connections, who may be proved to be implicated in his guilt, may have, or power of being able to make restitution and then commence a new prosecution for the same accordingly.

Begging leave here only to observe that, her judgment will naturally point out the manner of employing the proper persons to make or form such estimate – the documents for which can readily be furnished by Mr. Backman.

Respecting the cargo or goods in the hands of Messrs Ryberg & Co Mrs Imlay has only to consult the most experienced persons engaged in the disposition of such articles and then placing them at their disposal act as she may deem right and proper always I trust governing herself according to the best of her judgment in which I have no doubt but that the opinions of Messrs Ryberg & Co will have a considerable and due influence.

Thus confiding in the talents zeal and earnestness of my dear beloved friend and companion I submit the management of these affairs intirely and implicitly to her discretion – remaining most sincerely & affectionately hers truly,

> May 19th 1795
> G. Imlay[91]

Unsurprisingly, perhaps, Wollstonecraft's journey did not yield any concrete results – or, at least, not as far as we can tell, since key files from the Royal Commission not having survived. Assuming it was on board the *Maria and Margaretha* in the first place, the silver was never retrieved. Wollstonecraft did manage to interview the key players in the case, including the defendant, Peder Ellefsen, but he continued to deny he had any part in the disappearance of the silver. By the autumn of 1795 little progress had been made in the lawsuit against him. Even though Imlay's former landlord, John Wheatcroft, Jr, travelled all the way from Le Havre to Copenhagen – presumably to testify that Ellefsen had been his lodger and that the silver had been stored in his room – no verdict ever appears to have been reached in the case. As for the *Maria and Margaretha*, she turned our not to have sunk after all. She returned to Gothenburg, where she was re-registered on 6 October 1795 as the property of Imlay's partner, Elias Backman.[92] Wollstonecraft had previously come to an agreement with Backman concerning the sales price and the price for the repairs.[93]

After leaving Copenhagen, Wollstonecraft stopped over at Hamburg in early September. It was there that she was hoping meet up with Imlay, before travelling on together to Switzerland.[94] She knew that Imlay had to see Barlow in Paris around this time to 'settle [his] affairs', so a rendezvous in Germany would make sense.[95] Disgusted with Hamburg ('this whirlpool of gain'), Wollstonecraft was relieved to find a comfortable house in nearby Altona.[96] The house had been 'particularly recommended' by 'an acquaintance' of Imlay's, St. John de Crèvecoeur, who had moved to Altona early in 1795.[97] Undoubtedly assuming that Imlay would get the hint, Wollstonecraft reported in her *Short Residence in Sweden, Norway and Denmark* that she generally dined in the company of the celebrated author of *Letters of an American Farmer*, with the two of them entertaining the other diners with their 'declamations against commerce'.[98] But Wollstonecraft was far from light hearted. In fact, she was 'weary of travelling' and repeatedly reminded Imlay of his promise to meet her in the autumn.[99] 'Business alone has kept me from you. – Come to any port, and I will fly down to my two dear girls with a heart all their own', Imlay had written to her; but he would not act on it.[100] Ostensibly, 'the presence of the French army ... rendered [her] intended tour through Germany, on [her] way to Switzerland, almost impracticable'; in reality, Imlay had flatly refused to leave London.[101] Convinced that he had 'formed some new attachment', Wollstonecraft once more fortified herself to meet Imlay in London, stricken with 'extreme anguish'.[102]

On her return to England, Imlay met Wollstonecraft in London and took her to the lodgings he had arranged for her. His aloofness towards her confirmed her suspicions. Upon making further inquiries, she learnt from the cook he had hired for her that Imlay, indeed, had a new mistress. Having confronted Imlay at the furnished house he had provided for his new partner, Wollstonecraft resolved to throw herself into the Thames. Battersea Bridge being too public, she rented a rowing-boat to Putney, walked through the rain for a while so that her thoroughly soaked clothes might weigh her down, and then jumped off the bridge. The boatman and some local fishermen having seen her jump, Wollstonecraft was pulled out of the river, unconscious but alive. Alerted by the suicide note she sent him, Imlay sent a coach to pick her up from the Duke's Head Tavern where she was being look after and had her taken to the Christies' house in Finsbury Square.[103] There over the next few weeks Rebecca nursed her back to health.

If she had hoped her suicide attempt might have brought Imlay back to her, she was sorely disappointed: he avoided seeing her, even though before he had been quite a regular visitor at the Christies. As Wollstonecraft regained her strength, so did her dogged determination to make her relationship with Imlay work. No doubt with her latest suicide attempt still fresh on his mind, Imlay buckled under her renewed resolve and agreed to Wollstonecraft's suggestion that she and Imlay, along with his mistress, might form a ménage à trois. They even went to look for a suitable house together. On reflection, Imlay's mistress was less thrilled with the idea and the plan fell through. While Imlay and his mistress moved into the new house, Wollstonecraft found her own lodgings at 16 Finsbury Square. The move allowed her to remain close to Rebecca, while it enabled Imlay to visit the Christies again without the embarrassment of seeing her there. Even so, Wollstonecraft could not let Imlay go: 'let me see, written by yourself – for I will not receive it through any other medium – that the affair is finished'.[104]

In late November, at her request, Imlay returned Wollstonecraft's letters to him, and left for Paris with his mistress for three months. In his farewell note he tried to exonerate himself for his 'decided conduct, which appeared to [her] so unfeeling', asserting that he was acting on 'exalted' principles and was led by feelings 'the most refined'. She sneered at his 'theory of morals' and was convinced he had only 'been anxious to shake [her] off'. If he had hoped that she would not judge him 'coolly' for having absconded to the Continent, he was going to be disappointed: 'Even at Paris, my image will haunt you – You will see my pale face – and sometimes the tears of anguish will drop on your heart, which you have forced from me'.[105] She also pursued her fleeting lover with further letters, in which she alternatively expostulated with him and coaxed him – 'Let me see you once more!'[106] Imlay felt 'tormented' by her letters and apparently did not reply.[107] It was not until March 1796 that Wollstonecraft fully accepted that their relationship was 'now finished'. This time there was no suicide note: 'I now solemnly assure you', she wrote to him, 'that this is an eternal farewell. – Yet I flinch not from the duties which tie me to life.'[108] She had lost the real man but kept her faith in the ideal she had created of him:

> It is strange that, in spite of all you do, something like conviction forces me to believe, that you are not what you appear to be.
>
>   I part with you in peace.[109]

EPILOGUE: LOST IN SPECULATION

> I believe that no materials exist for a full and satisfactory biography of this man
> Herman Melville, 'Bartleby, the Scrivener'[1]

After the final break-up of their relationship in March 1796, Gilbert Imlay would see Mary Wollstonecraft one more time. As Godwin recounts, 'They met by accident upon the New Road [in London, now part of Euston Road]; he alighted from his horse, and walked with her for some time; and the rencounter passed, as she assured me, without producing in her any oppressive emotion'.[2] Thereafter, Imlay more or less disappears from historical sight. Aside from some scattered records of financial disputes with merchants in London court archives, very few traces of Imlay's activities or whereabouts have come to light after he separated from Mary Wollstonecraft – although there is a record of his death and burial on the Isle of Jersey, discovered in 1903, and the text of an epitaph which once appeared on his tombstone in the yard of St Brelade's Church, but which has only survived in transcript. Thus, despite extensive research carried out by several generations of Wollstonecraft and Imlay scholars on both sides of the Atlantic, the last three decades of Imlay's life remain a blank page.

Inevitably, in the absence of any hard facts, Imlay's later life has been the subject of considerable rumour and speculation. Writing to Lyman C. Draper in 1847, early Kentucky settler Thomas Rogers recalled that the common wisdom was that Imlay had died 'in Norfolk in England, some time previous to [his] brother John's death, which happened on the 16th April 1794'.[3] In 1805, a relative reported in passing that Gilbert Imlay was believed to be back in the United States and was expected to pay a visit to New Jersey some time soon.[4] More often than not, claims about Imlay's activities after the break-up of his affair with Wollstonecraft are simply the result of misinterpreting archival sources. Thus, it has been claimed that 'Imlay continued to buy up frontier land' and on 19 November 1810 'was granted a deed for 3400 acres in Kentucky'.[5] In fact, Imlay did not buy any land in Kentucky in 1810, or, indeed, at any other point after he left the United States (the deed anyway refers to Imlay as the 'grantor', *not* the 'grantee', so he was selling, not buying).[6] Much wilder claims have been made about Imlay's alleged spying activities, both in America and in Europe. Thus, the fact that Imlay resigned from the Continental Army in July 1778 has been interpreted as evidence that he may have been recruited into Washington's wartime network of spies (who were all conveniently 'sworn to permanent secrecy').[7] There has also been a persistent rumour that Imlay had Tory sympathies and was in fact a British spy during the Revolutionary War.[8] Inevitably, there are those who have claimed that Imlay was actually a double agent, who merely *appeared* to be spying for the British.[9] Continuing in this vein, it has been suggested that after his arrival in Europe, Imlay was in the pay of American and/or British intelligence services and that his commercial and shipping operations in London and Le Havre were merely a cover for his spying activities.[10]

Is it at least *possible* that Imlay was a spy, either during the Revolutionary War or the Anglo-French War – or both? Certainly, it is *possible*. Both sides in the American conflict used elaborate networks of formal and occasional spies. Imlay's second cousin, for instance, the wealthy and respectable Philadelphia-based shipping master and merchant John Imlay, gathered intelligence for Congress on British troop movements and British shipping in the Caribbean.[11] During the French Revolution a host of both British and American expats and Revolution tourists kept a close eye on events – and each other – on behalf of their governments. Thus, the British agent Major Semple, wearing the green cockade and pretending to be an Irish patriot, was found hovering around Thomas Paine's radical salon at the Philadelphia Hotel.[12] Nathaniel Cutting, the Massachusetts shipmaster and commercial agent for Nathaniel Tracy at Le Havre, acted as an informal confidential agent for the Department of State (Jefferson offered him the strategic post of American Consul to Le Havre but Cutting declined, preferring business to covert diplomacy).[13] So, yes, it is *possible* that Imlay in some capacity or other at some point in his life was in one way or another involved in activities that may be qualified as 'spying' for some nation. But if he was, this would not in any way have been uncommon or remarkable. However, the key point here is that there is no evidence to support any of the speculations about Imlay's alleged spying activities.

Much of the speculation about Imlay's activities after 1796 has focused on his supposed involvement in the seditious activities of General James Wilkinson. Thus, having first (wrongly) identified Imlay as the 'spy' Wilkinson 'affectionately' referred as 'Gilberto' (who was in reality neither Imlay, nor a spy), Gordon subsequently speculates in her biography of Wollstonecraft that in the mid-1790s Imlay may have been Wilkinson's agent promoting British interest in a scheme to capture Spanish Florida and the Louisiana Territory.[14] While it is true that Wilkinson had remained secretly in the pay of the Spanish authorities after his botched attempt – in 1787–8 – to turn the District of Kentucky into a satellite state of Spanish Louisiana, there is no indication whatsoever that Imlay was

in any way involved in the 'Spanish Intrigue' of 1794–5, or, indeed, in its pred-
ecessor, the 'Spanish Conspiracy' of 1778–88.[15] When in the course of 1804–5
Wilkinson became involved in what is now known as the 'Burr Conspiracy',
Imlay's participation is often almost automatically assumed on the basis of what
is, at best, circumstantial or tangential 'evidence'.

The Burr Conspiracy, in a nutshell, was a secessionist plot in the Old
Southwest, named after its presumed architect, Aaron Burr. After a distinguished career in the Revolutionary army and having served in the United
States' Senate from 1781 to 1797, in 1801 Burr became Vice-President under
Thomas Jefferson, with whom he had tied in electoral votes in the election
of 1800. In 1804 Burr's long-standing enmity with Alexander Hamilton culminated in a duel, in which Hamilton was killed. With his political career
in tatters, Burr turned his attention to the western territory, where there was
still plenty of opportunity for fame and gain. Although the ultimate aims of
the plot have never become known, they were identified at the time with the
separation of the trans-Appalachian states from the union and the creation a
vast independent empire in the south and west. In the spring of 1805, Burr
undertook a personal reconnaissance tour of the West. It was probably on this
trip that he first met Harman Blennerhassett, an eccentric Irish aristocrat who
lived in feudal splendour on an island in the Ohio River (an idea he may well
have derived from Imlay's description of 'Diamond Island' in *The Emigrants*).
Burr also visited James Wilkinson, then governor of the Louisiana Territory, as
well as several other government dignitaries. Funds for the plan were supplied
by Burr's son-in-law, Joseph Alston, and by Blennerhassett. By the summer of
1806, boats, supplies and men had been procured, mainly at Blennerhassett
Island, and Burr was ready to move. With some sixty followers, he set out to
join Wilkinson's men near Natchez, Mississippi. Coded letters from Burr were
on the way to Wilkinson, alerting him to be ready to move on Mexico, but
Wilkinson at the last minute decided to bail out of the plot and betray Burr
to President Jefferson. Burr and Blennerhassett were arrested and indicted on
charges of treason, but acquitted on a technicality in June 1807. By then both
men had lost their reputations as well as their fortunes; they would end their
lives in abject poverty.

There are two events in the aftermath of the Burr Conspiracy that have been
linked to Gilbert Imlay. The first concerns Burr himself. After Wollstonecraft's
death in 1798 from complications relating to the birth of their daughter Mary,
William Godwin adopted the three-year-old Fanny Imlay and raised her as his
own daughter alongside the new infant. In 1801 Godwin married Mary Jane
Clairmont, who had two children from her first marriage, Charles and Jane (later
Clair). Having fled to London in 1807 following the failed coup, Burr was taken
in by the extended Godwin family. Burr, an ardent disciple of Wollstonecraft's

theories on education, was particularly smitten with the three girls, whom he referred to as 'les Goddesses'.[16] When he returned to the United States the following year, he left the Godwins as if he were a member of the family. Was there more to Burr's warm relations with the Godwins than their charity and Burr's adoration of Wollstonecraft? If he knew, or had known, Fanny's father, would Burr have talked to her about Imlay? If, indeed, because there is no evidence that Imlay ever met or corresponded with Burr. Nor is there any indication that he ever had any contact with Fanny after he and her mother split up.

The other potential connection between Imlay and the Burr Conspiracy concerns Harman Blennerhassett and is even more tangential. Despite his aristocratic descent and considerable fortune, Blennerhassett had been a zealous Jacobin revolutionary, who had spent some time in France during the Revolution before emigrating to North America. He may well have been inspired to do so by Gilbert Imlay's writings about the Ohio Valley. The kind of idyllic paradise he created for himself and his wife on the north end of Backus (now Blennerhassett) Island bears a remarkable resemblance to the utopian retreat of Bellefont, to which the hero and heroine of *The Emigrants* retire in bucolic bliss. Having spent what remained of his inheritance on his defence against the charge of treason, Blennerhassett spent the rest of his life looking for employment by which he might recover some of his lost fortune. In 1827 his quest took him to the Isle of Jersey, where he lived for a brief time before making his home on nearby Guernsey. There he died in 1831 following a series of paralytic strokes. Did Blennerhassett visit the Isle of Jersey because he knew it was the home of Gilbert Imlay? Did the two exiles ever meet – the ideologue of the future American empire in the West and the man who had tried to realize his utopian vision with the help of gunpowder and bullets? It is ironic, to say the least, that they both died, impoverished and forgotten, on a Channel Island – neither in the Ohio Valley, nor in France, nor quite in Britain, either.

When Joel Barlow died in 1812, he left a list of his holdings, which included $115,540 in bank and corporate stocks as well as land claims totalling an estimated $175,000.[17] He had done quite well in the speculation trade, especially in Hamburg, and had then wisely invested his assets in French debt certificates (which he expected to rise in value once the Revolutionary wars were over and the Republic consolidated).[18] As we have seen, James Swan had done even better in the wartime trade between France and the United States, while Benjamin Hichborn – judging from Mary Wollstonecraft's observations and her repeated tirades against his avidity to make a fortune – appears to have come away with a neat sum as well. However, there is no indication that when Gilbert Imlay breathed his last breath on the Isle of Jersey, he was living there in regal splendour. Describing him as 'the most generous creature in the world', Mary Wollstonecraft reported that when they first met, Imlay was 'without fortune'.[19] Well over two years later he was apparently not much better off. For even though he 'continually' offered Wollstonecraft 'pecuniary assistance' and could afford to keep two furnished houses (one for Wollstonecraft and one for his new mistress), he was unable to lend any financial support to Wollstonecraft's father and her sisters Eliza and Everina, as she had asked him to do before she set off for Scandinavia.[20] Around the time the relationship ended, Imlay had executed a bond, the interest on which was intended to support Fanny. But nearly a year later, in March 1797, Wollstonecraft reported to her sister Everina that he had failed to pay even the 'first half-year's interest' on the bond. His creditors had even forwarded some bills to her – which, she added sarcastically, 'I take it for granted, he *forgot* to pay'.[21] Was Imlay really that badly off, or was he simply lavishing his money away on his mistress instead of spending it on his daughter's upbringing?

Though Imlay repeatedly acknowledged his duty to support his daughter, he never seems to have put much effort into it. Yet apparently he *had* come to an arrangement with Chalmers & Cowie, one of the firms he did business with on a regular basis, to the effect that Wollstonecraft could draw upon the proceeds of any future venture or cargo of his that might come into Cowie's hands in excess of £50, which Imlay still owed to his partner.[22] Godwin reported that in the spring of 1797 Chalmers & Cowie had, indeed, received goods belonging to Imlay, which at sale had fetched considerably more than expected – around £1,000.[23] Rather than a share of the profits, however, Wollstonecraft accepted a loan from Cowie. 'I want not protection without affection', she had told Imlay when they were still together; 'and support I need not, whilst my faculties are undisturbed'.[24] With Godwin now giving her both the protection and affection she had been seeking, she certainly was not going to accept any of the proceeds of Imlay's 'crooked business'. Wollstonecraft's close friend Joseph Johnson would be a lot less accommodating after her death in September 1797. In an effort secure the financial future of the three-year-old daughter of his deceased friend, Johnson demanded that Imlay put up the entire principal for the trust deed that he had issued for Fanny. Imlay must have refused to do so, whereupon Johnson threatened to publicly shame Imlay into compliance. Johnson apparently went to see Cowie in order to recover the money from him. But Godwin wanted to keep Fanny, for Wollstonecraft's sake, if not for her own. Imlay agreed to this arrangement, on condition that there would be no further financial claims on him. In a rare move, Imlay then wrote to Johnson urgently requesting that his name no longer be dragged through the mud:

> I like to be where I can be most useful – I believe the opinion of the world is always
> sufficiently secured by an upright & unequivocal conduct, though one should refuse
> to conform to some of its narrow & censorious maxims – I believe this observation

will apply in my case – if so, I beseech you to reflect how brotherly & considerate a conduct it is, to begin the senseless cry of scandal, & incite the world to consider that conduct as faulty, which, I believe, it is inclined to consider as innocent – observe also, that what is done is irremediable, & that, if I were to change my situation upon such a remonstrance as yours, I should encourage, not silence, the tongue of calumny[.][25]

Perhaps Imlay had more principles and a more sensitive conscience than his racketeering, land-jobbing and slave-trading might suggest.

Imlay may also have had a more practical reason for wanting to foil any calumnious reports about his private life. Imlay's business affairs appear to have taken a permanent turn for the worse after the debacle of the *Maria and Margaretha* venture. Whatever meagre information we can gather from the court archives suggests that Imlay had come down from the reckless realm of blockade running, international shipping and venture trading to the more humdrum world of a London shopkeeper. His trade now being local and retail, rather than anonymous and wholesale, gossip and slander would obviously hurt his business. The archives tell us that on 1 November 1796, one Nicholas Morel, an upholsterer from Great Marlborough Street, filed a complaint against Gilbert Imlay, Esq., in a court at Westminster for £600 'for divers goods, wares, and merchandise before that time sold and delivered by the said Nicholas to the said Gilbert'.[26] Judgement was returned in this case on 30 January 1797, when Imlay was ordered to pay £323.1.11 for damages and £24.18.1 for costs. On 21 November 1798, John Eldred, a cabinet and knife-case maker of Brick Lane, Old Street filed a complaint against Imlay for damages of £50 for 'diver goods, wares, and merchandises'.[27] Since Thomas Christie was a partner in his wife's grandfather's carpet manufacturing business in Finsbury Square, it is conceivable that Imlay and Christie were in some sort of household furnishings business together.[28] Christie died in Surinam in October 1796 while on business there, and Imlay may well have tried to continue the trade.

Imlay was still doing a bit of speculating on the side, of course, only on a smaller scale. It appears from a suit he brought in February 1798 against one George James, 'late of Harley Place', London, that Imlay had been investing money in a West Country coal mine. He lost the case, in which he had sued for £1,750 in dividends allegedly owed to him, when the defendant entered a counter-claim saying that Imlay owed him money for unpaid promissory notes.[29] Although Imlay's name does not appear in any of the London commercial directories and carrier lists for the relevant years, it is almost certain that he was in London and that his main source of income was through trade. Again, court records are our only guide. Thus, on 2 February 1801 William Wilkinson and John Rame brought a suit against Imlay, Alexander Sherieff and others 'of London'.[30] However, on 4 March 1801, Alexander Sherieff and others sued Imlay for £709.9.2 for damages and £36.10.10 for costs.[31] 'A. Sheriff & Son' are listed in various commercial directories as London orange merchants (some listings have 'Sheriff, A. Grocer'). This would suggest that by 1801 Imlay had shifted his business to the trade in fruit and produce. However, when in January 1812 a 'Gilbert Imlay' from 3 King's Row, Knightsbridge, took out insurance, he was listed as a 'preparer of the colouring used by brewers'.[32] It seems that he never remained in a line of trade for very long – most likely, given the evidence from the court archives, because he had a tendency not to pay his bills. Perhaps that is also the reason why he is not mentioned in any of the commercial directories; it is as if he wanted to be untraceable. What the evidence from archives also suggests is that Imlay's fortunes were in a progressively downward spiral. He definitely does not come across as a man sitting on a pile of silver: whatever happened to the *Maria and Margaretha*'s precious cargo, there are no signs that Imlay ever got his hands on it.

There is no evidence to suggest that Imlay ever went back to France, let alone returned to blockade running. When he got back from Hamburg in July 1795, Barlow never resumed his purveyance operation in Paris, leaving Imlay effectively without a job. However, the two men presumably did meet up in Paris in late July or early August to settle their affairs, as Wollstonecraft had reported.[33] Interestingly, in a letter to her brother of 28 June, Ruth Barlow, too, had mentioned that they would briefly stop at Paris on their way back home to the United States because Joel had 'some affairs to settle there'.[34] What Imlay precisely had to discuss with Barlow in Paris, is unknown, although it seems inevitable that it was in some way related to the fate of the missing silver. On 9 August, Wollstonecraft had written to Imlay from Tönsberg, probably while he was in Paris: 'I shall wait with some degree of anxiety till I am informed how your affairs terminate'.[35] If they *did* steal the silver, did Imlay and Barlow meet in Paris to divide the spoils? Had Wollstonecraft hoped that she and Imlay would from now on be able to live off the proceeds of what she believed to be Imlay's last venture? If so, had her trip to Scandinavia merely been an elaborate smoke-screen to make the French government and everybody else believe that Barlow's consortium had been robbed of the silver that it had in reality stolen? Or had she in fact gone to Scandinavia to receive and then to dispose of the silver?

The most likely scenario is that the silver was brought ashore at Arendal, probably by Ellefsen and Coleman. It is entirely possible that there had been a secret plan – Ellefsen's and/or Imlay's? – to subsequently stage the sinking of the *Maria and Margaretha* in order to cover up the theft. But, at the end of the day, the fate of the silver remains unknown. What archival evidence there is only allows us to pose some tantalizing questions. What *was* 'the cargo or goods in the hands of Messrs Ryberg & Co', Imlay's agents in Copenhagen, which was mentioned in Imlay's letter of attorney and which Wollstonecraft was authorized to dispose of as she deemed 'right and proper'?[36] Was Barlow's investment spree in the French capital – $34,000 in French government securities and $50,000 in two parcels of Paris real estate – only funded by the commissions he had raked in during his stay in Hamburg? Where had the money come from that Wollstonecraft accused Imlay of having 'lavished away' in the autumn of 1795?[37] And what exactly did Barlow mean when some time in late 1795 he wrote a memo to himself – the *only* reference to Imlay in his extensive business papers: 'Imlays 7 cases Ct – 25.8'? Did he mean 'ct' as in 'carat' and, if so, was he referring to the diamonds and precious stones confiscated by the Jacobins from disenfranchised or guillotined aristocrats and ecclesiasts?[38] The idea is less far-fetched than it may seem when put in the context of James Swan's 'Observations sur le Commerce National'. In this late 1793 memorandum, Swan suggested that rather than dispose of the diamonds and precious stones kept in the Convention's warehouses directly through dealers in The Netherlands, England and Portugal, the 'public fortune' could be used to greater advantage if the Commission des Subsistances bartered the stones for iron, leather and cereals in the trade with Denmark and Sweden.[39] It is a distinct possibility that the 'silver ship' was less unique to Imlay's mercantile enterprises than we have so far assumed. Were there 'diamond ships' in addition to 'silver ships'? Given Swan's insistence on absolute secrecy, it is unlikely we will ever find out.

It is not known when Imlay moved to the Isle of Jersey, or, indeed, why.[40] He may have gone into voluntary exile – perhaps in connection with debt or litigation – or he may have been attracted to the island's trade opportunities. Though Crown Dependencies, the Channel Islands have never been part of the United Kingdom as such. Norman, not British law applies on the islands, which are self-governing in internal affairs. During the eighteenth and nineteenth centuries, the Channel Islands were rife with privateering and smuggling, or 'free trade' as it is known locally. There is a certain logic in Gilbert Imlay ending up on the Isle of Jersey and spending his remaining years there. The earliest indication that Imlay was on Jersey is documented in a suit brought by Imlay and others on 21 June 1828 against one William Goff. Apparently, on 2 April of that year Imlay had loaned £50 to Goff, which the latter would not or could not repay.[41]

Gilbert Imlay died on the Isle of Jersey, 20 November 1828 and was buried in the St Brelade's churchyard on the 24th. He was survived by someone who knew him well enough to provide what Imlay's first biographer, Richard Garnett, described as, 'a curious epitaph in prose and verse'. The text of the epitaph was still legible on the tombstone in 1833, when the copy was made which Garnett reprinted in the *Athenaeum* in 1901. Unfortunately, like so many other witnesses to Imlay's life, it has not survived. The prose part read:

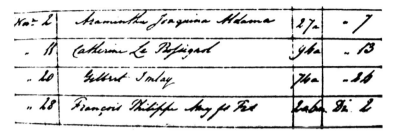

Figure 9. Burial Record of Gilbert Imlay. Burial Records,
St Brelade's Church, Jersey. Courtesy of the Jersey Archives.

Here was intered the perishable remains of Gilbert Imlay, Esq., who was born Feb. 9,
1758, and expired on the 20 Novr., 1828.[42]

The parish register of St Brelade's Church gives Imlay's age as '74' at the time
of his death, which would correspond with 1754, not 1758, as the year he was
born (Figure 9).[43] One likes to think that the minor poet who provided the verse
epitaph was Harman Blennerhassett, who had come over from Guernsey for the
day to give his final salute to his Jacobin pal and ideologue of America's western
Arcadia. Whoever it was, it is perhaps fitting that the epitaph commemorates
the high point of Gilbert Imlay's life, when he was, at least in one guise, an agent
of Liberty's dawn:

> Stranger intelligent! should you pass this way
> Speak of the social advances of the day –
> Mention the greatly good, who've serenely shone
> Since the soul departed its mortal bourne;
> Say of statesmen wise have grown, and priests sincere
> Or if hypocrisy must disappear
> As philosophy extends the beam of truth,
> Sustains rights divine, its essence, and the worth
> Sympathy may permeate the mouldering earth,
> Recal the spirit, and remove the dearth,
> Transient hope gleams even in the grave,
> Which is enough dust can have, or ought to crave
> Then silently bid farewell, be happy,
> For as the globe moves round, thou will grow nappy,
> Wake to hail the hour when new scenes arise,
> As brightening vistas open in the skies.[44]

NOTES

The following abbreviations are used throughout the Notes.

AAE Paris	Archives des Affaires Étrangères (Paris)
AHN Madrid	Archivo Histórico-Nacional (Madrid)
Beinecke	Beinecke Rare Book and Manuscript Library, Yale University (New Haven, CT)
Draper MSS	Draper Manuscript Collection, Wisconsin Historical Society (Madison, WI)
FHS	Filson Historical Society (Louisville, KY)
Blunt White	G. W. Blunt White Library, Mystic Seaport Museum (Mystic, CT)
Houghton	Houghton Library, Harvard University (Cambridge, MA)
Jefferson County CCO	Jefferson County Circuit Clerk's Office (Louisville, KY)
Kentucky LO	Kentucky Land Office (Frankfort, KY)
Kentucky SA	Kentucky State Archives, Kentucky Department for Library and Archives (Frankfort, KY)
LoC	Library of Congress (Washington, DC)
NA	National Archives (formerly Public Record Office, Kew, UK)
NARA	National Archives and Records Administration (Washington, DC)
Nelson County CCO	Nelson County Circuit Clerk's Office (Bardstown, KY)
New Jersey HS	New Jersey Historical Society (Newark, NJ)
New Jersey SA	New Jersey State Archives (Trenton, NJ)
Princeton	Princeton University Library, Rare Books and Special Collections (Princeton, NJ)

Prologue

1. In *The Collected Letters of Mary Wollstonecraft*, ed. J. Todd (London: Penguin Books, 2003), p. 295.

2. K. Marx, *The German Ideology*, in K. Marx and F. Engels, *Collected Works*, trans. C. Dutt, W. Lough and C. P. Magill, 50 vols (London: Lawrence and Wishart, 1976), vol. 5, p. 42. *The German Ideology* was originally written in 1845–6 and published in complete form in 1932.

3. E. F. Wyatt, 'The First American Novel', *Atlantic Monthly*, 144 (October 1929), pp. 466–75, on p. 466.

4. For details, see Chapters 7 and 9.

5. See Chapter 7 for further details.

6. At her request, Imlay returned Wollstonecraft's letters to him in November 1795 (Mary Wollstonecraft to Imlay, 27 November 1795, in *The Collected Letters of Mary Wollstonecraft*, p. 332). If Wollstonecraft did not destroy Imlay's letters herself, it is probable that William Godwin did so soon after her death, presumably in order to protect his wife's reputation from further calumny in the hostile popular press.

7. W. Godwin, *Memoirs of the Author of a Vindication of the Rights of Woman* (London: J. Johnson and G.G. and J. Robinson, 1798), p. 122. Godwin quotes from Shakespeare's *Othello*, V.ii.346–7.

8. The main sources for biographical information on Imlay are J. W. Townsend, *Kentuckians in History and Literature* (New York and Washington, DC: Neale Publishing Company, 1907), pp. 13–25; R. L. Rusk, 'The Adventures of Gilbert Imlay', *Indiana University Studies*, 10:57 (March 1923), pp. 3–26; O. F. Emerson, 'Notes on Gilbert Imlay, Early American Writer', *PMLA*, 39:2 (June 1924): pp. 406–39; W. C. Durant, 'A Supplement to *Memoirs of Mary Wollstonecraft*', in W. Godwin, *Memoirs of Mary Wollstonecraft*, ed. W. C. Durant (1798; London: Constable, 1927), pp. 135–334, on pp. 223–309; and J. L. Fant III, 'A Study of Gilbert Imlay (1754–1828): His Life and Works' (PhD thesis, University of Pennsylvania, 1984). Of these accounts, Rusk's, Emerson's and Fant's are the most thoroughly researched and hence the most reliable. However, although it expands on and corrects a number of errors in Emerson and Rusk, Fant's study is marred by suggestive speculation and hypothesis. For details about the background of Imlay's forebears, see Fant, 'A Study of Gilbert Imlay', pp. 3–11. Further information on Imlay can be gleaned from William Godwin's *Memoirs of the Author of a Vindication of the Rights of Woman* and from the letters Mary Wollstonecraft as published in *Letters Written during a Short Residence in Sweden, Norway, and Denmark* (London: J. Johnson, 1796), and in *Letters to Imlay*, ed. C. K. Paul (London: C. K. Paul, 1879), see also his introduction, pp. xxxvi–l. Most accounts of the life of Mary Wollstonecraft contain information on Imlay, but these are on the whole derived from the *Memoirs* and Wollstonecraft's letters.

1 War Child and Soldier

1. F. Parkman, *France and England in North America*, 2 vols (1884; New York: Library of America, 1983), vol. 2, p. 843.

2. Ibid., vol. 2, pp. 844–5.

3. Ibid., vol. 2, p. 947.

4. G. Imlay, *The Emigrants, &c.; or, The History of an Expatriated Family, Being a Delineation of English Manners, Drawn from Real Characters, Written in America*, 3 vols (London: A. Hamilton, 1793), vol. 1, p. 84.

5. Parkman, *France and England in North America*, vol. 2, pp. 1174–5.

6. 'Extract from a Letter from New-York', *Pennsylvania Gazette*, 15 August 1757.
7. Ibid.
8. *New American Magazine*, 31 May 1758; *Pennsylvania Gazette*, 6 July 1758.
9. *Pennsylvania Gazette*, 6 July 1758.
10. *New American Magazine*, 31 May 1758.
11. S. Smith, *The History of the Colony of Nova-Caesaria, or New-Jersey: Containing, an Account of its First Settlement, Progressive Improvements, the Original and Present Constitution, and other Events to the Year 1721. With some particulars since; and a Short View of its Present State* (Burlington, NJ: James Parker; sold also by David Hall, Philadelphia, 1765), p. 446.
12. D. L. Kemmerer, 'A History of Paper Money in Colonial New Jersey, 1668–1775', *Proceedings of the New Jersey Historical Society*, 74 (April 1956), pp. 107–44, on p. 144.
13. J. E. Pomfret, *Colonial New Jersey: A History* (New York: Scribner's Sons, 1973), pp. 178–9.
14. Roughly a third of New Jerseyans – around 50,000 citizens – supported the cause for independence; another third remained loyal to George III; and the final third considered themselves neutral in the conflict, in many cases because their faith forbade them to bear arms (as in the case of the large Quaker community).
15. For a copy of the full list of associators, see J. W. Barber and H. Howe, *Historical Collections of the State of New Jersey: Containing a General Collection of the Most Interesting Facts, Traditions, Biographical Sketches, Anecdotes, etc. Relating to its History and Antiquities, with Geographical Descriptions of Every Township in the State Illustrated by 120 Engravings* (New York: for the authors, by S. Tuttle, 1844), pp. 314–16.
16. T. F. Gordon, *Gazetteer of the State of New Jersey: Comprehending a General View of its Physical and Moral Conditions, Together with a Topographical and Statistical Account of its Counties, Towns, Villages, Canals, Rail Roads, etc., Accompanied by a Map* (1834; Cottonport, LA: Polyanthos, 1973), p. 161.
17. By the end of the nineteenth century, even the Imlay family burial ground, situated on the southerly bank of Doctor's Creek, a short distance below the mill, had fallen into decay. When genealogist and local historian Charles Hutchinson visited the site of the burial ground in April 1885, this is what he found: 'It is within the limits of the 480 acres which Capt. Richard Saltar conveyed to the first Peter (or Patrick) Imlay in 1710, and is apparently at about the northwesterly corner of the 111 acres which was the residence of his son Robert, and his son, Peter. If, however, any of that branch are buried there, nothing now indicates the fact. There appears to have once been quite a number of marble gravestones, only a few of which now remain. Several others are broken off at the base and fragments are plentifully scattered about. A roadway along the southerly side, where there is a fence, passes over a number of graves. The stone of Peter Imlay, son of William, and grandson of Peter [Patrick], which is the oldest now existing, is broken, and was found lying by the fence. The inscription is as follows: "In memory of Peter Imlay, who departed this life January 26th A.D. 1789, aged 57 years". The stone to the memory of Susanna, his wife, who died November 14, 1803, aged 70 years, is still standing. Of their children, I am told that the stone of William Eugene lies at the foot of the bank, but I did not find it. Samuel, son of Peter, and Mary his wife, have stones still standing, as also Nathaniel and Ann his wife. There are also stones to the memory of "Harriet Imlay, who departed this life March 30th A.D. 1821, in the 28th year of her age", and "Mary Ann, wife of Wm. B. Elliott, who departed this life September 9, A.D. 1848, aged 53 years". I

find no others.' In 1912 Hutchinson added this postscript to his original observations: 'How this evidently populous burial place should have ever been permitted to pass into the hands of strangers, and to be subjected to the wanton destruction that has occurred there, I cannot understand' (Charles R. Hutchinson Collection, 1788–1922, New Jersey HS, box 4, folder 5, book 3, p. 93).

18. Grant from James, Duke of York, to Carteret and Berkeley, 24 June 1664, *Records of the Council of Proprietors of the Western Division of New Jersey*, New Jersey SA, loose parchments and miscellaneous records, 1664–1815, nr. 2.

19. Ibid., Bound Volumes, nr. 1.

20. Cited in Pomfret, *Colonial New Jersey*, p. 57.

21. See Hutchinson Collection, New Jersey HS, bound oversized boxes, 'Family Records' ('Imlay'), series 3, book A, p. 366.

22. D. Dobson, *Scottish Emigration to Colonial America, 1607–1785* (Athens, GA: University of Georgia Press, 1994), p. 49.

23. Hutchinson Collection, New Jersey HS, bound oversized boxes, 'Family Records', series 3, book A, p. 366.

24. Minutes of Monmouth County, 1688–1721, Monmouth County Archives (County Clerk's Office, Manalapan, NJ), p. 252.

25. East Jersey Deeds, New Jersey SA, book F-2, p. 535.

26. Ibid., book D, p. 93.

27. Ibid., book H, p. 100.

28. Tracing members of the Imlay dynasty in the Jersey colonial records is further complicated by the existence in West New Jersey of the Emley family. The Emleys were descendents of William Emley, who was born in Blyth Parish, Nottinghamshire, in 1648. Persecuted for his Quaker faith, Emley became a commissioner from Yorkshire for the proprietors of New Jersey and in 1677 left for America to buy land from the Indians along the Delaware River, including one tract in Burlington County, near the present city of Trenton. A skilled surveyor, Emley was one of the commissioners appointed to determine the line between East and West Jersey. Many of his descendents remained in Burlington County, but some settled in Monmouth County. Conversely, some of the descendents of the Imlays, having first settled in north-eastern Monmouth County, later also established themselves in Burlington County. In provincial records, the Emleys indifferently spelled their names with an E or an I.

29. East Jersey Deeds, New Jersey SA, book D, pp. 393–4.

30. *Minutes of the Board of Proprietors of the Eastern Division of New Jersey, 1685–1794*, 4 vols (vols 1–3, Perth Amboy, NJ: Board of Proprietors of the Eastern Division of New Jersey, 1949–85; vol. 4, ed. M. N. Lurie and J. R. Walroth (Newark, NJ: New Jersey Historical Society, 1985.), vol. 1, p. 193.

31. Deeds, 1722–1947, Monmouth County Archives (County Clerk's Office, Manalapan, NJ), book F, p. 151.

32. East Jersey Deeds, New Jersey SA, book F, p. 181.

33. H. Imlay and N. Imlay, *The Imlay Family* (Zanesville, OH: n.p., 1958), pp. 14–15.

34. The deed (for 150 acres) was said to have been preserved among papers in the estate of George Imlay of Imlaystown (1886), See Hutchinson Collection, New Jersey HS, 'Family Records', series 2, book 2, p. 167. See also [W. H. P. Oliver], *A Brief Account of the American Ancestors and of Some Descendents of William Henry Imlay of Hartford, Connecticut, 1780–1858, Compiled for the Most Part from the Public Records by One of his Grandsons and Printed for Distribution in the Family* (privately printed, n.d.), p. 4.

35. Hutchinson Collection, New Jersey HS, 'Family Records', series 3, book A, p. 371 (map).
36. The property that was acquired by Peter Imlay in 1727 remained in the Imlay family until it was sold to the Hendrickson family around 1915. The house, known locally as 'The Imlay Mansion', is located on the north side of Doctors Creek, opposite the Happy Apple hotel. The current construction has early nineteenth-century origins (probably the section on the left) and was expanded with Italiante additions in the 1860–70s.
37. East Jersey Deeds, New Jersey SA, book L, p. 74.
38. Ibid., Book H, pp. 100, 101.
39. Imlay and Imlay, *The Imlay Family*, p. 46.
40. East Jersey Deeds, New Jersey SA, book H-2, p. 335; Imlay and Imlay, *The Imlay Family*, p. 46.
41. Hutchinson Collection, New Jersey HS, box 4, folder 5, book 3, pp. 69–70.
42. Imlay and Imlay, *The Imlay Family*, pp. 45–6.
43. Monmouth County Wills, 1751–1756, New Jersey SA, pp. 2021–6 (recorded in West Jersey Wills, book 7, pp. 525–6).
44. Ibid., p. 2025.
45. [Oliver], *A Brief Account of the American Ancestors and of Some Descendents of William Henry Imlay*, p. 10.
46. Monmouth County Wills, 1761–1763, New Jersey SA, p. 2649 (recorded in West Jersey Wills, book 11, p. 195).
47. On 25 January 1762 Peter executed a bond for £500 and took out a license to marry Mary Holmes. Marriage Bonds and Licenses, I, 1711–1795, New Jersey SA, p. 22.
48. Letter from W. T. B. S. Imlay (Brooklyn, NY) to W. Nelson (Paterson, NJ), 11 November 1906, Miscellaneous Manuscripts, 1664–1956, New Jersey HS, MSS MG 23.
49. Marriage Bonds and Licenses, I, New Jersey SA, p. 42.
50. This conjecture was first made by Ralph Leslie Rusk in 'The Adventures of Gilbert Imlay', p. 6, n.
51. Poulson's *American Daily Advertiser*, 13 September 1827, and *Saturday Evening Post*, 15 September 1827.
52. Enterremens de St Brelade Depuis Janvier 1825, Church Records, Jersey Archive (St Helier, Isle of Jersey), fol. 5.
53. East Jersey Deeds, New Jersey SA, book D-3, p. 65.
54. *Calendar of New Jersey Wills, Vols I–IX* (1730–1800), in *Documents Relating to the Colonial, Revolutionary and Post-Revolutionary History of the State of New Jersey* [various titles, commonly called the *New Jersey Archives*], vols 23, 30, 32–8, Archives of the State of New Jersey, 1st series, 42 vols (Newark and Paterson: various publishers, 1901, 1918, 1924–44), vol. 28: Calendar of New Jersey Wills, Vol. I, 1670–1730 (1901), ed. W. Nelson, p. 93.
55. Hutchinson Collection, New Jersey HS, 'Family Records', series 2, book 2, p. 166.
56. *Documents Relating to the Colonial History of the State of New Jersey*, 2nd series, vol. 2, ed. F. B. Lee (Trenton, NJ: John L. Murphy Publishing Co., 1903), p. 416.
57. Monmouth County Records, Hutchinson Collection, New Jersey HS, box 4, folder 1 (vol. 70.11, L).
58. Upper Freehold Town Book, book A, Hutchinson Collection, New Jersey HS, box 4, folder 1 (vol. 70.11, L).
59. West Jersey Deeds, New Jersey SA, book H, p. 692.
60. Hutchinson Collection, New Jersey HS, 'Family Records', series 2, book 2, p. 166.

61. *Pennsylvania Gazette*, 24 November 1784.
62. Hutchinson Collection, New Jersey HS, 'Family Records', series 2, book 2, p. 166. On 14 November 1792 the Allentown mill property was sold by the sheriff as the property of Robert Pidgeon to John Imlay, the wealthy trader from Allentown, who on 29 December of the same year conveyed it to Robert Evilman for £2,300. See Hutchinson Collection, New Jersey HS, box 4, folder 5, book 3, p. 88.
63. M. S. Adelberg, *Roster of the People of Revolutionary Monmouth County* (n.p., n.d.), p. 147.
64. *New Jersey Gazette*, 21 August 1782.
65. Adelberg, *Roster of the People of Revolutionary Monmouth County*, pp. 146–7. An Isaac Imlay signed a 'Petition for Urgent Action against the Disaffected' on 21 February and 14 March 1777.
66. See Daughters of the American Revolution, *DAR Patriot Index: Millennium Administration*, 3 vols (Baltimore, MD: Gateway Press, 2003), vol. 2, pp. 1430–1. See also Adelberg, *Roster of the People of Revolutionary Monmouth County*, pp. 146–7.
67. Monmouth County Militia, Compiled Military Service Records of Soldiers who Served in the American Army during the Revolutionary War, NARA, MS Wid. 466.
68. William Eugene Imlay was admitted to the degree of Bachelor of Arts on 27 September 1773. As part of the commencement festivities, he took part in a voluntary competition among the graduates, acting as opponent in a forensic disputation on the thesis, 'The Corruption of a State is not Hastened by the Improvement of Taste and Literature; but by the Introduction of Wealth'. See *Pennsylvania Gazette*, 13 October 1773, no. 2338, p. 2, and *Rivington's New-York Gazetteer*, 14 October 1773, no. 26, p. 2.
69. L. Sabine, *The American Loyalists, or Biographical Sketches of Adherents to the British Crown in the War of the Revolution; Alphabetically Arranged; with a Preliminary Historical Essay* (Boston, MA: Charles C. Little and James Brown, 1847), p. 379.
70. Compiled Service Records of Soldiers who Served in the American Army during the Revolutionary War, NARA, MS 1062.
71. Joseph L. Fant erroneously claims that this Peter Imlay was Gilbert's father in 'A Study of Gilbert Imlay', p. 14. It is highly unlikely that Gilbert's father, who was fifty-eight at the time and the father of five children and nine stepchildren, would have joined the militia in anything other than a mere ceremonial capacity. Besides, Peter Imlay was buying and selling land all through 1778, when he was supposed to be held prisoner. The Council for Safety agreed to exchange Peter Imlay for Anthony Woodward on 11 September 1778, while on 4 September of that year Peter was advertising the sale of a plantation in Upper Freehold. See Monmouth County Militia, Compiled Military Service Records of Soldiers who Served in the American Army during the Revolutionary War, NARA, MSS 1126, 3979, printed roster, p. 641; New Jersey Council of Safety Minutes, March 1777–October 1778, New Jersey SA, p. 278.
72. His warrant, signed by Colonel David Forman, is preserved in Revolutionary War MSS, NARA, MS 20413.
73. In early June 1778 the leader of the New Jersey Loyalists, Skinner, launched a raid from Staten Island into New Jersey in order to capture Burrows in Middletown Point (Matawan), following a tip-off from William Taylor, a Loyalist militia colonel and a relative to Burrowes. Burrowes managed to get away in the nick of time, after which the refugees captured Burrowes's father and some militia officers and took them to Staten Island. The Patriots retaliated by capturing William Taylor, upon which Sir Henry Clinton arranged for an exchange of prisoners.

74. Company Pay Roll, Office of Army Accounts, NARA, indexed in '*Compiled Service Records of Soldiers who served in the American Army during the Revolutionary War*', Record Group 93 (RG 93), reel 65.

75. F. B. Heitman, *Historical Register of Officers in the Continental Army during the War of the Revolution, April, 1775, to December, 1783* (1914; Baltimore, MD: Genealogical Publishing Co., 1967), p. 24; F. A. Berg, *Encyclopedia of Continental Army Units: Battalions, Regiments, and Independents Corps* ([Harrisberg, PA]: Stockpole Books, [1972]), p. 43; R. K. Wright, Jr, *The Continental Army* (Washington, DC: Center of Military History United States Army, 1983), p. 321.

76. Revolutionary War MSS, NARA, MS 18096.

77. Compiled Service Records of Soldiers who Served in the American Army during the Revolutionary War, NARA; W. S. Stryker, *The Battle of Monmouth*, ed. W. Starr Myers (Princeton, NJ: Princeton University Press, 1927), Appendix V.

78. New Jersey Council of Safety, Loose Papers, 1776–1781, New Jersey SA, MS 4126.

79. *The Papers of William Livingston*, gen. ed. C. E. Prince, 5 vols (Trenton, NJ: New Jersey Historical Commission, 1979), vol. 1, p. 377.

80. New Jersey Council of Safety Minutes, 18 March 1777–October 1778, New Jersey SA, Box 1.

81. Revolutionary War MSS, NARA, MS 18096.

82. Ibid., MS 17995.

83. N. Collin, *The Journal of Nicholas Collin, 1746–1831* (Philadelphia, PA: The New Jersey Society of Pennsylvania, 1936), p. 56.

84. Monmouth County Court, Common Pleas, Loose Papers, 1726–1927, Monmouth County Archives (Manalapan, NJ), box 49.

85. New Jersey Supreme Court, New Jersey SA, no. 16609.

86. *New Jersey Gazette*, 21 August 1782.

87. Ibid.

88. New Jersey Supreme Court, New Jersey SA, Minute Books, book 60, pp. 329, 340, 341.

89. Ibid., p. 392.

90. Monmouth County Court, Common Pleas, Loose Papers, Monmouth County Archives, box 50.

91. Ibid.

92. Ibid.

93. New Jersey Supreme Court, New Jersey SA, Minute Books, pp. 446, 467.

94. Extensive research in the Monmouth County Archives has shown that Gilbert Imlay is not mentioned as a defendant in the criminal records (Quarter Sessions). In the Monmouth County Deed Books he is not mentioned as either a grantee or as a grantor, which means he never legally held title to any land in the county, nor sold any such land.

95. [Oliver], *A Brief Account of the American Ancestors and of Some Descendents of William Henry Imlay*, p. 9.

96. See R. K. Murdoch, 'Benedict Arnold and the Owners of the *Charming Nancy*', *Pennsylvania Magazine of History and Biography Index*, 84 (January 1960), pp. 22–55.

97. L. B. Walker, '"Life of Margaret Shippen", Wife of Benedict Arnold', *The Pennsylvania Magazine of History and Biography* 24:4 (1900), pp. 257–66, 401–29, on pp. 417–18.

2 Land-Jobber à la Mode

1. Beall-Booth Family Papers, FHS, MSS A B365 5.

2. G. Imlay, *A Topographical Description of the Western Territory of North America; Containing a Succinct Account of Its Climate, Natural History, Population, Agriculture, Manners and Customs, with an Ample Description of the Several Divisions into which that Country is Partitioned, and an Accurate Statement of the Various Tribes of Indians that Inhabit the Frontier Country. To which is Annexed, a Delineation of the Laws and Government of the State of Kentucky, Tending to Shew the Probable Rise and Grandeur of the American Empire. In a Series of Letters to a Friend in England* (London: J. Debrett, 1792), p. 40. Note that all references to *A Topographical Description* are to the first edition, unless otherwise noted.

3. Rusk, 'The Adventures of Gilbert Imlay', p. 7.

4. Jefferson County Court Minute Books, Nelson County CCO, book 1 (6 April 1784 – December 1785), p. 3.

5. Imlay to Daniel Boone, [15 March 1783], Draper MSS, 25C83. Boone had paid £16,000 for treasury warrant 10,216, authorizing him to survey his 10,000 acres (Warrants, Surveys and Patents, Kentucky LO, survey book VA 7858); the fact that he sold his survey to Imlay for £2,000 can only mean that Boone had paid for his warrant in Virginia paper money, and that he sold the tract to Imlay for silver money.

6. See Imlay to William Triplet, 15 July 1784, Harry Innes Papers, 1752–1900, LoC, container 6, 12.253, (in which the purchase date of March 1783 is confirmed), and an untitled and undated document, in Imlay's handwriting, endorsed 'A List of the Land assigned by Holder and to be assigned by Imlay', Innes Papers, container 6, 12.265 (which lists the individual items involved in the deal and confirms the total acreage of 20,000).

7. See Matthew Walton's bill against Imlay, Henry Lee and Henry Banks, 11 May 1797, Miscellaneous Papers, Nelson County CCO, 4pp, unpaginated and uncatalogued.

8. Fayette County Entries (11 November 1783), Kentucky LO, book 3, pp. 36–7. All four tracts were surveyed for Imlay (Virginia surveys VA 8614, VA 8615, VA 8617, and OK 2937), but since he later disposed of the tracts, none of the grants are in his name.

9. Imlay to Daniel Boone, [15 March 1783], Draper MSS, 25C83.

10. N. O. Hammon (ed.), *My Father, Daniel Boone: The Draper Interviews with Nathan Boone*, intro. N. L. Dawson (Lexington, KY: University Press of Kentucky, 1999), p. 109.

11. L. C. Draper, *The Life of Daniel Boone*, ed., T. F. Belue (Mechanicsburg, PA: Stackpole Books, 1998), p. 441, p. 568. In December 1784 Hite attended the Kentucky Convention that met at Danville as a member from Lincoln County. He died in 1794.

12. Isaac Hite to Abraham Hite, 26 April 1783, Isaac Hite Family Papers, FHS, MSS C/H Hite, Isaac. On the map he would publish a year after Hite wrote to his father, John Filson marked the area north of Green River between Panther Creek and Rough Creek as having an 'Abundance of Iron Ore' (see J. Filson, *The Discovery, Settlement and Present State of Kentucky: And an Essay towards the Topography, and Natural History of that Important Country* (Wilmington, DE: printed by James Adams, 1784), 'Map of Kentucky').

13. Isaac Hite to Abraham Hite, 26 April 1783, Hite Family Papers, FHS, MSS C/H Hite, Isaac.

14. There are five known alternative spellings of Imlay's name in documents relating to his land-jobbing days: Emley, Imley, Emlay, Emly and Imly. A letter written by Imlay to Boone in 1786 is marked 'Gilbert Emley' in a contemporary hand – probably Boone's (Draper MSS, 26C153). One B. Gaines recollected in 1833, 'There was such a man as George Emley [superscribed 'Imlay'] in this country about the years 1784 & 5, he was on Old Revolutionary Captain; what became of him I know not; except that he wrote and

published a Novel, none of which was founded on fact' (B. Gaines to Mann Butler, 17 December 1833, Draper MSS, 9J2383). Writing in November 1785, William Christian refers to his 'near neighbour' Imlay as 'Captain Imley' (William Christian to his mother, sister and brother-in-law, 4 November 1785, Hugh Blair Grigsby Papers, 1745–1944, Virginia Historical Society (Richmond, VA), MSS 1 G8782 b 5751). Most of the records in the Kentucky Court of Appeals Deed Books and District of Kentucky Supreme Court Deed Books, in Kentucky SA, also use the spelling 'Emley'. In a letter from 13 November 1801 the Providence-based entrepreneur Silas Talbot referred to his former business partner as both 'Imlay' and 'Emlay' (Talbot to Nathaniel Russell, 13 November 1801, Silas Talbot Papers, Blunt White, collection 18, box 8, folder 12). When Ann Christian wrote to her sister, Ann Fleming, on 3 November 1785, she sent her letter by 'Capt Emly' (Hugh Blair Grigsby Papers, MSS 1 G8782 b 5813). In the Virginia Land Office Grants, Library of Virginia (Richmond, VA), there are two grants in the name of Gilbert 'Imly' (both dated 1 June 1786).

15. Court Minute Books, 1781–1794, Jefferson County CCO, book A, pp. 58–9.
16. T. P. Abernethy, *Western Lands and the American Revolution* (New York and London: D. Appleton-Century Co., 1937), p. 250. John May's sales trip to Philadelphia is reported in a letter from Lardner Clark to Samuel Beall, 19 November 1781, Beall-Booth Family Papers, FHS, MSS A B365 2.
17. H. Marshall, *The History of Kentucky, Exhibiting an Account of the Modern Discovery, Settlement, Progressive Improvement, Civil and Military Transactions, and the Present State of the Country*, 2 vols (Frankfort, KY: printed by Henry Gore, 1812), vol. 1, pp. 165–6.
18. John Floyd to William Preston, 28 March 1783, Draper MSS 17CC145.
19. Emerson and Rusk erroneously identified Imlay's business partner and agent Henry Lee as the famous General Henry Lee of Virginia ('Light-Horse Harry'), perhaps echoing an earlier suggestion by Townsend (*Kentuckians in History and Literature*, p. 15). However, Imlay *did* enlist the services of Henry Lee of Virginia as his legal attorney in November 1786, not long before he left the United States (see below).
20. Imlay to Henry Lee, 2 September 1784, Draper MSS, 6BB41.
21. Imlay to Henry Lee, 14 September 1784, Draper MSS, 6BB41[2].
22. Imlay to Henry Lee, 21 September 1784, Beinecke, Gen. MSS Misc., group 2444 F–1.
23. Imlay to Henry Lee, 10 October 1784, Draper MSS, 6BB42.
24. Imlay would not have been alone in his appreciation of Floyd's expertise and knowledge in locating the choicest tracts in Kentucky, many of whom he had surveyed for himself: John May was eager to buy Floyd's land for the same reason in January 1783 (John May to Samuel Beall, 9 January 1783, Beall-Booth Family Papers, FHS, MSS A B365 3).
25. The Virginia Land Office Grants, Library of Virginia (Richmond, VA), indicate that Imlay was granted, alone or in partnership with John Holder, Matthew Walton and Henry Lee, a total of 22,994 acres in Jefferson County, and 6,400 acres in Fayette County.
26. Imlay to Henry Lee, 2 September 1784, Draper MSS, 6BB41
27. Imlay to Henry Lee, 14 September 1784, Draper MSS, 6BB41[2].
28. See Supreme Court Order Books, 1787–1792, Kentucky SA, book A, p. 244 (Imlay v. William Peachy); p. 515 (Imlay v. William Preston); p. 516 (Imlay v. James Speed; Imlay v. William Shannon and William Johnson; Imlay v. John McGee; Imlay v. Richard Barbour).
29. Imlay to Skinner, 27 September 1784, Innes Papers, LoC, container 6, 12.254.
30. Imlay to Henry Lee, 10 October 1784, Draper MSS, 6BB42.

31. Cleveland v. Imlay and Lee, Old Circuit and Common Law Courts, Jefferson County CCO, File 5746 (Rusk, 'The Adventures of Gilbert Imlay', p. 8; the originals of these records have since been reported 'lost or mislaid'). See also Minute Books, Jefferson County CCO, book A, p. 81.

32. Old Circuit and Common Law Courts, Jefferson County CCO, File 546 (ibid.). See also Minute Books, Jefferson County CCO, book A, p. 64.

33. Order Book, 1784–1785, Jefferson County CCO, p. 287. For Sebastian's plea on behalf of Imlay, see Old Circuit and Common Law Courts, Jefferson County CCO, File 5746 (Rusk, 'The Adventures of Gilbert Imlay', p. 9).

34. Kentucky Supreme Court, Chancery Decrees, 1798–1800, Nelson County CCO, unnumbered document.

35. Ibid.

36. Deed Books, 1783–1806, Jefferson County CCO, book 1, 1783–1791, p. 190.

37. Ibid., p. 190.

38. Supreme Court Order Books, Kentucky SA, book D (March 1789–March 1790), p. 105.

39. Supreme Court Rule Docket Books, 1785–1792, Kentucky SA, book 2, pp. 244, 450.

40. Kentucky Supreme Court, Chancery Decrees, Nelson County CCO, unnumbered document.

41. Cf. Rusk, 'The Adventures of Gilbert Imlay', p. 10.

42. Imlay to Sebastian, letter of attorney, Bond and Power of Attorney Books, 1783–1805, Jefferson County CCO, book 1 (1783–1798), p. 169. Lewis's tract of 50,000 acres on Green River was entered on 19 December 1782 (see W. R. Jillson (ed.), *Old Kentucky Entries and Deeds: A Complete Index to all of the Earliest Land Entries, Military Warrants, Deeds and Wills of the Commonwealth of Kentucky* (1926; Baltimore, MD: Genealogical Publishing Co., 1969), p. 236).

43. Imlay to Sebastian, letter of attorney, Bond and Power of Attorney Books, Jefferson County CCO, book 1, p. 170.

44. Ibid., p. 171.

45. Ibid., p. 170.

46. Imlay to William Clark, 26 September 1785, Draper MSS, 1M125. On the eve of his campaign against the Indians in the Miami region, General Rogers Clark appointed William Clark of Clarksville his 'true and lawful Attorney', describing him as 'my trusty and loving friend' (Draper MSS, 1M133).

47. Imlay to William Clark, 5 November 1785, Draper MSS, 1M128.

48. Christian to his mother, 4 November 1785, Hugh Blair Grigsby Papers, Virginia Historical Society, MSS 1 G8782 b 5751.

49. Imlay to James Marshall, 6 November 1785, Innes Papers, LoC, container 6, 12.258.

50. Christian to his mother, 12 December 1785. Hugh Blair Grigsby Papers, Virginia Historical Society, MSS 1 G8782 b 5751–2. Christian was killed in April 1786 whilst leading a party of settlers in pursuit of a band of Indians who had stolen some of their horses.

51. Virginia Land Office Grants, Library of Virginia, Grants S (1785–1786), pp. 621–3, 638–40, 640–2; Grants U (1786), pp. 113–15, 115–17, 117–19, 121–3, 126–8, 128–30, 162–4.

52. Imlay to John Helm, 2 November 1785, Helm-Haycraft Collection, Lincoln Museum (Fort Wayne, IN), uncatalogued.

53. Samuel Beall to John May, 14 February 1786, Beall-Booth Family Papers, FHS, MSS A B365 5.
54. May first unfolded his grand scheme in letters to Samuel Beall dated 16 and 17 August 1779, Beall-Booth Family Papers, FHS, MSS A B365 1.
55. Virginia Land Law 1779, ch. XII, art. i, in *The Statutes at Large, Being a Collection of all the Laws of Virginia from the First Session of the Legislature in 1619*, ed. W. W. Hening, 13 vols (Richmond, VA: George Cochran, 1822), vol. 10, p. 35.
56. Virginia Land Law 1779, ch. XIII, art. ii, in *The Statutes at Large*, ed. Hening, vol. 10, p. 50.
57. John May to Beall, 15 March 1780, Beall-Booth Family Papers, FHS, MSS A B365 1.
58. Beall to John May, 14 June 1780, Beall-Booth Family Papers, FHS, MSS A B365 1.
59. Beall to John May, 11 November 1780, Beall-Booth Family Papers, FHS, MSS A B365 1.
60. In October 1781, for instance, May allowed Beall to dispose of 200,000 acres of land owned by their company. See John May to Beall, 17 October 1781, Beall-Booth Family Papers, FHS, MSS A B365 2.
61. See Beall to John May, 9 December 1782; John May to Beall, 9 January 1783, Beall-Booth Family Papers, FHS, MSS A B365 3.
62. The agreement lists the names of the persons for whom the company had located warrants, the quantity of land located and the proportions allocated to each of the partners. John Floyd, 'Land List, 1783', Kentucky Historical Society, Library, Special Collections and Archives (Frankfort, KY), MSS 88SC17.
63. Jefferson County Entries, Kentucky LO, book A, p. 267A, p. 267B; and Jillson (ed.), *Old Kentucky Entries and Deeds*, p. 250.
64. John May to Beall, 9 January 1783, Beall-Booth Family Papers, FHS, MSS A B365 3.
65. Beall to John May, 28 September 1784, Beall-Booth Family Papers, FHS, MSS A B365 3.
66. John May to Beall, 25 January 1785, Beall-Booth Family Papers, FHS, MSS A B365 4.
67. 'Memorandum of the Lands comprehended in an agreement entered into between Gilbert Imlay & John May the twentieth eighth day of February 1785', Beall-Booth Family Papers, FHS, MSS A B3654.
68. John May to Beall, 27 June 1786, Beall-Booth Family Papers, FHS, MSS A B365 5.
69. Memorandum in Beall's handwriting, undated, Beall-Booth Family Papers, FHS, MSS A B365 12. See also John May to Beall, 14 July 1786, Beall-Booth Family Papers, FHS, MSS A B365 6.
70. John May to Beall, 4 September 1786, Beall-Booth Family Papers, FHS, MSS A B365 6.
71. John May to Beall, 2 July 1785, Beall-Booth Family Papers, FHS, MSS A B365 4.
72. John May to Beall, 14 July 1786, and John May to Beall, 27 October 1786, Beall-Booth Family Papers, FHS, MSS A B365 6.
73. John May to Beall, 4 September 1785, Beall-Booth Family Papers, FHS, MSS A B365 4.
74. Imlay to Richard Woolfolk and John Helm, 20 July 1785, Helm-Haycraft Collection, Lincoln Museum, uncatalogued.
75. Beall to Imlay, 26 August 1785, Beall-Booth Family Papers, FHS, MSS A B365 4.
76. Beall to John May, 14 February 1786, Beall-Booth Family Papers, FHS, MSS A B365 5.
77. Thomas Rutland to Imlay, 5 June 1786, Thomas Rutland Letter Book, Maryland Historical Society (Baltimore, MD), MS 1726; John May to Samuel Beall, May 1786, and

Samuel Beall to John May, 14 February 1786, Beall-Booth Family Papers, FHS, MSS A B365 5. See also Amos Ogden to Isaac Hite, 28 July 1786, Chancery Decrees, 1798–1800, Nelson County CCO, unnumbered document.

78. See Amos Ogden to Isaac Hite, 28 July 1786, ibid.

79. Chancery Court, Deed Books, Nelson County CCO, book 1, pp. 96–125. Land traded after the grant had been issued, was filed in the records of Deeds and Wills on the county level. The indentures are all dated 1 June 1787, except one, which bears the date of 6 June 1787. However, these dates are not the dates of the actual transactions between Imlay and Talbot (which we know took place sometime prior to 7 September 1786), but reflect the time the original indentures were copied into the Nelson County Deed Book (Kentucky land sold outside of the district had to be recorded under Virginia law in the appropriate county).

80. John May to Beall, received in May 1786, Beall-Booth Family Papers, FHS, MSS A B365 5.

81. Ibid.

82. Imlay to Sebastian, letter of attorney, Bond and Power of Attorney Books, Jefferson County CCO, book 1, p. 169.

83. Supreme Court Deed Books, Kentucky SA, book A, pp. 102–3. The bond was 'ordered recorded' by the Court on 12 June 1786 (see Supreme Court Order Books, Kentucky SA, book A, p. 416).

84. Beall to George May, 23 May 1786, Beall-Booth Family Papers, FHS, MSS A B365 5.

85. Beall to Skinner, 13 June 1786, Beall-Booth Family Papers, FHS, MSS A B365 5.

86. John May to Beall, 27 June 1786, Beall-Booth Family Papers, FHS, MSS A B365 5.

87. Ibid.

88. John May to Beall, 14 July 1786, Beall-Booth Family Papers, FHS, MSS A B365 6.

89. Memorandum in Beall's handwriting, undated, Beall-Booth Family Papers, FHS, MSS A B365 12. See also John May to Beall, 14 July 1786, Beall-Booth Family Papers, FHS, MSS A B365 6.

90. Ibid.

91. John May to Beall, 9 October 1786, Beall-Booth Family Papers, FHS, MSS A B365 6.

92. Ibid.

93. John May to Beall, 27 October 1786, Beall-Booth Family Papers, FHS, MSS A B365 6.

94. John May to Beall, received 13 December 1786, Beall-Booth Family Papers, FHS, MSS A B365 6.

95. Ibid.

96. John May to Beall, 27 December 1786, Beall-Booth Family Papers, FHS, MSS A B365 6.

97. John May to Beall, 9 October 1786 (copy in Beall's handwriting), Beall-Booth Family Papers, FHS, MSS A B365 6.

98. L. N. Dembitz, *Kentucky Jurisprudence in Four Books: I. Constitutional and Political Law. II. The Law of Real Estate. III. Other Rights of Property. IV. Persons and their Obligations. With an Introduction on the Sources of Kentucky Law* (Louisville, KY: J. P. Morton, 1890), p. 185.

99. Virginia Land Office Grants, Library of Virginia, grant book 2 (1786), pp. 33–5, 35–6.

100. Ibid., pp. 241–5.

101. Ibid., pp. 351–2, 353–4; book 7 (1786–1787), pp. 141–3, 143–5.

102. 'Indenture, August 1, 1786. Gilbert Imley of Virginia, to James Wilkinson of Fayette County, for 500 pounds, 2,148 acres in Fayette County, beginning on the side of the Salt

Spring trace, in Jesse Hoges' preemption line, thence northeast to Stoners Fork of Licking. Recorded March 19, 1787' (Supreme Court Deed Books, Kentucky SA, book A, p.
289).

103. Indenture between Imlay and Arthur Lee, 26 September 1786, Blair-Lee Family Papers,
Papers of Samuel Phillips Lee (1812–1897), Princeton, MSS C0614, box 104, F 3. This
transaction is confirmed in an indenture dated 19 November 1810 (Court of Appeals
Deed Books, Kentucky SA, book N, p. 477), which was acknowledged at Alexandria,
District of Columbia, on 24 November 1810, and recorded by the Kentucky Court of
Appeals on 17 April 1811 (Court of Appeals Deed Books, Kentucky SA, book N, pp.
368–9).

3 Friends in High Places

1. Thomas Rutland Letter Book, Maryland Historical Society, MS 1726.
2. See Imlay's bond to Arthur Lee, dated 2 December 1786, Blair-Lee Family Papers, Papers
of Samuel Phillips Lee, Princeton, MSS C0614, box 104, F 3.
3. John Marshall to Arthur Lee, 5 March 1787, cited in R. H. Lee, *Life of Arthur Lee,
LL.D.*, 2 vols (Boston: Wells and Lilly, 1829), vol. 2, p. 321.
4. James Bagues to James Calbraith, 22 March 1788, Thomas Rutland Letter Book, 1787–
1789, William L. Clements Library, University of Michigan (Ann Arbor, MI).
5. Thomas Rutland to Imlay, 22 May 1786, 5 June 1786, 30 July 1786, Thomas Rutland
Letter Book, Maryland Historical Society, MS 1726.
6. James Bagues to Imlay, 8 February 1787, Thomas Rutland Letter Book, William L. Clements Library, University of Michigan.
7. See Rutland to John Bellio, 4 June 1787; Rutland to James Calbraith, 22 March 1788;
Rutland to Thomas Rutland, Jr, 7 January 1788; Rutland to Daniel Henry, 2 May 1788;
Rutland to Daniel Henry, 16 April 1789; and Rutland to Thomas McColloch, 24 June
1789, in Thomas Rutland Letter Book, William L. Clements Library, University of
Michigan.
8. Thomas Rutland to James Bagues, 11 December 1786, Thomas Rutland Letter Book,
Maryland Historical Society, MS 1726.
9. Rutland to Richard Henry Lee, 12 January 1788, Thomas Rutland Letter Book, William
L. Clements Library, University of Michigan.
10. James Wilkinson to Dr Hugh Shiell, 16 July 1784 and 20 July 1784, 'Letters of General
James Wilkinson', *Register of the Kentucky Historical Society*, 24:70 (January 1926), pp.
259–67, on pp. 262, 263.
11. W. Paxton, *The Marshall Family, or A Genealogical Chart of the Descendants of John Marshall and Elizabeth Markham, his Wife, Sketches of Individuals and Notices of Families
Connected with Them* (Platte City, MO: R. Clarke & Co, 1885), p. 51.
12. Supreme Court Deed Books, Kentucky SA, book A, pp. 102–3. The bond was 'ordered
recorded' by the Court on 12 June 1786 (see Supreme Court Order Books, Kentucky
SA, book A, p. 416).
13. 'Memorandum for James Marshall Esq. Relative to his Conduct with Capt. John Holder',
6 November 1785, Innes Papers, LoC, container 6, 12.258.
14. Abernethy, *Western Lands and the American Revolution*, p. 321. Harry Innes was born
in Caroline County, Virginia, on 15 January 1752. He was the son of Revd Robert
Innes and Catherine Richards. At the beginning of the American Revolution, Innes

was appointed by the Committee of Public Safety in Virginia to manage Chipil's lead mines. In 1779 he was appointed commissioner to hear land claims in the state's Abingdon district. In 1782 he was elected by the Virginia legislature as an assistant judge of the Supreme Court of Virginia for the District of Kentucky. But he did not move to Kentucky until 1783, where he resided in Danville. He resigned as presiding judge of the Supreme Court when he was appointed attorney general for the District of Kentucky in 1787. From 1787 to 1816, he was United States district judge for Kentucky. He died in Frankfort, Kentucky, on 20 September 1816. See also J. M. Brown, *The Political Beginnings of Kentucky: A Narrative of Public Events Bearing on the History of that State to the Time of its Admission into the American Union* (Louisville, KY: John P. Morton and Company, 1889), p. 71.

15. Wilkinson to James Hutchinson, 18 August 1787, 'Letters of Gen. James Wilkinson Addressed to Dr. James Hutchinson, of Philadelphia', *Pennsylvania Magazine of History and Biography*, 12:1 (1888), pp. 54–64, on p. 64.

16. Imlay to Sebastian, letter of attorney, Bond and Power of Attorney Books, Jefferson County CCO, book 1, p. 169.

17. For further details on these cases, see Chapter 2.

18. See Emerson, 'Notes on Gilbert Imlay', p. 413, n. 22.

19. Wilkinson to Shiell, 20 July 1784, 'Letters of General James Wilkinson', p. 263.

20. Marshall, *The History of Kentucky*, vol. 1, p. 165. Marshall does not say where Wilkinson was before he settled in Lexington, but he does say that Lexington was 'the object of his [Wilkinson's] *ultimate* destination' (italics added). The anonymous (but probably self-authored) *A Plain Tale, Supported by Authentic Documents, Justifying the Character of General Wilkinson, By a Kentuckian* ([New York: n.p., 1807], p. 8) confirms that 'Gen. W. had migrated to the western country in 1783'. See also Chapter 5, n. 64, below.

21. In his 20 July 1784 letter to Shiell, Wilkinson reported that the construction of his house was now so far advanced 'as to be in readiness to commence the raising of the logs on Monday next' ('Letters of General James Wilkinson', p. 263). Since it did not even have a roof by the end of July, the fact that Wilkinson's house is marked on Filson's map (in *The Discovery, Settlement and Present State of Kentucky*) may suggest that Filson did not leave Kentucky 'in the early summer of 1784', as John Walton observed in *John Filson of Kentucky* (Lexington: University of Kentucky Press, 1956), p. 29.

22. Marshall, *The History of Kentucky*, vol. 1, p. 244.

23. Ibid., p. 165. Humphrey Marshall had been quite active in the land business since his arrival in Kentucky (see the Fayette and Jefferson entries in Jillson (ed.), *Old Kentucky Entries and Deeds*, pp. 124, 245). Some of these enterprises were with General Wilkinson (see Fayette County Entries, Kentucky LO, book 4, p. 124).

24. Marshall, *The History of Kentucky*, vol. 1, pp. 244–5.

25. General J. Wilkinson, *Memoirs of My Own Times*, 3 vols (Philadelphia, PA: printed by Abraham Small, 1816), vol. 2, p. 109. See also Anon., *A Plain Tale*, p. 8.

26. Marshall, *The History of Kentucky*, vol. 1, p. 165.

27. J. R. Jacobs, *Tarnished Warrior: Major-General James Wilkinson* (New York: The Macmillan Company, 1938), p. 71.

28. W. R. Shepherd, 'Wilkinson and the Beginnings of the Spanish Conspiracy', *American Historical Review*, 9:3 (April 1904), pp. 490–506, on p. 493; Wilkinson to Shiell, 1784–1785, 'Letters of General James Wilkinson', pp. 259–65.

29. Abernethy, *Western Lands and the American Revolution*, p. 301; Wilkinson to Shiell, 20 July 1784, 'Letters of General James Wilkinson', p. 263. The location of the mill is marked on Filson's map (in *The Discovery, Settlement and Present State of Kentucky*), in Lincoln County, just south of Dick's River.

30. Between December 1783 and December 1786, Wilkinson, alone or with partners, entered a total of nearly 250,000 acres in Fayette County (Jillson (ed.), *Old Kentucky Entries and Deeds*, pp. 159–60). 'Wilkinson, Armstrong, Dunn & Co.' were also active in Jefferson County, where in 1786 they bought land from one James Patten of Louisville (see Bond and Power of Attorney Books, Jefferson County CCO, book 1, p. 64).

31. Wilkinson to Hutchinson, 20 June 1785, 'Letters of General James Wilkinson', p. 60.

32. Wilkinson to Hutchinson, 18 August 1785, 'Letters of General James Wilkinson', p. 64.

33. Ibid., p. 63.

34. Wilkinson to Matthew Irvine, 27 [28?] September 1784, Emmet Collection, New York Public Library, Em. Ser. VIII, 2018 [1 page].

35. Imlay to William Triplet, 15 July 1784, Innes Papers, LoC, container 6, 12.253; 'Memorandum for James Marshall Esq. Relative to his Conduct with Capt. John Holder', 6 November 1785, Innes Papers, container 6, 12.258; 'A List of the Land assigned by Holder and to be assigned by Imlay' [n.d.], Innes Papers, container 6, 12.265.

36. 'Memorandum for James Marshall Esq. Relative to his Conduct with Capt. John Holder', 6 November 1785, Innes Papers, LoC, container 6, 12.258. Incidentally, the reference to Green's wild goose chase after Holder's elusive acres, described on pp. 2–3 of the 'Memorandum', offers a further suggestion that Imlay was in Kentucky at least by the middle of 1783. In the document Imlay recalls that he had asked Green to call on Holder for directions to his entries in the autumn of 1783; he then goes on to say that Holder returned to Kentucky ('this Country') in the spring of 1784, having been absent for 'upwards of seven months without leaving an agent for his business with me' ('Memorandum', pp. 2–3).

37. Imlay to William Triplet, 15 July 1784, Innes Papers, LoC, container 6, 12.253.

38. Imlay to Dr Alexander Skinner, 27 September 1784, Innes Papers, LoC, container 6, 12.255.

39. His position was apparently desperate enough for Imlay to send the detailed, 4-page memorandum to his attorney James Marshall on 6 November, instructing him when and how to start litigation against Holder.

40. Imlay to Henry Lee, 28 May 1785, Draper MSS, 6BB43.

41. Warrants, Surveys and Patents, Kentucky LO, survey book VA 7858.

42. Imlay to Boone, 21 December 1786, Draper MSS, 26C152–53.

43. John Cleves Symmes had been an Associate Justice of the New Jersey Supreme Court (1777–83) and a Continental Congressman. He was in the north-west territory at this time, and would soon petition Congress for a two-million acre grant of land in Ohio, between the Miami and Little Miami Rivers (known as 'The Miami Purchase'). Imlay's deal with John Cleves Symmes is confirmed in a letter from Harry 'Light-Horse' Lee to Symmes dated 22 April 1787 (in *Letters of Delegates to Congress: 1774–1789*, ed. P. H. Smith, G. W. Gawalt, R. Fry Plakas and E. R. Sheridan, 26 vols (Washington, DC: Library of Congress, 1976–2000), vol. 24, p. 243). It is possible that Imlay knew Symmes from his days in the New Jersey militia. Between 1776 and 1779, Symmes was commander of three regiments of the New Jersey militia and was in charge of the forts on the New Jersey frontier. He also fought at many battles, including the Battle of Monmouth.

44. It must have been Wilkinson who ultimately paid the surveying fee, for the survey was registered in his name on 17 October 1788 (Warrants, Surveys and Patents, Kentucky LO, survey book VA 7858). A patent in Wilkinson's name was issued on 22 February 1790 (Virginia Land Office Grants, Library of Virginia, grant book 11, p. 347).

45. Warrants, Surveys and Patents, Kentucky LO, survey book VA 7858. Interestingly, given their involvement in the triangular contract with Isaac Hite and the Green River ironworks, the witness to this transaction was Imlay's associate Amos Ogden.

46. Cited in J. M. Faragher, *Daniel Boone: The Life and Legend of an American Pioneer* (New York: Henry Holt and Co., 1992), p. 247.

47. N. O. Hammon, 'Daniel Boone's Land Problems' (unpublished article). Fearing that it might be difficult to obtain title to the land, Wilkinson later instructed Harry Innes to convey Boone's tract to Harry 'Light-Horse' Lee, in connection with a 'conditional obligation' which he had given Imlay 'respecting that tract'. However, in March 1796, after Boone had indicated he was after all prepared to transfer title to the tract to him, Wilkinson regretted the conveyance – realizing that clear title to the tract, which was 'of first or second quality', would make it worth 'a fortune'. Wilkinson to Innes, 29 March 1796, Innes Papers, LoC, container 23, 2.5368–72.

48. The deed was acknowledged in Richmond, Virginia, on 10 November 1786, and certified in Richmond on 18 March 1816. It was finally recorded by the Kentucky Court of Appeals on 6 April 1816 (Court of Appeals Deed Books, Kentucky SA, book Q, pp. 449–51).

49. P. C. Nagel, *The Lees of Virginia: Seven Generations of an American Family* (New York: Oxford University Press, 1990), p. 162.

50. Henry Lee, Jr, to Washington, 31 March 1778, George Washington Papers, LoC, Series 4, General Correspondence, 1697–1799.

51. George Washington to President of Congress, 3 April 1778, in *The Writings of George Washington from the Original Manuscript Sources, 1745–1799*, ed. J. C. Fitzpatrick, 39 vols (Washington, DC: Government Printing Office, 1931–44), vol. 11, pp. 205–6.

52. George Washington to Henry Lee, 24 July 1780, Lee Family Papers, Virginia Historical Society (Richmond, VA), section 134, MSS 1 L51 f 605.

53. Isaac Hite to Abraham Hite, 26 April 1783, Hite Family Papers, FHS, MSS C/H Hite, Isaac.

54. Imlay to Henry Lee, 28 May 1785, Draper MSS, 6BB43. Because of Imlay's reference to 'Mr. Lees survey' in his letter to Henry Lee, Fant believed that the letter could not have been sent to Henry Lee of Mason County, but that it had somehow come into his possession. Since we now know that Imlay was in fact referring to Light-Horse Harry's survey, there is no reason to doubt that Imlay's letter was indeed addressed to the man whose name is endorsed on the envelope, 'Mr Henry Lee near Lexington' (see Fant, 'A Study of Gilbert Imlay', p. 32, n. 39).

55. Virginia military warrant no. 1937 authorized the survey of 7,777⅔ acres of Kentucky land. See Jillson (ed.), *Old Kentucky Entries and Deeds*, p. 344.

56. See Chapter 2, p. 54 and n. 85, above.

57. Beall to Skinner, 13 June 1786, Beall-Booth Family Papers, FHS, MSS A B365 5.

58. Henry Lee to John Cleves Symmes, 22 April 1787, in *Letters of Delegates to Congress*, ed. Smith et al., vol. 24, p. 243.

59. The indenture must have been drawn up somewhere in the East, possibly in Philadelphia. Having spent the best part of the summer in New Orleans, colluding with the Spanish authorities there to lay the groundwork for the handover of Kentucky to Spain, Wilkin-

son had not started his journey home until 16 September 1787, travelling via Charleston and Philadelphia en route to Kentucky – where he finally arrived in February 1788.

60. Bibb Family Papers, 1760–1887, FHS, MSS A B581 56.
61. Bill of Complaint, Matthew Walton against Gilbert Imlay, Henry Lee and Henry Banks, 11 May 1797, Miscellaneous Papers, Nelson County CCO, 4 pp, unpaginated and uncatalogued.
62. Jefferson County Entries, Kentucky LO, book A, pp. 269, 239; Virginia Land Office Grants, Library of Virginia, grant book U (1786), pp. 128–31. The grant was issued on 12 December 1785.
63. Bill of Complaint, Matthew Walton against Gilbert Imlay, Henry Lee and Henry Banks, 11 May 1797, Miscellaneous Papers, Nelson County CCO, 4 pp, unpaginated and uncatalogued.
64. Court of Appeals Deed Books, Kentucky SA, book A, p. 347. The deed was drawn up on 5 May 1795 and registered in Richmond on 13 May 1795; it was recorded by the Kentucky Court of Appeals on 11 July 1796.
65. Court of Appeals Deed Books, Kentucky SA, book A, p. 349. The deed was registered in Richmond on 13 May 1795, and acknowledged by the Kentucky Court of Appeals on 11 July 1796.
66. District and Supreme Court Documents, Nelson County CCO, unpaginated and uncatalogued.
67. Henry Banks, 'separate answer', Philadelphia, 2 December 1797 (sworn statement), attached to the proceedings of a session of the Kentucky Supreme Court, Bardstown District, held on 11 May 1798, Miscellaneous Papers, Nelson County CCO, 2 pp, unpaginated and uncatalogued. In the same archive is a contemporary copy of Banks's 'separate answer', 3 pp.
68. By the time Banks issued his statement, Light-Horse Harry had come to be known as 'General Lee'. In 1794 he had been asked by Washington to command the Virginia militia to put down the Whiskey Rebellion in western Pennsylvania. Never having risen beyond the rank of lieutenant-colonel in the regular army, it is from this mission with the Virginia militia that Lee derived the title of 'General'.
69. Henry Banks, 'supplemental answer' to Walton's bill of complaint, Richmond, 22 July 1797 (sworn statement), attached to the proceedings of a session of the Kentucky Supreme Court, Bardstown District, held on 19 July 1800, Miscellaneous Papers, Nelson County CCO, 4 pp, unpaginated and uncatalogued.
70. District and Supreme Court Documents, Nelson County CCO, unpaginated and uncatalogued.
71. See C. Royster, *Light-Horse Harry Lee and the Legacy of the American Revolution* (Baton Rouge, LA: Louisiana State University Press, 1981), pp. 171–85.
72. *The American Watchman and Delaware Republican*, 5 August 1812, cited in Royster, *Light-Horse Harry Lee*, p. 171.
73. Innes Papers, LoC, container 6, 'Papers re Gilbert Imlay's lands'.
74. John Cleves Symmes to Richard Clough Anderson, 21 June 1787, in *The Intimate Letters of John Cleves Symmes and His Family*, ed. B. W. Bond, Jr (Cincinnati, OH: The Historical and Philosophical Society of Ohio, 1956), p. 107. For Henry Lee's letter to Symmes, see note 58 above.
75. Indenture between Gilbert Imlay and Arthur Lee, 26 September 1786. MSS C0614, Blair-Lee Family Papers, Papers of Samuel Phillips Lee, Princeton, box 104, folder 3, unnumbered document.

76. Indenture between Gilbert Imlay, by his attorney Henry Lee, and Francis Lightfoot Lee, 19 November 1810, Blair-Lee Family Papers, Papers of Samuel Phillips Lee, Princeton, box 104, folder 3, unnumbered document.

77. Endorsement, in Arthur Lee's handwriting, to the Virginia Grant for 1,000 acres in Fayette (preemption warrant 197). Blair-Lee Family Papers, Papers of Samuel Phillips Lee, Princeton, box 104, folder 3, unnumbered document.

78. Lee had given the original deed to Henry Banks in May 1795, when he had sold all of Imlay's patents, surveys, entries and contracts to Banks. Blair-Lee Family Papers, Papers of Samuel Phillips Lee, Princeton, box 104, folder 3, unnumbered document.

79. Indenture between Gilbert Imlay, by his attorney Henry Lee, and Francis Lightfoot Lee, 19 November 1810, Blair-Lee Family Papers, Papers of Samuel Phillips Lee, Princeton, box 104, folder 3, unnumbered documents. Acknowledged at Alexandria, District of Columbia, 24 November 1810, and recorded by the Kentucky Court of Appeals, 17 April 1811, Court of Appeals Deed Books, Kentucky SA, book N, p. 477 ff.

80. *Commentator* (Frankfort, KY), 14 November 1821.

81. Filson entered a total of nearly 13,000 acres of land in December 1783 (yet never obtained a patent for any of it). See Jillson (ed.), *Old Kentucky Entries and Deeds*, p. 98.

82. As early as September 1775 John Floyd in a letter to Colonel William Preston was complaining about such activities by non-resident land-jobbers: 'They go about in companies & build 40 or 50 cabins a piece on the land where no surveying has yet been done, and I am convinced there can't be an officers claim of 2000 acres laid to any great advantage after this year' (John Floyd to William Preston, 1 September 1775, Draper MSS, 33S282–5). However, the practice continued. In May 1776, Floyd was again complaining about hundreds of land-jobbers building cabins and making improvements on behalf of 'some of the leading men northward' (John Floyd to William Preston, 19 May 1776, Draper MSS, 33S292–5).

83. Court of Appeals Deed Books, Kentucky SA, book D, p. 20. The tract concerned was sold by James Watson and his wife Elizabeth by deed dated 4 December 1802, which copies much of the text of the earlier indenture (see Court of Appeals Deed Books, Kentucky SA, book G, pp. 343–8). Admittedly, the evidence for inferring that that 'Emley's' on Filson's map is a reference to Gilbert Imlay depends entirely on the assumption that the 'Captain Imlay' mentioned in the Taylor-Watson deed is Gilbert Imlay. On the other hand, there is no reason to assume otherwise.

4 Slave Trader

1. Wollstonecraft, *Letters Written during a Short Residence in Sweden, Norway, and Denmark*, pp. 159–60.

2. Chancery Court, Deed Books, Nelson County CCO, book 1, pp. 96–125. Land traded after the grant had been issued was filed in the records of deeds and wills on the county level. The deeds for the sales were not registered in Nelson County Court Minute Books until 11 April 1787, and the transaction between Imlay and Talbot was only finalized on 12 June 1787, when the deeds drawn up in Philadelphia were acknowledged and ordered to be recorded by Nelson County Court (Chancery Court, Deed Books, Nelson County CCO, book pp. 96–125, and Court of Quarter Sessions, Minute Books, Nelson County CCO, book 1, pp. 401–2). On this occasion Imlay was represented by John Steele, acting as his attorney, while Talbot's payment in Pennsylvania paper money and Spanish silver dollars was received on Imlay's behalf by another attorney, Benjamin Sebastian.

3. The patents were issued on 9 and 12 December 1785. See, Virginia Land Office Grants, Library of Virginia, Grants S (1785–6), pp. 621–3, 638–40, 640–2; Grants U (1786), pp. 113–15, 115–17, 117–19, 121–3, 126–8, 128–30, 162–4.

4. On Talbot's ventures in the post-revolutionary Atlantic seaboard trade, see W. M. Fowler, Jr, *Silas Talbot: Captain of Old Ironsides* (Mystic, CT: Mystic Seaport Museum, 1995), pp. 66–7.

5. *Charleston Evening Gazette*, 14 September 1785, vol. 1, no. 57, p. 1.

6. Cyprian Sterry to Talbot, bill of sale, 25 August 1785, in Silas Talbot Papers, Blunt White, collection 18, box 1, folder 14. The *Industry* had been built at Rehoboth, Maryland, in 1783, and had been registered in Providence on 20 October of that year. Its original owners were two Providence merchants, John Murray and Cyprian Sterry, and its first master was Thadeus Swain. See *Ship Registers and Enrollments of Providence, Rhode Island, 1773–1939*, 2 vols (Providence, RI: The National Archives Project, 1941), vol. 1, p. 531. A Brown alumnus, Cyprian Sterry was a trustee ('curator') of Brown University from 1792 until 1813. Following the 1794 Federal Slave Trade Act, Sterry disavowed the slave trade, in contrast to fellow slave trader John Brown, who gained the dubious honour of being the first Rhode Islander to be prosecuted for violating the Slave Trade Act (but was acquitted in June 1798).

7. Talbot to Nathaniel Russell, 16 November 1786, Silas Talbot Papers, Blunt White, collection 18, box 1, folder 17.

8. Imlay had sold his nine patents for £750 Pennsylvania money and 12,771 Spanish silver dollars. The exchange rate for the Spanish dollar in the later colonial period was 7s. 6d. Pennsylvania, which meant that Imlay had received £750 plus £4,789, or £5,539, for his land.

9. Ibid.

10. 'The Concessions and agreement of the Lords Proprietors of New Jersey, to and with all and every of the adventurers, and all such as shall settle and plant there', Part V, art. 2, in *Documents Relating to the Colonial, Revolutionary and Post-Revolutionary History of the State of New Jersey* (commonly known as *New Jersey Archives*), 1st series, 42 vols (Newark and Paterson, NJ: various publishers, 1880–1949), vol. 1, pp. 241–67.

11. Pomfret, *Colonial New Jersey*, p. 210.

12. Monmouth County Court, Common Pleas, Loose Papers 1757–1758, New Jersey SA, box 12.

13. Bill of sale, in Mary A. Fisk Papers, cited in Hutchinson Collection, New Jersey HS, box 4, folder 5, book 3, pp. 88–9.

14. J. Coughtry, *The Notorious Triangle: Rhode Island and the African Slave Trade, 1700–1897* (Philadelphia, PA: Temple University Press, 1981), p. 262.

15. Benjamin Hicks to Talbot, 19 January 1786, in Silas Talbot Papers, Blunt White, collection 18, box 1, folder 15. Hicks had been at Kormantine for thirteen days when he wrote this letter.

16. Ibid.

17. Benjamin Hicks to Talbot, 21 February 1786, Silas Talbot Papers, Blunt White, collection 18, box 1, folder 15.

18. The *Charleston Evening Gazette* listed the *Industry* as 'Entered Inwards' in the 'Custom-House' column of its 1 August issue (*Charleston Evening Gazette*, vol. 2, no. 332, p. 2). Similar entries appeared on 2 August in the *Charleston Morning Post, and Daily Advertiser* (p. 2) and on 3 August in the *Columbian Herald, or The Independent Courier of North America* (South Carolina; no. 199, p. 3).

19. The bill of sale specifies among the charges that duty was paid for seventy-two slaves. See Nathaniel Russell to Talbot, bill of sale, 9 September 1786, Silas Talbot Papers, Blunt White, collection 18, box 1, folder 17.

20. Murray, Mumford & Bower to Talbot, 6 September 1786, Silas Talbot Papers, Blunt White, collection 18, box 1, folder 17. According to Coughtry, 'truly devastating mortality rates', such as the loss sustained by the owners of the *Industry* on this trip, were 'rare'. For an analysis of the mortality rates among slaves aboard the slavers, see *The Notorious Triangle*, pp. 145–50. In 1808 the abolitionist Thomas Clarkson observed that the mortality rates during the Middle Passage and immediately after the voyage were so great that, 'if it were only general for a few months, would entirely depopulate the globe' (T. Clarkson, *The History of the Rise, Progress, and Accomplishment of the Abolition of the Slave-Trade by the British Parliament*, 2 vols (London: Longman, Hurst, Rees and Orme, 1808), vol. 2, p. 363).

21. Nathaniel Russell (1738–1820) was originally from Bristol, Rhode Island. He arrived in Charleston in 1765, where he became an agent for Providence merchants. Later he became one of Charleston's wealthiest and most influential citizens.

22. Nathaniel Russell to Talbot, bill of sale, 9 September 1786, Silas Talbot Papers, Blunt White, collection 18, box 1, folder 17. Fevers, flux (dysentery) and smallpox were among the most common and most deadly diseases aboard slavers.

23. According to the bill of sale, the gross proceeds of the sale of sixty-seven slaves were £2,835 (the expenses came to £389). At an average price of just over £42 per head, Imlay, Sterry and Talbot could have made £7,560 on the voyage (minus expenses) had all 180 slaves on the *Industry* survived the Middle Passage.

24. Talbot must have arrived in Kentucky sometime in April, for on 2 May he endorsed an order to pay £28.3.10 'Virginia Currency' to Hare, McCaughey & Co, dated 'Falls of the Ohio' (Talbot to Hewes & Anthony, 2 May 1786, Silas Talbot Papers, Blunt White, collection 18, box 1, folder 15).

25. Cyprian Sterry to Talbot, 19 June 1786, Silas Talbot Papers, Blunt White, collection 18, box 1, folder 15.

26. Cyprian Sterry to Benjamin Hicks, 9 May 1786, Silas Talbot Papers, Blunt White, collection 18, box 1, folder 15.

27. Cyprian Sterry to Talbot, 19 June 1786, Silas Talbot Papers, Blunt White, collection 18, box 1, folder 15.

28. Cyprian Sterry to Talbot, 6 September 1786, Silas Talbot Papers, Blunt White, collection 18, box 1, folder 17.

29. Talbot to Nathaniel Russell, 16 November 1786, Silas Talbot Papers, Blunt White, collection 18, box 1, folder 17.

30. Nathaniel Russell to Talbot, 3 January 178[7], in Silas Talbot Papers, Blunt White, collection 18, box 1, folder 15. Internal evidence – notably Russell's acknowledgement of having received Talbot's letter of 16 November 1786 – indicates that the letter is erroneously dated '3 January 1786'.

31. Nathaniel Russell to Talbot, 12 March 1787, Silas Talbot Papers, Blunt White, collection 18, box 2, folder 1.

32. Imlay to Talbot, 5 March 1787, Silas Talbot Papers, Blunt White, collection 18, box 2, folder 1.

33. W. J. Mills, *Historic Houses of New Jersey* (Philadelphia, PA, and London: J. B. Lippincott, 1902), p. 170.

34. Imlay to Talbot, 7 March 1787 (postscript to Imlay to Talbot, 5 March 1787), Silas Talbot Papers, Blunt White, collection 18, box 2, folder 1.

35. Ibid.
36. Talbot to Nathaniel Russell, 13 November 1801, Silas Talbot Papers, Blunt White, collection 18, box 8, folder 12.
37. Isaac Dunn to Talbot, 1 May 1788, Silas Talbot Papers, Blunt White, collection 18, box 2, folder 5.
38. Robert Johnston to Talbot, 22 October 1787, Silas Talbot Papers, Blunt White, collection 18, box 2, folder 3.
39. D. Hart to Talbot, 19 May 1787, Silas Talbot Papers, Blunt White, collection 18, box 2, folder 2.
40. South Carolina Judgment Rolls, South Carolina Department of Archives and History (Columbia, SC), S136002, box 137A, #208A–1.
41. Ibid., box 137A, # 208A–2.
42. Ibid.
43. Ibid., box 137A, # 208A–5.
44. See P. M. Marsh, *Philip Freneau: Poet and Journalist* (Minneapolis, MN: Dillon Press, 1967), p. 100, p. 104.
45. Russell to Talbot, 15 December 1787, Silas Talbot Papers, Blunt White, collection 18, box 2, folder 3.
46. This time frame is corroborated by information contained in the letters of the Annapolis-based merchant Thomas Rutland. In an attempt to redeem a £300 debt, Rutland in the course of 1787–9 launched an intensive and prolonged search for Imlay up and down the East Coast (see also Chapter 3). However, no sightings of Imlay were reported to him after May/June 1787. See Rutland to James Calbraith, 22 March 1788, and Rutland to Thomas McColloch, 24 June 1789, in Thomas Rutland Letter Book, William L. Clements Library, University of Michigan. By April 1789, Rutland was 'sure' that Imlay was 'in London'. Rutland to Daniel Henry, 22 April 1789, in Thomas Rutland Letter Book, William L. Clements Library. In a letter to Richard Henry Lee of 12 January 1788, Rutland claimed that he had received information to suggest that Imlay had 'lately been at New York'. This *might* suggest that Imlay left for Europe at a date after the late spring or early summer of 1787, were it not for the fact that Rutland's letter to Lee was deliberately worded so as to trick Lee into revealing Imlay's whereabouts. See Rutland to Thomas Rutland, Jr, 22 March 1788, in Thomas Rutland Letter Book, William L. Clements Library. More likely than not, Rutland simply made up the report about the 'late' sighting of Imlay in New York because he needed an excuse to write to Lee, who was serving as a member of the United States Congress (then in session in New York).

5 Authority on the American West

1. Imlay, *The Emigrants*, vol. 1, pp. v–vi.
2. Review of *The Emigrants* in *Monthly Review; or Literary Journal*, n.s. 11 (August 1793), p. 468.
3. Ibid.
4. W. Wordsworth, *The Prelude, or, Growth of a Poet's Mind* (1850), ed. E. de Selincourt (Oxford: Oxford University Press, 1926), book XI, ll. 693–701.
5. Anon., *The Periodical Press of Great Britain and Ireland: or, An Inquiry into the State of the Public Journals, Chiefly as Regards their Moral and Political Influence* (London: Hurst, Robinson & Co., 1824), p. 24.

6. H. N. Brailsford, *Shelley, Godwin, and Their Circle* (London: Williams and Norgate, 1913), p. 7.
7. Ibid., p. 18.
8. J. M. S. Tompkins, *The Popular Novel in England, 1770–1800* (London: Constable, 1932), p. 300.
9. The timing of its composition would certainly warrant placing the *Topographical Description* within the context of contemporary writings through to late 1791. Despite the text's claim that the letters were written from Kentucky, internal evidence suggests that the book was written (at least in part, but probably in its entirety) long after the author had left both Kentucky and America in the course of 1787. The book is dated most specifically by a number of references to events in recent American and British history. Thus, a reference in Letter III to 'the federal city on the Potowmac' indicates a date of composition well after February 1791, when the French engineer Pierre Charles L'Enfant first arrived in Washington at the request of George Washington to begin his site reconnaissance for what was to become the nation's capital (Congress had enacted the legislation authorizing the president to establish a permanent location for the seat of government on the Potomac River on 12 July 1790). A remark in Letter II to the effect that 'it is at length agreed, that [Kentucky] is to be admitted into the federal union in June 1792' also suggests a date of composition after February 1791, since it was not until 4 February that Congress passed the act which awarded Kentucky statehood by 1 June 1792. References to the boycott of West Indian sugar following the government's refusal to pass legislation to abolish the slave trade (Letter IX) and to the detrimental effects this was having on the state's revenue from import duty (Letter X) suggest that these passages were written well after the publication of William Fox's pamphlet *An Address to the People of Great Britain on the Propriety of Abstaining from West India Sugar & Rum* (London: M. Gurney, 1791). The most recent historical event referred to in the text is the defeat of the Governor of the Northwestern Territory, General Arthur St Clair, during an ambush carried out by a combined Indian force just north of Fort Jefferson (slightly to the west of the Great Miami River). News of this event, which took place on 4 November 1791, could not have reached England much before the end of the year – if not later. There is, in fact, only one historical reference that would suggest an earlier date of composition, and that is a reference in Letter VIII to the first Kentucky consensus, which apparently at that time had yet to take place. The first census was actually taken in 1790 (when the District of Kentucky turned out to have 73,617 inhabitants, of which 61,113 were free white citizens).
10. Thus, for the radical playwright, novelist and pamphleteer Thomas Holcroft hardly a day went by during this period that he did not go into Debrett's to read the newspapers, discuss recent publications and catch up on the latest political and military news. John Debrett published Holcroft's radical play *The Road to Ruin* in 1792.
11. I. Maxted, *The London Book Trades, 1775–1800: A Preliminary Checklist of Members* (Folkestone, Kent: William Dawson and Sons, 1977), pp. 64, 3.
12. Ibid., p. 215.
13. Among the publications listed are: *An Authentic Copy of the New Constitution of France, adopted by the National Convention, July 1793, in English and French*; a new edition of *A Plan of the New Constitution of the United States of America*; *Letters from Paris, written during the Summer of 1791 and 1792*; *A History of the French Revolution*, translated by James White from the French of J. P. Rabaut; and the ninth edition of Thomas Holcroft's play *The Road to Ruin*. The list also includes a half-page announcement of the second

edition of the *Topographical Description*. See, J. Debrett, *New Publications Printed for J. Debrett, Opposite Burlington House, Piccadilly* (London: J. Debrett, 1973).

14. Imlay, *A Topographical Description*, title page.

15. J. H. St John de Crèvecoeur, *Letters from an American Farmer: Describing Certain Provincial Situations, Manners, and Customs, Not Generally Known* ..., new edn (London: Thomas Davies and Lockyer Davis, 1783), pp. 24, 19.

16. Imlay, *A Topographical Description*, p. iv.

17. Ibid., title page, p. 2.

18. Ibid., p. iv.

19. Ibid., p. 1.

20. Crèvecoeur, *Letters from an American Farmer*, p. 303.

21. Ibid., pp. 63, 64.

22. Imlay, *A Topographical Description*, title page, p. 108.

23. Ibid., pp. 53, 54.

24. Crèvecoeur, *Letters from an American Farmer*, pp. 57, 65.

25. Ibid., p. iii. For a discussion (and subsequent dismissal) of the various possible sources for Imlay's account of the western territory, see Fant, 'A Study of Gilbert Imlay', pp. 82–94.

26. Thus, for instance, Filson's mention of the 'celebrated anatomist' Dr Hunter (*The Discovery, Settlement and Present State of Kentucky*, p. 35) is echoed in the *Topographical Description*, p. 220 ('your celebrated anatomist, the late Dr. Hunter'). In the Preface to the second English edition of the text, Imlay (or, more likely, his editor/publisher) flatly denies that the *Topographical Description* was based on Filson's 1784 text (which it reprints in an appendix) – this is in sharp contrast, or so he alleges, to 'Morse and all other writers ... since that aera' (*A Topographical Description of the Western Territory of North America: Containing a Succinct Account of its Soil, Climate, Natural History, Population, Agriculture, Manners, and Customs. With an Ample Description of the Several Divisions into which that Country is Partitioned. To which are Added, The Discovery, Settlement, and Present State of Kentucky. And an Essay towards the Topography, and Natural History of that Important Country. By John Filson. To which is Added, I. The Adventures of Col. Daniel Boon ... II. The Minutes of the Piankashaw Council ... III. An Account of the Indian Nations ... By George Imlay ... Illustrated with correct Maps of the Western Territory of North America*, 2nd edn (London: J. Debrett, 1793), p. xv. Its inclusion in the appendix to the second edition of Imlay's *Topographical Description* was the first printing of Filson's influential text on Kentucky in England.

27. Even in those passages in which topographical or other facts – as well as the order in which are presented – appear to be based on Filson's *The Discovery, Settlement and Present State of Kentucky*, Imlay's text frequently adds details that are not mentioned by Filson and that only someone who was quite familiar with the terrain would have known about (see, for instance, Imlay's detailed description of the Rapids of the Ohio at Louisville and the surrounding area in *A Topographical Description*, pp. 46–50).

28. Ibid., pp. 58, 122, 38.

29. Ibid., pp. 216, 217, 242–3. In an essay aimed at revealing that the *Dictionary of American English* incorrectly cited the third edition of Imlay's *Topographical Description* (1797) as the source for the first or early occurrences of a number of Americanisms, John T. Krumpelmann inadvertently directed us to another authority Imlay relied on for his description of the natural history of the western territory. Several of Imlay's descriptive tags of species of plants and animals appear to have been translated from Le Page du Pratz's *Histoire de la Louisiane* (Paris, 1758), or are verbatim citations

from the abridged English translation, which appeared in London in 1763. See J. T. Krumpelmann, 'Du Pratz's *History of Louisiana* (1763), a Source of Americanisms, Especially of those Attributed to Imlay', *American Speech*, 20:1 (February 1945), pp. 45–50.

30. Imlay, *Topographical Description*, pp. 61, 62.
31. Ibid., p. 63.
32. Ibid., p. 124.
33. Ibid., p. 133.
34. Ibid., pp. 33, 37, 38, 39.
35. Ibid., pp. 41, 44–5.
36. Ibid., p. 45.
37. Ibid., pp. 47, 49.
38. Ibid., p. 48.
39. Ibid., p. 14.
40. Ibid., pp. 144, 153.
41. Ibid., p. 105.
42. Ibid., pp. 99–100.
43. G. Imlay, *A Topographical Description of the Western Territory of North America: Containing a Succinct Account of its Soil, Climate, Natural History, Population, Agriculture, Manners, and Customs. With an Ample Description of the Several Divisions into which that Country is Partitioned. With Great Additions*, 3rd edn (London: J. Debrett, 1797), p. xii.
44. Imlay, *A Topographical Description*, pp. 107–8.
45. Ibid., p. 97.
46. Ibid., pp. 133, 185, 187, 201.
47. *The Adventures of Col. Daniel Boone; containing a Narrative of the Wars of Kentucky*, in Filson, *The Discovery, Settlement and Present State of Kentucky*, pp. 54–5.
48. Ibid., pp. 39–40.
49. Ibid., p. 108.
50. Imlay, *A Topographical Description*, 3rd edn, p. xi.
51. Imlay, *A Topographical Description*, p. v.
52. Ibid., p. ix.
53. Ibid., p. xi.
54. Ibid., pp. xii–xiii.
55. Ibid.
56. Authorship of the petition is identified by Marshall, *The History of Kentucky*, vol. 1, p. 335.
57. Ibid., p. 245. Humphrey Marshall's book is a notoriously one-sided, fiercely partisan account of the formative years in Kentucky's history, in which Marshall mainly wanted to settle the score with his former political enemies, notably Wilkinson, Innes and Brown. However, although his impressions and conclusions are often biased or wrong, the facts he presents are usually correct.
58. Wilkinson to James Hutchinson, 18 August 1787, 'Letters of Gen. James Wilkinson Addressed to Dr. James Hutchinson', p. 63.
59. Marshall, *The History of Kentucky*, vol. 1, p. 245; Brown, *The Political Beginnings of Kentucky*, p. 71.

60. James Wilkinson to Diego Gardoqui y Arriquibar, 1 January 1789, James Wilkinson Letters to Esteban Miró, and Related Documents, 1788–1793, Beinecke, WA MSS S–1985, folder 6.

61. Marshall, *The History of Kentucky*, vol. 1, p. 258. Gardoqui had been commissioned as Spanish chargé d'affaires in the United States on 27 September 1784; his opposite number in Spain was William Carmichael.

62. Ibid., vol. 1, p. 259, p. 260.

63. Ibid., vol. 1, pp. 263–4.

64. According to the anonymous author of *A Plain Tale*, the General's financial hopes at the time of his trip to New Orleans were '*jeopardized*', and this was the reason why he was 'determined to look abroad for what he had not found at home' (*A Plain Tale*, p. 8). It is perfectly feasible, as Daniel Clark suggests, that Wilkinson himself was the author of *A Plain Tale*. See D. Clark, *Proofs of the Corruption of Gen. James Wilkinson and of his Connexion with Aaron Burr, with a Full Refutation of his Slanderous Allegations in Relation to the Character of the Principal Witness against him* (Philadelphia, PA: Wm. Hall, jun. & Geo. W. Pierie, 1809), p. 9.

65. Wilkinson, *Memoirs*, vol. 2, p. 109.

66. Anon., *A Plain Tale*, p. 13.

67. Wilkinson was introduced to Miró and other officers of the Spanish government by Daniel C. Clark, with whom he and his partner, Isaac B. Dunn, would enter into a contract in August 1787 whereby they gained a monopoly of the American trade through New Orleans. See Clark, *Proofs of the Corruption of Gen. James Wilkinson*, notes (numbered separately), p. 105.

68. Miró and Navarro to Valdez, 25 September 1787, Papeles de Estado, AHN Madrid, Legajo 3893 A.

69. Navarro to the King, 30 April 1789, Papeles relativos á la Lusiana, AHN Madrid, Seccion de Ultramar, vol. III.

70. Navarro, dispatch, 12 February 1787, cited in C. Gayarré, *The History of Louisiana*, 4 vols (vols 1–2, New York: Redfield; vols 3–4, W. J. Widdleton, 1854), vol. 3, p. 182.

71. Miró to the Marquis La Sonora, March 1787, cited in Gayarré, *The History of Louisiana*, vol. 3, p. 184.

72. Navarro, dispatch, 10 October 1787, cited in Gayarré, *The History of Louisiana*, vol. 3, p. 190.

73. Imlay, *A Topographical Description*, p. 85.

74. 'Proposals of John Fitch to enable Sd. Fitch to erect a steam Engine for rowing a Boat', John Fitch Papers, 1783–1854, LoC, no. 53.

75. See [J. Fitch], 'The Original Steam-Boat Supported; or, A Reply to Mr. James Rumsey's Pamphlet. Shewing the True Priority of *John Fitch*, and the False Datings, &c. of *James Rumsey*' (Philadelphia, PA: printed by Zachariah Poulson, Junr., 1788).

76. P. L. Phillips, *The Rare Map of the Northwest 1785, By John Fitch, Inventor of the Steamboat: A Bibliographical Account with Facsimile Reproduction Including some Account of Thomas Hutchins and William McMurray* (Washington, DC: W. H. Lowdermilk & Co., 1916), p. 16.

77. Gardoqui, dispatch to Marquis La Sonora, no. 19, 3 September 1785, cited in Gayarré, *The History of Louisiana*, vol. 3, p. 199.

78. Brown, *The Political Beginnings of Kentucky*, p. 97.

79. In 1788, Crèvecoeur, realizing that Fitch's invention could be of great strategic and commercial importance to France, attempted to secure financial backing for Fitch's

experiments. In January of that year he wrote to the Duke d'Harcourt urging him to inquire with the minister of the navy whether they knew about Fitch's invention. He also approached Franklin on the matter, hoping that his endorsement would persuade the French government to take the invention seriously. See G. W. Allen and R. Asselineau, *St. John de Crèvecoeur: The Life of an American Farmer* (New York: Viking, 1987), pp. 153–7.

80. Wilkinson finished the memorial on 21 August, a day before he took the oath that made him a Spanish citizen. See Miró and Navarro to Wilkinson, 6 September 1787, Papeles de Estado, AHN Madrid, Legajo 3893 A.

81. Miró and Navarro to Wilkinson, 6 September 1787, Papeles de Estado, AHN Madrid, Legajo 3893 A. A translation of the permit of trade signed by Miró is reprinted in Brown, *The Political Beginnings of Kentucky*, p. 101.

82. Miró and Navarro to Valdez, 25 September 1787, Papeles de Estado, AHN Madrid, Legajo 3893 A.

83. Marshall, *The History of Kentucky*, vol. 1, p. 233.

84. Ibid., vol. 1, p. 313.

85. Miró to Valdez, 15 June 1788, Papeles de Estado, AHN Madrid, Legajo 3893 A.

86. Wilkinson, 'Memorial', 22 August 1787, Papeles de Estado, AHN Madrid, Legajo 3893 A. In his *Memoirs*, Wilkinson flatly denied, 'in the face of God and man', that he ever 'conceded a tittle of honour or interests of [his] own country', or ever having omitted 'to employ [his] ascendancy over the officers of Spanish Louisiana, to render them subservient to the interest, and accommodation of the United States' (vol. 2, p. 115).

87. Marshall, *The History of Kentucky*, vol. 1, p. 286. The Virginia convention ratified the constitution by a vote of 89 to 79.

88. Ibid., vol. 1, p. 305. Gardoqui's account of his meetings with John Brown is reprinted in Brown, *The Political Beginnings of Kentucky*, pp. 146–8. Though some (including J. M. Brown) later denied they had taken place, John Brown's negotiations with Gardoqui about obtaining free navigation of the Mississippi if Kentucky were to declare itself independent were widely reported in the newspapers in the East at the time, where both Brown's and Gardoqui's duplicity were regarded as a potentially serious threat to the union and the future of the Atlantic states (see for instance 'American Intelligence: Alexandria, Jan. 22', *New-York Weekly Museum*, 42 (28 February 1789), p. 2).

89. Ibid., vol. 1, pp. 310–11. Accusing Marshall of waging a personal vendetta against them, J. M. Brown launched a vindication of John Brown and Harry Innes, denying that they had any involvement in the Spanish conspiracy (*The Political Beginnings of Kentucky*, pp. 203–18). However, Wilkinson's letters to Miró – which came to light after *The Political Beginnings of Kentucky* was published – reveal that both Brown and Innes, as well as Alexander Bullitt, were aware of the purpose of Wilkinson's visit to New Orleans and of his negotiations with Miró and Navarro. Wilkinson had also shared the contents of his memorial with them. In a letter to Esteban Miró, dated 15 May 1788, Wilkinson confirmed that Innes and Bullitt were 'perfectly accord with [them] in sentiment of policy: as soon as the form of Government is organized & adopted by the people, they will proceed to elect a Governor, Legislative Body & other officers, and will I have no doubt appoint a political Agent, with powers to treat on the connexion which we have in contemplation, and I think these points will be accomplished, by March next' (James Wilkinson Letters to Esteban Miró, Beinecke, WA MSS S–1985, folder 2). In a letter to John Brown

of 7 December 1787, Innes in no uncertain terms states his conviction that 'the God of Nature having made that River [the Mississippi] the only outlett to this Western World, we are intitled to a free navigation thereof upon this principle that it was intended for a Common from the Creation, & that no Government ~~could have a right~~ <ought> to monopolize it solely' (Harry Innes to John Brown, 7 December 1787, Kentucky Historical Society, Library, Special Collections and Archives (Frankfort, KY), MSS 97SC190). In a letter to Miró dated 14 February 1789 Wilkinson described Brown, who had just been re-elected as the district's delegate to Congress, 'as a Spy on the Conduct of that Body' (James Wilkinson Letters to Esteban Miró, Beinecke, WA MSS S–1985, folder 7).

90. Gayarré, *The History of Louisiana*, vol. 3, p. 238.
91. See Pierre Tardiveau to General George Rogers Clark, 23 November 1795, Draper MSS, 55J.
92. Brown, *The Political Beginnings of Kentucky*, p. 220.
93. The Kentucky Constitution was framed by the Tenth Convention (the First Constitutional Convention) held at Danville, 2–19 April 1792. Colonel Isaac Shelby was elected Kentucky's first governor on 4 May. Kentucky was admitted into the union as the fifteenth state on 1 June. Governor Shelby was inaugurated when the first legislature met in Lexington on 4 May.
94. Wilkinson to Miró, 17 September 1789, James Wilkinson Letters to Esteban Miró, Beinecke, WA MSS S–1985, folder 10.
95. The decision of the Council of State on Wilkinson's first memorial, dated 20 November 1788, is in Papeles de Estado, AHN Madrid, Legajo 3893 A.
96. Wilkinson's second memorial is in James Wilkinson Letters to Esteban Miró, Beinecke, WA MSS S–1985, folder 10. There is a copy in Spanish in Papeles de Estado, AHN Madrid, Legajo 3893 B.
97. Wilkinson to Miró, 18 September 1789, Papeles de Estado, AHN Madrid, Legajo 3893 B. The list of proposed pensioners varies from those who 'are my confidential friends and support my plan' (they include Harry Innes, Benjamin Sebastian, John Brown, Caleb Wallace and John Fowler), to those who 'favor separation from the United States and a friendly connection with Spain' (they include Benjamin Logan and Isaac Shelby), to those who 'favor separation from Virginia but do not carry their views any further' (among them Light-Horse Harry Lee), to a list of those who are opposed to separation, some of whom 'have British leanings', others favour 'the interests of Congress', but all are 'our enemies' and 'hence it is necessary to win them over' (they include Thomas Marshall, Humphrey Marshall and George Muter). The list specifies how much each pensioner was to be paid. See W. R. Shepherd, 'Papers on Wilkinson's Relations with Spain', *American Historical Review*, 9:4 (July 1904), pp. 748–66, on pp. 764–6.
98. See, for instance, L. Gordon, *Mary Wollstonecraft: A New Genus* (London: Little, Brown, 2005), pp. 198–9.
99. Of course, several of Wilkinson's letters and other documents from this period were in cipher, but Imlay's name does not appear in any of the code lists that have survived (see James Wilkinson Letters to Esteban Miró, Beinecke, WA MSS S–1985, folder 16). Gordon has suggested that 'Gilberto' (code name '37') may in fact have been Gilbert Imlay. This is mere speculation. In fact, 'Gilberto' was presumably Wilkinson's confidant and personal translator 'Don Gilberto' Leonard, rendered in English as Gilbert Leonard. Don Gilberto was paymaster of the army in the early 1790s and later rose to the post of intendant and comptroller of the Province of Louisiana.

100. Imlay, *A Topographical Description*, p. 75.

101. Ibid., p. 77.

102. Ibid.

103. Fitch's observation is recorded by Charles Whittlesey in his *Life of John Fitch*, in Jared Sparks (ed.), *Library of American Biography*, 2nd series, vol. 6 (Boston, MA: Little, Brown and Co., 1845), pp. 81–166, on p. 108.

104. Imlay, *A Topographical Description*, p. 66.

105. Ibid., p. 68. In 1790, when the district's first census was taken, Kentucky had a population of 73,677, of which 61,113 were free white persons.

106. Ibid., p. 84.

107. Ibid., p. 85.

108. Ibid., p. 155.

109. T. Jefferson, *Notes on the State of Virginia* (1781), ed. W. Peden (Chapel Hill, NC, and London: University of North Carolina Press, 1982), Query VIII.

110. T. R. Malthus, *An Essay on the Principle of Population* (1798), in *The Works of Thomas Robert Malthus*, ed. E. A. Wrigley and D. Souden, 8 vols (London: Pickering & Chatto, 1986), vol. 1, p. 39.

111. Ibid., vol. 1, p. 41.

112. Ibid., vol. 1, p. 9.

113. Ibid., vol. 1, p. 65. The phrases in quotation marks are from Shakespeare's *The Tempest*, IV.i.151–3.

114. Imlay, *A Topographical Description*, p. 184. The motion by William Wilberforce to abolish the slave trade was put to the vote in the House of Commons on 18 April 1791. Although it had the support of Charles Fox and Prime Minister William Pitt, Wilberforce's motion failed by a margin of 163 to 88 votes, with many Members of Parliament prejudiced against the bill by recent slave insurrections on Saint Domingue, Martinique and Dominica.

115. Ibid., p. 185. Contemporary accounts confirm that William Fox's call for a boycott of West Indian sugar and rum had a considerable impact on the buying habits of English consumers. Thus in January 1792, one of Britain's leading abolitionists, Thomas Clarkson, wrote to Josiah Wedgwood that he had not travelled anywhere where Fox's pamphlet 'had not produced an astonishing effect' (*Correspondence of Josiah Wedgwood, 1781–1794*, ed. K. Eufemia and L. Farrer (London: privately printed, 1906), p. 183). Clarkson noted that around this time '25,000 Persons have left off Sugar & Rum' and that the 'Sugar Revenue by Report had fallen off 200,000£ this Quarter'. In his history of the abolition of the slave trade Clarkson later estimated that 'not fewer than three hundred thousand persons' in England 'had abandoned the use of sugar' (*The History of the Rise, Progress, and Accomplishment of the Abolition of the Slave-Trade*, vol. 2, p. 350). Although the Commons had voted to end the slave trade in 1792, the West Indian plantation lobby in the House of Lords managed to block full passage of the bill. Despite opposition in the Lords, Parliament managed to restrict the slave trade in 1806, and abolished it entirely in 1807.

116. Imlay, *A Topographical Description*, p. 185.

117. Ibid., pp. 187–8.

118. Ibid.

119. Ibid., p. 201.

120. Ibid., p. 193.

121. Ibid., p. 197.

122. Ibid., p. 201.
123. Ibid., p. 158.
124. Ibid., pp. 182, 158.
125. Ibid., p. 167.
126. Ibid., pp. 168, 166–7.
127. Ibid., p. 168.
128. T. Paine, *Rights of Man: Being an Answer to Mr. Burke's Attack on the French Revolution* (1791), ed. H. Collins (Harmondsworth: Penguin, 1969), p. 24.
129. Imlay, *A Topographical Description*, p. 163.
130. Ibid., pp. 163, 161.
131. Ibid., pp. 169–70.
132. Ibid., pp. 176, 180, 177, 179, 180.
133. *European Magazine*, 22 (July 1792), pp. 35–8; *Analytical Review*, 13 (August 1792), pp. 382–6; *Monthly Review*, n.s. 8 (August 1792), pp. 390–401; *Literary Magazine and British Review*, 9 (October 1792), pp. 300–3; *English Review*, 22 (July 1793), pp. 42–3; *Critical Review; or, Annals of Literature*, n.s. 9 (September 1793), pp. 53–8. Although the reviews in the *English Review* and the *Critical Review* may have appeared in response to the publication of the Dublin reprint of the first edition and of Debrett's second edition (1793), the reviewers in both cases commented on the first Debrett edition of 1792.
134. *American Museum; or, Universal Magazine*, 12 (November 1792), pp. 265–71; *Universal Asylum and Columbian Magazine*, 9 (November 1792), pp. 307–11; *New York Magazine; or, Literary Repository*, 4:9 (September 1793), pp. 542–9.
135. *Analytical Review*, 11 (September 1791), pp. 37–43.
136. *European Magazine*, 22 (July 1792), p. 35.
137. *Critical Review*, n.s. 9 (September 1792), pp. 54, 55, 56, 57.
138. *Analytical Review*, 13 (August 1792), p. 384.
139. *Monthly Review*, n.s. 8 (August 1792), pp. 390, 391, 400.

6 Jacobin Novelist and Defender of the Rights of Woman

1. Imlay, *The Emigrants*, vol. 1, p. 65.
2. H. J. Pye, *The Aristocrat, A Novel*, 2 vols (London: Sampson Low, 1799), vol. 1, p. 131.
3. W. Enfield, review of *Caleb Williams*, *Monthly Review*, n.s. 15 (September 1794), pp. 145, 149.
4. Godwin's *Enquiry Concerning Political Justice* was published in February 1793. *The Emigrants* was advertised as published 'this day' on the front page of the *Morning Chronicle* for Tuesday, 12 March 1793. The novel was listed in the 'Catalogue of Books & Pamphlets Published in Great-Britain and Ireland During the first six months of 1793', which was appended to the *Analytical Review*, 16 (1793), p. 541. However, the imprint was probably post-dated. See also note 95 below.
5. W. Hazlitt, *The Spirit of the Age or Contemporary Portraits* (1825; Oxford: Oxford University Press, 1928), p. 18.
6. Ibid., p. 20.
7. *Critical Review*, n.s. 9 (October 1793), p. 155.
8. Ibid.
9. *Monthly Review*, n.s. 11 (August 1793), pp. 468–9.

10. J. Seelye, *Beautiful Machine: Rivers and the Republican Plan 1755–1825* (New York and Oxford: Oxford University Press, 1991), p. 156.
11. Imlay, *The Emigrants*, vol. 3, p. 75.
12. Ibid., vol. 1, p. 49.
13. Ibid., vol. 1, p. 154.
14. Ibid.
15. Ibid., vol. 1, p. 186.
16. Ibid., vol. 1, pp. 186–7.
17. Ibid., vol. 3, pp. 129, 128.
18. Ibid., vol. 3, pp. 129–30.
19. Ibid., vol. 3, p. 131.
20. Ibid., vol. 3, pp. 132–3.
21. Imlay, *A Topographical Description*, p. 178.
22. Imlay, *The Emigrants*, vol. 1, p. 100.
23. Ibid., vol. 1, p. 65.
24. Ibid., vol. 1, pp. 200, 201; vol. 2, pp. 57–8.
25. Ibid., vol. 2, p. 72.
26. Imlay's account is quite accurate, for, as Lawrence Stone notes, 'especially in the period 1740–1820, the damages awarded were so much beyond the defendant's capacity to pay that the verdict was tantamount to a sentence of life imprisonment for debt' (*Broken Lives: Separation and Divorce in England 1660–1857* (Oxford and New York: Oxford University Press, 1993), p. 23).
27. Imlay, *The Emigrants*, vol. 2, p. 73.
28. See V. Jones (ed.), *Women in the Eighteenth Century* (London and New York: Routledge, 1990), p. 219.
29. W. Blackstone, *Commentaries on the Laws of England*, 4 vols (Oxford: Clarendon Press, 1765–9), vol. 1, p. 442.
30. M. Wollstonecraft, *A Vindication of the Rights of Woman: With Strictures on Political and Moral Subjects* (London: J. Johnson, 1792), pp. 331, 355; *Maria; or The Wrongs of Woman* (1798), in *Mary and The Wrongs of Woman*, ed. G. Kelly (Oxford: Oxford University Press, 1976), p. 74; *Vindication of the Rights of Woman*, p. 329.
31. Imlay, *The Emigrants*, vol. 1, p. 214 (italics added).
32. Ibid., vol. 2, p. 11.
33. Ibid., vol. 1, pp. 136, 138. Mary Hays in her *Letters and Essays, Moral and Miscellaneous* (London: T. Knott, 1793), p. 29, published in the same year as *The Emigrants*, compares husbands and West Indian plantation owners, both of whom have a vested interest in resisting legal reform of their property-owning rights. Also published in the same year were Blake's anti-slavery tracts, 'America' and 'Visions of the Daughters of Albion', the latter poem explicitly combining issues of slavery with those of gender oppression.
34. Extract in J. Breen, *Women Romantics 1785–1832: Writing in Prose* (London: Dent, 1996), p. 123.
35. Imlay, *The Emigrants*, vol. 2, pp. 23, 24.
36. Ibid., vol. 2, p. 33.
37. Ibid., vol. 2, p. 35.
38. Ibid., vol. 2, pp. 37–8.
39. Ibid., vol. 1, p. 203 (italics in original).
40. Ibid., vol. 1, p. 101.
41. Ibid., vol. 2, pp. 80, 83.

42. Ibid., vol. 2, p. 145. See also vol. 3, pp. 179–80.

43. Ibid., vol. 2, p. 147. Wollstonecraft memorably sympathizes with Matilda in Letter 18 of *Letters Written during a Short Residence in Sweden, Norway, and Denmark*, as do many other writers of the period.

44. Imlay, *The Emigrants*, vol. 1, p. ii.

45. Ibid., vol. 2, p. 117.

46. Ibid., vol. 2, p. 121.

47. Ibid., vol. 3, p. 141.

48. Ibid., vol. 3, pp. 141–2.

49. This episode is much extended in the later novel, where we see the husband berating the purchaser for his sexual timidity (see, Wollstonecraft, *The Wrongs of Woman*, pp. 158–63).

50. Imlay, *The Emigrants*, vol. 3, p. 180.

51. As Lawrence Stone notes, the 'shift from physical violence against, or challenge to duel with, one's wife's lover to a suit for monetary damages from him' is a 'sign of a change from an honour-and-shame society to a commercial society' (*Broken Lives*, p. 23).

52. Imlay, *The Emigrants*, vol. 1, pp. 36, 217.

53. Ibid., vol. 3, p. 139. See Mary Wollstonecraft's use of Defoe's phrase to describe marriage as a 'legal prostitution' (*Vindication of the Rights of Woman*, p. 338).

54. Imlay, *A Topographical Description*, p. 162.

55. Imlay, *The Emigrants*, vol. 3, p. 139. Ironically, Imlay's critique of the detrimental effects of the commercial spirit sounds very like Wollstonecraft's complaints about him in her *Letters to Imlay* and her anxieties about commercial society in *Letters Written during a Short Residence in Sweden, Norway, and Denmark*.

56. Imlay, *The Emigrants*, vol. 3, p. 144.

57. Ibid., vol. 3, pp. 79, 138.

58. Ibid., vol. 3, p. 156.

59. Ibid., vol. 3, p. 145.

60. L. Stone, *Road to Divorce, England 1530–1987* (Oxford: Oxford University Press, 1990), p. 428. In his case-studies – which read like short stories – Stone recounts the case of Beaufort v. Beaufort, subtitled 'The impotent duke and the adulterous duchess, 1729–1742', in which the duke proves his maligned virility in front of witnesses (see *Broken Lives*, pp. 117–38).

61. Stone, *Road to Divorce*, pp. 360, 362.

62. J. Fliegelman, *Prodigals and Pilgrims: The American Revolution against Patriarchal Authority, 1750–1850* (Cambridge: Cambridge University Press, 1982), p. 137.

63. Ibid., p. 137. Arguments for the reform or abolition of marriage as an important element in the future state of society to which they aspired are a significant feature of Jacobin novels; Thomas Holcroft's *Anna St Ives* (1792), for example, contends that, 'Of all the regulations which were ever suggested to the mistaken tyranny of selfishness, none perhaps to this day have surpassed the despotism of those which undertake to bind not only body to body but soul to soul, to all futurity, in despite of every possible change which our vices and our virtues might effect, or however numerous the secret corporal or mental imperfections might prove which a more intimate acquaintance should bring to light!' (*Anna St Ives: A Novel* (1792), ed. W. Verhoeven, in *The Novels and Selected Plays of Thomas Holcroft*, 5 vols, gen. ed. W. Verhoeven (London: Pickering and Chatto, 2007), vol. 2, pp. 245–6). William Godwin argued, in *Enquiry Concerning Political Jus-*

tice (1793), that in a future state, marriage would be the free choice of two partners, to last as long as the rational inclinations of both partners wished (Book 8, ch. 8).

64. Fliegelman, *Prodigals and Pilgrims*, p. 134.
65. Cited in ibid., p. 125.
66. Imlay, *The Emigrants*, vol. 3, p. 169–70. See, too, Mrs W—'s exclamation to Miss R—, 'Come to these Arcadian regions [west of the Alleghenies] where there is room for millions' (vol. 1, p. 92). It is possible that the character of Eliza owes something to that of Mary Wollstonecraft's sister of the same name, whom she persuaded to leave her husband, the brutal Mr Bishop, and for whom she cared during 1782.
67. Ibid., vol. 3, p. 184.
68. L. Colley, *Britons: Forging the Nation 1707–1837* (New Haven, CT: Yale University Press, 1992), p. 252.
69. R. Polwhele, *The Unsex'd Females: A Poem, Addressed to the Author of The Pursuits of Literature* (London: Cadell and Davies, 1798), p. 19. For further discussion of Williams, and of the issue in general, see, V. Jones, 'Women Writing Revolution: Narratives of History and Sexuality in Wollstonecraft and Williams', in S. Copley and J. Whale (eds), *Beyond Romanticism* (London and New York: Routledge, 1992), pp. 178–99.
70. Imlay, *The Emigrants*, vol. 2, p. 73. Cf. David Humphrey's poem 'On the Happiness of America' (1786), wherein this national happiness is predicated in part on the fact that the women do not suffer 'Eastern' bondage (cited in Fliegelman, *Prodigals and Pilgrims*, p. 143).
71. Imlay, *A Topographical Description*, pp. 3, 2.
72. Imlay, *The Emigrants*, vol. 3, p. 138.
73. The novel does make pragmatic suggestions to improve the condition of women, especially in its support of female education. Wollstonecraft argued that women are kept in the educational dark to prepare them for 'the slavery of marriage', a slavery the novel explicitly wishes to banish. Writing to her sister, Caroline cites the 'injudicious' 'education of women' as circumscribing their understanding and constraining them to 'colloquial charms' (ibid., vol. 1, p. 174); her uncle advocates the moral reform of male education, which would lead to the 'amelioration' of female education (ibid., vol. 2, pp. 44–51).
74. Cited in Jones, 'Women Writing Revolution', p. 181. Cf. the comments of Sir Thomas Mor—ley in the novel, who, while acknowledging the defects British marital law, nevertheless considers 'that no women in Europe enjoy so many privileges, or have so much consequence in the common affairs of life' as English women (Imlay, *The Emigrants*, vol. 3, pp. 180–1).
75. Imlay, *The Emigrants*, vol. 2, p. 156.
76. Ibid., vol. 1, p. 67.
77. Ibid., vol. 2, p. 45.
78. The captivity narrative occurs between the stories of Juliana and Eliza, and takes up only a few pages: Caroline is captured on page 19 of volume 3 and is back in Arl—ton's protection by page 36 of the same volume.
79. Ibid., vol. 3, pp. 25–6.
80. Ibid., vol. 3, p. 39.
81. Ibid., vol. 3, p. 36.
82. Ibid., vol. 3, p. 41.
83. Ibid., vol. 3, pp. 26, 47, 50, 64.
84. Ibid., vol. 3, p. 50.

85. *The Emigrants* provides one of the earliest captivity narratives in American fiction: Christopher Castiglia cites Ann Eliza Bleeker's *The History of Maria Kittle* (1793) as the first, and he argues that women writers 'popularized the wilderness of fiction' and exploited the possibilities of 'gender critique' offered by the captivity narrative (*Bound and Determined: Captivity, Culture-Crossing, and White Womanhood from Mary Rowlandson to Patty Hearst* (Chicago, IL, and London: University of Chicago Press, 1996), p. 112). Imlay's novel was published well before those by Brockden Brown and Fenimore Cooper, which traditional literary history has credited with bringing captivity, and the American 'wilderness', into fiction, and is contemporaneous with the women's writing analysed by Castiglia.

86. L. Kerber, *Women of the Republic: Intellect and Ideology in Revolutionary America* (Chapel Hill, NC: University of North Carolina Press, 1980), p. 184.

87. Columbia College commencement oration of 1795 entitled 'Female Influence'; cited in Kerber, *Women of the Republic*, p. 230. Especially significant in America was the figure of Republican motherhood, paradigmatically represented in *The Emigrants* by Mrs W—.

88. Castiglia, *Bound and Determined*, p. 158 (with reference to the work of Paul Michael Rogin).

89. Imlay, *The Emigrants*, vol. 3, pp. 129–36. Compare this with Il—ray's early insight that British tyranny is exacerbated precisely because the oppressed lack institutional representation (vol. 1, pp. 62–3).

90. Ibid., vol. 3, p. 134.

91. Wollstonecraft, *The Wrongs of Woman*, p. 159.

92. Imlay, *The Emigrants*, vol. 1, p. 63.

93. *The Adams Family Correspondence*, ed. L. H. Butterfield and M. Friedlaender, 8 vols (Cambridge, MA: Harvard University Press, 1963–2007), vol. 1, pp. 370, 382.

94. Imlay, *A Topographical Description*, p. 181.

95. *The Emigrants* was advertised as published in the *London Chronicle*, 72, 4–6 December 1792, p. 538, and in the *St James's Chronicle*, 4–6 December 1792 (it was re-advertised in *St James's Chronicle*, 5–7 September 1793). Post-dating on title pages was a standard trick in the eighteenth-century book trade, suggesting that a publication was of a more recent date than it actually was. See P. Garside, J. Raven and R. Schöwerling (gen. eds), *The English Novel 1770–1829: A Bibliographical Survey of Prose Fiction Published in the British Isles*, 2 vols (Oxford: Oxford University Press, 2000), vol. 1, p. 82–4.

96. Maxted, *The London Book Trades, 1775–1800*, p. 99.

97. *British Critic, A New Review*, 1 (July 1793), p. 341.

98. *Critical Review*, n.s. 9 (October 1793), p. 156.

99. Ibid., p. 155.

100. *Monthly Review*, n.s. 11 (August 1793), p. 468.

101. Ibid., p. 469.

102. Ibid., p. 468.

103. Imlay, *The Emigrants*, vol. 1, p. ii.

104. The use of the term 'the Mountain' for what is in fact a mountain range over fifty miles across, has in the past been cited as 'evidence' that Imlay could not have written the novel himself (see *The Emigrants (1793), Traditionally Ascribed to Gilbert Imlay but, More Probably, By Mary Wollstonecraft*, ed. R. R. Hare (Gainesville, FL: Scholars' Facsimiles & Reprints, 1964), p. 43. Twelve Mile Island is identified on a map in Draper MSS, 1M131. Major Erkuries Beatty identifies Six Mile Island as 'Diamond Island' in 'Diary of Major Erkuries Beatty [1786–7]', *Magazine of American History*, 1 (1877), pp. 239–41.

105. See Shane's interview (1859) with Robert Wickliffe, Sr, in Draper MSS, 15CC83, and Captain B. Gaines to Mann Butler, 17 December 1833, in Draper MSS, 9J2383. Wickliffe's claim that Gilbert Imlay was a first cousin of Mrs Robert Barr was also accurate. Robert Ross Barr had married Rebecca Tilton of Philadelphia in 1778; Rebecca was the daughter of Margaret Imlay and Peter Tilton. Margaret Imlay was the sister of Gilbert's father, Peter Imlay.

106. F. W. Grayson, 'The Grayson Family', *Tyler's Quarterly Historical and Genealogical Magazine*, 5 (1923–4), pp. 195–208, 261–8, on p. 261.

107. *The Filson Club Compilation of Jefferson County, Virginia/Kentucky Early Marriages, book 1 (1781–July, 1826)* (Louisville, KY: Filson Historical Society, 1941), pp. 2–3.

108. Kentucky Supreme Court, Chancery Decrees, 1798–1800, Nelson County CCO, uncatalogued and numbered documents.

109. See *The Emigrants*, ed. Hare, 'Introduction'. Lacking any kind of positive proof, Hare also claims that Wollstonecraft authored the *Topographical Description*. See also J. R. Cole, 'Imlay's Ghost: Wollstonecraft's Authorship of *The Emigrants*', *Eighteenth-Century Women: Studies in Their Lives, Work, and Culture*, 1 (2001), pp. 263–98.

110. Wollstonecraft to Imlay, 10 February 1795, in *The Collected Letters of Mary Wollstonecraft*, p. 283.

7 Expat Radical and Conspirator

1. *Nachrichten von dem westlichen lande der Nordamerikanischen freistaaten, von dem klima, den naturprodukten, der volksmenge, den sitten und gebraüchen desselben, nebst einer angabe der indianischen völkerstämme, die an den gränzen wohnen, und einer schilderung von den gestetzen und der regierung des staates Kentucky. In briefen an einen freund in England*, trans. E. A. W. Zimmermann (Berlin: In der Vossischen buchhandlung, 1793).

2. 'Letters of Christoph Daniel Ebeling', ed. W. C. Lane, *Proceedings of the American Antiquarian Society*, n.s. 35 (October 1925), pp. 272–451, on p. 301.

3. 'Conting't Exp's. p'd for Imlay's Hist. of Kentucky for Mrs. W— ..... $ 0.87', in 'Washington's Household Account Book, 1793–1797', *Pennsylvania Magazine of History and Biography*, 31 (1907), pp. 53–82, on p. 68.

4. Anon., *Berkeley Hall: or, The Pupil of Experience* (1796), ed. W. M. Verhoeven, in *Anti-Jacobin Novels*, gen. ed. W. M. Verhoeven, 10 vols (London: Pickering & Chatto, 2005), vol. 6; G. Walker, *The Vagabond, A Novel* (1799), ed. W. M. Verhoeven (Peterborough, Ontario: Broadview Press, 2004).

5. See R. B. Heilman, *America in English Fiction, 1760–1800: The Influence of the American Revolution* (Baton Rouge, LA: Louisiana State University Press, 1937), pp. 80–2.

6. *The Emigrants* was not reprinted until 1998. See G. Imlay, *The Emigrants, &c.; or, The History of an Expatriated Family, Being a Delineation of English Manners, Drawn from Real Characters, Written in America* (1793), ed. W. M. Verhoeven and A. Gilroy (New York: Penguin, 1998).

7. A. Fitzroy, *The Discovery, Purchase, and Settlement of the Country of Kentuckie, in North America, so Famous for its Fertility of Soil, Produce, Climate, Minerals, Quadrupedes, Curiosities, Trade, Rapid Population, Religion, &c. &c. The Whole Illustrated by a New and Accurate Map Annexed* (London: printed by H. Goldney, 1786).

8. Imlay, *A Topographical Description*, 2nd edn, p. xv.

9. See *European Magazine*, 22 (July 1792), p. 36; *Monthly Review*, n.s. 8 (August 1792), pp. 400–1; *English Review*, 22 (July 1793), p. 42.
10. *Monthly Review*, n.s. 8 (August 1792), pp. 400–1.
11. See, for instance, Fant, 'A Study of Gilbert Imlay', p. 73.
12. Imlay was still in London on 2 February 1793, for on that day – if it is authentic – he addressed a letter to Harry Toulmin, who, by way of endorsement, attached extracts of it to his *A Description of Kentucky, in North America: To which are Prefixed Miscellaneous Observations Respecting the United States* ([London]: n.p., 1792) (which, according to the title page, was 'printed in November, 1792').
13. Imlay, *A Topographical Description*, 2nd edn, p. 400.
14. Ibid., pp. 103–5, n.
15. Ibid., p. 112, n.
16. Ibid., p. 118, n.
17. Ibid., p. 124, n., p. 125, n.
18. Ibid., p. 123, n.
19. Ibid., pp. 123–4, n.
20. Ibid., p. 118, n.
21. Imlay, *A Topographical Description*, 3rd edn, pp. 82–129, 219–21, 144–65, 296–305.
22. Ibid., pp. viii–ix.
23. Ibid., pp. vii, 13.
24. C. Pigott, *A Political Dictionary: Explaining the True Meaning of Words* (London: D. I. Eaton, 1795), pp. 17, 113.
25. J. Thelwall, *The Tribune* (1795), in *The Politics of English Jacobinism: Writings of John Thelwall*, ed. G. Claeys (University Park, PA: Pennsylvania State University Press, 1985), pp. 69, xxv.
26. Thus, in its issue for May 1793 the *Gentlemen's Magazine* reported, 'Several of our periodical publications have of late abounded with essays written to prove the superior felicity of American farmers, and to recommend our husbandmen to quit their native plains, and seek for happiness and plenty in the Transatlantic desarts' (*Gentlemen's Magazine*, 63 (1793), p. 401). The same periodicals, however, frequently carried essays warning against the dubious activities of British and American land-jobbers, who were trying to tempt potential emigrants to settle in the New World, and sell them land to which they held the rights. Thus, in September 1793 the *Gentlemen's Magazine* published a review abstract of *Letters on Emigration, By a Gentleman Lately Returned from America*, which, according to the reviewer, 'contain[s] much good admonition to the several classes of men who are disposed to emigrate'. Commenting on the large numbers of emigrants that returned to Britain destitute and disillusioned, the reviewer can only conclude that 'this land of universal promise is the land of general disappointment' (*Gentlemen's Magazine*, 65 (1793), p. 760). The travelling gentleman himself ends his *Letters* on an equally dismissive note: 'But, it may be asked, ought no description of persons to emigrate? The reply is obvious – The guilty *must*, and the very unfortunate *will*, though the prejudices of the natives are too apt to confound the latter with the former' (*Letters on Emigration, By a Gentleman Lately Returned from America* (London: C. and G. Kearsley, 1794), p. 76). For detailed analyses of pre-Revolutionary emigration to British North America, see B, Bailyn, *The Peopling of British North America: An Introduction* (New York: Alfred A. Knopf, 1986), and *Voyagers to the West: A Passage in the People of America on the Eve of the Revolution* (New York: Alfred A. Knopf, 1986).

27. Samuel Coleridge to Robert Southey, 1 September 1794, in *Collected Letters of Samuel Taylor Coleridge*, ed. E. L. Griggs, 4 vols (Oxford: Clarendon Press, 1956–9), vol. 1, p. 99.

28. *British Critic*, 5 (January 1795), p. 27. It was the emigration of fellow radicals Joseph Priestley and Thomas Cooper to Pennsylvania that finally persuaded Coleridge in October 1794 to opt for the banks of the Susquehanna. However, in the end the Pantisocratic scheme collapsed before it was put into practice. Rising land prices, disagreement between the two architects of the scheme, and lack of funds caused the 'Pantisocratic Plan' to be shelved indefinitely by early 1795.

29. James Swan (1754–1830) was a Scottish-born merchant and financier from Boston, who after 1788 was engaged in a wide range of commercial and speculative enterprises. From 1794 to 1796 Swan was the official purchasing agent of the French government in the United States. See Chapter 8 for more details.

30. J. Keane, *Tom Paine: A Political Life* (London: Bloomsbury, 1995), p. 370.

31. M. D. Conway, *The Life of Thomas Paine; With a History of his Literary, Political, and Religious Career in America, France, and England ... To which is added a Sketch of Paine by William Cobbett (hitherto unpublished)*, 2 vols (New York and London: G. P. Putnam's Sons, 1892), vol. 2, pp. 61–76, 'A Garden in the Faubourg St. Denis'. Paine's intimate friend Thomas Clio Rickman lists 'Captain Imlay', along with Joel Barlow, among Paine's 'American friends' during this period (T. C. Rickman, *The Life of Thomas Paine* (London: T. C. Rickman, 1819), p. 41).

32. S. Schama, *Citizens: A Chronicle of the French Revolution* (New York: Alfred A. Knopf, 1989), pp. 581–7.

33. D. Malone, *The Public Life of Thomas Cooper, 1783–1839* (New Haven, CT: Yale University Press, 1926), pp. 19–29.

34. Ibid., pp. 34–40.

35. Schama, *Citizens*, pp. 582–3.

36. J. P. Brissot de Warville, *New Travels in the United States of America. Performed in 1788 ...*, trans. [J. Barlow] (London: J. S. Jordan, 1792), p. 46.

37. Ibid., pp. 478–9.

38. Ibid., p. 479.

39. Ibid., pp. 479–80, 480.

40. See F.-A. Aulard (ed.), *Recueil des actes du comité de Salut Public avec la correspondance officielle des représentants en mission, et le registre du conseil exécutif provisoire*, 16 vols (Paris: Imprimerie nationale, 1889–1904), vol. 2, pp. 10, 82.

41. F. J. Turner, 'The Origin of Genet's Projected Attack on Louisiana and the Floridas', *American Historical Review*, 3:4 (July 1898): p. 655.

42. In 1797 Otto claimed that it had been Brissot who had proposed Genet as minister to the United States. See Correspondance Politique, Espagne, AAE Paris, vol. 635, doc. 295.

43. Schama, *Citizens*, pp. 688–9.

44. Otto, who was in fact Crèvecoeur's son-in-law, had returned to Paris in late 1792 from the United States, where he had been private secretary to Count Luzerne during his American mission (1779–84). In 1785 he had returned there to become chargé d'affaires at the French embassy in New York. Otto had written to Lebrun on 2 January 1793 asking for a job, and Lebrun had appointed him on January 29 in what was one of the most important jobs in the ministry. See Allen and Asselineau, *St. John de Crèvecoeur*, pp. 159–60, 179–80.

45. 'I refer to you Captain Imlay, an American of the state of Kentucky, who has been recommended to me by the honourable Cooper from Manchester; he wishes to talk to me about the expedition into Mississippi. He strikes me as someone quite capable to provide you with intelligence regarding the manner in which this plan might be executed. After you have spoken to him, we can make an appointment with the Minister for a more general discussion of this topic.' Brissot to Otto, 26 March 1793, Correspondance Politique, Espagne, AAE Paris, vol. 635, doc. 295.

46. Ibid., vol. 634, doc. 202. The document is endorsed '1792', but this must be an error, because in the second paragraph it talks about the advantages in future peace negotiations with Spain if France were to conquer Louisiana.

47. Correspondance Politique, États-Unis, Louisiane et Florides, 1792–1803, AAE Paris, vol. 7, doc. 1, pp. 4–9.

48. 'He fears, however, that the documents relating to this topic that were presented to your Committee by Minister Le Brun may not have been examined, given that your incessant labours barely meet the demands put on you by the people's Safety.' Ibid., p. 4.

49. 'Observations du Cap. Imlay, Traduites de L'Anglais', Correspondance Politique, Espagne, AAE Paris, vol. 634, doc. 202 (my translations).

50. Draper MSS, 12J60.

51. Born in Ireland and trained as a physician in Edinburgh, Dr James O'Fallon had arrived in America to fight on the side of the Americans in the Revolutionary War, both as a soldier and a pamphleteer. At the close of the Revolution, he settled in Charleston, where he got involved in land speculation. He became a promoter of the famous South Carolina Yazoo Company, which had managed to obtain a grant of over fifty thousand acres on the Mississippi below the Yazoo River. His attempts to persuade settlers to buy the Company's plots were seriously compromised by Spain's claims to the region. He even went so far as to conspire with Wilkinson in the latter's treasonable dealings with the Spanish, and sent a letter to Miró in which he promised that the settlers would willingly pledge allegiance to the King of Spain in exchange for being allowed to take up their land claims. In the spring of 1790 he appeared in Kentucky, presumably to persuade some of the restless settlers there to relocate further south, in the Yazoo region. He got on well with the locals, many of whom were Revolutionary War veterans, and in February 1791 married General Clark's youngest sister, Frances. But Wilkinson thought he was a lightweight in the world of international political intrigue and advised Miró to avoid him. Undaunted, O'Fallon thereupon changed allegiance from Spain to Revolutionary France, and joined General Clark's plan to free Louisiana and hand it to the French. See L. P. Kellogg, 'Letter of Thomas Paine, 1793', *American Historical Review*, 29:3 (April 1924), pp. 501–3; and Gayarré, *The History of Louisiana*, vol. 3, pp. 272–93.

52. Draper MSS, 12J60. When he arrived in Charleston on 8 April, Genet found awaiting him the original letter that General Clark had written to the French Minister to the United States from the Falls of the Ohio on 2 February, in which he offered a detailed plan to expel the Spanish from Louisiana (a copy of which O'Fallon had forwarded with his own letter to Paine – which was the copy Paine shared with the Convention and with Genet). See Turner, 'The Origin of Genet's Projected Attack on Louisiana and the Floridas', p. 665. Clark's letter is reproduced in 'Selections from the Draper Collection in the Possession of the State Historical Society of Wisconsin', *Annual Report of the American Historical Association*, 1 (1896), pp. 930–1107, on pp. 967–1.

53. Correspondance Politique, Espagne, AAE Paris, vol. 635, doc. 316.

54. Lyonnet's 'Additional Considerations', Correspondance Politique, Espagne, AAE Paris, vol. 635, doc. 317. Lyonnet to Lebrun, [received] 4 April 1793, Correspondance Politique, Espagne, AAE Paris, vol. 635, doc. 37.

55. Ibid., vol. 635, doc. 313. The document recommends that Barlow, Sayre, Beaupoil and Lyonnet be sent immediately on a 'secret mission' to Philadelphia, where they would raise an army that would conquer Louisiana and ultimately complete Miranda's grand ambition, the complete liberation of all Spanish colonies in America.

56. Correspondance Politique, Espagne, AAE Paris, vol. 635, doc. 195. The plan is dated 4 March 1793.

57. Ibid., vol. 636, doc. 37, doc. 101, doc. 205.

58. Ibid., vol. 636, doc. 205.

59. 'Citizen Minister, Captain Imlay, who is delivering this letter to you, informs me that nothing has yet been decided regarding the expedition to Mississippi. I must confess that in my opinion this tardiness is quite detrimental to the public cause. If the Captain and others involved in this plan do not depart within a fortnight, it will be necessary to abort the mission, and since the Republic would seriously have to reproach itself for having abandoned it, I urge you to come to a firm decision. Financial concerns should not hold you back at this point. Should you need the advice of the Council [of ministers], I would be happy to turn to them to promote the advantages of the scheme but I beg you not to lose the occasion. J. P. Brissot.' Ibid., vol. 635, doc. 295.

60. 'They are men burning with the Fire of liberty, who are embittered against Spain, which continues to violate their rights, by erecting barriers against their natural rise to prosperity and by paralysing key industrial activity and competion.' Correspondance Politique, États-Unis, Louisiane et Florides, AAE Paris, vol. 7, doc. 1.

61. For further details on Genet's mission to the United States, see Turner, 'The Origin of Genet's Projected Attack on Louisiana and the Floridas', and C. C. O'Brien, *The Long Affair: Thomas Jefferson and the French Revolution, 1785–1800* (Chicago, IL, and London: University of Chicago Press, 1996), ch. 5, 'French Revolution in America: The Mission of Citizen Charles-Edmond Genet'.

62. Correspondance Politique, Etats-Unis supplément, 21–4, AAE Paris, vol. 39, doc. 144. See also, H. Ammon, *The Genet Mission* (New York: Norton, 1973), p. 44.

8 Purveyor to the French Revolution

1. Wollstonecraft, *Letters Written during a Short Residence in Sweden, Norway, and Denmark*, p. 30.

2. 'Scheme to take Louisiana without any cost to the nation'; 'in the name of the French republic'. Correspondance Politique, Espagne, AAE Paris, vol. 636, fol. 391.

3. O'Brien, *The Long Affair*, pp. 231, 307.

4. J. Barlow, 'Letter to the People of Piedmont', in *The Political Writings of Joel Barlow, Containing 'Advice to the Privileged Orders', 'Letter to the National Convention', 'Letter to the People of Piedmont', 'The Conspiracy of Kings'* (New York: Fellows & Adam, Thomas Greenleaf, and Naphtati Judah, 1796), p. 216 n.

5. A. C. Clauder, 'American Commerce as Affected by the Wars of the French Revolution and Napoleon, 1793–1812' (PhD thesis, University of Pennsylvania, 1932), p. 34.

6. See ibid., pp. 27–50.

7. Memoranda, 1795–1796, Joel Barlow Papers, Houghton, series I, item 7.

8. Seelye, *Beautiful Machine*, p. 117.
9. Cited in J. H. James, 'Introduction', in M. Cutler, *Ohio in 1788. A Description of the Soil, Productions, etc., of that Portion of the United States Situated Between Pennsylvania, the Rivers Ohio and Scioto and Lake Erie. Translated from the French*, trans. and intro. J. H. James (Columbus, OH: A. H. Smythe, 1888), p. 12. This volume is James's translation of the French edition of Manasseh Cutler's *An Explanation of the Map which Delineates that Part of the Federal Lands Comprehended between Pennsylvania West Line, the Rivers Ohio and Scioto, and Lake Erie*, which appeared anonymously in Paris in 1789. Since they were actively promoting emigration to the Ohio country during the autumn of 1789, it is quite possible that Barlow and Playfair were somehow involved in the publication of the French translation of Cutler's text.
10. For more details on the Ohio and Scioto land companies, see W. Havinghurst, *Wilderness for Sale: The Story of the First Western Land Rush* (New York: Hastings House, 1956), pp. 147–61; S. Livermore, *Early American Land Companies: Their Influence on Corporate Development* (New York: The Commonwealth Fund, 1939), pp. 134–46; A. M. Sakolski, *The Great American Land Bubble: The Amazing Story of Land-Grabbing, Speculations, and Booms from Colonial Days to the Present Time* (New York and London: Harper & Brothers, 1932), pp. 99–123.
11. Sakolski, *The Great American Land Bubble*, p. 36.
12. Washington to Marquis de Lafayette, 28 May 1788, in *The Writings of George Washington*, vol. 29, p. 506. The letters to Marquis de la Luzerne and Comte de Rochambeau were also dated 28 May 1788 (ibid., pp. 503–4; p. 503). Although he made no mention of the Scioto project and recommended Barlow to his correspondents only on the grounds of his poetical talent, Washington observed in a letter of 19 June 1788 to Richard Henderson (chief promoter of the ill-fated Transylvania Company in the 1770s) 'that there is a gentleman (to wit Mr. Joel Barlow) gone from New York by the last French Packet, who will be in London in the course of this year, and who is authorized to dispose of a very large body of land in that Country [the north-west territory]' (ibid., p. 521).
13. For more details on the history of Ohiopiomingo and the trade in similar utopian wilderness communities in Kentucky in the 1790s, see my *Americomania, or, Illusions of Liberty: British Radicals and American Lands, 1789–1800* (forthcoming: Chapel Hill, NC: University of North Carolina Press, 2008).
14. [W. Playfair], *Prospectus pour l'établissement sur les rivières d'Ohio et de Scioto, en Amérique* [with appended 'Époque des Paiemens' and 'Plan des achats des Compagnies de L'Ohio et de la Scioto'] (Paris: Prault, 1789). On the text's authorship, see J. Moreau-Zanelli, *Gallipolis: histoire d'un mirage americain au xviiie siècle* (Paris and Montreal: L'Harmattan, 2000), p. 98. Prault printed at least one other promotional tract for Barlow and Playfair: *Avis intéressant aux amateurs de l'agriculture: 120,000 journaux de terres à vendre, en tout ou en partie, & dont les acquéreurs peuvent tirer un grand produit* (Paris: Prault, 1789). The text begins: 'La Compagnie du Scioto, établie à Paris pour l'exploitation & la vente de trois millions d'acres anglais de terres ...' ('The Scioto Company, established in Paris for the development and sale of three million English acres of land ...').
15. J. Woodress, *A Yankee's Odyssey: The Life of Joel Barlow* (Philadelphia, PA, and New York: J. B. Lippincott Company, 1958), p. 103.
16. For Barlow's letters to Duer, see T. T. Belote, *The Scioto Speculation and the French Settlement at Galliopolis: A Study in Ohio Valley History* (Cincinnati, OH: University of Cincinnati Press, 1907), pp. 65–82.

17. With investments in paper assets, stocks, government warrants, state securities, and currencies and securities on the consolidated national debt, Duer's speculative empire finally collapsed when the government sued him for two unbalanced accounts. He was arrested in 1792 and spent the last seven years of his life in prison. Duer's crash triggered 'the panic of 1792', the first major financial panic in New York's history.

18. C. F. de Volney, *A View of the Soil and Climate of the United States of America* (1803), trans. C. Brockden Brown (Philadelphia: J. Conrad & Co., 1804), p. 325, p. 327.

19. Joel Barlow to Ruth Barlow, 20 July 1789, cited in C. B. Todd, *Life and Letters of Joel Barlow, L.L.D., Poet, Statesman, Philosopher, with Extracts from his Works and Hitherto Unpublished Poems* (New York: G. P. Putnam's Sons, 1886), p. 87.

20. *Archives parlémentaires de 1787 à 1794, Recueil complet des debats legislatifs et politique des Chambres Francaises*, 1st series, 82 vols (Paris, 1884), vol. 17, p. 40.

21. Cited in Woodress, *A Yankee's Odyssey*, p. 118.

22. William Godwin's diary for 1792, cited in C. K. Paul, *William Godwin: His Friends and Contemporaries*, 2 vols (London: H. S. King, 1876), vol. 1, p. 71.

23. *Advice to the Privileged Orders*, in Barlow, *The Political Writings of Joel Barlow*, p. 109.

24. Woodress, *A Yankee's Odyssey*, p. 117.

25. Brissot de Warville, *New Travels in the United States of America*, trans. [Barlow], p. vii.

26. Ibid., pp. ix–x, viii.

27. Ibid., pp. 476–8, n.

28. Barlow to Abraham Baldwin, 17 October 1791, Joel Barlow Papers, Houghton, series III, item 66.

29. *The Trial of Thomas Hardy for High Treason, at the Sessions House in the Old Bailey ... November 1794 ... Taken in Short-Hand, by Joseph Gurney*, 4 vols (London: Martha Gurney, 1794–5), vol. 4, pp. 423, 424.

30. *The Parliamentary History of England from the Earliest Period to the Year 1803. Volume 30, Comprising the Period from the Thirteenth of December 1792, to the Tenth of March 1794* (London: Longman, 1817), p. 110. In a letter to her husband dated 9 January 1793, Ruth Barlow reported Burke's use of the phrase 'prophet Joel' in Parliament. Cited in M. R. Adams, 'Joel Barlow, Political Romanticist', *American Literature*, 9:2 (May 1937), pp. 113–52, on p. 135.

31. Woodress, *A Yankee's Odyssey*, p. 119.

32. Wollstonecraft to William Roscoe, 14 February 1792, in *The Collected Letters of Mary Wollstonecraft*, p. 196.

33. Adams, 'Joel Barlow, Political Romanticist', p. 133.

34. Woodress, *A Yankee's Odyssey*, p. 138.

35. Barlow to Ruth Barlow, 8 July 1796, Joel Barlow Papers, Houghton, series III, item 271.

36. Diary, 25 May–12 September [1788], Joel Barlow Papers, Houghton, series I, item 9.

37. Ibid.

38. Barlow expressed his ideas on economic liberalism most clearly in Part V of the *Advice to the Privileged Orders*, which deals with revenue and expenditure, particularly under conditions of war. Following physiocrats such as Brissot and Clavière, Barlow argued that taxes should not be the end but the means of government and that they should be derived from the productive element, land. Any national 'funding system' should be based on direct taxation of land and free trade. For, at the end of the day, it is 'the spirit of commerce' that is the best guarantor of liberty and man's natural rights.

39. Y. Bizardel, *Les Américains à Paris pendant la révolution* (Paris: Calmann-Lévy, 1972), p. 247.

40. James Monroe to James Madison, 30 June 1795, in *The Papers of James Madison*, gen. ed. W. T. Hutchinson and W. M. E. Rachal, 17 vols (Chicago, IL: University of Chicago Press, 1962–91), vol. 16: 27 April 1795–27 March 1797, ed. J. C. A. Stagg, T. A. Mason and J. K. Sisson, p. 33.
41. Bizardel, *Les Américains à Paris pendant la révolution*, p. 42.
42. J. Swan, *Causes qui se sont opposées aux progrès du commerce entre la France et les États-Unis de l'Amérique, avec les moyens de l'accélérer ... en six lettres adressées à M. le marquis de La Fayette. Traduit sur le manuscrit anglais du colonel Swan ...* (Paris: printed by L. Potier, 1790).
43. On 28 November 1793, Swan wrote a memorandum in response to a question from the commission concerning the possibilities of importing gunpowder, food supplies and other necessaries (Archives Nationales (Paris), F11 292–3; a duplicate copy can be found in F11 223, mémoire 51). Amongst many other goods, Swan assured the members of the commission that his Boston-based company could supply a million quintals of American wheat and flower to the Republic, on condition that the operation could be carried on in secrecy. To support his case, he included a copy of a letter to Gautier at the Ministry of War, in which he alluded to existing business contacts with the Ministry of the Navy. Also on 28 November 1793, Dallarde, Swan & Company sent a memorandum to the Committee for Agriculture and Commerce in which they claim to have already imported more than eighty shiploads of provisions into France and request that in return they be allowed to export luxury goods to Philadelphia (F. Gerbaux and C. Schmidt (eds), *Procès-verbaux des comités d'agriculture et de commerce de la Constituante, de la Législative et de la Convention*, 4 vols (Paris: Imprimerie Nationale, 1906–10), vol. 4, p. 244). On 12 December 1793 Swan addressed a long memorandum to the joint Committees of Public Safety and Finances in which he outlined what goods he could import into France from both neutral and enemy nations; what goods he could export from France; how he would go about executing these transactions; and how payment might be arranged (Archives Nationales (Paris), F11 223, mémoire 1). In a follow-up memorandum he provided details about how the plan might be implemented (ibid., mémoire 2).
44. 'Observations sur le Commerce National', Archives Nationales (Paris), F11 223, mémoire 82.
45. James Swan to the 'Agents de commerce', 10 January 1794, Archives Nationales (Paris), F11 223, no. 60.
46. Ibid., mémoire 51. See also H. C. Rice, 'James Swan: Agent of the French Republic, 1794–1796', *New England Quarterly*, 10:3 (September 1937), pp. 464–86, on pp. 470–1.
47. P. Caron, *La Commission des subsistances de l'an II: procès-verbaux et actes* (Paris: E. Leroux, 1924–5), pp. 658–70.
48. Correspondance Politique, États-Unis supplement, AAE Paris, 23, fol. 156. Imlay and Wollstonecraft knew the Swiss banker Johann Schweizer through his wife, Madeleine, formerly Magdalena Hess, the sister of Martha Hess, who had been the lover of Henry Fuseli, the Swiss painter with whom Wollstonecraft had proposed to start a platonic relationship in late 1792. In September 1794, Wollstonecraft in a letter to Imlay told him that Madeleine Schweizer, who was reading a copy of the German translation of his *Topographical Description* by her side, 'desire[d] [her] to give her love to [him], on account of what [he] [had said] of the negroes' (Wollstonecraft to Imlay, 23 September 1794, in *The Collected Letters of Mary Wollstonecraft*, p. 266).

49. The activities of 'Agence Swan' are documented in papers contained in Correspondance Politique, États-Unis supplement, AAE Paris, 21–4.

50. See Rice, 'James Swan', pp. 472ff. 'Swan & Schweizer' went into administration in January 1796, after France's financial crisis had caused funding for the purchasing agency to dry up. Swan's outstanding claim on the French government for 1 million *livres* was eventually honoured as part of Bonaparte's sale of Louisiana in 1803, when the United States agreed to pay $12 million as well as to assume all claims American citizens had on France.

51. Caron, *La Commission des subsistances de l'an II*, index.

52. Ibid., p. 88, p. 102.

53. Ibid., pp. 662–3.

54. P. Nyström, *Mary Wollstonecraft's Scandinavian Journey*, trans. G. R. Otter, Acta Regiae Societatis Scientiarum et Litterarum Gothoburgensis, Humaniora 17 (Gothenburg: Royal Society of Arts and Sciences, 1980), p. 20. Gouverneur Morris had business dealings with Chalmers & Cowie, and was wined and dined by both Mr Chalmers and Mr Cowie on several occasions (see *A Diary of the French Revolution by Gouverneur Morris, 1752–1816, Minister to France during the Terror*, ed. B. C. Davenport, 2 vols (London: George G. Harrap & Co., 1939).

55. T. Christie, *Letters on the Revolution of France, and on the New Constitution Established by the National Assembly: Occasioned by the Publications of the Right Hon. Edmund Burke, M.P. and Alexander de Calonnne, Late Minister of State* ..., 2 vols (London: J. Johnson, 1791).

9 Blockade Runner and Infamous Lover

1. *The Collected Letters of Mary Wollstonecraft*, p. 277.

2. The most comprehensive accounts of Wollstonecraft's life are J. Todd, *Mary Wollstonecraft: A Revolutionary Life* (London: Weidenfeld & Nicolson, 2000), and Gordon, *Mary Wollstonecraft*. Being biographies of Mary Wollstonecraft, not Gilbert Imlay, these works reflect little original research into Imlay's life, particularly relating to the period before he met Wollstonecraft. As a result, they repeat several inaccuracies and mistakes introduced by previous biographers of Wollstonecraft and add a few new ones of their own.

3. See *The Collected Letters of Mary Wollstonecraft*, p. xiv.

4. Mary Wollstonecraft to William Roscoe, 12 November 1792, in ibid., p. 208.

5. Wollstonecraft had adopted the title 'Mrs' following the publication of *The Rights of Woman* in 1792; unmarried women of around forty would do so to signal that they were no longer on the marriage market.

6. Godwin, *Memoirs of the Author of a Vindication of the Rights of Woman*, p. 98.

7. Wollstonecraft to Imlay, 12 June 1795, in *The Collected Letters of Mary Wollstonecraft*, p. 298.

8. Wollstonecraft to Imlay, 29 December 1794, in ibid., p. 274; Wollstonecraft to Imlay, *c.* 10 October 1795, in ibid., p. 327; Wollstonecraft to Imlay, 10 February 1795, in ibid., p. 283.

9. Wollstonecraft to Imlay, 20 August 1794, in ibid., p. 260. In her *Vindication* Wollstonecraft had argued that women were not artful and devious by nature but that it was educating girls to be weak and passive (as propagated by Rousseau) and the

'frivolous practice of gallantry or vanity of protectorship' that had led to a 'system of cunning and lasciviousness' (*A Vindication of the Rights of Woman*, p. 172). In *Émile*, Rousseau had identified cunning as 'the natural gift' of the ideal woman (J.-J. Rousseau, *Émile; or On Education* (1762), trans. A. Bloom (New York: Basic Books, 1979), p. 334).

10. Godwin, *Memoirs of the Author of a Vindication of the Rights of Woman*, p. 104.
11. Wollstonecraft, *A Vindication of the Rights of Woman*, pp. 40–4. See also Godwin, *Memoirs of the Author of a Vindication of the Rights of Woman*, p. 82.
12. Ibid., pp. 103, 79
13. Ibid., p. 113.
14. Barlow to Ruth Barlow, 19 April 1793, Joel Barlow Papers, Houghton, series III, item 210.
15. Wollstonecraft, *A Vindication of the Rights of Woman*, p. 8.
16. Ibid., p. 342.
17. Barlow to James Watson, 1 October 1792, Joel Barlow Papers, Houghton, series III, item 210.
18. Wollstonecraft to Eliza Wollstonecraft, 13 June 1793, in *The Collected Letters of Mary Wollstonecraft*, pp. 225–6.
19. Wollstonecraft to Imlay, 10 February 1795, in ibid., p. 282.
20. Wollstonecraft to Everina Wollstonecraft, 10 March 1794, in ibid., p. 249. Apparently, Wollstonecraft had been recommending Imlay on several occasions as 'a brother [she] would love and respect' (Wollstonecraft to Everina Wollstonecraft, 20 September 1794, in ibid., p. 262).
21. Playing the Émile card was evidently a routine part of Imlay's self-promotion. Thus, in a letter to Harry Toulmin of 2 February 1793, which Toulmin appended to his *Description of Kentucky* (presumably to boost the sale of the book), Imlay claimed that he had 'lived in the woods half the period of [his] life'. The book's 'editor' similarly claims in his Preface that the Imlay was 'a man who had lived until he was more than five and twenty years old, in the back parts of America', 'except during the period he had served in the army' (*A Description of Kentucky, in North America*, pp. 118, iv).
22. Wollstonecraft to Imlay, 20 August 1794, in *The Collected Letters of Mary Wollstonecraft*, p. 260.
23. Wollstonecraft to Imlay, *c.* August 1793, in ibid., p. 228; Wollstonecraft to Imlay, 19 August 1794, in ibid., p. 258. Cf. her teenage effusion to her friend Jane Arden: 'I am a little singular in my thoughts of love and friendship; I must have the first place or none' (Wollstonecraft to Jane Arden, *c.* mid-late 1773–16 November 1774, in ibid., p. 13).
24. Wollstonecraft to Imlay, 22 September 1794, in ibid., pp. 263–4.
25. Bizardel, *Les Américains à Paris pendant la révolution*, p. 197.
26. Wollstonecraft to Imlay, 22 September 1794, in *The Collected Letters of Mary Wollstonecraft*, p. 264; Wollstonecraft to Imlay, 23 September 1794, in ibid., p. 266.
27. Godwin, *Memoirs of the Author of a Vindication of the Rights of Woman*, p. 108.
28. No record of Imlay's registration of their 'marriage' has survived, and there is no mention among Morris's extensive consular records that he ever saw or was in touch with either Imlay or Wollstonecraft (see Fant, 'A Study of Gilbert Imlay', pp. 149–150, n.). This could suggest that Imlay registered Wollstonecraft at the United States Consulate in Paris, rather than the Legation. However, of the fourteen volumes of Morris's diary, one

- volume five, which would have covered the period 6 January 1793–11 October 1794
– is missing.

29. Wollstonecraft would retain the name of 'Imlay' until she married Godwin in 1797.

30. As was required of all foreigners at the time, Imlay registered with the police at Le Havre, identifying himself as an American 'négociant', the day after his arrival there on 15 brumaire II (5 November 1793). See Police Générale, Déclarations des propriétaires et principaux locataires des étrangers logeant chex eux, 1793, An II (29 septembre 1793–22 nivoise An II [11 January 1794]), Archives Municipals du Havre (Le Havre), Archives Municipales de la Période Révolutionnaire.

31. Barlow and Swan had offices in the same building at 63, rue de la Réunion. A letter from Wollstonecraft to Ruth Barlow confirms that the Swans were on quite familiar terms with both the Barlows and the Imlays (Wollstonecraft to Ruth Barlow, 8 July 1794, in *The Collected Letters of Mary Wollstonecraft*, p. 255).

32. H. M. Williams, *Letters Containing a Sketch of the Politics of France, from the Thirty-First of May 1793, till the Twenty-Eighth of July 1794, and of the Scenes which have Passed in the Prisons of Paris*, 2 vols (London: G. G. and J. Robinson, 1795), vol. 2, p. 155, p. 163.

33. Wollstonecraft to Imlay, *c.* November 1793, in *The Collected Letters of Mary Wollstonecraft*, pp. 232–3.

34. 'I hate commerce', Wollstonecraft wrote in a letter to Imlay on 1 January 1794, in ibid., p. 238.

35. Wollstonecraft to Imlay, 14 January 1794, in ibid., p. 245.

36. Police Générale, Déclarations des propriétaires et principaux locataires des étrangers logeant chex eux, 1793, An II (23 nivoise–12 germ. [12 January–1 April 1794]), Archives Municipals du Havre (Le Havre).

37. État Civil, Naissances, An II (18 nivose–29 fructidor), Archives Municipals du Havre (Le Havre), Archives Municipales de la Période Révolutionnaire. Following France's administrative protocol of double registration of vital statistics (first introduced in 1667), a duplicate copy of Fanny's birth certificate is kept in the Archives départementales. See Notaires, communes, état civil, officiers publics et ministériels, Archives départementales de Seine-Maritime (Rouen), série E

38. Wollstonecraft to Ruth Barlow, 20 May 1794, in *The Collected Letters of Mary Wollstonecraft*, p. 254.

39. Some of the detail in this paragraph is derived from Mary Wollstonecraft's letter to the Danish Prime Minister A. P. Bernstorff, 5 September 1795, Department of Foreign Affairs (1770–1848), Danish National Archives (Copenhagen), Box 893 (1795–1846), Miscellanea, letter I ('Madame Imlays sag 1795–96' ['The case of Madam Imlay']). Further details can be found in Nyström, *Mary Wollstonecraft's Scandinavian Journey*.

40. Wollstonecraft to Ruth Barlow, 27 April 1794, in *The Collected Letters of Mary Wollstonecraft*, p. 251. See also Wollstonecraft to Ruth Barlow, 8 July 1794, in ibid., p. 254.

41. The estimate is by Imlay, in a letter to Elias Backman, 24 October 1794. The sum was first mentioned in Nyström, *Mary Wollstonecraft's Scandinavian Journey*, p. 23. See also p. 24.

42. Using Ellefsen as his front, Imlay made sure his name did not appear in either the deed of purchase for the ship nor in the ship's Danish papers. See ibid., pp. 22–3.

43. According to Nyström, Ellefsen told the Danish Consulate that the *Maria and Margaretha* was bound for Copenhagen (ibid., p. 22). Other sources suggest that Elsinore was the official destination.

44. See Clauder, 'American Commerce as Affected by the Wars of the French Revolution and Napoleon', p. 56.

45. Mary Wollstonecraft to Danish Prime Minister A. P. Bernstorff, 5 September 1795, Department of Foreign Affairs (1770–1848), Danish National Archives (Copenhagen), Box 893 (1795–1846), Miscellanea, letter I ('Madame Imlays sag 1795–96' ['The case of Madam Imlay'], p. 2. Letter of instruction from Gilbert Imlay to Peder Ellefsen, 13 August 1794, Town Magistrate, Notary Protocol 8 (1794–1804), fols 131a, 131b.

46. Nyström, *Mary Wollstonecraft's Scandinavian Journey*, p. 24.

47. Letter of recommendation from Francis Delamotte to Elias Backman, 13 August 1794, Town Magistrate, Notary Protocol 8 (1794–1804), Statsarkivet i Kristiansand, Kristiansand byrett, Notarialprotokoll 8 (1792–1804), fol. 100 ('Havre 26 Thermidor År 2'), Kristiansand Provincial Archives (Norway), published by the Chief of Police, Sorensen. The letter is a translation into Norwegian of an original in either French or English.

48. Delamotte was used to diplomatic ruses and international intrigue. Thomas Jefferson, who was Secretary of State in the first administration of George Washington until his resignation on 31 December 1793, used to send his secret messages to Gouverneur Morris in Paris via Delamotte, as opposed to his regular letters, which went via the English packet (*A Dairy of the French Revolution by Gouverneur Morris*, vol. 2, p. 399).

49. This method of 'neutralizing' a ship and its cargo was standard practice in James Swan's agency and is described in detail in his December 1793 Memorandum to Joint Committee of Public Safety and Finances. No ship would leave France carrying a purchase order that might reveal what the real destination of the cargo was. The bills of lading of vessels sailing from French ports would typically be dated 'London' and would be signed by a person who was personally known to the company's agent in Hamburg, who would act in accordance with instructions he had previously received from Swan. All correspondence would be couched in such terms that, even if a letter were to be opened, it could in no way compromise the ship's cargo. In addition, a system of coded place-names would be used in all correspondence (the code name for Le Havre was 'Falmouth'; 'St Sebastian' was in fact Brest). Swan's memorandum also confirms that the company's agents in the various European ports had been instructed to maintain close relations with the consuls and other public officers of America, Spain, The Netherlands and France and to seek their assistance and protection whenever necessary. It is almost certain that Delamotte was in cahoots with Swan's agents at Le Havre. See Archives Nationales (Paris), F11 223, mémoire 1.

50. Gordon, *Mary Wollstonecraft*, pp. 235–6.

51. See ibid., p. 233.

52. P. Verlet, *Le mobilier royal française*, 4 vols (Paris: Librarie Plon), vol. 3, p. 89.

53. Correspondance Politique, États-Unis supplement, AAE Paris, 23.

54. Elias Backman to the Swedish Regent, Duke Carl, 15 March 1794, Biographica, 'Backman', Swedish National Archives (Gothenburg), microfiche card E012194/7. See also Nyström, *Mary Wollstonecraft's Scandinavian Journey*, p. 30.

55. Ibid., p. 30.

56. Wollstonecraft, *Letters Written during a Short Residence in Sweden, Norway, and Denmark*, pp. 249, 250.

57. Ibid., p. 251.

58. Ibid., p. 260.

59. G. I. Gallop, 'Politics, Property and Progress: British Radical Thought, 1760–1815' (D.Phil. thesis, Oxford University, 1983), p. 144.

60. Ibid., pp. 22, 23.

61. Ibid., p. 24.

62. T. Paine, *Rights of Man. Part the Second. Combining Principle and Practice* (London: J. S. Jordan, 1792), p. 82.

63. M. Durey, 'Thomas Paine's Apostles: Radical Emigrés and the Triumph of Jeffersonian Republicanism', *William and Mary Quarterly*, 3rd series, 44:4 (October 1987), pp. 661–88, on pp. 679, 680. There was considerable overlap between radical 'commission commerce' and the more mainstream Whig economic order of 'progressive commercialization'. Thus, the economist and cleric Josiah Tucker, Dean of Gloucester and later of Bristol, argued that commerce was perfectly compatible with God's providential plan. A man well-read in the writings of Francis Hutcheson and other Scottish intellectuals, Tucker sought to link spiritual and economic activities of working men *and* women in what he called a 'System of universal Commerce', thus making 'Self-Interest and Social coincide' (see J. Tucker, 'On the Connection and Mutual Relation between, Christian Morality, Good Government, and National Commerce' (1774), cited in K. Sutherland, 'Hannah More's Counter-Revolutionary Feminism', in K. Everest (ed.), *Revolution in Writing: British Literary Responses to the French Revolution* (Milton Keynes and Philadelphia: Open University Press, 1991), pp. 27–63, on p. 57).

64. Wollstonecraft to Ruth Barlow, 8 July 1794, in *The Collected Letters of Mary Wollstonecraft*, p. 255.

65. Wollstonecraft to Imlay, *c.* March 1794, in ibid., p. 250 (italics added).

66. Wollstonecraft to Ruth Barlow, 27 April 1794, in ibid., p. 251 (italics added).

67. Wollstonecraft to Ruth Barlow, 20 April 1794, postscript, in ibid., p. 254 (italics added).

68. Wollstonecraft to Ruth Barlow, 8 July 1794, in ibid., p. 254.

69. Wollstonecraft to Imlay, 22 September 1794, in ibid., p. 263.

70. Wollstonecraft to Imlay, 20 August 1794, in ibid., p. 259.

71. Barlow was writing to Ruth from Altona on 12, 22 and 29 August (with further letters to her on 17, 18 and 19 August from an unspecified location, presumably also Altona). See Joel Barlow Papers, Houghton, series III, items 215, 219, 220. Wollstonecraft had never taken to Barlow. When she first met him she thought he had a 'very benevolent, affectionate heart, and tolerable understanding', but upon further acquaintance she decided that he was 'a worthy man, but devoured by ambition' (Wollstonecraft to Everina Wollstonecraft, 20 June 1792, in *The Collected Letters of Mary Wollstonecraft*, p. 200; Wollstonecraft to Everina Wollstonecraft, 14 September 1792, in ibid., p. 203). She felt he was too rational and calculating, and totally obsessed with making a name for himself as well as a large fortune.

72. Wollstonecraft to Ruth Barlow, 20 May 1794, in ibid., p. 253.

73. Ruth Barlow to Joel Barlow, 14 January 1796, Joel Barlow Papers, Houghton, series IV, item 543.

74. Wollstonecraft to Imlay, 28 September 1794, in *The Collected Letters of Mary Wollstonecraft*, p. 267.

75. Wollstonecraft to Imlay, 22 September 1794, in ibid., p. 264; Wollstonecraft to Imlay, 23 September 1794, in ibid., p. 265; before she had spoken of his 'money-getting face' (Wollstonecraft to Imlay, *c.* November 1793, in ibid., p. 234); Wollstonecraft to Imlay, 22 September 1794, p. 264.

76. Wollstonecraft to Imlay, 28 September 1794, in ibid., p. 268.

77. Wollstonecraft to Imlay, 28 December 1794, in ibid., p. 272.

78. Wollstonecraft to Imlay, 9 February 1795, in ibid., p. 281.

79. Wollstonecraft to Imlay, 10 February 1795, in ibid., p. 282.

80. Wollstonecraft to Imlay, 19 February 1795, in ibid., p. 285.

81. Godwin, *Memoirs of the Author of a Vindication of the Rights of Woman*, p. 119.

82. Wollstonecraft to Imlay, 28 December 1794, in *The Collected Letters of Mary Woll-stonecraft*, p. 272.

83. Wollstonecraft to Imlay, 29 December 1794, in ibid., p. 274; Wollstonecraft to Imlay, 9 January 1795, in ibid., p. 277.

84. Wollstonecraft to Imlay, 22 September 1794, in ibid., p. 264.

85. Wollstonecraft to Imlay, 19 February 1794, in ibid., p. 284.

86. En route to London Wollstonecraft stopped at Le Havre. According to her registration with the police, she had received her passport in Paris on 30 March and had arrived in Le Havre on 5 April, where she stayed at the Maison Poulet (Police Générale, Déclarations des propriétaires et principaux locataires des étrangers logeant chex eux, An III (9 germ.–30 mess. [29 March–18 July 1795]), Archives Municipals du Havre (Le Havre), Archives Municipales de la Période Révolutionnaire.

87. Godwin, *Memoirs of the Author of a Vindication of the Rights of Woman*, p. 127.

88. Wollstonecraft to Imlay, 22 March 1795, in *The Collected Letters of Mary Wollstonecraft*, p. 292.

89. Godwin, *Memoirs of the Author of a Vindication of the Rights of Woman*, p. 128.

90. Ibid.

91. Abinger Collection, Bodleian Library (Oxford), Dep.b.210/4.

92. Gothenburg Regional Archives ('Landsarkivet', Gothenburg, Sweden).

93. Backman paid 1,210 *kroner* (around £250) for the ship; the repairs cost 3,202 *kroner* (Kommerskollegium Huvudarkivet 1795 F IIb, Riksarkivet (Stockholm).

94. Wollstonecraft to Imlay, 1 July 1795, in *The Collected Letters of Mary Wollstonecraft*, p. 308; Wollstonecraft to Imlay, 27 September 1795, in ibid., p. 322.

95. Wollstonecraft to Imlay, 1 July 1795, in ibid., p. 308.

96. Wollstonecraft, *Letters Written during a Short Residence in Sweden, Norway, and Denmark*, p. 259.

97. Ibid., p. 254. Where and when Imlay and Crèvecoeur got acquainted has not been established. It may have been in America, or in Paris, or possibly at Le Havre.

98. Ibid.

99. Wollstonecraft to Imlay, 6 September 1795, in *The Collected Letters of Mary Woll-stonecraft*, p. 320; Wollstonecraft to Imlay, 27 September 1795, in ibid., p. 322.

100. Wollstonecraft to Imlay, *c.* December 1795, in ibid., p. 335.

101. Wollstonecraft, *Letters Written during a Short Residence in Sweden, Norway, and Denmark*, p. 261.

102. Wollstonecraft to Imlay, 4 October 1795, in *The Collected Letters of Mary Wollstonecraft*, p. 324.

103. Wollstonecraft to Imlay, *c.* October 1795, in ibid., pp. 327–8.

104. Wollstonecraft to Imlay, *c.* November 1795, in ibid., p. 330.

105. Wollstonecraft to Imlay, 27 November 1795, in ibid., pp. 332–3.

106. Wollstonecraft to Imlay, *c.* December 1795, in ibid., p. 336.

107. Wollstonecraft to Imlay, *c.* December 1795, in ibid., p. 335.

108. Wollstonecraft to Imlay, *c.* March 1796, in ibid., p. 339.

109. Ibid.

Epilogue

1. H. Melville, 'Bartleby, the Scrivener: A Tale of Wall Street', in H. Melville, *Billy Budd and Other Stories* (Harmondsworth, Middlesex: Penguin Books, 1967), p. 59.
2. Godwin, *Memoirs of the Author of a Vindication of the Rights of Woman*, p. 145.
3. Thomas Rogers to Lyman C. Draper, 3 September 1847, Draper MSS, 10J1201.
4. Clark Family Paper, 1776–1931, Rutgers University Library (New Brunswick, NJ).
5. Gordon, *Mary Wollstonecraft*, p. 382.
6. On 19 November 1810 the Court of Appeals of the State of Kentucky registered a new deed by which Henry ('Light-Horse Harry') Lee, acting as Imlay's pro forma attorney, reconveyed to Francis Lee four tracts comprising 3,400 acres of land which had been patented to Imlay in July and November 1786 and which he had originally sold by deed to Arthur Lee – Francis Lee's brother – in May 1787 (again through Lee's mediation). That deed having been lost, Francis Lee had asked Henry Lee to execute a new deed, and it was that deed that the Supreme Court acknowledged on 19 November 1810. See Chapter 3 for details. Gordon also claims that Imlay was selling land on 27 December 1789 and in 1791 (ibid., p. 198); in fact, he had sold all the land he ever owned in Kentucky several years before and these late 'sales' were merely part of Henry Lee's attempts to sort out some of the legal entanglements caused by Imlay's convoluted transactions. Lee acted on his own accord and there is no hint anywhere that he and Imlay were ever in touch after early 1787.
7. Ibid., p. 193.
8. Imlay and Imlay, *The Imlay Family*, p. 188. Basically a family memoir, *The Imlay Family* contains much information that is plainly incorrect and the book is therefore not a reliable source for details on Gilbert Imlay.
9. Gordon, *Mary Wollstonecraft*, p. 194, n.
10. Ibid., pp. 215–16, 243.
11. On 4 April 1781 John Imlay wrote to senior Congressman John Witherspoon that he had received intelligence from New York that 'another Expedition was preparing at N. York' under the command of General Clinton and that its aim was to take the Delaware Bay. Imlay must have been a long-standing and trusted source, for Witherspoon immediately passed the information on the 'President of Congress', Samuel Huntington (formally, at this point, the 'President of the United States in Congress Assembled'), and to the 'President of the State' (governor), William Livingston. See John Witherspoon to William Livingston, 5 April 1781, *Letters of Delegates to Congress*, ed. Smith et al., vol. 17, pp. 133–4.
12. Conway, *The Life of Thomas Paine*, vol. 2, p. 64. See also Rickman, *The Life of Thomas Paine*, p. 129.
13. Cutting knew many of the people Imlay had dealings with at Le Havre: he was well acquainted with Francis DelaMotte, and did business with John Wheatcroft, James Swan and Samuel Blackden (Nathaniel Cutting Journal and Letterbooks, 1786–1798, Massachusetts Historical Society (Boston, MA), *passim*).
14. Gordon, *Mary Wollstonecraft*, pp. 198, 241–2.
15. See A. P. Whitaker, 'Harry Innes and the Spanish Intrigue: 1794–1795', *Mississippi Valley Historical Review*, 15:2 (September 1928), pp. 236–48.
16. Gordon, *Mary Wollstonecraft*, p. 417.
17. Adams, 'Joel Barlow, Political Romanticist', p. 141.
18. Barlow to Ruth Barlow, 8 July 1796, Joel Barlow Papers, Houghton, series III, item 276.

19. Wollstonecraft to Eliza Bishop, *c.* 23 April 1795, in *The Collected Letters of Mary Wollstonecraft*, p. 290; see also, Wollstonecraft to Everina Wollstonecraft, 27 April 1795, in ibid., p. 292.

20. Wollstonecraft to Imlay, 8 December 1795, in ibid., p. 335.

21. Wollstonecraft to Everina Wollstonecraft, 22 March 1797, in ibid., p. 403.

22. William Godwin to Cowie, 2 April 1798, Abinger Collection, Bodleian Library (Oxford), Dep.b.227/8.

23. Gordon claims that the £1,000 'must have come from the silver ship, since this was the only Imlay venture in which Mary took part' (*Mary Wollstonecraft*, p. 286), yet she offers no evidence to support his claim. Surely, the one cargo Imlay would never have signed away unseen and uninspected would have been the silver from the *Maria and Margaretha*.

24. Wollstonecraft to Imlay, 26 August 1795, in *The Collected Letters of Mary Wollstonecraft*, p. 319.

25. Imlay to Joseph Johnson, forwarded by the latter to William Godwin, 22 April 1798, Abinger Collection, Bodleian Library (Oxford), Dep.b.229/(b).

26. Morel v. Imlay, Court of King's Bench, Plea Side – Plea Rolls or 'Judgment Rolls', NA, KB 122: Roll 494. Morel upholstery business in Great Marlborough Street is listed in *The Post Office Annual Directory for the Year 1803* as well as in *Holden's Triennial Directory for the Years 1802, 1803 and 1804*.

27. Eldred v. Imlay, Court of King's Bench, Plea Side – Plea Rolls or 'Judgment Rolls', NA, KB 122, Rolls 702–4.

28. Imlay may have had dealings with Christie's company while he was still in France. On 20 September 1794, Mary Wollstonecraft wrote a letter to her sister Everina, c/o 'M. J. Moore & Co., Finsbury Square, London' (Everina may have worked for Moore & Co.). The letter was carried by Imlay, who was on his way to London. M. J. Moore was Rebecca Christie's grandfather.

29. Imlay v. George James, 10 February 1798, Court of Chancery, Six Clerks Office: Pleadings 1758 to 1800, NA, C12/2188/14; James v. Imlay, 5 March 1798, Court of King's Bench, Plea Side – Entry Books of Judgments, NA, Ind. 9666.

30. Wilkinson and Rame v. Imlay, Sherieff, et al., Court of King's Bench, Plea Side – Entry Books of Judgments, NA, Ind. 9669.

31. Sherieff et al. v. Imlay, Court of King's Bench, Plea Side – Docket Books, NA, no. 6295.

32. Records of Sun Fire Office, Guildhall Library (London), MS 11936/459/867077. In a way, Imlay was again involved in wartime trade. In the early nineteenth century colouring was used in the production of porter, a strong beer that derived its dark colour from the use of brown malt. When the malt tax was successively increased to help pay for the Napoleonic Wars, brewers looked for ways to produce a dark beer but use less malt. The solution was to use a proportion of pale malt and add colouring to obtain the desired hue. There were various ways of producing beer colouring. Some brewers used a small amount of highly roasted malt that had been darkened to the point of being scorched and burnt; others would dissolve burnt brown sugar in water; another method was to evaporate wort until what remained had the colour and consistency of treacle. Imlay cannot have had much business after 1816, when a law was passed allowing only malt and hops to be used in the production of beer.

33. Wollstonecraft to Imlay, 1 July 1795, in *The Collected Letters of Mary Wollstonecraft*, p. 308.

34. The Barlows had returned to Paris in July. On 28 June Ruth wrote to her brother: 'We leave this country in about a fortnight for France. Mr. B. has some affairs to settle there, and they should not detain him too long, we intend sailing [for home] in September, but France always [has] something fascinating to the dear Man, and I much fear he will stay until the season shall be too far advanced to make the passage' (Ruth Barlow to Abraham Barlow, 28 June 1795, Baldwin Family Papers, 1779–1886, Henry E. Huntington Library and Art Gallery (San Marino, CA)).

35. Wollstonecraft to Imlay, 9 August 1795, in *The Collected Letters of Mary Wollstonecraft*, p. 318.

36. Abinger Collection, Bodleian Library (Oxford), Dep.b.210/4.

37. Wollstonecraft to Imlay, 8 December 1795, in *The Collected Letters of Mary Wollstonecraft*, p. 335.

38. Memoranda [v.p., 1795–1796], Joel Barlow Papers, Houghton, series I, item 7. Gordon mistook the middle long 's' in 'cases' for an 'f', and concluded somewhat bizarrely that 'Imlay had marked out seven Parisian cafés', wondering, 'For what purpose?' Indeed. Of course, it would all make sense, Gordon muses, 'were [Imlay] part of a new secret service, run by the President himself' (Gordon, *Mary Wollstonecraft*, pp. 307, 308).

39. 'Observations sur le Commerce National', Archives Nationales (Paris), F11 223, mémoire 82.

40. The following records at the Jersey Archive were searched but yielded no reference to Imlay: Probate Records, Wills and Testaments; Almanacs; PRIDE database (containing records of house ownership going back two hundred years); rates lists; General Don's Military census 1806; General Don's Military census 1815; Sinnatts records (containing details of the deaths of certain people); Cour du Decret (registers concerning bankruptcy); Cour d'Heritage (registers concerning real property and ownership); Cour du Billets (registers concerning debts and promissory notes); Poursuites Criminelles (registers concerning crimes committed); Cour du Samedi (registers concerning debts).

41. Table du S. A. Medi CLVII, Records of the Royal Court, Greffe's Office, Jersey Archive (St Helier, Jersey), no. 4, 1818–1829.

42. R. Garnett, 'Gilbert Imlay', *Athenaeum*, 3955 (15 August 1903), pp. 219–20, on p. 219.

43. Enterremens de St Brelade Depuis Janvier 1825, Church Records, Jersey Archive (St Helier, Isle of Jersey), fol. 5.

44. Garnett, 'Gilbert Imlay', p. 219.

BIBLIOGRAPHY

Manuscripts

Abraham Lincoln Presidential Library, formerly Illinois State Historical Library (Springfield, IL)
Pierre Menard Papers, 1741–1910
Barthélemi Tardiveau Papers

Allentown-Upper Freehold Historical Society (Allentown, NJ)
Charles R. Hutchinson Papers (microfilm)

Archives départementales de Seine-Maritime (Rouen)
Notaires, communes, état civil, officiers publics et ministériels

Archives des Affaires Étrangères (Paris)
Correspondance Politique
Espagne
États-Unis supplément, 21–24
États-Unis, Louisiane et Florides, 1792–1803

Archives Canada of Canada (Ottawa)
Colonial Office Records, Series Q, Vol. XLI, p. 283, No. 107; XLII, p. 13, No. 112

Archives Diplomatiques (Nantes)
Actes notariés (Notarised deeds)
Archives des postes diplomatiques, consulaires, culturels et de coopération
État civil (Public Records)

Archives Municipals du Havre (Le Havre), Archives Municipales de la Période Révolutionnaire
Commerce et Industrie, Marchandises anglaises, An II
État Civil, Naissances, An II (18 nivose–29 fructidor)
Police Générale. Déclarations des propriétaires et principaux locataires des étrangers logeant chez eux, 22 nivose An II–30 messidor An III

Archives Nationales (Paris)
F^{11}, 223, Memoranda 1, 2, 51, 60, 82

Archivo General de Indias (Seville)
Archivo de la Capitanía General de Cuba (Florida y Luisiana), Papeles de Cuba (1770–1834), Legajos 1400–1699

Archivo Histórico-Nacional (Madrid)
    Papeles de Estado
    Papeles relativos á la Lusiana

Beinecke Rare Book and Manuscript Library, Yale University (New Haven, CT)
    Barlow Papers, Yale Collection of American Literature
    Gen. MSS Misc., group 2444 F–1
    James Wilkinson Letters to Esteban Miró and Related Documents, 1788–1793

Bodleian Library (Oxford)
    Abinger Collection

British Library

Butler Rare Books and Manuscript Library, Columbia University (New York)
    Gouverneur Morris Papers, 1768–1816

Chicago Historical Society (Chicago, IL)
    The James Wilkinson Collection, 1779–1823

Cincinnati Historical Society (Cincinnati, OH)
    Gallipolis Papers

Danish National Archives (Copenhagen)
    Department of Foreign Affairs (1770–1848), Box 893 (1795–1846), Miscellanea, letter
    I ('Madame Imlays sag 1795–96' ['The case of Madam Imlay']

David Library of the American Revolution (Washington Crossing, PA)
    Compiled Service Records of Soldiers who served in the American Army during the Revolu-
    tionary War, Record Group 93, Reel 65

Filson Historical Society (Louisville, KY)
    Beall-Booth Family Papers
    Bibb Family Papers, 1760–1887
    Gorin Family Papers
    Isaac Hite Family Papers
    The Political Club Records, 1786–1790

Gothenburg Regional Archives ('Landsarkivet', Gothenburg, Sweden)

Guildhall Library (London)
    Records of Sun Fire Office

G. W. Blunt White Library, Mystic Seaport Museum (Mystic, CT)
    Silas Talbot Papers

Houghton Library, Harvard University (Cambridge, MA)
    Arthur Lee Papers
    Christophe Daniel Ebeling Papers
    Joel Barlow Papers

Henry E. Huntington Library and Art Gallery (San Marino, CA)
    Baldwin Family Papers, 1779–1886
    Collection of Correspondence of Nathanael Greene, 1775–1786
    Papers of William Sullivan, 1795–1822

Jefferson County Circuit Clerk's Office (Louisville, KY)

County Court
    Minute Books, 1781–1794
    Deed Books, 1783–1806
    Entry Books
    Order Book, 1784–1785
    Will Books 1784–1846
Old Chancery Court
    Bond and Power of Attorney Books, 1783–1805

Jersey Archive (St Helier, Jersey)
    Almanacs
    Cemetery Details, St Brelade's Church
    Church Records, Burial register for the parish church of St Brelade
    Cour du Billets (registers concerning debts and promissory notes)
    Cour du Decret (registers concerning bankruptcy)
    Cour d'Heritage (registers concerning real property and ownership)
    Cour du Samedi (registers concerning debts)
    General Don's Military census 1806
    General Don's Military census 1815
    Poursuites Criminelles (registers concerning crimes committed)
    PRIDE database (contains records of house ownership going back 200 years)
    Probate Records (registers wills and testaments), Judicial Greffe, 1660–1948
    Royal Court Records, *Table du S. A. Medi* CLVII, Greffe's Office, No. 4 (1818 à 1829)
    Rates lists
    Sinnatts records (contains details of the deaths of certain people)

John Carter Brown Library (Providence, RI)
    A Map of Part of the State of Kentucky
    A Plan of the Township of Franklinville

Kentucky Historical Society, Special Collections and Archives Library (Frankfort, KY)
    John Floyd, Land List, 1783
    Harry Innes, Letter to John Brown, 7 December 1787
    James Wilkinson Letters

Kentucky Land Office (Frankfort, KY)
    Jefferson County Entries, Book A
    Fayette County Entries
    Warrants, Surveys and Patents

Kentucky State Archives, Kentucky Department for Library and Archives (Frankfort, KY)
    Supreme Court Deed Books
    Supreme Court Rule Docket Books, 1785–1792
    Supreme Court Docket Book, 1785–1786
    Supreme Court Order Books, 1787–1792
    Court of Appeals Deed Books

Kristiansand Provincial Archives ('Statsarkivet', Kristiansand, Norway)
    Testimony of crew *Marie and Margaretha*
    Letter from Imlay to Elias Backman from Le Havre

Letter of instruction from Gilbert Imlay to Peder Ellefsen, 13 August 1794, Town Magistrate, Notary Protocol 8 (1794–1804), fols 131a, 131b
Letter of recommendation from Francis Delamotte to Elie Backman, 13 August 1794, Town Magistrate, Notary Protocol 8 (1794–1804), fol. 100b

Library of Congress (Washington, DC)
George Washington Papers, 1741–1799
Harry Innes Papers, 1752–1900
James Wilkinson Papers, 1780–1824
John Fitch Papers, 1764–1963
John Fitch Papers, 1783–1854
Patrick Henry Papers, 1776–1818
Robert Morris Papers

Library of Virginia (Richmond, VA)
Harry Innes Papers, 1772–1850
Virginia Land Office Grants

Lincoln Museum (Fort Wayne, IN)
Helm-Haycraft Collection

Louisiana State University Libraries
James Brown Papers 1764–1829

Maryland Historical Society (Baltimore, MD)
Thomas Rutland Letter Books

Massachusetts Historical Society (Boston, MA)
Nathaniel Cutting Journal and Letterbooks, 1786–1798

Meirs, Leslie V. (Flemington, NJ)
Bruere Imlay Family Papers. Formerly in possession of Mrs Elizabeth (Bruere) Imlay (1881)

Missouri Historical Society (St Louis, MO)
Clark Family Collection, 1766–1991
George Rogers Clark Papers, Box 3–5
William Clark Papers, Box 11
Clemens Family Collection, 1737–1954, Jeremiah Clemens Papers
James Wilkinson Collection, 1788–1932

Monmouth County Archives (County Clerk's Office, Manalapan, NJ)
Common Pleas, Loose Papers, 1726–1927
Common Pleas, Minute Books, 1735–1943
Deeds, 1722–1947
Deed Books, 1669–1955
Insolvent Debtors, 1755–1898
Minutes of Monmouth County, 1688–1721
Quarter Sessions, Minute Books, 1667–1948

Monmouth County Historical Association (Freehold, NJ)
Charles R. Hutchinson Papers (microfilm)
Philip Freneau Papers, 1661–1939

National Archives (formerly Public Record Office, Kew, UK)
Colonial Office Papers
Court of Chancery
Court of King's Bench
Customs Papers
East Florida Papers, East Florida Claims Commission: Papers and Reports
Foreign Office Papers
Treasury Papers
War Office Papers

National Archives and Records Administration (Washington, DC)
Compiled Military Service Records of Soldiers who Served in the American Army during the Revolutionary War
Revolutionary War MSS

National Archives of Sweden ('Riksarkivet', Stockholm)
Elias Backman to Duke Carl, 15 March 1794, Biographica, 'Backman', microfiche E01219 4/7
Kommerskollegium, Huvudarkivet 1795 F IIb

Nelson County Circuit Clerk's Office (Bardstown, KY)
Chancery Court, Deed Books
Chancery Decrees, 1798–1800
Court of Quarter Sessions, Minute Books, Book 1
District and Supreme Court Documents
Nelson County, Deed Books, 7A and 7B
Miscellaneous Papers, unnumbered and uncatalogued, Research Box EEEEE
Original Deeds, unnumbered and uncatalogued

Newberry Library (Chicago, IL)
Edward E. Ayer Manuscript Collection

New Jersey Historical Society (Newark, NJ)
Charles R. Hutchinson Collection, 1788–1922
Miscellaneous Manuscripts, 1664–1956
Montgomery-Burnet Family Papers

New Jersey State Archives (Trenton, NJ)
County Records, 1667–1997
East Jersey Deeds
Federal Records, 1791–1998
Judiciary, 1704–1993
Legislature, 1703–1993
Marriage Bonds and Licenses, I, 1711–1795
Monmouth County Court, Common Pleas, Loose Papers 1757–1758
Monmouth County Wills, 1751–1756; 1761–1763
Municipal Records, 1692–1997
New Jersey Council of Safety, Loose Papers, 1776–1781
New Jersey Council of Safety Minutes, March 1777–October 1778
New Jersey Council of Safety Records, Oaths of Allegiance and Abjuration, and Performance Bonds, 1776–1783

New Jersey Supreme Court Records
  Newspapers, 1771–2001
  Records of the Council of Proprietors of the Western Division of New Jersey
  West Jersey Deeds
  Wills and Inventories, *c.* 1670–1900

New Jersey State Library (Trenton, NJ)
  Archives and History Bureau

New Orleans Public Library
  City Archives, Miscellaneous Record Book of New Orleans, 1760–1830

New York Public Library
  Carl H. Pforzheimer Collection of Shelley and His Circle
  Circulars, American Agency, London
  Emmet Collection
  James Wilkinson Papers
  Joel Barlow Papers

Philadelphia City Archives
  Deed Books, 1777–1799

P. K. Yonge Library of Florida History, University of Florida (Gainesville, FL)
  East Florida Papers, 1784–1821

Princeton University Library, Rare Books and Special Collections (Princeton, NJ)
  Blair-Lee Family Papers, Papers of Samuel Phillips Lee

Rhode Island Historical Society (Providence, Rhode Island)
  Aaron Lopez Collection
  Benjamin Talbot Papers
  Rowland and Mary Hazard Papers
  Ship's Logs Collection
  Silas Talbot Papers

Rutgers University Library (New Brunswick, NJ)
  Clark Family Paper, 1776–1931
  Neilson Family Papers, 1768–1908
  Philip Freneau Papers

South Carolina Department of Archives and History (Columbia, SC)
  South Carolina Judgment Rolls

South Carolina Historical Society (Charleston, SC)
  Columbian Herald
  Ravenel Family Papers, 1695–1925, Secretary of State Daybook, 1788–1789

University of Virginia (Charlottesville)
  Lee Family Papers

Virginia Historical Society (Richmond, VA)
  Henry Banks Papers, 1781–1817
  Hugh Blair Grigsby Papers, 1745–1944
  Lee Family Papers
  Virginia Supreme Court, District of Kentucky, Order Books (1783–1792), Books A, D, F

William L. Clements Library, University of Michigan (Ann Arbor, MI)
Thomas Rutland Letter Book, 1787–1789

Wisconsin Historical Society (Madison, WI)
Draper Manuscript Collection
Daniel Boone Papers
George Rogers Clark Papers
William Clark Papers
Simon Kenton Papers
Kentucky Papers

Newspapers and Periodicals

American Museum; or, Universal Magazine (Philadelphia)

American Watchman and Delaware Republican (Wilmington)

Analytical Review (London)

British Critic, A New Review (London)

Charleston Evening Gazette

Charleston Morning Post, and Daily Advertiser

Columbian Herald, or The Independent Courier of North-America (South Carolina)

Commentator (Frankfort, KY)

Courier Journal (Louisville)

Critical Review; or, Annals of Literature (London)

English Review (London)

European Magazine (London)

Literary Magazine and British Review (London)

London Chronicle

Magazine of American History

Monthly Review; or Literary Journal (London)

Morning Chronicle

New American Magazine (Perth Amboy)

New Jersey Gazette (Burlington)

New Jersey Journal, and Political Intelligencer (Elizabeth Town)

New York Magazine; or, Literary Repository

New-York Weekly Museum

Pennsylvania Gazette (Philadelphia)

Philadelphia Monthly Magazine; or, Universal Repository of Knowledge and Entertainment

Poulson's American Daily Advertiser (Philadelphia)

Rivington's New-York Gazetteer

St James's Chronicle (London)

Saturday Evening Post (Philadelphia)

Universal Asylum and Columbian Magazine (Philadelphia)

Bibliographical Sources

Andrews, C. M., *Guide to the Materials for American History to 1783 and the Public Record Office of Great Britain*, 2 vols (Washington, DC: Carnegie Institution of Washington, 1912–14).

Andrews, C. M., and F. G. Davenport, *Guide to the Manuscript Materials for the History of the United States to 1783, in the British Museum, in minor London Archives, and in the Libraries of Oxford and Cambridge* (Washington, DC: Carnegie Institution of Washington, 1908).

Atkins. P. J., *The Directories of London, 1677–1977* (London: Mansell, 1990).

Boyle's City and Commercial Companion to the Court Guide (London: P. Boyle, 1802, 1804, 1818).

Boyle's City Companion to the Court Guide (London: P. Boyle, 1798, 1800).

Boyle's City Guide or Commercial Directory (London: P. Boyle, 1797).

Brookes-Smith, J., *Index for Old Kentucky Surveys & Grants* (Frankfort, KY: Kentucky Historical Society, 1975).

Calendar of New Jersey Wills, Vols I–IX (1730–1800), in *Documents Relating to the Colonial, Revolutionary and Post-Revolutionary History of the State of New Jersey* [various titles, commonly called the *New Jersey Archives*], vols 23, 30, 32–8, Archives of the State of New Jersey, 1st series, 42 vols (Newark and Paterson: various publishers, 1901, 1918, 1924–44).

Documents Relating to the Colonial History of the State of New Jersey, 2nd series, vol. 2, ed. F. B. Lee (Trenton, NJ: John L. Murphy Publishing Co., 1903).

The Filson Club Compilation of Jefferson County, Virginia/Kentucky Early Marriages, Book 1 (1781–July, 1826) (Louisville, KY: Filson Historical Society, 1941).

Garside, P., J. Raven and R. Schöwerling (gen. eds), *The English Novel 1770–1829: A Bibliographical Survey of Prose Fiction Published in the British Isles*, 2 vols (Oxford: Oxford University Press, 2000).

Harper, J. L. (ed.), *Guide to the Draper Collection* (Madison, WI: State Historical Society of Wisconsin, 1983).

Hill, R. R., *Descriptive Catalogue of the Documents relating to the History of the United States in the Papeles de Cuba, deposited in the Archivo General de Indias at Seville* (Washington, DC: Carnegie Institution of Washington, 1916).

Holden's Triennial Directory (London: W. Holden, 1799–1800, 1802–4, 1805–7, 1809–11).

Holden's Triennial Directory, Supplement (London: W. Holden, 1808).

Jillson, W. R. (ed.), *Old Kentucky Entries and Deeds: A Complete Index to all of the Earliest Land Entries, Military Warrants, Deeds and Wills of the Commonwealth of Kentucky* (1926; Baltimore, MD: Genealogical Publishing Co., 1969).

—, *The Kentucky Land Grants: A Systematic Index to all of the Land Grants Recorded in the State Land Office at Frankfort, Kentucky, 1782–1924*, 2 vols (1925; Baltimore, MD: Genealogical Publishing Co., 1971).

Johnstone's London Commercial Guide and Street Directory (London: D. Johnstone, 1817).

Leland, W. G., *Guide to Materials for American History in the Libraries and Archives of Paris*, 2 vols (Washington, DC: Carnegie Institution of Washington, 1932–43).

Kent's Directory For the Year (London: Kent, 1778–99, 1800–28).

Lowndes's London Directory (London: T. and W. Lowndes, 1783–99).

McDowell, S. (ed.), *Calendar of the George Rogers Clark Papers of the Draper Collection of Manuscripts* (Utica, KY: McDowell Publications, 1985).

Marriage Records, 1665–1800: Documents Relating to the Colonial History of the State of New Jersey 1st series, vol. 22, ed. W. Nelson (Paterson, NJ: Press Printing and Publishing Co., 1900).

Parker, D. W., *Guide to Materials for United States History of Canadian Archives* (Washington, DC: Carnegie Institution of Washington, 1913).

Patents and Deeds and other Early Records of New Jersey, 1664–1703 (1899), ed. W. Nelson (Baltimore, MD: Genealogical Publishing Co., 2007).

Paxton, F. L., and C. O. Paullin, *Guide to Materials in London Archives for History of the United States since 1783* (Washington, DC: Carnegie Institution of Washington, 1914).

Pigot's & Co.'s London and Provincial New Commercial Directory (J. Pigot & Co., Manchester, 1822–23, and 1826–27).

The Post Office Annual Directory (London: Ferguson and Sparke, 1801–15; London: Critchett and Woods, 1816–50).

Robson's London Commercial Directory, Street Guide, and Carriers' List (London: W. Robson and Co., 1819, 1822, 1830, 1836).

Ship Registers and Enrollments of Providence, Rhode Island, 1773–1939, 2 vols (Providence, RI: Work Projects Administration, 1941).

State of New Jersey Index of Wills, Inventories, Etc., in the Office of the Secretary of State Prior to 1901, 3 vols (1913; Baltimore, MD: Genealogical Publishing Company, 1969).

Swan, N. L., *Ellis Index ... to the History of Monmouth County, New Jersey, by Franklin Ellis, 1885* (Lincroft, NJ: Brookdale Community College Press, 1973).

Universal British Directory of Trade and Commerce, Comprehending Lists of Inhabitants of London, Westminster and Borough of Southwark, 4 vols (London: P. Barfoot and J. Wilkes, 1790–2).

Universal British Directory of Trade and Commerce, and Manufacture, vol. 3 (London: P. Barfoot and J. Wilkes, 1794).

Universal British Directory of Trade, Commerce and Manufacture, vol. 5 (London: P. Barfoot and J. Wilkes, 1798).

US National Archives and Records Administration (NARA), University of Maryland (College Park, MD), indexed in *Compiled Service Records of Soldiers who served in the American Army during the Revolutionary War.*

Wakefield's Merchant and Tradesman's General Directory (London: R. Wakefield, 1794).

Primary Sources

The Adams Family Correspondence, ed. L. H. Butterfield and M. Friedlaender, 8 vols (Cambridge, MA: Harvard University Press, 1963–2007).

Anon., 'Extract from a Letter from New-York', *Pennsylvania Gazette*, 15 August 1757.

—, *Articles of an Association by the Name of the Ohio Company* (New York: printed by Samuel and John Loudon, 1787).

—, *Avis intéressant aux amateurs de l'agriculture: 120,000 journaux de terres à vendre, en tout ou en partie, & dont les acquéreurs peuvent tirer un grand produit* (Paris: Prault, 1789).

—, 'Short Account of the Life and Character of Thomas Hutchins, late Geographer-General to the United States', *American Museum; or, Universal Magazine*, 7:4 (April 1790), pp. 212–13.

—, 'Some Particulars Relative to the Soil, Situation, Productions, &c. of Kentucky. Extracted from the Manuscript Journal of a Gentleman not long since Returned from those Parts', *American Museum; or, Universal Magazine*, 11:1 (January 1792), pp. 11–15.

—, *Letters on Emigration, By a Gentleman Lately Returned from America* (London: C. and G. Kearsley, 1794).

— [T. Cooper?], *Thoughts on Emigration, in a Letter from a Gentleman in Philadelphia, to his Friend in England* (London, 1794).

—, *A View of the Relative Situation of Great Britain and the United States of North America: By a Merchant* (London: printed by H. L. Galabin, 1794).

—, 'Plan of Association of the North American Land Company. Established February, 1795' (Philadelphia: printed by R. Aitken and Son, 1795).

—, *Berkeley Hall: or, The Pupil of Experience* (1796), ed. W. M. Verhoeven, in *Anti-Jacobin Novels*, gen. ed. W. M. Verhoeven, 10 vols (London: Pickering & Chatto, 2005), vol. 6.

— [T. Clio Rickman?], *Emigration to America, Candidly Considered. In a Series of Letters, from a Gentleman, Resident there, to his Friend, in England* (London: printed by Thomas Clio Rickman, 1798).

—, *Henry Willoughby. A Novel*, 2 vols (London: G. Kearsley, 1798).

—, 'Situation, Feelings, and Pleasures, of an American Farmer', *Philadelphia Monthly Magazine; or, Universal Repository of Knowledge and Entertainment*, 1:6 (June 1798), pp. 327–33.

—, *Terms, Conditions, and Circumstances, Touching Lands for Sale in the United States of America* ([Philadelphia?], 1798).

—, *A Plain Tale, Supported by Authentic Documents, Justifying the Character of General Wilkinson, By a Kentuckian* ([New York, 1807]).

—, *The Periodical Press of Great Britain and Ireland: or, An Inquiry into the State of the Public Journals, Chiefly as Regards their Moral and Political Influence* (London: Hurst, Robinson & Co., 1824)

Archives parlémentaires de 1787 à 1794, Recueil complet des débats législatifs et politique des Chambres Françaises, 1st series, 82 vols (Paris, 1884).

Aulard, F.-A. (ed.), *Recueil des actes du comité de Salut Public avec la correspondance officielle des représentants en mission, et le registre du conseil exécutif provisoire*, 16 vols (Paris: Imprimerie nationale, 1889–1904).

—, *Hermsprong; Or, Man As He Is Not* (London: William Lane, 1796).

Barber, J. W., and H. Howe, *Historical Collections of the State of New Jersey: Containing a General Collection of the Most Interesting Facts, Traditions, Biographical Sketches, Anecdotes, etc. Relating to its History and Antiquities, with Geographical Descriptions of Every Township in the State Illustrated by 120 Engravings* (New York: for the authors, by S. Tuttle, 1844).

Barlow, J. *The Political Writings of Joel Barlow, Containing 'Advice to the Privileged Orders', 'Letter to the National Convention', 'Letter to the People of Piedmont, 'The Conspiracy of Kings'* (New York: Fellows & Adam, Thomas Greenleaf, and Naphtati Judah, 1796).

Barrell, C. and H. Servanté, *Observations on the North-American Land-Company, Lately Instituted in Philadelphia* (London: C. Barrell and H. Servanté, American Agents, 1796).

Beatty, E., 'Diary of Major Erkuries Beatty [1786–7]', *Magazine of American History*, 1 (1877), pp. 239–41.

Blackstone, W., *Commentaries on the Laws of England*, 4 vols (Oxford: Clarendon Press, 1765–9).

Brissot de Warville, J. P., *New Travels in the United States of America. Performed in 1788 ...*, trans. [J. Barlow] (London: J. S. Jordan, 1792).

—, *The Commerce of America with Europe; Particularly with France and Great Britain; Comparatively Stated and Explained*, trans. [J. Barlow] (London: J. S. Jordan, 1797).

Burke, E., *Reflections on the French Revolution* (London: J. Dodsley, 1790).

Butler, Capt. L., 'Letters to Mrs. Joseph Cradock' [1784–1788], *Magazine of American History*, 1 (1877), pp. 40–7.

Caron, P., *La Commission des subsistances de l'an II: procès-verbaux et actes* (Paris: E. Leroux, 1924–5).

—, *Paris pendant la Terreur: rapports des agents secrets du ministre de l'Intérieur*, 6 vols (Paris: Librairie Alphonse Picard [and others], 1910–64).

Christie, T. *Letters on the Revolution of France, and on the New Constitution Established by the National Assembly: Occasioned by the Publications of the Right Hon. Edmund Burke, M.P. and Alexander de Calonnne, Late Minister of State ...*, 2 vols (London: J. Johnson, 1791).

Clark, D., *Proofs of the Corruption of Gen. James Wilkinson and of his Connexion with Aaron Burr, with a Full Refutation of his Slanderous Allegations in Relation to the Character of the Principal Witness against him* (Philadelphia, PA: Wm. Hall, jun. & Geo. W. Pierie, 1809).

Clark, G. R., *George Rogers Clark Papers, 1771–1781*, ed. J. A. James, Collections of the Illinois State Historical Library, vol. 8; Virginia Series, vol. 3 (Springfield, IL: Illinois State Historical Library, 1912).

—, *George Rogers Clark Papers, 1781–1784*, ed. J. A. James, Collections of the Illinois State Historical Library, vol. 19; Virginia Series, vol. 4 (Springfield, IL: Illinois State Historical Library, 1926).

Clarkson, T., *The History of the Rise, Progress, and Accomplishment of the Abolition of the Slave-Trade by the British Parliament*, 2 vols (London: Longman, Hurst, Rees and Orme, 1808).

Coleridge, S. T, *The Collected Letters of Samuel Taylor Coleridge*, ed. E. L. Griggs, 4 vols (Oxford: Clarendon Press, 1956–59).

Collin, N., *The Journal of Nicholas Collin, 1746–1831* (Philadelphia, PA: The New Jersey Society of Pennsylvania, 1936).

Condorcet, M. J. A. N. Caritat, marquis de, *Esquisse d'un tableau historique des progrès de l'esprit humain* (Paris: Agasse, 1795).

Cooper, T., *Some Information Respecting America* (Dublin: P. Wogan; and London: J. Johnson, 1794).

Coxe, T., *A View of the United States of America, In a Series of Papers, Written at Various Times Between the Years 1787 and 1794 ... Interspersed with Authentic Documents: The Whole Tending to Exhibit the Progress and Present State of Civil and Religious Liberty, Population, Agriculture, Exports, Imports, Fisheries, Navigation, Ship-Building, Manufactures, and General Improvement* (1794; London: J. Johnson, 1795).

Crèvecoeur, J. H. St John de, *Letters from an American Farmer: Describing Certain Provincial Situations, Manners, and Customs, Not Generally Known ...*, new edn (1782; London: Thomas Davies and Lockyer Davis, 1783).

—, *Lettres d'un cultivateur américain*, 3 vols (Paris: Cuchet, 1787).

—, *Voyage dans la haute Pensylvanie et dans l'état de New-York: par un membre adoptif de la nation Onéida / Traduit et publie par l'auteur des Lettres d'un cultivateur américain*, 3 vols (Paris : Maradan, 1801).

Cutler, M., *Life, Journals and Correspondence of Rev. Manasseh Cutler, LL.D*, ed. W. Parker and J. Perkins Cutler, 2 vols (Cincinnati, OH: Robert Clarke & Co., 1888).

—, *Ohio in 1788. A Description of the Soil, Productions, etc., of that Portion of the United States Situated Between Pennsylvania, the Rivers Ohio and Scioto and Lake Erie. Translated from the French*, trans. and intro. J. H. James (Columbus, OH: A. H. Smythe, 1888).

[Cutler, M.], *An Explanation of the Map which Delineates that Part of the Federal Lands Comprehended between Pennsylvania West Line, the Rivers Ohio and Scioto, and Lake Erie; Confirmed to the United States by Sundry Tribes of Indians, in the Treaties of 1784 and 1786, and Now Ready for Settlement* (Salem, MA: printed by Dadney and Cushing, 1787).

Debrett, J., *New Publications Printed for J. Debrett, Opposite Burlington House, Piccadilly* (London: J. Debrett, 1973).

'Documents on the Relations of France to Louisiana, 1792–1795', ed. F. J. Turner, *American Historical Review*, 3:3 (April 1898), pp. 490–516.

Documents Relating to the Colonial, Revolutionary and Post-Revolutionary History of the State of New Jersey [various titles, commonly called the *New Jersey Archives*], Archives of the State of New Jersey, 1st series, 42 vols (Newark and Paterson, NJ: various publishers, 1880–1949).

Dorchester, L., 'Observations upon the Colony of Kentucky', in J. Brown, *The Political Beginnings of Kentucky. A Narrative of Public Events Bearing on the History of that State up to the Time of its Admission into the American Union* (Louisville, KY: J. P. Morton and Co., 1889).

Early Western Travels, 1748–1846: A Series of Annotated Reprints of Some of the Best and Rarest Contemporary Volumes of Travel, Descriptive of the Aborigines and Social and Economic Conditions in the Middle and Far West, during the Period of Early American Settlement, ed. R. Gold Thwaites (Cleveland, OH: A. H. Clark, 1904–7).

Ebeling, C. D., 'Letters of Christoph Daniel Ebeling', ed. W. C. Lane, *Proceedings of the American Antiquarian Society*, n.s. 35 (October 1925), pp. 272–451.

Fitzroy, A., *The Discovery, Purchase, and Settlement of the Country of Kentuckie, In North America, so Famous for its Fertility of Soil, Produce, Climate, Minerals, Quadrupedes, Curiosities, Trade, Rapid Population, Religion, &c. &c. The Whole Illustrated by a New and Accurate Map Annexed* (London: printed by H. Goldney, 1786).

Filson, J., *The Discovery, Settlement and Present State of Kentucky: And an Essay towards the Topography, and Natural History of that Important Country* (Wilmington, DE: printed by James Adams, 1784).

—, 'A Journal of two Voyages from the Falls of Ohio to Post St Vincent ...' [1785], Draper MSS 10CC35–46, in B. W. Bond, 'Two Westward Journeys of John Filson, 1785', *Mississippi Valley Historical Review*, 9:4 (March 1923), pp. 320–30.

[Fitch, J.], 'The Original Steam-Boat Supported; or, A Reply to Mr. James Rumsey's Pamphlet. Shewing the True Priority of *John Fitch*, and the False Datings, &c. of *James Rumsey*' (Philadelphia, PA: printed by Zachariah Poulson, Junr., 1788).

Fleming, Col. W., *Journal of Travels in Kentucky, 1779–1780*, in N. D. Mereness (ed.), *Travels in the American Colonies* (New York: Antiquarian Press, 1961).

—, *Journal of Travels in Kentucky, 1783*, in *Travels in the American Colonies*, in N. D. Mereness (ed.), *Travels in the American Colonies* (New York: Antiquarian Press, 1961).

Floyd, J., '"In a Dangerous Situation": Letters of Col. John Floyd, 1774–1783', ed. N. O. Hammon and J. R. Harris, *Register of the Kentucky Historical Society*, 83:3 (Summer 1985), pp. 202–36.

Fox, W., *An Address to the People of Great Britain on the Propriety of Abstaining from West India Sugar and Rum* (London: M. Gurney, 1791).

Freneau, P., *An Historical Sketch, to the End of the Revolutionary War, of the Life of Silas Talbot, Esq., of the State of Rhode-Island, Lately Commander of the United States Frigate, the Constitution, and of an American Squadron in the West-Indies* (New-York: H. Caritat, 1803).

Gerbaux, F., and C. Schmidt (eds), *Procès-verbaux des comités d'agriculture et de commerce de la Constituante, de la Législative et de la Convention*, 4 vols (Paris: Imprimerie Nationale, 1906–10).

Godwin, W., *Enquiry Concerning Political Justice, and its Influence on Modern Morals and Happiness* (1793), in *Political and Philosophical Writings of William Godwin*, ed. M. Philp, 7 vols (London: Pickering & Chatto, 1993), vol. 3.

—, *Things As They Are; or, The Adventures of Caleb Williams* (London: B. Crosby, 1794).

—, *Memoirs of the Author of a Vindication of the Rights of Woman* (London: J. Johnson and G.G. and J. Robinson, 1798).

Gordon, T. F., *Gazetteer of the State of New Jersey: Comprehending a General View of its Physical and Moral Conditions, Together with a Topographical and Statistical Account of its Counties, Towns, Villages, Canals, Rail Roads, etc., Accompanied by a Map* (1834; Cottonport, LA: Polyanthos, 1973).

Hamilton, A., *The Papers of Alexander Hamilton*, ed. H. C. Syrett and J. E. Cook, 27 vols (New York and London: Columbia University Press, 1961–87).

Hays, M., *Letters and Essays, Moral and Miscellaneous* (London: T. Knott, 1793).

Hazlitt, W., *The Spirit of the Age or Contemporary Portraits* (1825; Oxford: Oxford University Press, 1928).

Holcroft, T., *Anna St Ives: A Novel* (1792), ed. W. M. Verhoeven, in *The Novels and Selected Plays of Thomas Holcroft*, 5 vols, gen. ed. W. M. Verhoeven (London: Pickering and Chatto, 2007), vol. 2.

Hutchins, T., *A Topographical Description of Virginia, Pennsylvania, Maryland, and North Carolina* (1778), ed., F. C. Hicks (Cleveland, OH: The Burrows Brothers Co., 1904).

Imlay, G., A., 'Observations du Cap. Imlay, Traduites de L'Anglais', *Archives de Affaires Étrangères, Correspondance Politique, Espagne*, 634 (1791), p. 462.

—, Letter to Harry Toulmin, 'London, Feb. 2, 1793', in H. Toulmin, *A Description of Kentucky, in North America: To which are Prefixed Miscellaneous Observations Respecting the United States* ([London], 1792), pp. 117–19.

—, *Topographical Description of the Western Territory of North America; Containing a Succinct Account of Its Climate, Natural History, Population, Agriculture, Manners and Customs, with an Ample Description of the Several Divisions into which that Country is Partitioned, and an Accurate Statement of the Various Tribes of Indians that Inhabit the Frontier Country. To which is Annexed, a Delineation of the Laws and Government of the State of Kentucky, Tending to Shew the Probable Rise and Grandeur of the American Empire. In a Series of Letters to a Friend in England* (London: J. Debrett, 1792).

—, *The Emigrants, &c.; or, The History of an Expatriated Family, Being a Delineation of English Manners, Drawn from Real Characters, Written in America*, 3 vols (London: A. Hamilton, 1793).

—, *The Emigrants (1793), Traditionally Ascribed to Gilbert Imlay but, More Probably, By Mary Wollstonecraft*, ed. R. R. Hare (Gainesville, FL: Scholars' Facsimiles & Reprints, 1964).

—, *The Emigrants, &c., or The History of an Expatriated Family, Being a Delineation of English Manners, Drawn from Real Characters, Written in America* (1793), ed. W. M. Verhoeven and A. Gilroy (New York: Penguin Books, 1998).

—, 'Mémoire sur la Louisiane, présenté au Comité de Salut public par un Citoyen Américain', *Archives de Affaires Étrangères, Correspondance Politique, États-Unis*, Supplement, 7 (1793), pp. 4–9.

—, *Nachrichten von dem westlichen lande der Nordamerikanischen freistaaten, von dem klima, den naturprodukten, der volksmenge, den sitten und gebräuchen desselben, nebst einer angabe der indianischen völkerstämme, die an den gränzen wohnen, und einer schilderung von den gestetzen und der regierung des staates Kentucky. In briefen an einen freund in England*, trans. E. A. W. Zimmermann (Berlin: In der Vossischen buchhandlung, 1793).

—, *A Topographical Description of the Western Territory of North America: Containing a Succinct Account of its Soil, Climate, Natural History, Population, Agriculture, Manners, and Customs. With an Ample Description of the Several Divisions into which that Country is Partitioned. To which are Added, The Discovery, Settlement, and Present State of Kentucky. And an Essay towards the Topography, and Natural History of that Important Country. By John Filson. To which is Added, I. The Adventures of Col. Daniel Boon ... II. The Minutes of the Piankashaw Council ... III. An Account of the Indian Nations ... By George Imlay ... Illustrated with correct Maps of the Western Territory of North America*, 2nd edn (London: J. Debrett, 1793).

—, *A Topographical Description of the Western Territory of North America: Containing a Succinct Account of its Soil, Climate, Natural History, Population, Agriculture, Manners, and Customs. With an Ample Description of the Several Divisions into which that Country is Partitioned. With Great Additions*, 3rd edn (London: J. Debrett, 1797).

Jacson, F., *Disobedience. A Novel*, 4 vols (London: William Lane, 1797).

Jefferson, T., *Notes on the State of Virginia*, ed. W. Peden (1781; Chapel Hill, NC, and London: University of North Carolina Press, 1982).

Jefferson, T., A. Adams and J. Adams, *The Adams-Jefferson Letters: The Complete Correspondence between Thomas Jefferson and Abigail and John Adams*, ed. L. J. Cappon (1959; Chapel Hill, NC, and London: University of North Carolina Press, 1987).

Journals of the Continental Congress, 1774–1789, ed. C. W. Ford, G. Hunt, J. C. Fitzpatrick, R. R. Hill, K. E. Harris and S. D. Tilley, 34 vols (Washington, DC: United States Government Printing Office, 1904–37).

Kentucky Court of Appeals Deed Books, ed. M. L. Cook and B. A. Cook (Evansville, IN: Cook Publications, 1985).

Lee, R. H. *Life of Arthur Lee, LL.D.*, 2 vols (Boston: Wells and Lilly, 1829).

Letters of Delegates to Congress: 1774–1789, ed. P. H. Smith, G. W. Gawalt, R. Fry Plakas and E. R. Sheridan, 26 vols (Washington, DC: Library of Congress, 1976–2000).

Livingston, W., *The Papers of William Livingston*, gen. ed. C. E. Prince, 5 vols (Trenton, NJ: New Jersey Historical Commission, 1979).

Mackintosh, J., *Vindiciae Gallicae. Defence of the French Revolution and its English Admirers against the Accusations of ... Edmund Burke* (London: G. G. J. & J. Robinson, 1791).

Madison, J., *The Papers of James Madison*, ed. W. T. Hutchinson and W. M. E. Rachal, 17 vols (Chicago, IL: University of Chicago Press, 1962–91).

—, *The Writings of James Madison, Comprising his Public Papers and his Private Correspondence, Including Numerous Letters and Documents now for the First Time Printed*, ed. G. Hunt, 9 vols (New York: G. P. Putnam's Sons, 1900–10).

Malthus, T. R. *An Essay on the Principle of Population* (1798), in *The Works of Thomas Robert Malthus*, ed. E. A. Wrigley and D. Souden, 8 vols (London: Pickering & Chatto, 1986).

Marshall, H., *The History of Kentucky. Including an Account of the Discovery, Settlement, Progressive Improvement, Political and Military Events, and Present State of the Country*, 2 vols (Frankfort, KY: printed by Henry Gore, 1812).

Marx, K., *The German Ideology*, in K. Marx and F. Engels, *Collected Works*, trans. C. Dutt, W. Lough and C. P. Magill, 50 vols (London: Lawrence and Wishart, 1976).

May, J., *The Western Journals of John May: Ohio Company Agent and Business Adventurer*, ed. D. L. Smith (Cincinnati, OH: Historical and Philosophical Society of Ohio, 1961).

Melville, H., 'Bartleby, the Scrivener: A Tale of Wall Street', in H. Melville, *Billy Budd and Other Stories* (Harmondsworth, Middlesex: Penguin Books, 1967), p. 59.

Minutes of the Board of Proprietors of the Eastern Division of New Jersey, 1685–1794, 4 vols (vols 1–3, Perth Amboy, NJ: Board of Proprietors of the Eastern Division of New Jersey, 1949–85; vol. 4, ed. M. N. Lurie and J. R. Walroth (Newark, NJ: New Jersey Historical Society, 1985).

Minutes of the Provincial Congress and the Council of Safety of the State of New Jersey (Trenton, NJ: printed by Naar, Day & Naar, 1879).

Monroe, J., *The Writings of James Monroe: Including a Collection of his Public and Private Papers and Correspondence now for the First Time Printed*, ed. S. M. Hamilton, 7 vols (New York and London: G. P. Putnam's Sons, 1899–1903).

Morris, G., *A Diary of the French Revolution by Gouverneur Morris, 1752–1816, Minister to France during the Terror*, ed. B. C. Davenport, 2 vols (London: George G. Harrap & Co., 1939).

Morris, R., *The Papers of Robert Morris, 1781–1784*, ed. E. J. Ferguson et al., 8 vols (Pittsburgh, PA: University of Pittsburgh Press, 1973–).

Morse, J., *The American Geography; or, A View of the Present Situation of the United States of America* (Elizabeth Town, NJ: printed by Shepard Kollock, for the Author, 1789).

Paine, T., *Rights of Man: Being an Answer to Mr. Burke's Attack on the French Revolution* (1791), ed. H. Collins (Harmondsworth: Penguin, 1969).

—, *Rights of Man. Part the Second. Combining Principle and Practice* (London: J. S. Jordan, 1792).

The Parliamentary History of England from the Earliest Period to the Year 1803. Volume 30, Comprising the Period from the Thirteenth of December 1792, to the Tenth of March 1794 (London: Longman, 1817).

Parsons, E., *The Voluntary Exile*, 5 vols (London: William Lane, 1795).

Pigott, C., *A Political Dictionary: Explaining the True Meaning of Words* (London: D. I. Eaton, 1795).

[Playfair, W.], *Prospectus pour l'établissement sur les rivières d'Ohio et de Scioto, en Amérique* [with appended 'Époque des Paiemens' and 'Plan des achats des Compagnies de L'Ohio et de la Scioto'] (Paris: Prault, 1789).

Polwhele, R., *The Unsex'd Females: A Poem, Addressed to the Author of The Pursuits of Literature* (London: Cadell and Davies, 1798).

Pownall, T., *A Topographical Description of such parts of North America as are Contained in the (Annexed) Map of the Middle British Colonies, &c. in North America* (London: J. Almon, 1776).

Price, R., *A Discourse on the Love of our Country, Delivered on Nov. 4, 1789, at the Meeting-House in the Old Jewry, to the Society for Commemorating the Revolution in Great Britain* (London: T. Cadell, 1789).

Priestley, J., *An Essay on the First Principles of Government, and on the Nature of Political, Civil, and Religious Liberty* (London: J. Dodsley, T. Cadell and J. Johnson, 1768).

—, *The Case of Poor Emigrants Recommended, in a Discourse, Delivered at the University Hall in Philadelphia, on Sunday, February 19, 1797* (Philadelphia, PA: printed by Joseph Gales, 1797).

Pye, H. J., *The Democrat: Interspersed with Anecdotes of Well Known Characters*, 2 vols (London: William Lane, 1795).

—, *The Aristocrat, A Novel*, 2 vols (London: Sampson Low, 1799).

Rickman, T. C., *The Life of Thomas Paine* (London: T. C. Rickman, 1819).

Rousseau, J.-J., *Émile; or On Education* (1762), trans. A. Bloom (New York: Basic Books, 1979).

Rumsey, J., 'A Plan Wherein the Power of Steam Is Fully Shown ...', appended to J. Fitch, *The Original Steam-Boat Supported* (1788; Tarrytown, NY: W. Abbatt, 1926), pp. 1–20.

Sabine, L., *The American Loyalists, or Biographical Sketches of Adherents to the British Crown in the War of the Revolution; Alphabetically Arranged; with a Preliminary Historical Essay* (Boston, MA: Charles C. Little and James Brown, 1847).

'Selections from the Draper Collection in the Possession of the State Historical Society of Wisconsin, to Elucidate the Proposed French Expedition under George Rogers Clark against Louisiana, in the Years 1793–94', *Annual Report of the American Historical Association*, 1 (1896), pp. 930–1107.

Shepherd, W. R., 'Papers Bearing on James Wilkinson's Relations with Spain, 1787–1816', *American Historical Review*, 9:4 (July 1904), pp. 748–66.

Smith, C., *The Young Philosopher*, 4 vols (London: T. Cadell, Jr, and W. Davies, 1798).

Smith, S., *The History of the Colony of Nova-Caesaria, or New-Jersey: Containing, an Account of its First Settlement, Progressive Improvements, the Original and Present Constitution, and other Events to the Year 1721. With some particulars since; and a Short View of its Present State* (Burlington, NJ: James Parker; sold also by David Hall, Philadelphia, 1765).

The Statutes at Large, Being a Collection of all the Laws of Virginia from the First Session of the Legislature in 1619, ed. W. W. Hening, 13 vols (Richmond, VA: George Cochran, 1822).

Swan, J., _Causes qui se sont opposées aux progrès du commerce entre la France et les États-Unis de l'Amérique, avec les moyens de l'accélérer ... en six lettres adressées à M. le marquis de La Fayette. Traduit sur le manuscrit anglais du colonel Swan_ ... (Paris: printed by L. Potier, 1790).

Symmes, J. C., _The Correspondence of John Cleves Symmes, Founder of the Miami Purchase_, ed. B. W. Bond, Jr (New York: Historical and Philosophical Society of Ohio, 1926).

—, _The Intimate Letters of John Cleves Symmes and His Family_, ed. B. W. Bond, Jr. (Cincinnati, OH: The Historical and Philosophical Society of Ohio, 1956).

Thelwall, J., _The Tribune_ (1795), in _The Politics of English Jacobinism: Writings of John Thelwall_, ed. G. Claeys (University Park, PA: Pennsylvania State University Press, 1985).

[Toulmin, H.], _Thoughts on Emigration. To which are Added, Miscellaneous Observations Relating to the United States of America: and a Short Account of the State of Kentucky_ ([London], 1792).

—, _A Description of Kentucky, in North America: To which are Prefixed Miscellaneous Observations Respecting the United States_ ([London], 1792).

—, _The Western Country in 1793: Reports on Kentucky and Virginia_, ed. M. Tinling and G. Davies (San Marino, CA: [Henry E. Huntington Library and Art Gallery], 1948).

The Trial of Thomas Hardy for High Treason, at the Sessions House in the Old Bailey ... November 1794 ... Taken in Short-Hand, by Joseph Gurney, 4 vols (London: Martha Gurney, 1794–5).

Tucker, J., _The Elements of Commerce and Theory of Taxes_ (1755), in _Josiah Tucker: A Selection of his Economic and Political Writings_, ed. R. Livingston Schuyler (New York: Columbia University Press, 1931).

Virginia Supreme Court: District of Kentucky Order Books, 1783–1792, ed. M. L. Cook and B. A. Cook (Evansville, IN: Cook Publications, 1988).

Volney, C. F. de., _A View of the Soil and Climate of the United States of America_ (1803), trans. C. Brockden Brown (Philadelphia, PA: J. Conrad & Co., 1804).

Walker, G., _The Vagabond, A Novel_ (1799), ed. W. M. Verhoeven (Peterborough, Ontario: Broadview Press, 2004).

Washington, G., 'Washington's Household Account Book, 1793–1797', _Pennsylvania Magazine of History and Biography_ 31 (1907), pp. 53–82.

—, _The Writings of George Washington from the Original Manuscript Sources, 1745–1799_, ed., J. C. Fitzpatrick, 39 vols (Washington, DC: Government Printing Office, 1931–44).

Wedgwood, J., _Correspondence of Josiah Wedgwood, 1781–1794_, ed. K. Eufemia and L. Farrer (London: privately printed, 1906).

Whittlesey, C., _Life of John Fitch_, in Jared Sparks (ed.), _Library of American Biography_, 2nd series, vol. 6 (Boston, MA: Little, Brown and Co., 1845), pp. 81–166.

Wilkinson, J., *Memoirs of My Own Times*, 3 vols (Philadelphia, PA: printed by Abraham Small, 1816).

—, 'Letters of Gen. James Wilkinson Addressed to Dr. James Hutchinson, of Philadelphia', *The Pennsylvania Magazine of History and Biography*, 12:1 (1888), pp. 54–64.

—, 'Letters of General James Wilkinson', *Register of the Kentucky Historical Society*, 24:70 (January 1926), pp. 259–67.

Williams, H. M., *Letters Containing a Sketch of the Politics of France, from the Thirty-First of May 1793, till the Twenty-Eighth of July 1794, and of the Scenes which have Passed in the Prisons of Paris*, 2 vols (London: G. G. and J. Robinson, 1795).

Winterbotham, W., *An Historical, Geographical, Commercial, and Philosophical View of the American United States, and the Settlements in America and the West-Indies*, 4 vols (London: J. Ridgway, H. D. Symonds and D. Holt, 1795).

—, *The American Atlas* (New York: John Reid, 1796).

Wollstonecraft, M., *A Vindication of the Rights of Men, in a Letter to the Right Honorable Edmund Burke occasioned by his Reflections on the Revolution in France* (London: J. Johnson, 1790).

—, *A Vindication of the Rights of Woman: With Strictures on Political and Moral Subjects* (London: J. Johnson, 1792).

—, *Letters Written during a Short Residence in Sweden, Norway, and Denmark* (London: J. Johnson, 1796).

—, *Maria; or The Wrongs of Woman* (1798), in *Mary and The Wrongs of Woman*, ed. G. Kelly (Oxford: Oxford University Press, 1976).

—, *Letters to Imlay*, ed. C. K. Paul (London: C. K. Paul, 1879).

—, *Political Writings*, ed. J. Todd (Oxford: Oxford University Press, 1994).

—, *The Collected Letters of Mary Wollstonecraft*, ed. J. Todd (London: Penguin Books, 2003).

Wordsworth, W., *The Prelude, or, Growth of a Poet's Mind* (1850), ed. E. de Selincourt (Oxford: Oxford University Press, 1926).

Secondary Sources

Abernethy, T. P., *Western Lands and the American Revolution* (New York and London: D. Appleton-Century Co., 1937).

Adams, M. R., 'Joel Barlow, Political Romanticist', *American Literature*, 9:2 (May 1937), pp. 113–52.

Adelberg, M. S. *Roster of the People of Revolutionary Monmouth County* (n.p., n.d).

—, *Roster of the People of Revolutionary Monmouth County [New Jersey]*, expanded and revised (unpublished, Monmouth County Archives, County Clerk's Office, Manalapan, NJ).

Adkinson, K., 'The Kentucky Land Grant System', *Circuit Rider* (Historical Confederation of Kentucky), 13:3 (May–June 1990), pp. i–iv.

Allen, G. W., and R. Asselineau, *St. John de Crèvecoeur: The Life of an American Farmer* (New York: Viking, 1987).

Ammon, H., *The Genet Mission* (New York: Norton, 1973).

Aron, S., 'Pioneers and Profiteers: Land Speculation and the Homestead Ethic in Frontier Kentucky' *The Western Historical Quarterly* 23:2 (May 1992), pp. 179–98.

—, *How the West Was Lost: The Transformation of Kentucky from Daniel Boone to Henry Clay* (Baltimore, MD: Johns Hopkins University Press, 1996).

Bailyn, B., *The Peopling of British North America: An Introduction* (New York: Alfred A. Knopf, 1986).

—, *Voyagers to the West: A Passage in the People of America on the Eve of the Revolution* (New York: Alfred A. Knopf, 1986).

Bakeless, J. E., *Daniel Boone* (New York: W. Morrow and Company, 1939).

Bauer, R., *The Cultural Geography of Colonial American Literatures: Empire, Travel, Modernity* (Cambridge and New York: Cambridge University Press, 2003).

Belote, T. T., *The Scioto Speculation and the French Settlement at Galliopolis: A Study in Ohio Valley History* (Cincinnati, OH: University of Cincinnati Press, 1907).

Bemis, S. F., 'The London Mission of Thomas Pinckey, 1792–1796', *American Historical Review*, 28:2 (January 1923), pp. 228–47.

Berg, F. A., *Encyclopedia of Continental Army Units: Battalions, Regiments, and Independents Corps* ([Harrisberg, PA]: Stockpole Books, [1972]).

Billington, R. A., 'The Origin of the Land Speculator as a Frontier Type', *Magazine of Agricultural History*, 18 (January 1944), pp. 204–21.

Bizardel, Y., *Les Américains à Paris pendant la révolution* (Paris: Calmann-Lévy, 1972).

Bond, B. W., 'Two Westward Journeys of John Filson, 1785', *Mississippi Valley Historical Review*, 9:4 (March 1923), pp. 320–30.

Bowman, A. H., *The Struggle for Neutrality: Franco-American Diplomacy during the Federalist Era* (Knoxville, TN: University of Tennessee Press, 1974).

Brock, L. V., 'The Colonial Currency, Prices, and Exchange Rates', *Essays in History*, 34 (1992), pp. 74–132.

Brown, J. M., *The Political Beginnings of Kentucky: A Narrative of Public Events Bearing on the History of that State up to the Time of its Admission into the American Union* (Louisville, KY: J. P. Morton and Co., 1889).

Brailsford, H. N. *Shelley, Godwin, and Their Circle* (London: Williams and Norgate, 1913).

Breen, J., *Women Romantics 1785–1832: Writing in Prose* (London: Dent, 1996).

Castiglia, C., *Bound and Determined: Captivity, Culture-Crossing, and White Womanhood from Mary Rowlandson to Patty Hearst* (Chicago, IL, and London: University of Chicago Press, 1996).

Clark, J. C. D., *English Society, 1660–1832: Religion, Ideology and Politics During the Ancien Régime* (Cambridge and New York: Cambridge University Press, 1985).

Clarke, T. W., *Émigrés in the Wilderness* (New York: Macmillan Company, 1941).

Clauder, A. C., 'American Commerce as Affected by the Wars of the French Revolution and Napoleon, 1793–1812' (PhD thesis, University of Pennsylvania, 1932).

Coke, B. H., *John May, Jr. of Virginia: His Descendants and Their Land* (Baltimore, MD: Gateway Press, 1975).

Cole, J. R., 'Imlay's Ghost: Wollstonecraft's Authorship of *The Emigrants*', *Eighteenth-Century Women: Studies in Their Lives, Work, and Culture*, 1 (2001), pp. 263–98.

Colley, L., *Britons: Forging the Nation 1707–1837* (New Haven, CT: Yale University Press, 1992).

Collin, N. C., *The Journal and Biography of Nicholas Collin, 1746–1831*, trans. A. Johnson, intro. F. H. Stewart (Philadelphia, PA: New Jersey Society of Pennsylvania, 1936).

Conway, M. D., *The Life of Thomas Paine; With a History of his Literary, Political, and Religious Career in America, France, and England ... To which is added a Sketch of Paine by William Cobbett (hitherto unpublished)*, 2 vols (New York and London: G. P. Putnam's Sons, 1892).

Coughtry, J., *The Notorious Triangle: Rhode Island and the African Slave Trade, 1700–1807* (Philadelphia, PA: Temple University Press, 1981).

Daughters of the American Revolution, *DAR Patriot Index: Millennium Administration*, 3 vols (Baltimore, MD: Gateway Press, 2003).

Dembitz, L. N., *Kentucky Jurisprudence in Four Books: I. Constitutional and Political Law. II. The Law of Real Estate. III. Other Rights of Property. IV. Persons and their Obligations. With an Introduction on the Sources of Kentucky Law* (Louisville, KY: J. P. Morton, 1890).

Dickinson, H. T. (ed.), *Politics and Literature in the Eighteenth Century* (London: Dent, 1974).

Dobson, D., *Directory of Scots Banished to the American Plantations 1650–1775* (Baltimore, MD: Genealogical Publishing Co., 1983).

—, *Scottish Emigration to Colonial America, 1607–1785* (Athens, GA: University of Georgia Press, 1994).

Dorfman, J., 'Joel Barlow: Trafficker in Trade and Letters', *Political Science Quarterly*, 59:1 (March 1944), pp. 83–100.

Draper, L. C., *The Life of Daniel Boone*, ed. T. F. Belue (Mechanicsburg, PA: Stackpole Books, 1998).

Durant, W. C. 'A Supplement to *Memoirs of Mary Wollstonecraft*', in W. Godwin, *Memoirs of Mary Wollstonecraft*, ed. W. C. Durant (1798; London: Constable, 1927), pp. 135–334.

Durden, R. F., 'Joel Barlow in the French Revolution', *William and Mary Quarterly*, 3rd series, 8:3 (July 1951), pp. 327–54.

Durey, M., 'Thomas Paine's Apostles: Radical Emigrés and the Triumph of Jeffersonian Republicanism', *William and Mary Quarterly*, 3rd series, 44:4 (1987), pp. 661–88.

Durrett, R. T., *John Filson: The First Historian of Kentucky: An Account of His Life and Writings, Principally from Original Sources*, Filson Club Publications No. 1 (Louisville, KY: Filson Club, 1884).

Echeverria, D., *Mirage in the West: A History of the French Image of American Society to 1815* (Princeton, NJ: Princeton University Press, 1957).

Eckert, A. W., *The Frontiersmen: A Narrative* (Ashland, KY: Jesse Stuart Foundation, 2001).

Edwards, O. D., and G. A. Shepperson, *Scotland, Europe and the American Revolution* (Edinburgh: Edinburgh University Student Publications, 1976).

Ellis, F., *History of Monmouth County, New Jersey, Illustrated* (Philadelphia, PA: R. T. Peck & Co., 1885).

Emerson, O. F., 'Notes on Gilbert Imlay, Early American Writer', *PMLA*, 39:2 (June 1924), pp. 406–39.

Euginia, S., 'Coleridge's Scheme of Pantisocracy and American Travel Accounts', *PMLA*, 45:4 (December 1930), pp. 1069–84.

Everest, K., *Revolution in Writing: British Literary Responses to the French Revolution* (Milton Keynes and Philadelphia, PA: Open University Press, 1991).

Fant, J. L., III. 'A Study of Gilbert Imlay (1754–1828): His Life and Works' (PhD thesis, University of Pennsylvania, 1984).

Faragher, J. M., *Daniel Boone: The Life and Legend of an American Pioneer* (New York: Henry Holt and Co., 1992).

Fliegelman, J., *Prodigals and Pilgrims: The American Revolution against Patriarchal Authority, 1750–1850* (Cambridge: Cambridge University Press, 1982).

Fowler, W. M., Jr, *Silas Talbot: Captain of Old Ironsides* (Mystic, CT: Mystic Seaport Museum, 1995).

Franklin, W., *Discoverers, Explorers, Settlers: The Diligent Writers of Early America* (Chicago, IL, and London: University of Chicago Press, 1979).

Gallop, G. I., 'Politics, Property and Progress: British Radical Thought, 1760–1815' (D.Phil. thesis, Oxford University, 1983).

Garnett, R., 'Gilbert Imlay', in *Dictionary of National Biography*, ed. L. Stephen and S. Lee, 63 vols (New York, 1885–1900).

—, 'Gilbert Imlay', *Athenaeum*, 3955 (15 August 1903), pp. 219–20.

Gates, P. W., 'The Role of the Land Speculator in Western Development', *Pennsylvania Magazine of History and Biography*, 66 (1942), pp. 314–33.

—, 'Tenants of the Log Cabin', *Mississippi Valley Historical Review*, 49:1 (June 1962), pp. 3–31.

Gayarré, C., *The History of Louisiana*, 4 vols (vols 1–2, New York: Redfield; vols 3–4, W. J. Widdleton, 1854).

Gerlach, L. R. (ed.), *New Jersey in the American Revolution, 1763–1783: A Documentary History* (Trenton, NJ: New Jersey Historical Commission, [c. 1975]).

Gerson, N. B., *Light-Horse Harry: A Biography of Washington's Great Calavry Man, General Henry Lee* (Garden City, NY: Doubleday & Co., 1966).

Gordon, L., *Mary Wollstonecraft: A New Genus* (London: Little, Brown, 2005).

Grayson, F. W., 'The Grayson Family', *Tyler's Quarterly Historical and Genealogical Magazine*, 5 (1923–4), pp. 195–208, 261–8.

Greene, J. P., *Pursuits of Happiness: The Social Development of Early Modern British Colonies and the Formation of American Culture* (Chapel Hill, NC: University of North Carolina Press, 1988).

Gregory, A., *The French Revolution and the English Novel* (New York: G. P. Putnam's Sons, 1915).

Hammon, N. O., 'Land Acquisition on the Kentucky Frontier', *Register of the Kentucky Historical Society*, 78:4 (Autumn 1980), pp. 297–321.

—, 'Settlers, Land Jobbers, and Outlyers: A Quantitative Analysis of Land Acquisition on the Kentucky Frontier', *Register of the Kentucky Historical Society*, 84:3 (Summer 1986), pp. 241–62.

— (ed.), *My Father, Daniel Boone: The Draper Interviews with Nathan Boone*, intro. N. L. Dawson (Lexington, KY: University Press of Kentucky, 1999).

Harrison, L. H., 'A Virginian Moves to Kentucky, 1793', *William and Mary Quarterly*, 3rd series, 15:2 (April 1958), pp. 201–13.

Havinghurst, W., *Wilderness for Sale: The Story of the First Western Land Rush* (New York: Hastings House, 1956).

Heilman, R. B., *America in English Fiction, 1760–1800: The Influence of the American Revolution* (Baton Rouge, LA: Louisiana State University Press, 1937).

Heitman, F. B., *Historical Register of Officers in the Continental Army during the War of the Revolution, April, 1775, to December, 1783* (1914; Baltimore, MD: Genealogical Publishing Co., 1967).

Hindemaker, E., *At the Edge of Empire: The Backcountry in British North America* (Baltimore, MD: Johns Hopkins University Press, 2003).

Imlay, H., and N. Imlay, *The Imlay Family* (Zanesville, OH: n.p., 1958).

Jackson, J. W., *With the British Army in Philadelphia, 1777–1778* (San Rafael, CA, and London: Presidio Press, 1979).

Jacobs, J. R., *Tarnished Warrior: Major-General James Wilkinson* (New York: The Macmillan Company, 1938).

Jillson, W. R., *The Kentucky Country: An Historical Exposition of Land Interest in Kentucky Prior to 1790, Coupled with Facsimile Reproductions of the London 1786 Brochure of Alexander Fitzroy, and the 'Whatman' Edition of John Filson's Map* (Washington, DC: H. L. & J. B. McQueen, 1931).

—, *A Transylvanian Trilogy: The Story of the Writing of Harry Toulmin's 1792 'History of Kentucky', Combined with a Brief Sketch of his Life and a New Bibliography* (Frankfurt, KT: Kentucky State Historical Society, 1932).

Jones, V. (ed.), *Women in the Eighteenth Century* (London and New York: Routledge, 1990).

—, 'Women Writing Revolution: Narratives of History and Sexuality in Wollstonecraft and Williams', in S. Copley and J. Whale (eds), *Beyond Romanticism* (London and New York: Routledge, 1992), pp. 178–99.

Kates, G., *The Cercle Social, the Girondins, and the French Revolution* (Princeton, NJ: Princeton University Press, 1985).

Keane, J., *Tom Paine: A Political Life* (London: Bloomsbury, 1995).

Kellogg, L. P., 'Letter of Thomas Paine, 1793', *American Historical Review*, 29:3 (April 1924), pp. 501–5.

Kemmerer, D. L., 'A History of Paper Money in Colonial New Jersey, 1668–1775' *Proceedings of the New Jersey Historical Society*, 74 (April 1956), pp. 107–44.

Kerber, L., *Women of the Republic: Intellect and Ideology in Revolutionary America* (Chapel Hill, NC: University of North Carolina Press, 1980).

Kraus, M., 'America and the Utopian Ideal in the 18th Century', *Mississippi Valley Historical Society Review*, 22:4 (1936), pp. 487–504.

—, 'Literary Relations between Europe and America in the Eighteenth Century', *William and Mary Quarterly*, 3rd series, 1:3 (July, 1944), pp. 210–34.

Krumpelmann, J. T., 'Du Pratz's *History of Louisiana* (1763), a Source of Americanisms, Especially of those Attributed to Imlay', *American Speech*, 20:1 (February 1945), pp. 45–50.

Little, W., *Reprints of Littell's Political Transactions in and concerning Kentucky and Letter of George Nicholas to his Friend in Virginia, also General Wilkinson's Memorial*, intro. T. Bodley (Louisville, KY: J. P. Morton & Company, 1926).

Livermore, S., *Early American Land Companies: Their Influence on Corporate Development* (New York: The Commonwealth Fund, 1939).

Maginnis, E. Van H. O., *The Manor of Buckhole: A History of Imlaystown* ([Allentown, NJ, 1972]).

Malone, D., *The Public Life of Thomas Cooper, 1783–1839* (New Haven, CT: Yale University Press, 1926).

Marsh, P. M., *Philip Freneau: Poet and Journalist* (Minneapolis, MN: Dillon Press, 1967).

Maxted, I., *The London Book Trades, 1775–1800: A Preliminary Checklist of Members* (Folkestone, Kent: W. Dawson and Sons, 1977).

Mereness, N. D. (ed.), *Travels in the American Colonies* (New York: Antiquarian Press, 1961).

Miller, V. C., *Joel Barlow: Revolutionist, London, 1791–92* (Hamburg: Friederichsen, de Gruyter & Co., 1932).

Mills, W. J., *Historic Houses of New Jersey* (Philadelphia, PA, and London: J. B. Lippincott, 1902).

Molden, G., 'Sølvbriggen Maria Margrete – ut av historiens mørke' ['Maria Margrete – New Historical Light on the Silver Brig'], *Årbok for Norsk Sjøfartsmuseum 1995* [*Yearbook for Norwegian Maritime Museum*] (Oslo: Norsk Sjøfartsmuseum, 1996), pp. 139–54.

—, 'Sølvskipet på vei ut av historiens mørke' ['The Silver Ship Emerging out of the Darkness of History'], *Agderposten* (31 August 1996).

—, 'Arvingene fikk ingen rikdom' ['No Riches for the Descendants'], *Agderposten* (31 August 1996).

—, 'Gjennomførte ikke forliset' ['Did not Carry out the Wrecking (of the ship)'], *Agderposten* (11 April 1997).

Moreau-Zanelli, J., *Gallipolis: histoire d'un mirage américain au xviiie siècle* (Paris and Montreal: L'Harmattan, 2000).

Murdoch, R. K., 'Benedict Arnold and the Owners of the *Charming Nancy*', *Pennsylvania Magazine of History and Biography Index*, 84 (January 1960), pp. 22–55.

Nagel, P. C., *The Lees of Virginia: Seven Generations of an American Family* (New York: Oxford University Press, 1990).

National Archives Microfilm Publications, 'Pamphlet Describing M 881', in *Compiled Service Records of Soldiers who Served in the American Army During the Revolutionary War* (Washington, DC: National Archives Trust Fund Board, 1976).

Nyström, P., *Mary Wollstonecraft's Scandinavian Journey*, trans. G. R. Otter, Acta Regiae Societatis Scientiarum et Litterarum Gothoburgensis, Humaniora 17 (Gothenburg: Royal Society of Arts and Sciences, 1980).

O'Brien, C. C., *The Long Affair: Thomas Jefferson and the French Revolution, 1785–1800* (Chicago, IL, and London: University of Chicago Press, 1996).

[Oliver, W. H. P.], *A Brief Account of the American Ancestors and of Some Descendents of William Henry Imlay of Hartford, Connecticut, 1780–1858, Compiled for the Most Part from the Public Records by One of his Grandsons and Printed for Distribution in the Family* (privately printed, n.d).

Park, M. C., 'Joseph Priestley and the Problem of Pantisocracy' (PhD thesis, University of Pennsylvania, 1947).

Parkman, F., *France and England in North America*, 2 vols (1884; New York: Library of America, 1983).

Paul, C. K., *William Godwin: His Friends and Contemporaries*, 2 vols (London: H. S. King, 1876).

Paxton, W., *The Marshall Family, or A Genealogical Chart of the Descendants of John Marshall and Elizabeth Markham, his Wife, Sketches of Individuals and Notices of Families Connected with Them* (Platte City, MO: R. Clarke & Co., 1885).

Phillips, P. L., *The First Map of Kentucky, by John Filson* (Washington, DC: W. H. Lowdermilk & Co, 1916).

—, *The Rare Map of the Northwest 1785, By John Fitch, Inventor of the Steamboat: A Bibliographical Account with Facsimile Reproduction Including some Account of Thomas Hutchins and William McMurray* (Washington, DC: W. H. Lowdermilk & Co., 1916).

Pusey, W. A., *The Wilderness Road to Kentucky: Its Location and Features* (New York: George H. Doran Co., 1921).

Pomfret, J. E., *The New Jersey Proprietors and their Lands, 1664–1776* (Princeton, NJ: Princeton University Press, 1964).

—, *Colonial New Jersey: A History* (New York: Scribner's Sons, 1973).

Rice, H. C., 'James Swan: Agent of the French Republic, 1794–1796', *New England Quarterly*, 10:3 (September 1937), pp. 464–86.

—, *Barthélemi Tardiveau: A French Trader in the West* (Baltimore, MD: Johns Hopkins University Press, 1938).

Rohrbough, M. J., *The Land Office Business: The Settlement and Administration of American Public Lands, 1789–1837* (New York: Oxford University Press, 1968).

Royster, C., *Light-Horse Harry Lee and the Legacy of the American Revolution* (Baton Rouge, LA: Louisiana State University Press, 1981).

Rusk, R. L., 'The Adventures of Gilbert Imlay', *Indiana University Studies*, 10:57 (March 1923), pp. 3–26.

Sakolski, A. M., *The Great American Land Bubble: The Amazing Story of Land-Grabbing, Speculations, and Booms from Colonial Days to the Present Time* (New York and London: Harper & Brothers, 1932).

Schama, S., *Citizens: A Chronicle of the French Revolution* (New York: Alfred A. Knopf, 1989).

Seelye, J., *Beautiful Machine: Rivers and the Republican Plan, 1755–1825* (New York and Oxford: Oxford University Press, 1991).

Sheenan, B. W., 'Paradise and the Noble Savage in Jeffersonian Thought', *William and Mary Quarterly*, 3rd series, 26:3 (July 1969), pp. 327–59.

Shepherd, W. R., 'Wilkinson and the Beginnings of the Spanish Conspiracy', *American Historical Review*, 9:3 (April 1904), pp. 490–506.

Smith, C. N., 'Virginia Land Grants in Kentucky and Ohio, 1784–1799', *National Genealogical Society Quarterly*, 61:1 (March 1973), pp. 16–27.

Smith, W. B., *The Sterry Family of America, 1670–1970* (Middleboro, MA: for the author, 1973).

Speed, T., *The Wilderness Road: A Description of the Routes of Travel by which the Pioneers and Early Settlers First Came to Kentucky*, Filson Club Publications No. 2 (Louisville, KY: Filson Club, 1886).

Stone, L., *Road to Divorce, England 1530–1987* (Oxford: Oxford University Press, 1990).

—, *Broken Lives: Separation and Divorce in England 1660–1857* (Oxford and New York: Oxford University Press, 1993).

Stryker, W. S., *Official Register of the Officers and Men of New Jersey in the Revolutionary War, Compiled under Orders of His Excellency Theodore F. Randolph, Governor*, rev. and compiled J. W. S. Campbell (1872; Baltimore, MD: Genealogical Publishing Co., 1967).

—, *The Battle of Monmouth*, ed. W. Starr Myers (Princeton, NJ: Princeton University Press, 1927).

Sutherland, K., 'Hannah More's Counter-Revolutionary Feminism', in K. Everest (ed.), *Revolution in Writing: British Literary Responses to the French Revolution* (Milton Keynes and Philadelphia: Open University Press, 1991), pp. 27–63.

Talbert, C. G., *Benjamin Logan: Kentucky Frontiersman* (Lexington, KY: University of Kentucky Press, 1962).

Todd, C. B., *Life and Letters of Joel Barlow, L.L.D., Poet, Statesman, Philosopher, with Extracts from his Works and Hitherto Unpublished Poems* (New York: G. P. Putnam's Sons, 1886).

Todd, J., *Mary Wollstonecraft: A Revolutionary Life* (London: Weidenfeld & Nicolson, 2000).

Tompkins, J. M. S., *The Popular Novel in England, 1770–1800* (London: Constable, 1932).

Toohey, R. E., *Liberty and Empire: British Radical Solutions to the American Problem, 1774–1776* (Lexington, KY: University Press of Kentucky, 1978).

Townsend, J. W., *Kentuckians in History and Literature* (New York and Washington, DC: Neale Publishing Company, 1907).

Treat, P. J., *The National Land System, 1785–1820* (1910; New York: Russell & Russell, 1967).

Turner, F. J., 'The Origin of Genet's Projected Attack on Louisiana and the Floridas', *American Historical Review*, 3:4 (July 1898), pp. 650–71.

Verhoeven, W. M. (ed.), *Revolutionary Histories: Transatlantic Cultural Nationalism, 1775–1815* (Houndmills, Hampshire, and New York: Macmillan/Palgrave, 2002).

—, *Americomania, or, Illusions of Liberty: British Radicals and American Lands, 1789–1800* (forthcoming: Chapel Hill, NC: University of North Carolina Press, 2008).

Verlet, P., *Le mobilier royal française*, 4 vols (Paris: Librarie Plon, 1955).

Walker, L. B., '"Life of Margaret Shippen", Wife of Benedict Arnold', *Pennsylvania Magazine of History and Biography*, 24:4 (1900), pp. 257–66, 401–29.

Walton, J., *John Filson of Kentucky* (Lexington, KY: University of Kentucky Press, 1956).

Westcott, T., *Life of John Fitch: The Inventor of the Steam-Boat* (1857; Philadelphia, PA: J. B. Lippincott, 1878).

Whitaker, A. P., 'Harry Innes and the Spanish Intrigue: 1794–1795', *Mississippi Valley Historical Review*, 15:2 (September 1928), pp. 236–48.

Woodress, J., *A Yankee's Odyssey: The Life of Joel Barlow* (Philadelphia, PA, and New York: J. B. Lippincott Company, 1958).

Woodward, R. L., and W. F. Craven, *Princetonians, 1784–1790: A Biographical Dictionary* (Princeton, NJ: Princeton University Press, 1991).

Wright, R. K., Jr, *The Continental Army* (Washington, DC: Center of Military History United States Army, 1983).

Wyatt, E. F., 'The First American Novel', *Atlantic Monthly*, 144 (October 1929), pp. 466–75.

INDEX